The Ballad as Song

The Ballad as Song

by

Bertrand Harris Bronson

•

University of California Press
Berkeley and Los Angeles 1969

University of California Press
Berkeley and Los Angeles, California

University of California Press, Ltd.
London, England

Copyright © *1969, by*
The Regents of the University of California
Standard Book Number: 520-01399-9
Library of Congress Catalog Card Number: 74-84045
Printed in the United States of America

To M. S. B.

"O what is longer than the way?"

Preface

FORTY-ODD years ago, when the writer of these occasional pieces began to interest himself in traditional ballads, there was little acknowledgment—at least in academic circles—that the study of balladry demanded more than the slightest recognition of the musical side of the subject. Beginning with a simple liking for folk-song in general, and an interest in the Child ballads in particular, it seemed to him natural to wish to bring the two together and collect such records as had survived of the tunes to which the old ballads had been traditionally sung. The project looked neither very large nor very challenging: the question was rather whether enough had been saved to make it worth while. At any rate, it appeared an innocent, if somewhat solitary, amusement, and was casually undertaken as a private hobby. Since, moreover, by definition traditional song was in the public domain, there were no visible obstacles except the limits of curiosity and time, and one could set out with a light heart. What sings Autolycus?

> A merry heart goes al the day,
> Your sad tires in a mile-a.

But this footpath proved longer than was anticipated.

The contents of the present volume are offshoots of the author's persistent efforts to control the material collected and to gain a better understanding of various aspects of an inexhaustible field. His center of research has continued to be that in which his serious work commenced, the Child ballads. The main body of evidence has meanwhile been set out in other volumes in a more orderly fashion. He cannot pretend that the basic orientation has been much altered by the revolutionary changes of attitude that have encompassed the subject in the last three decades. Perhaps this is evidence of an obstinate inflexibility, of an inability to learn from the march of events; and I may confess to a mild embarrassment, seeing these scattered pieces now gathered together, in finding them returning with "damnable iteration" to the same fundamental positions, too often without seeking the relief of fresh illustrations, when for a fresh audience an old instance served the argument as well. It was certainly never expected that they would be read in succession; nor yet need they be now. But as they stand here, they constitute an honest history of the stages of a student's attempts to explain and defend a consistent point of view. For that reason, it has seemed best to put them in chronological order, rather than try to give them a specious but confused appearance of timeliness by rearrangement and up-dating. Homogeneity they may claim, but never the organic unity of a monograph proceeding step by step. Each is self-contained and in its own limited terms self-sufficient. Painful repetition one hopes at least to have mitigated by excision and slight verbal alteration; but otherwise, in the main they appear, apart from two papers hitherto unpublished (nos. 16 and 18), as they were originally printed.

It may be objected that, because they do not answer to the winds of social concern currently prevailing, they do not bespeak the notice of those who (as Chaucer would say) "ride al of the newe jet," or dance to a modern pipe. But even for the latter there may be some profit in looking back. Tradition, so long as it remains such, cannot live entirely divorced from its roots. Folk-song did not begin yesterday; and they who make it a serious occupation today can profit by the historical perspective. Indeed, the present essays, as they took shape, appeared to the writer to be addressing contemporary assumptions and problems; and they may serve to sharpen, and help to define, the current moment, whether by contrast or by raising issues that are still moot.

Analytical questions and methods, at any rate, do not go out of date overnight. The problems of melodic identity, of taxonomy and classification, of traditional transmission and variation, are likely to be with us for a long time. The interaction of tunes and texts is a subject that has received far too little attention. The question of modal shifts in the course of traditional transmission is one that, so far as I know, has never been studied, however much the modes in themselves may have been discussed. Morphology and comparative analysis are still in the primary stages of musicological notice in the area of folk-song. The writer may claim some credit for initiating inquiry in these directions and for suggesting ways of handling the multiform methodological questions that arise in their investigation. Over all, in fact, one may justifiably conjecture that as yet we are only at the threshold of serious study on a broad but solid comparative base.

B. H. B.

Contents

1. "Edward, Edward. A Scottish Ballad" and a Footnote   1

2. Samuel Hall's Family Tree   18

3. The Interdependence of Ballad Tunes and Texts   37

4. Mrs. Brown and the Ballad   64

5. Folk-Song and the Modes   79

6. Habits of the Ballad as Song   92

7. On the Union of Words and Music in the "Child" Ballads   112

8. Two Reviews: George Pullen Jackson and the Shaped-Note Spirituals   133

9. The Morphology of the Ballad Tunes   144

10. About the Most Favorite British Ballads   162

11. Toward the Comparative Analysis of British-American Folk-Tunes   172

12. Folk-Song and Live Recordings   202

13. Two Reviews: Frank Brown and North Carolina Folklore   211

14. "All this for a Song?"   224

15. Folk-Song in the United States, 1910–1960   243

16. Fractures in Tradition among the "Child" Ballads   257

17. Cecil Sharp and Folk-Song   273

18. "Of Ballads, Songs, and Snatches"   282

    Index   315

"Edward, Edward. A Scottish Ballad"
and a Footnote

Edward" has justly held a place of honor among ballads ever since it was first given to the world, in 1765, in the *Reliques* of Thomas Percy. For many persons, indeed, it has come to typify the whole category, so that "Edward" is what they think of when the popular ballad is mentioned. Ballad-lovers who wish to win converts are likely to point first to "Edward" as exemplifying more strikingly than any other piece the peculiar merits of this kind of literature. No class in public speaking neglects it; no concert baritone but includes it in his repertory. All this is sufficient testimony to its universal appeal.

Its right to these laurels was confirmed by the great master, Francis James Child. "Edward," he said, "is not only unimpeachable, but has ever been regarded as one of the noblest and most sterling specimens of the popular ballad." [1] Child's approbation is the hallmark of balladry; and since he pronounced "Edward" sterling, few indeed have been rash enough to announce their suspicion of an alloy in the metal. Yet before Child's "I have said" doubts had been expressed more than once, and after almost sixty years of respectful silence, during which period the ways of oral tradition have been explored with results richly informative, it may be permissible once again to raise the question. "Return, Alpheus, the dread voice is past."

Percy printed the ballad as "from a MS. copy transmitted from Scotland"; and supplemented that information, in his fourth edition, with a further note: "This curious Song was transmitted to

[1] F. J. Child, *The English and Scottish Popular Ballads*, I (1882), 167.

the Editor by Sir David Dalrymple, Bart. late Ld. Hailes, a Lord of
Session" [2]—the same Lord Hailes who revealed the secret of Lady
Wardlaw's composition of "Hardyknute" when the rest of the
world believed it to be a genuine old ballad discovered, in a vault,
on scraps of paper "wrapped round the bottoms of clues." Lord
Hailes had an active interest in old Scots ballads, and had himself
printed such pieces from time to time. He supplied Percy with
some of the finest ballads that adorn the *Reliques*—all from manuscript copies of unspecified origin, or, at best, deriving from the
"memory of a lady since dead." A "lady," be it noted, not a peas-
ant. Lord Hailes was not the man to spend valuable time taking
down songs from the mouths of the peasants in order to get the
exact words of unvarnished tradition. It was not yet generally
known that the common people were the residuary legatees of
things of this sort; nor, if it had been, would it have appeared desirable to perpetuate clumsy ineptitudes where improvement was
easy. Percy put the general attitude frankly enough in the Preface
to his fourth edition: "the old copies, whether MS. or printed, were
often so defective or corrupted, that a scrupulous adherence to
their wretched readings would only have exhibited unintelligible
nonsense, or such poor meagre stuff, as neither came from the
Bard, nor was worthy the press; when, by a few slight corrections
or additions, a most beautiful or interesting sense hath started
forth, and this so naturally and easily, that the Editor could seldom
prevail on himself to indulge the vanity of making a formal claim
to the improvement." [3]

In his failure to be specific about sources, Lord Hailes was no
more careless than his contemporaries, including Scott and excepting Ritson. Nor is there the slightest reason to suppose that he
would have been any more likely to respect the letter than were his
contemporaries, again including Scott and excepting Ritson. Percy
himself, as is abundantly clear, was almost incredibly unscrupulous
in this matter. A text, therefore, which comes to us, as "Edward"
comes, through the medium of the *Reliques*, must provide itself
with incontrovertible vouchers for its authenticity. Nothing in that
work can be accepted merely on trust: literally everything has to
be tested by other authority, as the publication of Percy's Folio
manuscript demonstrated beyond contradiction.

[2] T. Percy, *Reliques of Ancient English Poetry*, I (1794), 61.
[3] *Ibid.*, I, xvi–xvii.

"The affectedly antique spelling in Percy's copy," writes Child in his headnote to "Edward," "has given rise to vague suspicions concerning the authenticity of the ballad, or the language: but as spelling will not make an old ballad, so it will not unmake one. We have, but do not need, the later traditional copy to prove the other genuine." [4] But, of course, the existence of a later traditional copy will not by itself prove Percy's copy genuine, nor anything like it. The closer it is to Percy's copy, the more likely it is either to have been derived from that copy, or to have been influenced by it— and the *Reliques* was one of the most widely known books of its half-century. And the more *un*like such a traditional copy is to its printed predecessor, the less serviceable it becomes in proving the authenticity of the *ipsissima verba* of the earlier version. The most it will do is offer corroborative evidence of the existence of such a ballad in traditional circulation.

The traditional copy to which Child refers was picked up by William Motherwell from the recitation of an old woman in Kilbarchan, sixty years after the publication of the *Reliques*. There are wide differences between it and the Percy version. Parricide has become fratricide, and the tragedy is revealed as having its origin in a casual quarrel "about the cutting of a willow wand." Thus any suggestion of guilt on the mother's part becomes rather pointless; and in fact this version does not accuse her of evil counsel to justify the bequest of "a fire of coals." One may therefore choose between supposing either that the ballad was so old that the lines of the plot had become obliterated in transmission, or that the suggestion of the mother's guilt was due to contamination by the Percy version. The latter supposition would be supported by the fact that wherever else the ballad has been found—in Sweden, Denmark, Finland, or America—the mother remains unimplicated in her son's crime.

In other respects, too, the traditional version differs from Percy's. The name of the protagonist has become "Davie." In printing his version, Motherwell observes that "there is reason to believe, that his Lordship [Lord Hailes] made a few slight verbal improvements on the copy he transmitted, and altered the hero's name to Edward, a name which, by-the-bye, never occurs in a Scottish ballad, except where allusion is made to an English King." [5] Whether or not Lord Hailes made the alterations suspected, it can

[4] Child, *loc. cit.*
[5] W. Motherwell, *Minstrelsy: Ancient and Modern* (1827), p. 340.

be confidently stated that Motherwell's copy is entirely lacking in the magic of Percy's version. Motherwell himself says he prints it chiefly to introduce the melody to which it is traditionally sung—a promise which he curiously and regrettably neglected to redeem in his appendix of tunes; and probably no educated reader, from that day to this, has thought his version worth memorizing in preference to the other. Nevertheless it is his version, rather than Percy's, which has been unmistakably perpetuated in oral tradition.

About the middle of the last century, Robert Chambers attempted to cast doubt on the folk origins of all the Scottish romantic ballads and propounded the theory—which has nowhere found acceptance—that the whole body of them was written by one person, about the commencement of the eighteenth century, and that that person was probably Lady Wardlaw. Thus, "Sir Patrick Spens," "Gil Morrice," "Edward," "Young Waters," "Edom o' Gordon" and the rest are cheaply provided with a parent. It was perhaps with Chambers's untenable theory in mind, as well as in allusion to Motherwell's comment, quoted above, that Child wrote his headnote to "Edward," asserting its genuineness in the face of vague suspicions.

Now if Child's remarks were prompted by the thought of some general theory like that of Chambers as it bore on the authenticity of such a ballad as "Edward," a possibility arises which is of very considerable importance to our discussion. It becomes possible, it even begins to look probable, that Child has been generally misunderstood. He may not, after all, have been asserting his belief in the authenticity, in the confined sense of the term, of the Percy-Hailes version, but rather his certainty that "Edward," regarding all its versions as a single entity—"Child no. 13"—was a genuine popular ballad. In saying that the traditional version proved the Percy version "genuine," he may not have meant to imply his acceptance of the latter, word for word in the form in which it appears in the *Reliques*, as the product of the popular muse uncontaminated by "literary" influences, but only his belief that basically it was not a poem of individual authorship. When he went on to declare that "Edward" was "unimpeachable," he may have had the larger concept still more entirely in his view. If he were defending this multiform entity, with its continental analogues, from a general attack like Chambers', he would not so easily have noticed the ambiguity of his words. He could pass insensibly from a discussion of the Percy version to the ballad taken as the sum of its versions, without marking the distinction. And, in fact, he does allow that the word "brand," in Percy's first stanza, "is possibly more literary than popular," though he goes no farther in that direction. "Further than this," he declares, "the language is entirely fit." The "language," that is, the vocabulary: he does not say whether he harbors any suspicion of subtler kinds of literary influence.

If this be the drift of Child's remarks—I do not insist that it is—he has certainly been misapprehended, for in common reference his praise of this ballad is always applied specifically to Percy's version, while the other versions are ignored or forgotten. Assurance that his words were to be interpreted as I have suggested that they may be, would at least be comforting to a critic who is not at all bent on showing that the ballad's life began with Lord Hailes's manuscript copy, but only that that copy is itself open to the gravest suspicion. Whatever Child thought of it, we must now scrutinize this version for evidence of literary rehandling.

In estimating the degree of literary influence that may be present in Percy's "Edward," we ought not at the start, on the strength of a knowledge of the habit of ballads, to ignore the superior artistry of this ballad over others of similar pattern, nor to minimize the skill with which the technique is employed here, even if we think the process largely unconscious. Too much emphasis on the virtues of the method tends to make one discount the value of the result, because, in spite of our era, most of us still respect conscious contrivance more highly than we do a mechanical necessity. In this ballad, we have been told, what seems the cunning of art in the ordonnance of the narrative is simply the product of ballad machinery. Given a familiar story, plus the ballad conventions of the climax of relatives and the legacy formula, "Edward" is the automatic result. Thus, in an otherwise admirable introduction to the ballads, we read:

. . . the telling unexpectedness at the close of *Edward* is due, not to conscious art, but rather to the instinctive use of formulas widespread and well established in ballad literature. Much, then, that looks like the last word in modern narrative method,—the concentration of attention upon a single situation, the use of concrete terms, the omission of explanation and of all unessential, or even essential, matter, the development of the situation with due regard to suspense and climax,—all this is natural and unconscious in the ballad.[6]

By thus seeming to emphasize the mechanics of the ballad as being in large measure responsible for its success, the critic involuntarily does it an injustice. Much in the ballad that "looks like the last word in modern narrative method" *is* the last word in modern narrative method—though not necessarily the final word. Let us not overstate the unconsciousness of the process: ballads do not make themselves in any esoteric sense; their employment of convention is deliberate and proceeds with foreknowledge of the intended result —which is to get their story told in their own fashion. The folk who sing the ballads never, if memory serves, lose sight of the story. We must disagree with the opinion that the singers of the ballad "Edward" had a greater interest in making lyrical comment on the story than in telling the story itself, or that they took the story for granted. Such an assumption is contradicted by the experience of every one who has collected ballads from the mouths of the people. And it leads to a false estimate of the importance to the folk-singer and his normal audience of the elements of suspense and surprise in the ballads. Naive minds are just as susceptible to these appeals as educated minds, probably more susceptible. As every one has noticed in children, suspense and surprise have their way with the hearer, no matter how familiar the story or how numerous the repetitions. With such listeners, at least, the pleasures of suspense are just as vivid whether or not the outcome is known, and the surprise is re-experienced at every fresh telling. Even the cultivated reader responds in some degree to these appeals, so long as a work of art that possesses them continues to exert any hold on him. Under the spell of the art-experience, he imaginatively resumes the condition of ignorance even while he knows the issue. He knows but he does not know. This divided consciousness, which actually enriches his experience, is no more contradictory,

---

[6] W. M. Hart, *English Popular Ballads* (1916), p. 16. The author of the passage has taken friendly exception to my understanding of his words. The phrase *instinctive use*, he feels, makes due allowance for the play of the artistic sense, and he would not deny the presence of such an element in the shaping of the ballads. I would suggest, however, that the more importance one is willing to grant to the presence of this element, the less one leaves of any such distinction between the ballads and works of "conscious art."

and no less real, then the "willing suspension of disbelief," and no less vital to full enjoyment of the work of art. We must have become deadened to the experience of "Edward" if we do not, every time we read the ballad, feel the atmosphere grow more and more charged as question and answer succeed one another, until the final revelation chills us with a fresh shock of horror. And if we with our comparatively objective attitude react in this fashion, we cannot doubt the force of these appeals on minds that lack our detachment and yield themselves to the story with unconstrained spontaneity.

But, whatever the degree of surprise, it is safe to declare that the complexity of pattern wherein the suspense is built up and the skill with which the terrible secret is withheld to the last is *sui generis* in the whole range of popular balladry. To be sure, the devices here employed are the familiar ones of incremental repetition, the legacy formula, the climax of relatives. Nevertheless, no other ballad makes use of them with anything like the same sophistication. "Lord Randal," for example, an admirable ballad, employs the same devices, in a similar pattern. But the effect is naive when compared with "Edward." In "Lord Randal," the questions of the mother are answered by the son in a straightforward manner; the truth in the case is early divined through Randal's insistence on his weariness, or sickness, immediately after his admission that he has been with his sweetheart; and there is no melodramatic and unlooked-for revelation at the close.

In the ordering of the questions and answers in "Edward," the degree of art over and above the ballad norm must be neither overlooked nor minimized. At the ordinary level, the questions of the mother would conventionally be asked in threes and so answered. Thus, for example:

> O hae ye killed your hauke sae guid,
> Or hae ye killed your reid-roan steid,
> Or hae ye killed your fadir deir.
> My deir son, now tell me O.

> I hae nae killed my hauke sae guid,
> Nor hae I killed my reid-roan steid,
> But I hae killed my fadir deir,
> Alas, and wae is me O.

Fortunately, instead of this, each question here has its answer in turn (taking the double question at the outset as one) before the next question is asked. No mere mechanical principle directs the selection of the more effective arrangement. Then, for the ordinary straightforward answer there is substituted a lying evasion, which, in turn, is answered by a statement of incredulity that in each case does duty for another question. Moreover, the form of the mother's reply to each successive evasion is unusual in balladry. We should ordinarily find her expressing her disbelief with much more directness, as, for instance:

> Ye lee, ye lee, my bonny son,
>   Sae loud's I hear ye lee O:
> Your haukis bluid was neir sae reid,
>   My deir son, I tell thee O.

Or she might even omit altogether the reason for her disbelief, letting the accusation of untruth stand alone. But here, instead, she omits the accusation itself and merely states the reasons, leaving the rest to inference:

> Your haukis bluid was nevir sae reid,

and again,

> Your steid was auld, and ye hae gat mair,
>   Sum other dule ye drie O.

Once more, when the legacy motive is employed, we do not find it in its normal form. We should expect, as in "Lord Randal," a series like

> What'll ye leave to your brither,
>   Edward, Edward . . . .
> What'll ye leave to your sister, . . . to your
>   bairns, . . . to your wife, . . . to your
>   mother . . .

Instead of this normal procedure, the mother's questions are framed in such a fashion as to catch up into themselves the material of the usual ballad reply, thereby in turn prompting replies of an imaginative reach far beyond the ordinary ballad compass. Hence, instead of something like

> 'What'll you leave to your bairns and your wife,
>   Edward, Edward?

> What'll you leave to your bairns and your wife,
>> My dear son, now tell me O.'
> 'I'll leave them baith my houses and lands,
>> Mither, Mither,' &c.

we find—it is a vast difference—

> And what wul ye doe wi your towirs and your ha?

followed by a most unconventional, but highly dramatic, reply:

> I'll let thame stand tul they doun fa.

And next:

> And what wull ye leive to your bairns and
>> your wife? . . .
> The warldis room, late them beg thrae life, &c.

And finally, the thrilling and awful conclusion, which gains still greater effectiveness by two features that are, once again, out of the ordinary. First, there is the mother's implication of an emotional bond between herself and her son, so that, instead of a question put with the usual impersonality, we have

> What wul ye leive to your *ain* mither *deir*?

The other feature is the son's turning upon his mother the full force of direct address, instead of continuing the third personal reference of her question, or avoiding the use of the pronoun:

> The curse of hell frae me sall ye beir, . . .
> Sic counseils ye gave to me O.

Contrast the effect of this with that of the final stanza in Motherwell's version:

> 'What wilt thou leave to thy mother dear,
>> Son Davie, son Davie?'
> 'A fire o coals to burn her, wi hearty cheer,
>> And she'll never get mair o me.'

The last line of Percy's version—"Sic counseils ye gave to me O"—raises another matter for consideration: the artistic substitution of a new and appropriate line at each repetition for the last part of the refrain. Thus, we might have expected something like

> My deir son, now tell me O

to keep recurring throughout the ballad in the alternate quatrains. Instead, we find the following:

> And why sae sad gang yee O? . . .
> My deir son I tell thee O. . .
> Sum other dule ye drie O. . .
> My deir son now tell me O. . .
> That were sae fair to see O. . .
> Whan ye gang ovir the sea O. . .

Similarly with the corresponding line in the intermediate quatrains: instead of a formula, as in "Lord Randal," we find continual change:

> And I had nae mair bot hee O. . .
> That erst was sae fair and frie O. . .
> Alas, and wae is mee O! . . .
> And Ile fare ovir the sea O. . .
> For here nevir mair maun I bee O. . .
> For thame nevir mair wul I see O. . .
> Sic counseils ye gave to me O.

It need hardly be said that this use of the refrain, instead of providing points of rest, or opportunities for choral assistance by the audience—the customary habit of ballads which have preserved their refrains—offers instead additional material on which the hearers would not be expected—nor indeed be able—to encroach. A similar use of the refrain occurs in Deloney's version of the "Fair Flower of Northumberland" and in a few other ballads where literary influence is to be presumed. The richness and irregularity of the refrain material in the present ballad is further elaborated by the alternation of "Edward, Edward" with "Mither, Mither" in the other half of the refrain—an exploitation of the dramatic possibilities of the refrain which can scarcely be paralleled elsewhere in ballads.

The antique spelling in which Percy (or Lord Hailes) saw fit to dress the ballad need not disturb us any more than it did Professor Child. But certain points of style and phraseology should not be overlooked. There is first the word *brand*, which Child himself noted as "possibly more literary than popular." The usual ballad word for a man's weapon is *blade* or *sword*, not *brand*—except *passim* in Peter Buchan's versions of the ballads. Again, the form of the first question invites attention: instead of

What bluid's that upon your sword?

or

How gat ye that bluid upon your sword?,

the extraordinary rhetoric of

Why dois your brand *sae drap wi bluid*?

Is this the language of oral tradition or of an embryonic Macbeth? It will hardly pass muster as good ballad diction. Again, for this question to be followed immediately by the further query, with its unheroic, not to say sentimental, implications, so unlike the ancient habit,

And why sae sad gang yee O,—

where *sad*, one may well feel, carries connotations of an eighteenth-century melancholy rather than of medieval hardihood: this, too, is surely worthy of remark. Even though the word *sad* be allowed the weight of an older habit, it will still seem somewhat out of key with the right tone of the tragic ballad, seem inappropriate to the unintrospective, unbrooding acceptance of grim realities in a stern and hostile world.

Possibly the next point is too subjective to find ready acceptance. One reader, at any rate, has the feeling that the closely knit sequence of the lines,

Your steid was auld, and ye hae gat mair,
Sum other dule ye drie O,

is much more reasonably argumentative than it has any business to be for good traditional ballad style. The point is tied up with the unnatural richness of the questions and answers. And it has already been suggested that here and throughout the remainder, this ballad, in its whole ordonnance, is the apotheosis of convention, pushing the devices it employs quite beyond their traditional manners and uses.

Motherwell's suggestion that Lord Hailes changed the original name of the hero to Edward is very brusquely dismissed by Professor Child. "Dalrymple, at least," he writes, "would not be likely to change a Scotch for an English name. The Bishop might doubtless prefer Edward to Wat, or Jock, or even Davie. But as there is no evidence that any change of name was made, the point need not be discussed." [7] Quite true; but if Motherwell is right in saying that the name does not elsewhere occur in a Scots ballad, it may still be permissible to wonder if it belongs in this one. The doubts which Child himself raises as to the authenticity of many lines and stanzas in Walter Scott's versions of the ballads he printed rest on exactly the same sort of grounds: a feeling as to what is or is not appropriate to the proper style of the pieces in question.

We should not care to go so far as the late T. F. Henderson, who after calling attention to this ballad's "utter linguistic superiority to the average Scottish traditional ballad versions," its "masterly wording" and "the admirable art of its construction," roundly declares it to be "verse with which the desecrating muse of popular tradition has had, so far as can be discerned, no commerce." [8] It is a fact, however, whether the fact mean much or little, that the ballad cannot be shown to have existed in British tradition before the publication of Percy's *Reliques*. Since Percy's time, "Edward" seems to have had a very limited circulation. In Scotland, it was found once by Motherwell (about 1825) and a fragment of it was picked up, at about the same time, by Alexander Laing. Since then it has not, so far as I know, been found by Scottish collectors.[9] Gavin Greig's sixty-odd volumes (MS.) of traditional verse gathered at the turn of the century contain no trace of it. It has apparently never gained a foothold in England.[10] In the southern mountains of the United States, however, it has been recovered several times in our own day. Cecil Sharp found it some eight times, in the Appalachians, more or less complete and in a form far closer to Motherwell's version than to Percy's. In this southeastern form, Edward (who is never named) kills his brother in a quarrel concerning a bush that might have made a tree. Although, as we have seen, in Mother-

[7] Child, *loc. cit.*

[8] T. F. Henderson, *The Ballad in Literature* (1912), pp. 25–26.

[9] This is now (1968) no longer true. Several versions have been found by Scottish collectors: that sung and recorded by Jeannie Robertson, out of Aberdeen, titled "My Son David," is now well known. Cf. Tradition Records, TLP. 1047, Side 1, band 7, Recorded by Hamish Henderson, 1951.

[10] A textually confused variant has lately been collected in Hampshire (Aldershot).

well's version the mother's guilt is suggested, the American versions bear no trace of this aspect of the plot. Since the Scandinavian variants also lack that Æschylean feature, it is natural to surmise that the implicating of the mother in the crime may not be a traditional element of the ballad, but may be rather some individual's stroke of genius, to give the due measure of pity and terror. Without it, at any rate, the ballad is left an undistinguished story in which an unpremeditated murder of a brother drives a man to flight from his home and family. Few things could be more tasteless, or more lacking in the tragic qualm, than these American versions. One example will serve for all:

How came that blood on the point of your
    knife?
My son, come tell to me.
It is the blood of my old coon dog
That chased the fox for me, me, me,
That chased the fox for me.

How come that blood, &c.
It is the blood of that old horse
That ploughed that field for me, &c.

How come that blood, &c.
It is the blood of one of my brothers
Which fell out with me, &c.

What did you fall out about? &c.
We fell out about a holly-bush
That would have made a tree, &c.

What will you do when your father comes
    home? &c.
I'll put my foot in a bunkum boat
And sail across the sea.

What will you do with your dear little wife? &c.
I'll put her foot in a bunkum boat
And sail across the sea.

What will you do with your dear little babe? &c.
I'll leave it here in this lone world
To dandle on your knee.

And what will you do with your old gobbler? &c.
I'll leave it here with you when I'm gone
To gobble after me.[11]

One cannot resist calling attention to that last stanza, with its introduction of new material into the ballad. Here is the "epical process" *in esse!*

Professor Child was wont to declare that the popular ballad was inimitable. Looking at "Edward," whether in Percy's version or in that of Mrs. Meg Shook, one inclines, for divergent reasons, to agree with Child. One feels, at any rate, that, as sent to Percy by Lord Hailes, it was, *so far as its form is concerned*, very close to its fountainhead. And its form, apart from its formulas, is what makes all the difference between Percy's version and the inept Appalachian variants.

[11] C. J. Sharp and M. Karpeles, *English Folk Songs from the Southern Appalachians*, I (1932), 49. Version sung by Mrs. Meg Shook, Clyde, North Carolina, August 2, 1917.

A Footnote to "Edward, Edward"

Dare one ask those who believe Percy's version of "Edward" to be the natural product of unsophisticated folk composition whether they have fully considered the implications of their position?

So far as I am aware, no one is disposed to quarrel with Professor W. M. Hart's admirably lucid analysis of the elements of the ballads, which he has ranked according to the degree of their narrative complexity. Except, perhaps, in the heroic ballads, most examples of which are Danish, he finds greatest attention to the element of character in the *Gest of Robyn Hode*, where the hero displays qualities of humor, loyalty, piety, rudimentary notions of social justice and class consciousness, besides the more physical attributes of hardihood, bravery, and so on. The simpler stages of balladry, in due proportion, are shown to lack this elaboration of character. Thus we learn that in the Robin Hood cycle "description of States of Mind is still an 'undeveloped element'"; that the border heroes "rise to the dignity of a type, embody popular ideals"; that in the Simple Ballads, the hero is a "mere doer of deeds, . . . nothing more." [12] Of this least complex class of ballads, where there is no emphasis on character, and where the focus of interest lies entirely in event or situation, "Edward" has been cited as an outstanding example.

The superiority of "Edward"—I speak only of Percy's version —is chiefly due to its surprise ending, which delays the climax to the very end, administering the shock of horrible revelation when the hearer believes he already knows all the essential facts in the story, so that he must reconstruct his attitude to everything that has preceded. Without this ending, the climax occurs in the middle of the ballad, and the dénouement is inartistically protracted. The violence of the readjustment which the ending forces upon us has possibly hindered our drawing certain necessary inferences relating to the conduct of the narrative and to the character of the persons involved in the ballad.

It is obvious that the whole dialogue, in the light of the final implication of the mother in her son's guilt, is converted into an intellectual fencing bout. The mother already knows everything. Her son knows she knows. Why, then, does she ask her questions?

[12] W. M. Hart, *Ballad and Epic* (1907), pp. 77, 70, 53.

Why does he postpone admission of the truth by lies and evasions? To answer these questions plausibly, from the point of view of character, is to construct psychological portraits of considerable complexity. One cannot justify the dialogue without presuming two highly self-conscious beings. From the psychological point of view, there is no simple explanation of such reticence and indirection as theirs.

But, from the narrative point of view, there is a simpler explanation. It may be argued that the dialogue is so arranged, not to exhibit any subtlety of character—and manifestly not to clarify the facts in the minds of either mother or son—but with deliberate cunning, to keep the hearer in the dark so that he may be surprised by the ending.

Either explanation is unacceptable to the orthodox view of the traditional ballad and its ways. The first compels us to assume a subtlety of character portrayal absolutely without parallel, not only among simple ballads of situation, but even in the classes of greatest complexity. People ask questions in ballads in order to learn what they do not know, or—in the case of the riddling ballads—because they believe the persons questioned do not know and cannot answer. "Lord Randal" and "Riddles Wisely Expounded" exemplify the types. Where else than in "Edward," on the contrary, can one find a character in a ballad asking for information which he or she knows that the informant knows that the questioner already possesses? But if we take the second explanation, we have to acknowledge a narrative technique of highly sophisticated artistry, quite uncharacteristic of the "natural and instinctive" use of conventional formulae in the traditional ballad. Where else can one observe a deliberate withholding of the crucial fact in the story? If the reader shies at the word *deliberate*, he is thrown back upon the other horn of the dilemma. And if it be argued that such a degree of narrative craft is not beyond the presumable skill of a popular singer steeped in the best ballad tradition, we may reasonably ask for other evidence of the same technique in the best ballad tradition.

Earlier, I have pointed out what seem to me good grounds for regarding Percy's "Edward" with suspicion, if proposed as an authentic exemplar of traditional balladry. I am glad to find that Professor Archer Taylor, in a scholarly and ingenious comparison of all the available variants of the ballad, in whatever language, has already arrived, by an entirely different route, at a similar conclusion: that the ending of Percy's version must be "surrendered as a contamination," and that in other respects as well the same version is "disordered." [13]

1940

[13] Archer Taylor, *"Edward" and "Sven i Rosengård"* (1931), pp. 26, 36, 38.

Samuel Hall's Family Tree

EVERYONE is aware of the difficulties confronting any attempt to trace a popular ballad or song to its beginnings. Even the anchors of place names and dated events often fail to hold fast. One is likely to find that such elements have entered late, and are in fact mere adaptations to new circumstances. In the search for reliable holds upon this sandy bottom, the common ballad quatrain or couplet is of course no assistant. But once in a while a particular verse pattern serves to mark an individual identity, all the more if coupled with a typical subject matter; and it is both amusing and instructive to pursue such a song to the point where it vanishes on the horizon of the past.

Such a song is the inelegant but very generally known "Samuel Hall," versions of which are sung traditionally and vociferously on the West Coast at the present time, and which may be found on phonograph records and in many printed collections. As the writer learned it from tradition, years ago and in a comparatively enfeebled version, the song went as follows:

O my name is Samuel Hall,
  Samuel Hall, Samuel Hall,
O my name is Samuel Hall
And I hate you one and all,
You're a gang of muckers all,
  Damn your hide.

O I killed a man, 'tis said,
  So 'tis said, so 'tis said,
O I killed a man, 'tis said,
And I hit him on the head,
And I left him there for dead,
  Damn his hide.

O they put me in the quad,
  In the quad, in the quad,
O they put me in the quad
And they chained me to a rod
And they left me there, by God,
  Damn their hide.

O the Preacher he did come,
  He did come, he did come,
O the Preacher he did come
And he looked so very glum
As he talked of Kingdom Come,
  Damn his hide.

O the Sheriff he came too,
  He came too, he came too,
O the Sheriff he came too,
With his boys all dressed in blue;
They're a gang of muckers, too,
  Damn their hide.

To the gallows I must go,
  I must go, I must go,
To the gallows I must go,
With my friends all down below
Saying, "Sam, I told you so,"
  Damn their hide.[1]

Much more full-bodied versions may be examined in Lomax's *American Ballads and Folk Songs* and in the melodramatic rendition of Carl Sandburg on a phonograph record.[2] A version close to the above, but with three other stanzas in place of the last, is printed, presumably from a Victorian music-hall specimen, in

---

[1] Without doubt, the "hide" of the refrain in this version is a bit of college slang, unconsciously substituted for an earlier "eyes," which had come to seem antiquated to the singers.

[2] Lomax (1934), p. 133; Musicraft Record no. 207–A, Album no. 11; "Gallows Song."

Harold Scott's *English Song Book*.[3] The tune, though perhaps distantly related, is different in effect, and carries an additional phrase which is necessary to the more typical verse pattern:

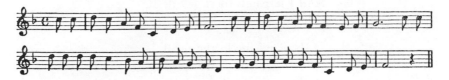

So up the rope I go, up I go,
So up the rope I go, up I go,
So up the rope I go, with my friends all down below,
Saying, "Sam, we told you so!"
              Damn their eyes!

I saw Molly in the crowd, in the crowd,
I saw Molly in the crowd, in the crowd,
I saw Molly in the crowd, so I hollered right out loud,
"Molly, ain't yer bloody proud?"
              Damn your eyes!

So this shall be my knell, be my knell,
So this shall be my knell, be my knell,
So this shall be my knell, and I'll meet you all in Hell,
And I hope you sizzle well—
              Damn your eyes!

Now, as the song was sung at Harvard, in the time of the Civil War, it presents some interesting variations:

My name it is Sam Hall,
  Chimney-sweep, chimney-sweep;
My name it is Sam Hall,
  Chimney-sweep.
My name it is Sam Hall,
And I robs both great and small;
But now I pays for all,
  Chimney-sweep.

Then the parson he will come . . .
With looks so bloody glum,
And talk o' what's to come,
  Chimney-sweep.

[3] Harold Scott (1926), pp. 84–85.

Then the sheriff he'll come too . . .
With all his bloody crew,
Their bloody work to do,
  Chimney-sweep.

Then up the drop we'll go . . .
While the people all below
'll say 'Sam Hall, I told you so,'
  Chimney-sweep.[4]

In this version we are carried back to a time when robbery was a capital offense. Moreover, the criminal is now provided with a calling: he is a chimney sweep who has taken to evil courses. This tradition is confirmed by a version of about 1851 printed on a broadside by Ryal and Company, Seven Dials, London, entitled, "Jack the Chimney Sweep," and beginning "My name it is Jack 'All, chimney sweep, chimney sweep." [5] The song, we learn from the late Frank Kidson, had been popularized about that time (1845–1850) by a comic singer of the music halls named G. W. Ross; [6] it was also printed in Howe's *100 Comic Songs*, p. 31, and in the *The Sam Hall Songster*, ca. 1850. The prevalent music-hall tune was possibly the one given by Harold Scott, as above. Doubtless, the recent currency of this general version of the song derives in the main from its music-hall popularity.

There are three elements to be noted, each of which may be followed as a clue to the further history of the song: (*a*) the chimney sweep, (*b*) the criminal hero, and (*c*) the stanza pattern. We shall take them in turn.

CHIMNEY SWEEP

In the more familiar recent American versions the chimney sweep has disappeared. This is natural for communities where the ancient mystery of chimney sweeping has ceased to be practised, especially since the element contributes nothing essential to the narrative. In England, however, chimney sweeps still look like chimney sweeps, and in the versions of the song which Cecil Sharp picked up from

---

[4] William Hayes, *Selected Songs Sung at Harvard College* (1866), pp. 58–59. The tune is not given.

[5] Sabine Baring-Gould Collection of Broadsides, British Museum, L. R. 271. a. 2, Vol. IX, fol. 225.

[6] Cf. the note contributed by Kidson, in Sharp's *Folk Songs from Somerset*, 4th series (1908), p. 77.

folk singers in Somerset, about the beginning of our century, the criminal was always designated as a sweep. Sharp gathered four versions, and it is noteworthy that they perpetuate a purer traditional strain, untouched by the music-hall influence. The hero's name is Jack Hall, and his song begins in the common way; but the end is carried farther than usual:

> O I rode up Tyburn Hill in a cart, in a cart,
> O I rode up Tyburn Hill in a cart.
> O I rode up Tyburn Hill, and 'twas there I made my will,
> Saying: The best of friends must part, so farewell, so farewell,
> Saying: The best of friends must part, so farewell.
>
> Up the ladder I did grope, that's no joke, that's no joke,
> Up the ladder I did grope, that's no joke.
> Up the ladder I did grope, and the hangman spread the rope,
> O but never a word said I coming down, coming down,
> O but never a word said I coming down.[7]

The tune which Sharp recorded is as follows:

It may be compared with a variant, "Johnny Hall," from County Tyrone in the last century, in the great Petrie Collection, no. 747:

----

[7] C. J. Sharp, *Folk-Songs from Somerset*, 4th series (1908), p. 20; also *One Hundred English Folk Songs* (1916), p. 182.

I am unable to point to any record or trace of the song about the iniquitous sweep named Hall in the earlier part of the nineteenth, or in the latter part of the eighteenth, century. Frank Kidson, however, who also took down the song from tradition, determined the fact that the hero's name was altered in the music halls from Jack to Sam; and discovered that at the end of the seventeenth century there was a historical Jack Hall who was sold as a child to a chimney sweeper for a guinea, who thereafter took to burglary and, while still a young man, was hanged on Tyburn Tree in the year 1701.[8] Kidson called attention to a song in D'Urfey's *Pills to Purge Melancholy*, called "The Moderator's Dream,"—"the Words [says D'Urfey] made to a pretty tune, called Chimney Sweep": that is, a new song set to an old tune of that title.[9] There was, then, a song about a chimney sweep in existence at that date. D'Urfey regrettably fails to print the tune, but the stanza pattern of his new words demonstrates the relationship of the lost song with the one that we know. "The Moderator's Dream" commences thus:

> Four Cardinals in Caps,
> *Save the Queen, save the Queen,*
> Four Monks with bloated Chaps,
> *Save the Queen:*
> Four Capuchins in Bays,
> And to make the People gaze,
> Two Hundred Lights to blaze;
> *Save the Queen, save the Queen.*

Kidson does not mention another song in the sixth and last volume of the *Pills*, with the identical stanza pattern, called simply "A Song" and beginning, "A young man and a maid."[10] The tune here is unnamed, but it is in all probability the one we are seeking, of "Chimney Sweep." It goes as follows:

[8] Cf. Kidson's note cited in footnote 6, above.
[9] *Pills*, II (1719), p. 182.
[10] *Pills*, VI (1720), p. 251.

So far as concerns Jack Hall the chimney sweep, it will be difficult to amplify the foregoing record. If the historical character
who died in 1701 actually gave rise to this particular branch of the
song, we may assume a lost broadside of that year or the next, set
to the tune above, as the parent from which all the songs so far
cited ultimately derive. But other branches of the song will considerably widen the prospect, and to these we shall now turn.

CRIMINAL HERO AND NATIONAL HERO

In the Harvard songbook mentioned above there is, as it happens,
another song about a criminal in the same stanza pattern. It celebrates the misdeeds of the famous buccaneer, Captain Kidd—
Robert in the song, but historically William Kidd.[11] "Captain
Kidd" has likewise circulated widely in traditional singing. There is
a very full version of it in W. R. Mackenzie's *Ballads and Sea-
Songs from Nova Scotia*.[12] The Harvard version contains seven
stanzas only, but the Nova Scotian one has twenty-five, of which
the following five will provide the skeleton of the song:

> (1) My name was Robert Kidd when I sailed, when I sailed,
> My name was Robert Kidd when I sailed.
> My name was Robert Kidd,
> God's laws I did forbid,
> And so wickedly I did when I sailed, when I sailed,
> And so wickedly I did when I sailed.
>
> (7) I murdered William Moore as I sailed, as I sailed . . .
> I murdered William Moore
> And left him in his gore,
> Not many leagues from shore as I sailed . . .
>
> (20) Thus being o'ertaken at last, I must die, I must die . . .
> Thus being o'ertaken at last,
> And into prison cast,
> And sentence being passed, I must die . . .
>
> (23) To Execution Dock I must go, I must go . . .
> To Execution Dock
> Will many thousands flock,
> But I must bear the shock, I must die . . .

---

[11] Hayes, pp. 16–18.
[12] Mackenzie (1928), pp. 278 ff., with many other references.

(25) Take warning now by me, for I must die, I must die . . .
Take warning now by me
And shun bad company,
Lest you come to hell with me, for I must die . . .[13]

Here we have a narrative which, *mutatis mutandis*, follows the same course as "Jack Hall," is told autobiographically, and told in the same stanza pattern. The chief difference is that the hero is a water criminal instead of a land criminal. But the resemblances are so marked as to put a relationship beyond doubt.

The popularity of "Captain Kidd" as a sailor song in comparatively recent years is attested by both Captain Whall and John Masefield.[14] We can follow the song back in cheap songsters and broadsheets printed in this country for about a hundred years; and a broadside printed in England carries it back to the year 1701, when it was directed to be sung to the tune of "Coming Down." [15] We need not look for it any earlier, for at low water, on May 23, 1701, Captain Kidd met his doom at Execution Dock. Jack Hall and Captain Kidd, then, paid the final penalty for their wrongdoing on the gallows in the same year. It would be difficult to say which song got the start of the other.

To return for a moment to the twentieth century: we learn from Cecil Sharp that of the four versions of "Jack Hall" which he collected, three were sung to a tune which properly belonged to a ballad about the naval hero, Admiral Benbow. The question arises, Why this association?

Benbow was a national figure: he rose, as had very few commanders before his day, from butcher's apprentice to admiral; he fought the French in the West Indies, in August 1702; was treacherously deserted by his own captains, all but one of whom turned tail in the battle and put for home. Benbow's right leg was carried away by chain shot, but he had himself carried up onto the quarterdeck to see the fight through. He died of his wounds, in November 1702.

[13] Though this version was taken down from singing, the tune is not given.
[14] W. B. Whall, *Sea Songs and Shanties*, 6th ed. (1927), p. xi; J. Masefield, *A Sailor's Garland* (ed. of 1928), p. xviii. For other versions, with tunes, cf. Gardner and Chickering, *Ballads and Songs of Southern Michigan* (1939), p. 318; J. Colcord, *Roll and Go* (1924), p. 69, and *Songs of American Sailormen* (1938), p. 141; E. H. Linscott, *Folk Songs of Old New England* (1939), p. 131. There was even a *Captain Kidd's Songster* (n.d.).
[15] An exemplar, perhaps unique, is in the Crawford Collection. It is reprinted in C. H. Firth's *Naval Songs and Ballads* (1908), p. 134–137. The tune is not known, but its title suggests the last phrase of Sharp's version of "Jack Hall."

There is little likeness between this heroic story of a famous admiral and the ignominious tale of an obscure chimney sweep turned criminal. The link by which they came to be related would appear to be Captain Kidd. The ballad of Captain Kidd was certainly in full flower by the time Benbow's story swept the nation. Wishing to take advantage of the breeze, some ballad writer turned for a model to a current sea song—the ballad of "Captain Kidd"—and made a new ballad to the same tune and stanza pattern. A half-sheet of the early eighteenth century provides our earliest text, and the tune has been recovered by William Chappell:

Come all you sailors bold, Lend an ear, lend an ear,
Come all you sailors bold, lend an ear.
It's of our Admiral's fame,
Brave Benbow called by name,
How he fought on the main You shall hear, you shall hear,
How he fought on the main you shall hear.

Brave Benbow he set sail For to fight . . .
Brave Benbow he set sail,
With a fine and pleasant gale,
But his Captains they turn'd tail In a fright . . .

Says Kirby unto Wade, "I will run . . .
"I value not disgrace,
Nor the losing of my place,
My enemies I'll not face With a gun . . ."

'Twas the Ruby and Noah's Ark Fought the French . . .
And there was ten in all,
Poor souls they fought them all,
They valued them not at all, Nor their noise . . .

It was our Admiral's lot With a chain shot . . .
Our Admiral lost his legs,

And to his men he begs,
"Fight on, my boys," he says, " 'Tis my lot . . ."

While the surgeon dress'd his wounds, Thus he said . . .
"Let my cradle now in haste
On the quarter-deck be plac'd,
That my enemies I may face Till I'm dead . . ."

And there bold Benbow lay, Crying out . . .
"Let us tack about once more,
We'll drive them to their own shore,
I value not half a score, Nor their noise . . ." [16]

This Benbow ballad is a good sturdy song, and we might expect it to serve as a model for other songs about naval figures. So it proves. At the time of the popular resentment against Admiral Byng over the loss of Minorca, in 1757, a song on the same pattern got started; first, doubtless, on broadsides, and later passing into tradition. It was current in Aberdeenshire at the opening of the nineteenth century, and was printed, finally, from old tradition, in Christie's *Traditional Ballad Airs*, with four stanzas of text, as follows, under the name, "Admiral Byng and Brave West":

I said unto brave West, "Take the van, take the van,"
I said unto brave West, "Take the van."
I said unto brave West,
"As you love fighting best;
I in the rear will rest,
  Take the van."

Brave West did boldly act in the van. . . .
As he did boldly act,
I call'd my own ships back;
Else he'd put the French to wrack
  Near Mahon.

Oh! woe to cursèd gold! ohon! . . .
Oh! woe to cursèd gold;
For Minorca I have sold,
That gallant place of old,
  With Mahon!

It's decreed by the King, I do hear, I do hear,
He's decreed it the nation to please,

[16] Chappell, *Popular Music of the Olden Time*, original edition, II (1855–59), 678–679.

It's decreed by the King,
I'll be shot by my marines,
For the misdeed I have deen
On the seas.[17]

There appears to be a telescoping in the last stanza; and one may also assume a good deal of forgetful abridgment.

Still later, the same pattern was employed for a song on the American hero, Paul Jones. It began, "You've all heard of Paul Jones, have you not? have you not?" [18] And again, after Nelson's victory at Copenhagen, a new adaptation appeared on the same plan. This song, called "The Battle of Copenhagen," contained twenty-seven stanzas, and was written early in 1805 by no less a poet than Thomas Campbell. It began as follows:

Of Nelson and the North
Sing the day,
When their haughty powers to vex
He engaged the Danish decks,
And with twenty floating wrecks
Crowned the fray.[19]

Campbell was dissatisfied with his first effort and afterwards re-wrote the song in a different meter. The improved version is still familiar, under the title of "The Battle of the Baltic."

All these, we may suppose, are offspring of the Admiral Benbow or the Captain Kidd ballad. The evidence from the tunes is scant-ier. Certainly, the eighteenth-century tune printed by Chappell for "Benbow," though perhaps related, shows little resemblance to D'Urfey's tune for "Chimney Sweep"; nor is it very close to the "Benbow" tune collected recently by Sharp.[20] The last named is as follows:

---

[17] W. Christie, *Traditional Ballad Airs*, II (1881), 260–261, with the tune.
[18] Cf. G. F. Graham, *Songs of Scotland*, I (1849), 28–29.
[19] Cf. *Poetical Works of Thomas Campbell*, Oxford edition (1907), pp. 192 ff.; Firth, *Naval Songs and Ballads* (1908), pp. 290 ff.
[20] *Folk-Songs from Somerset*, 3d series (1906), p. 51; *One Hundred English Folk Songs* (1916), p. 200.

We know, however, that "Benbow" and "Jack Hall" were being
sung to the same tune when Sharp was collecting in Somerset. And
Captain Whall tells us that in his day (*ca.* 1875–?), at sea, "Benbow" was being sung to the tune of "Captain Kidd." [21] But he
does not print the tune which he had heard. In fact, so far as I
know, there are before 1920 only one or two printings of the
words of "Captain Kidd" together with a tune.[22] These have been
inaccessible to me. They are American, as are most of the printed
texts of this ballad. Nevertheless, we need not give up hope of finding identifiable and early versions of the tune for "Captain Kidd."
If we search the early hymnbooks of the "shaped-note" kind, we
shall find in some of them a hymn with a first stanza as follows:

> Through all the world below
> God is seen all around;
> Search hills and valleys through,
>   There he's found.
> The growing of the corn,
> The lily and the thorn,
> The pleasant and forlorn,
> All declare God is there,
> In the meadows drest in green
>   There he's seen.[23]

The title of this hymn is "Captain Kidd," and the name might conceivably have puzzled a good many pious singers to account for.
The melody is as follows:

STANZA PATTERN

The text of the hymn of "Captain Kidd" takes us out of the proper
subject matter which we have been following. But the stanza pattern is so distinctive and recognizable that we may reasonably infer

[21] Whall, *Sea Songs and Shanties* (ed. of 1927), p. 81.

[22] Cf. Mackenzie's *Ballads and Sea Songs from Nova Scotia*, pp. 278–279, for
references.

[23] Cf. William Walker, *Southern Harmony* (1835), *et an. seq.*, reprinted as a
W.P.A. publication (1939), p. 50.

relationships where it occurs. It remains to inquire whither and how far back this vehicle will carry us.

Beginning at our own end of things, we shall find, if we look about, a fair number of popular traditional songs on miscellaneous subjects written to this pattern. There is, for example, the well-known "Oh, the eagles they fly high In Mobile, in Mobile." In a recent collection of songs from Mississippi there is a fragment beginning, "Oh, I had an apple pie," which exists in fuller form in a version of 1844:

> Oh, I had an apple pie,
>> Over there, over there.
> Oh, I had an apple pie,
> And the crust was made of rye,
> And 'twas eat that or die,
>> Over there, over there.
>
> Oh, the potatoes they grow tall,
>> Over there, over there.
> Oh, the potatoes they grow tall,
> And they plant them in the fall,
> And they eat them tops and all,
>> Over there, over there.[24]

This song is evidently a variant of the Irish Famine song,

> O the praties they are small
> Over here, over here, etc.

Several English collections of our own century have traditional songs on the same pattern. One of the most widely disseminated is "Three maidens a milking did go," which was found by Frank Kidson in Yorkshire, by Cecil Sharp in Somerset, by Alfred Williams on the Thames.[25] This stem is itself fairly old, for it exists on mid-nineteenth-century broadsides.[26] Incidentally, the tune preserved by Kidson can be seen in a variant form with the fairly common nonsense song, "I was born almost ten thousand years

[24] A. P. Hudson, *Folk-Songs of Mississippi* (1936), pp. 216–217. The earlier version was published by Atwill in New York (1844), four stanzas with music. Cf. also Howe, *100 Comic Songs*, p. 31; Sigmund Spaeth, *Read 'em and Weep* (1926), pp. 33–34.
[25] Kidson, *Traditional Tunes* (1891), p. 73; Sharp MSS., Clare College, Cambridge, fols. 1207, 1476; Williams, *Folk Songs of the Upper Thames* (1923), p. 229; Sandburg (1927), pp. 330–331.
[26] E.g., S. Baring-Gould Collection, British Museum, L.R. 271. a. 2, Vol. III, fol. 29 (a Newcastle broadside printed by Williamson).

ago," in Carl Sandburg's *American Song-Bag*, 1927, though here the stanza pattern has been obscured in the text.

Looking further among the popular hymns current in this country in the last century particularly, we can see how welcome the pattern was for pious uses. Walker's *Southern Harmony*, convenient for inspection because recently reprinted, yields other examples besides "Captain Kidd." Thus, "Solemn Thought" contains words that might have been taken straight from a version of "Kidd" or "Jack Hall":

> Remember, sinful youth, you must die, you must die,
> Remember, sinful youth, you must die.
> Remember, sinful youth,
> Who hate the way of truth,
> And in your pleasures boast, you must die, you must die,
> And in your pleasures boast, you must die.[27]

Another example is "The Saints Bound for Heaven," beginning, "Our bondage it shall end by and by, by and by," and so on.[28] Another is the beautiful "Wondrous Love":

> What wondrous love is this, oh! my soul! oh! my soul!
> What wondrous love is this, oh! my soul!
> What wondrous love is this!
> That caused the Lord of bliss
> To bear the dreadful curse for my soul, for my soul,
> To bear the dreadful curse for my soul.[29]

In the Old World the pattern had already been employed for religious purposes. A carol introduced by Thomas Hardy into *Under the Greenwood Tree* (Pt. I, chap. 4) makes use of the stanza. The carol is "Remember O thou Man"; it is still current in tradition, and was probably the pattern for "Remember, sinful youth." It

[27] Walker, p. 29.
[28] Walker, p. 258.
[29] Walker, p. 252.

was printed in early nineteenth-century collections like Sandys' *Christmas Carols*, 1833; Bedford's *Excellency of Divine Musick*, 1733, carries it back another century; Forbes's *Aberdeen Cantus*, 1662, three-quarters of a century further; and Ravenscroft's *Melismata*, 1611, another half century yet.[30]

Returning once more to the nineteenth century, and leaving the religious texts for the present, we can point to a Manx song, "Marrinys yn Tiger," the tune of which is a variant of "Benbow" as collected by Sharp.[31] Again, the Welsh have a song on the same stanzaic pattern, with a tune markedly reminiscent of D'Urfey's "Chimney Sweep," here called "The Vale of Clwyd." [32]

The Orkney Islanders had a song, very popular in the last century and current in many versions, but usually called "Germany Thomas." It was likely to commence somewhat as follows:

> Oh, my luve's in Germany, Send him hame, send him hame,
> Oh, my luve's in Germany, Send him hame.
> Oh, my luve's in Germany,
> Long leagues o' land and sea
> Frae Westray and frae me—Send him hame.

The tune that goes with this song is, in the following version,[33] unquestionably a member of the same family as D'Urfey's:

The Jacobites, who at least in Scotland, had a quick ear for a good tune, held this one dear. For it Robert Burns wrote his vigorous "Ye Jacobites by name," sent to Johnson's *Scots Musical Museum* in 1792.[34]

---

[30] Cf. *Oxford Book of Carols* (1927), No. 42.
[31] W. H. Gill, *Manx National Song-Book* (1896), p. 4.
[32] C. V. Stanford, *National Song Book* (1906), Welsh Songs, p. 240. The tune is separately named "The Missing Boat."
[33] Alfred Moffat, *Minstrelsy of Scotland*, 2d ed. (1896), p. 115.
[34] Vol. IV, No. 371. Cf. also J. C. Dick (ed.), *The Songs of Robert Burns* (1903), pp. 264, 464.

Another song, "Aikendrum," shows that the Jacobites had already appropriated the tune and stanza for upwards of half a century before Burns wrote. "Aikendrum" describes the situation immediately before the battle of Sheriffmuir, 1715. It commences:

> Ken you how a Whig can fight, Aikendrum, Aikendrum?
> Ken you how a Whig can fight, Aikendrum?
> He can fight, the hero bright,
> With his heels and armour light,
> And his wind of heav'nly might, Aikendrum, Aikendrum,
> Is not Rowley in the right, Aikendrum? [35]

In variant forms, the tune of this was used with the "Paul Jones" ballad, about 1780; [36] it appears also above with Christie's version of "Admiral Byng"; and it has recently been used in the North of Scotland with "Barbara Allan." [37]

An Orkney version of "Germany Thomas" was published in Col. D. Balfour's *Ancient Orkney Melodies* in 1885. There is also an Irish variant of the tune with the title of "They say my love is dead," in the Petrie Collection (no. 698) as collected from a fiddler and lacking the words. Stenhouse declared, with that positiveness which belied his frequent errors, that "Germany Thomas" had been written by Hector Macniell, as Macniell himself had informed him; and also that it had been published on an Edinburgh single sheet as by a lady, upon the death of an officer in 1794. But the Orkney tradition held that it was written by a certain Colonel Traill, who was an officer in the army of Gustavus Adolphus—a tradition which, if credible, would move the song a full century further back, to about the year 1625.

At any rate, there is among the Thorn-Drury Broadsides at Harvard, with the MS. date of November 7, 1659, a ballad entitled "The Arraignment of the Divell for stealing away President Bradshaw." This song, directed to be sung to the tune of "Well-a-day, well-a-day," preserves the stanza pattern in question, and ends with a Tyburn conclusion relating it more closely to "Captain Kidd" and "Jack Hall." The last two stanzas:

[35] J. Hogg, *Jacobite Relics*, 2d series (1821), pp. 22 ff.
[36] Cf. William Stenhouse, *Illustrations of the Lyric Poetry and Music of Scotland* (1853), p. 343.
[37] Cf. G. Greig and A. Keith, *Last Leaves of Traditional Ballads* (1925), p. 70, tune 2.

(18) You must die out of hand,
          Satanas, Satanas,
This our Decree shall stand,
          without Controll,
And we for you will pray,
Because the Scriptures say,
When some men curse you, they
          curse their own soul.

(19) The Fiend to Tiburn's gone,
          There to die, there to die,
Black is the North anon,
          great storms will be:
Therefore together now
I leave him and th' Gallow:
So Newes-man take 'em thou,
          Soon they'l take thee.[38]

Here we appear to have an ancestor, but not an original, for our eighteenth-century hanging ballads.

The communistic group of Social Levellers, know as "Diggers," led by Winstanley, 1649–1652, already had a song on the same pattern, called "Stand up now, Diggers All." The words of it may have been written by Winstanley himself. It contained the following lines:

The gentry are all round, stand up now, stand up now,
The gentry are all round, stand up now.
The gentry are all round, on each side they are found,
Their wisdom's so profound, to cheat us of our ground,
          Stand up now, stand up now.

The clergy they come in, stand up now, . . .
The clergy they come in, and say it is a sin,
That we should now begin, our freedom for to win,
          Stand up now, Diggers all.

To conquer them by love, come in now, . . .
To conquer them by love, as it does you behove,
For He is King above; no power like to love.
          Glory here, Diggers all.[39]

---

[38] The ballad was reprinted in full in C. Mackay, *The Songs and Ballads of the Cavaliers* (1864), pp. 124 ff.

[39] G. M. Trevelyan, *England under the Stuarts* (1904), pp. 282–283, with other references.

Among the Pepys Broadsides (Vol. I, fol. 111) is a ballad on the death of Sir Walter Raleigh, October 29, 1618, which is directed to be sung to the same tune as was "The Arraignment of the Divell," namely, "Well-a-day." This song, besides being a still earlier example of the dying confessions type, preserves the same general pattern. It commences:

> Courteous kind Gallants all, pittie me, pittie me,
> My time is now but small,
>   here to continue:
> Thousands of people stay,
> To see my dying day,
> Sing I then welladay,
>   wofully mourning.[40]

The slight variation in the stanza here brings the song closer in form to the religious branch perpetuated by "Remember O thou Man" than to the more familiar secular variants. The tune of "Well a-day" was a familiar tune in Shakespeare's time, much employed for songs of this kind, and elsewhere called "Essex's Last Good-Night." [41]

We can carry the pattern still further back. In Edinburgh, in 1567, appeared that very curious book called "Ane Compendius Buik of Godly and Spirituall Sangis Collectit out of sundrye partes of the Scripture, with sundrye uther Ballatis changeit out of prophaine sangis in godly sangis for avoyding of sin and harlatry, with augmentation of syndrye gude and godly ballatis." The primary object of this work was to *religify* secular folk-songs by substituting for the sinful words of love and merriment new pious words, keeping the patterns so that the same tunes could be used, because "the Devil had all the good tunes." The "Gude and Godly Ballatis" contains the pattern we have been pursuing:

> All my lufe, leif me not,
>   Leif me not, leif me not,
> All my lufe, leif me not,
>   This myne allone:
> With ane burding on my bak,
> I may not beir it, I am sa waik;

[40] Cf. H. E. Rollins, *A Pepysian Garland* (1922), pp. 89 ff.
[41] A version of it was printed in Chappell's *Popular Music*, I, 176. On the tune and its uses, see Claude M. Simpson, *The English Broadside Ballad and Its Music* (1966), pp. 747-748.

Lufe, this burding fra me tak,
Or ellis I am gone.[42]

One further step into the dark backward and abysm of time remains to be taken. In the quaint book entitled *The Complaynt of Scotlande*, published about 1549, mention is made of a song beginning,

My lufe is lyand seik, send hym ioy, send hym ioy.[43]

Here we reach the very sea mark of our utmost sail, as, so far as I have perused earlier collections, the pattern we have followed does not appear in them. Where it had its beginning therefore remains a mystery; but at times the stanzaic experiments of the earlier carol writers approach it, and we may perhaps assume, pending further light, that our wayward ballad of "Samuel Hall," thoroughly acclimated now in California, took its rise ultimately in the bosom of the Church, in England, at some time in the later Middle Ages.

1942

[42] *Op. cit.*, ed. A. F. Mitchell, Scottish Text Society (1897), p. 220. Cf. also A. G. Gilchrist, "Sacred Parodies of Secular Folk Songs," in the *Journal of the English Folk Dance and Song Society*, Vol. III, No. 3 (December 1938).
[43] *Op. cit.*, ed. J. A. H. Murray, Early English Text Society (1872), p. 65.

The Interdependence of
Ballad Tunes and Texts

HISTORY, doubtless, has its logic, if a man could but find it out. After fifty years of arduous and enthusiastic effort in the collection of British folk-tunes, and, behind that, another hundred and fifty devoted with increasing scholarly assiduity to the collection and detailed comparative study of ballad texts, nothing but the apparent unreason of history could justify the absurdity of recommending at this date that for their proper comprehension it is necessary to study texts and tunes together. For that is so logically and so obviously the initial point of departure! And before any other approach was thinkable an unnatural divorce had to be effected between two elements which had always existed, not side by side, but so inextricably interwoven that even Psyche's "confused seeds" were not more intermixed. The absurdity of urging an axiom for acceptance rests on a greater absurdity: namely, that the greatest scholar in the field, the acknowledged "prince" of ballad students, could all but complete his lifework on the subject without a single word of analysis or description of the traditional music—the vitalizing, breath-giving half of balladry.

Latterly, however, thanks to the sound work of individual collectors and folk-song societies, there has been plenty of interest in folk-music, and some pious exhortation from older students of the ballad not to neglect the tunes. If I am justified in taking as my theme the elementary interdependence of ballad tunes and ballad texts, it is because throughout the country too many academic courses in the ballad still proceed on the basis of textual study alone, with perhaps for a final flourish an hour or so devoted to the

37

concert rendition of a few selected numbers, or the playing of such commercial phonograph records, unaccompanied by critical remarks, as the instructor may have chanced to scrape together—with the acquiescence, one hopes, of a wife indulgent to his extravagance. But as for the exhaustive accumulation of records of the same song for comparative or analytical study of traditional variation, where are the English or Music departments that have budgeted for this?

Yet, I insist, if the student of the ballad is not prepared to give equal attention to the musical, as to the verbal, side of his subject, his knowledge of it will in the end be only half-knowledge. If he lacks the necessary acquaintance with musical rudiments, or is indisposed or unable to enlist the active and continual collaboration of others properly equipped, he had better turn to other fields. For he dismisses the ballad music at his peril. In spite of the scanty and undependable records which have survived from earlier centuries, there is always a possibility that some illumination may be thrown on a particular problem by what is known or can be deduced from ballad music. And, for our own century, for the study of the ballad as something else than a fossil deposit, there is available a fairly large mass of evidence awaiting critical examination. In the present brief survey, I shall devote most of my space to supporting these contentions by characteristic examples.

Take first the elementary matter of the ballad stanza, the unit which matches each complete repetition of the tune, of which it must be the exact counterpart. What is the nature of this unit? What is its irreducible minimum, what are its constituent parts, how is it to be divided? How is a scholarly editor to dispose it upon his page? Ordinarily, as every one knows, it consists of fourteen stresses, with a pause after the seventh, set off by a rhyme between the seventh and fourteenth. The pause may be, and frequently is, filled in by another stress, in which case a corresponding stress will also be added at the end. Metrically, the iambic is the usual pattern, but other types of feet are so freely substituted in easygoing popular verse that it is best not to overemphasize the metrical unit. Hymnodists call these two varieties of stanza "common metre" and "long metre," respectively, or CM and LM. In actual length, however, they do not differ, because the length of the added foot, or stress, in LM—that is, the eighth and sixteenth stresses—precisely equals the length of the pause or sustained note in cm. Both forms, that is to say, are sixteen pulses long. The pause which occurs at the halfway point of the stanza corresponds with the most obvious structural feature of a tune of this sort, the mid-pause, or middle cadence, which in the majority of our tunes comes on the dominant—musically the most satisfying point of rest after the tonic.

As ballads are generally printed, the stanza is divided into four lines, alternately of four and three stresses, or, in lm, of four and four. And for this division also there is as a rule musical justification; for subordinate pauses, or cadences, ordinarily occur in a tune at just those points, so that we feel a natural division into four musical phrases. This scheme is so ubiquitous in English and Scottish folk-song that where it does not occur—unless the departure is according to some well-defined pattern, as in the case of five-, six-, or eight-phrase tunes—we may almost assume that something has gone wrong with the traditional machinery, whether from forgetfulness of text or tune, or from some extraneous influence.

There is no sign that there has been any appreciable variation in this structural norm for ballad tunes since the beginning of the record. During its whole known history, that is to say, the ballad tune has shown no inclination to transcend or exceed in any manner the structural bounds that we know today. But also, during its whole history, this folk-tune pattern has shown no preference for ballads, or *narrative* songs, over any other kind of traditional song text, whether work song, carol, or personal lyric. There is no evidence, or inherent probability, that in the beginning it belonged to the ballad alone, unless we maintain that in the beginning there was only narrative ballad—which is to me unthinkable. Without stopping to muster arguments, it seems obvious that the narrative ballad, in the form in which we know it—and be it remembered that we deny the name when the form is lacking—cannot have existed before the musical vehicle which sustains it had been invented. By definition the ballad is a song. The first ballad, therefore, was sung to a tune. Regardless of whether that particular tune came into existence simultaneously with the first ballad, the form of the tune—this ubiquitous musical pattern found with nearly every kind of popular song—was already in existence. For the proponent of the theory of communal ballad origins it is even more necessary to believe this to be true than it is for the believer in individual composition.

For a group can join in communal singing only when the members of it are in approximate agreement about the tune.

I do not propose to enter upon the question of communal origins. At this distance from Harvard University I dare, indeed, to call the theory metaphysical moonshine, in so far as it has any bearing upon the popular ballad of recorded history—the ballad as represented, for example, by any known variant of any of Child's three hundred and five, including "The Maid freed from the Gallows." Let me then revert to the four-phrase musical form which we take as the norm for our ballad of tradition.

When we find a ballad text which notably fails to conform to this pattern of a minimum of four equivalent phrases, what is to be concluded? Child, following Motherwell, prints his A text of "The False Knight upon the Road" (no. 3) in this fashion:

> (1) "O whare are ye gaun?"
>   Quo the fause knicht upon the road:
> "I'm gaun to the scule,"
>   Quo the wee boy, and still he stude.
>
> (2) "What is that upon your back?" quo, etc.
> "Atweel it is my bukes," quo, etc.
>
> (3) "What's that ye've got in your arm?"
> "Atweel it is my peit."

And so on. Now it is obvious that the first and third lines are in general abnormally short. To lengthen them, nothing seems detachable from the alternating refrain lines, because we can hardly borrow less than the two-stress phrases, "Quo the fause knicht" and "Quo the wee boy," and borrowing so much would leave us in worse case than before, with only two stresses for the refrain lines. Moreover, the refrain lines look as if they were to be regarded as proper four-stress lines as they stand. Can we, then, put any trust in this text as one actually sung? On the contrary, when we turn to Motherwell's Appendix of tunes, we find a tune for this ballad with variant words for the first stanza as follows:

> "O whare are ye gaun?" quo' the false knight,
>   And false false was his rede.
> "I'm gaun to the scule," says the pretty little boy,
>   And still still he stude.

The evidence of this variant suggests that the first was given inaccurately, either to save space or to avoid unnecessary repetition. Unless there was a sharp cleavage in the tradition, we should suppose that "quo the fause knicht" was after all part of the first line, and was repeated to fill out the second. Thus:

> "O whare are ye gaun?" quo the fause knicht
> [Quo the fause knicht] upon the road:
> "I'm gaun to the scule," quo the wee boy,

and so on. Motherwell's "quo, etc." on the same line of text, after the first stanza, might hint corroboration. Looking for further light, we come upon a North Carolina variant collected by Sharp in 1916. (The first, of course, was Scottish, 1827.) The first two phrases of the music carry the following text:

> "Where are you going?" says the knight in the road.
> "I'm going to my school," said the child as he stood.

A Virginia variant confirms this pattern, as do others, from Tennessee and Indiana. A connection in the melodic tradition can be traced through all these with one another and with Motherwell's tune. One would consider the case closed, therefore, were it not for an odd little circular tune preserved by Macmath from Scottish tradition about the end of last century. This tune has the look of being much worn down in tradition, but as it stands it carries the exact counterpart of Motherwell's first text, and so ought finally to settle the question of line adjustment. Well, it does! It proves that the stanzas should be printed as long couplets, and that it is a violence to split them in two. For the tune is one of those which forgo any real first and third cadence, and bring you to the midpoint without a break. Any fixing of first and third cadence would have to be arbitrarily determined by the words, for it would have no musical significance. Musically, an arbitrary cadence point would be possible on any one of four successive beats—which is but to say again that there is no real cadence. If we divided exactly in half, which would be the musical norm, we should get the textual absurdity of

> "O whare are ye gaun?" says
>   The fause knicht upon the road.
> "I'm gaun to the scule," says
>   The wee boy; and still he stude.

But the musical phrase, I repeat, begs not to be divided at all: then why should the words? There is, I might add in lieu of further discussion, a melodic connection between this tune and a Nova Scotian one; and since that is connected with the Appalachian variants, we can link the whole series onto the traditional melodic chain—though not in a straight line of descent.

A textual problem of a somewhat different sort arises in connection with the ballad of "Clerk Colvill" (no. 42). Child's A text of this ballad comes from the famous Mrs. Brown of Falkland, who supplied Jamieson and Scott with some of their choicest and rarest texts. A few years ago, Ritson's transcript of a lost manuscript collection of Mrs. Brown's ballads was turned up in the auction rooms, was bought by Dr. Rosenbach, and was presented to Harvard. The transcript preserves the tunes to which this lady sang her ballads, set down, unfortunately, by a confessedly inexpert hand, but, in the lack of anything better, a valuable record, as indeed anything of the sort before 1800 must necessarily be.[1] "Clerk Colvill," it will be remembered, is the ballad of a mortal man who meddled with a beautiful water-sprite, incurring her enmity with fatal results. A headache set in, which only grew worse when she gave him a piece of her sark to bind about his head for a cure. He had barely time to reach home before death overtook him. Keats's "La Belle Dame" is perhaps an educated cousin of this ballad. Mrs. Brown's text is in LM, quatrains of four-stress lines, rhyming on the second and fourth. There is no refrain, internal or external, and there is no indication in the manuscript that a refrain was sung. The words are not written under the notes: the tune is given first, by itself, and the text follows after, separately. Now, the tune is composed of two phrases of equal length followed by a repeat mark, and then a longer phrase, also marked for repetition. It is hard to see how a quatrain could have been sung to such a tune. A line of text corresponds well enough to either of the first two phrases. Then what of the repeat? It is quite against custom to sing the first two lines of a stanza through twice. The repeat, then, must mean that the second half of the stanza was sung to the same two phrases. But that leaves the second part of the tune unaccommo-

---

[1] The original MS, of which Ritson's is a faithful copy, has been rediscovered in the library at Aldourie Castle. A photographic copy is on loan to the National Library of Scotland.

dated with words. Two lines of text could with an effort be squeezed into this second part, but there are convincing reasons against it. One is that there is no phrasal correspondence between the first and second part of the tune. Another is that the second part must be divided just where two notes are tied together (by the only tie which the writer took pains to insert in this half). A third is that the second half is four bars long, as against six bars in the first half—a very odd fact, if equal lines of text are to be carried by it. And a fourth is that the second half is felt to be naturally only one long phrase. It appears to me, therefore, that no part of the text as we have it was sung to this second half. The only deduction possible, then, is that it must have carried a refrain which Mrs. Brown's copyist, her nephew, never bothered to set down. Presumably, if the words or syllables had made sense, he would have done so: we may infer that they were nonsense syllables. And for such a case there are parallels in Greig's collection of Aberdeenshire tunes.[2] But the fact that Mrs. Brown's nephew left out the refrain without the least hint of omission raises a question about other ballads which have come down from her, only one of which in this manuscript has a refrain. Two, in particular, are in the form of tetrameter couplets. Now, so far as I remember, although it is a common practice to omit an alternating internal refrain after the first stanza, in printing, so that the rest of the ballad *reads* in short couplets, no ballad has ever been taken down from actual folk singing, by careful and accurate collectors like Sharp and Greig, in this short-couplet form. If the refrain comes inside the quatrain, on lines 2 and 4, there is of course no sign of the fact in the tune alone. The fact that the tunes of these ballads of Mrs. Brown appear to be of the usual four-phrase sort (in one case ABAB, or two phrases repeated) consequently throws no light on the question. But in view of the general rule, and the all-but-demonstrable omission in the case just discussed, it appears strongly probable that Mrs. Brown sang "Willy's Lady" (no. 6) and "Gil Brenton" (no. 5) with an interlaced refrain. Moreover, the same probability appears to me to hold in all similar cases of early texts in short couplet form, taken down without their proper tunes. Such a conclusion would affect,

[2] For the tune in question, and further discussion of it, cf. *California Folklore Quarterly*, I (1942), 188–190; or better, the author's *The Traditional Tunes of the Child Ballads*, I (1959), p. 334.

to name no lesser things, the A* text (*ca.* 1450) of "Riddles Wisely Expounded" (no. 1), supposing it to have been sung, and "Earl Brand" in its first and most important text. But the same would *not* hold for the long couplets—really a half-stanza to the line—of "St. Stephen and Herod" (no. 22), "Judas" (no. 23), and "Bonnie Annie" (no. 24).

The question of patterns in refrain has obvious importance for the melodic tradition of a ballad. Had Child been concerned to establish the singing tradition of his ballads, it is clear that he must have given more attention to their refrains than he did. In many cases, such concern would have resulted in a rearrangement of his variants. For, obviously, where there has been a shift in the type of refrain, as from interlaced refrain at the second and fourth lines to refrain as an added fifth line, or to a more complicated interlacing, there must also have occurred a corresponding alteration in the melodic vehicle. A change of this kind could not be a gradual transition, such as produces the multiplicity of related variants. It must have been single and sudden, a conscious shift from one tune to another. This sort of aberration is not ordinarily included in the conventional description of the traditional process. Nevertheless, the evidence is sufficient to show that, whatever the motives, the phenomenon is not uncommon; and it must be reckoned with as an important factor of change in oral transmission.[3]

For illustration we may use "The Twa Sisters" (no. 10), a ballad unusually rich in changes of refrain. One would guess from the record that the earlier type of refrain here was the simple interlaced pattern at the second and fourth lines. The earliest English texts (of mid-seventeenth century provenience) are of this kind, and the majority of Child's Scottish and Irish texts belong to it. (In all, he takes account of about forty texts.) All the variants of the "Binnorie" group fall into this category. Incidentally, it might be noted that the currency of the "Binnorie" refrain appears mainly in the wake of Scott's *Minstrelsy*, 1802. It does not appear in the Herd manuscripts, nor in the *Scots Musical Museum*, and Pinkerton is the only authority—he is not often entitled to the name—to make use of it before Scott. And Scott, as his manuscripts prove, engrafted it upon his primary copy of the ballad from another.

Of this same type of refrain we have various styles: "With a hie

[3] Cf. further on this point, essay sixteen in this collection.

downe downe a downe-a" (in the seventeenth century); "Fal the lal the lal laral lody" (English of the nineteenth, and probably eighteenth, century); "Norham, down by Norham," or "Nonie an' Benonie," coupled with "By the bonnie mill-dams o Norham," or "Benonie"; "Hey with a gay and a grinding O" and "About a' the bonny bows o London"; "Cold blows the wind, and the wind blows low" with "And the wind blows cheerily around us, high ho"; "Oh and ohone, and ohone and aree" with "On the banks of the Banna, ohone and aree"; "Hech hey my Nannie O" with "And the swan swims bonnie O." The last two styles are especially Celtic, and the swan refrain would be particularly favored in Ireland, where they go in for swans. Child's suggestion that the explanation of the obscure name, "Binnorie," may possibly lie in the phrase, "On the banks of the Banna, ohone and aree," is supported neither by the rhythm nor by the Irish tunes, which appear fairly distinct from the Binnorie group. As a final example of this type of refrain, a variant found in Michigan, in 1934, might be cited: "Viola and Vinola," with "Down by the waters rolling"—wherein the proper names turn out to be those of the rival sisters. It is to be hoped that the gloss of commercialism on these names is too high to be perpetuated in traditional memory.

This ballad still persists in vigorous life in our own country, especially in the Appalachian region. There its association with dancing is attested by the words of a refrain of a different type, prevalent wherever the "play-party" tradition has been current, and probably elsewhere. Here the pattern is of a stanza of double length, the interlaced refrain coming on the second, fourth, seventh, and eighth lines. There is a threefold repetition of the first line of text, on lines one, three, and five; so that the narrative advances only two lines with each stanza. Here is a characteristic example, from Kentucky:

> There lived an old lord by the Northern Sea,
>   Bowee down!
> There lived an old lord by the Northern Sea,
>   Bow and balance to me!
> There lived an old lord by the Northern Sea,
> And he had daughters one, two, three,
>   I'll be true to my love,
>   If my love'll be true to me! [4]

[4] James Watt Raine, *Land of Saddle-Bags* (1924), p. 118.

Musically, this stanza implies a double-strain, or eight-phrase air, with the middle cadence coming after the second element of re-frain. It is especially apt for dancing, for the greater length gives space for the figures to develop, and the slow rate of narrative pro-gression permits concentration rather on the dance than on the story. Many of the seventeenth-century English country-dance tunes in Playford and elsewhere are of this form. But it is older than the seventeenth century and has associations with a number of early ballads and songs, such as "The Wedding of the Frog and the Mouse," "The Friar in the Well," "The Three Ravens." That its perennial serviceability is not yet spent is proved by the currency of "Mademoiselle from Armentières" ("Hinky Dinky, Parlez Vous"). And that the demoiselle is in the direct line from an Eliza-bethan daughter of Eve can be proved by a morality-play of about 1568. In William Wager's *The Longer Thou Livest the More Fool Thou*, Moros, whose head is stuffed only with idle mischief, enters singing snatches from the popular songs he has picked up from his pothouse companions. He gets through the first stanza of one of these, as follows:

> There was a mayde cam out of Kent,
>> Daintie loue, daintie loue,
> There was a mayde cam out of Kent,
>> Daungerous be:
> There was a mayde cam out of Kent,
> Fayre, propre, small and gent,
> As euer vpon the grounde went,
>> For so should it be.

That is the earliest appearance of the full-blown "Twa Sisters" stanza known to me; but there may well be earlier cases, for many early carol texts, assuming natural repetitions, would fall into the same form. It is doubtless evidence of a depraved taste to confess that one would give the rest of Wager's play in exchange for the rest of Moros's ballad.

As for "bow and balance": how old are the names of these pos-tures in the dance can perhaps be settled by the historians of that subject. In its present connection, the question is complicated by several ambiguous possibilities. The earliest trace of the Appala-chian refrain which I have noted with this ballad goes back to Kent, as it happens, about the year 1770. Among the Percy papers there is a copy of that locality and date, with refrain on 2, 4, 7, and 8 as follows:

> . . . Hay down down derry down
> . . . And the bough it was bent to me
> . . . I'll prove true to my love
>   If my love will prove true to me.

There can be no doubt of the connection between these refrains. But the earlier one has no indication of the dance-step. From a Yorkshire variant of the later nineteenth century comes a new suggestion:

> . . . Low down, derry down dee
> . . . Valid we ought to be
> . . . And I'll be true to my love
>   If my love will be true to me.

Here are neither bent knees nor bent boughs. But in another variant of about the same time and place as the last comes this:

> . . . Bow down, bow down
> . . . As the bough doth bend to me
> . . . And I'll be true to my true love
>   If my love will be true to me.

This last gives us a consistent reading, but it is not easy to prove that it is the original consistency. Certainly "hey down down derry down" has ancient precedent behind it, notably in the Robin Hood cycle; whilst "low down" in such a context has little or none. Nor does "low down" seem likely to have led to "bow down." Yet "down" by itself contains the suggestion of "low"; and if "hey" were ever pronounced "hi" by singers, someone sooner or later would be sure to change "hi down" to "low down." Again, there is on record among such singers the pronunciation "bo" for "bow": "he bo'd his breast and swum." The sequence is therefore possible, if barely so. On the other hand, "the bough was bent to me" might of itself induce the "bow down" of the other line; and in its turn "bow down" might suggest in oral tradition the other image, as it obviously has in one recorded variant, "Bow your bends to me." From this to "bow and balance" is but a skipping step in a dancing community. But the "Valid we ought to be" can hardly have been corrupted *into* "balance and bo(w) to me": it must have been the other way round, where the dance terms were unfamiliar. So that a greater antiquity may be indicated for "bow and balance" than any of which we have record. Nevertheless, *boughs* that bend, and *bōws*—whether elbows or bows of yew— have ancient and legitimate connections with balladry, and may well contain the radical images. Moreover, the American variants continue the confusion between *bōws* and *boughs*. *Balance*, however, comes not in such a questionable shape; and when "the *boys* are bound for me," as in certain late variants, they wear their folk etymology upon their sleeves.

At any rate, the variants with these refrains—there are between three and four dozen of them on record—all belong to one melodic family, which can never have been related to the "Binnorie" group. The "bow down" pattern has shown an occasional tendency, as exhibited in about a dozen additional recorded variants, to abridge itself to a six-phrase pattern, generally by omitting one repetition of the first line, together with the second element of the refrain. As thus, in a Berkshire version:

> A varmer he lived in the West Countree,
> > With a hey down, bow down:
> A varmer he lived in the West Countree,
> And he had daughters, one two, and three,
> > And I'll be true to my love,
> > If my love 'll be true to me.

That this is not actually a new pattern, but a corruption of the former one, is proved by the fact that every case of it is an incomplete and usually disordered member of the same melodic family.

Finally, a separate Scottish tradition as old as the eighteenth century makes use of the same eight-phrase interlaced stanza pattern, but with place names for the refrain, and (apparently) a distinct melodic tradition. Thus Mrs. Brown's text:

> There was twa sisters in a bowr,
> > Edinburgh, Edinburgh,
> There was twa sisters in a bowr,
> > Stirling for ay
> There was twa sisters in a bowr,
> There came a knight to be their wooer.
> > Bonny St. Johnston
> > stands upon Tay.

The same refrain is found with several other ballads.

It will perhaps be a relief if I turn to another aspect of my subject, another way in which texts and tunes are interrelated. It not infrequently appears that, just as a refrain will get attached to more than one ballad, so variants of one and the same tune will be discovered in association with the texts of different ballads. What are the possible explanations of such a phenomenon, and what legitimate inferences may be drawn from it?

There are undoubtedly certain tunes, or tune families, which are so strongly and ineradicably rooted in traditional singing that, like the commonest sorts of weed, they tend to crop up everywhere and take possession of any available space, crowding out the less hardy plants. Such, for example, are the common tunes for "Lady Isabel and the Elf Knight" (no. 4) and "Lord Thomas and Fair Eleanor" (no. 73), which are found all over the ballad landscape. From these I can draw no significant inference, other than the obvious one that certain tunes are so catchy and easy to remember that, once heard, they cannot be shaken off. Like burrs, they cling to every passerby and are carried far and wide.

But there are other tunes which require a congenial soil for transplantation, and sometimes reveal an interesting lineal connection. There may be fortuitous resemblances between tunes which cause them to gravitate and coalesce. Equally, there may be verbal or narrative connections between ballad texts which facilitate a borrowing by one ballad of the other's tune. Or, again, there may be tunes which, from a relationship half-consciously sensed by the singer, act as the disintegrating and reintegrating agents that gradually win away elements of a ballad, and reestablish these in new contexts, modifying the conduct of the narrative, or otherwise effecting a crossing that produces a new and different species. Many of these textual interconnections have been remarked in Child's headnotes. But it can hardly be doubted that the tunes have been responsible for the linkages perhaps as often as have parallels of situation.

Sometimes related tunes suggest or lend confirmation to a suspected connection between ballads. A case in point is Child's no. 27, "The Whummil Bore." Child introduces it with the dubious remark: "This ballad, if it ever were one, seems not to have been met with, or at least to have been thought worth notice, by anybody but Motherwell." As the piece is very short, it may be quoted here:

(1) Seven lang years I hae served the king,
  Fa fa fa fa lilly
And I never got a sight of his daughter but ane.
  With my glimpy, glimpy, glimpy eedle,
  Lillum too tee a ta too a tee a ta a tally

(2) I saw her thro a whummil bore,
And I neer got a sight of her no more.

(3) Twa was putting on her gown,
And ten was putting pins therein.

(4) Twa was putting on her shoon,
And twa was buckling them again.

(5) Five was combing down her hair,
And I never got a sight of her nae mair.

(6) Her neck and breast was like the snow,
Then from the bore I was forced to go.

This appears to be an example of pawky fun at the expense of high romance, like "Sir Eglamore," "The Twa Corbies," (no. 26) or "Kempy Kay" (no. 33). For this sort of thing there is, of course, high precedent in Chaucer's *Sir Thopas*, to name but one out of multitudes. "The Whummil Bore" appears to me a by-blow of a serious romantic ballad. The evidence of its tune indicates where its affiliations lie. Here is Motherwell's tune:

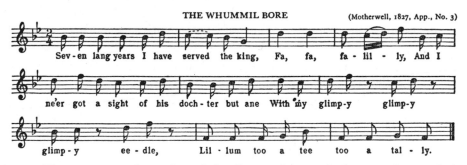

THE WHUMMIL BORE   (Motherwell, 1827, App., No. 3)

Sev-en lang years I have served the king, Fa, fa, fa-lil-ly, And I ne'er got a sight of his doch-ter but ane With my glimp-y glimp-y glimp-y ee-dle, Lil-lum too a tee too a tal-ly.

If we reverse the order of the first and second phrases, the result is a fairly close parallel to Miss Minnie Macmath's tune for "Hind Horn" (no. 17), amounting almost to identity in the third phrase. The Motherwell tune, flown with insolence, repeats its third phrase with variation, and ends with a fifth phrase which would supply an equally appropriate termination for the Macmath tune, which in fact seems to have forgotten its proper conclusion:

HIND HORN   (Child, I, 503, and V, 413)

She gave him a gay gold ring, Hey lil- le lu and how lo__ lan, But he gave her a far bet-ter thing, Wi my hey down and a hey did-dle down- ie.

Child, incidentally, did not miss the fact that some versions of "Hind Horn" contained a curious reference to Horn's seeing his love through some small aperture, e.g., an augur bore, or a gay gold ring, and conjectured that the detail was borrowed from "The Whummil Bore," where it manifestly comes in more appropriately. He did not, however, suggest that a much greater obligation lay in the opposite direction, which to me appears altogether probable. "Hind Horn" is an ancient and honorable ballad, and its tune, in one variety or another, is well established and consistently associated with it.

The ballad of "Lizie Wan" (no. 51) is one which has not often been found. It first appears in Herd's manuscripts and has been recovered half a dozen times in our century in this country, and once in England. As Herd gives it, it tells an unpleasant story: Lizie sadly confesses to her father that she is with child. By comes her brother, and she charges him with equal guilt:

> There is a child between my twa sides,
> Between you, dear billy, and I.

When he finds out that she has revealed her state, he draws his sword and cuts her to pieces. His mother asks him, later, why he acts so distraught. He replies, first, that he has killed his greyhound, and next, under pressure, that he has slain Lizie Wan.

> "O what wilt thou do when thy father comes hame,
>   O my son Geordy Wan?"
> "I'll set my foot in a bottomless boat,
>   And swim to the sea-ground."
>
> "And when will thou come hame again,
>   O my son Geordy Wan?"
> "The sun and the moon shall dance on the green
>   That night when I come hame."

The parallel in the latter part of this ballad with the much more famous "Edward" (no. 13) is obvious. It is therefore interesting to find a similar parallel between the tune collected by Sharp in his Appalachian version of "Lizie Wan" and one of the tunes which he got in the same region for "Edward":

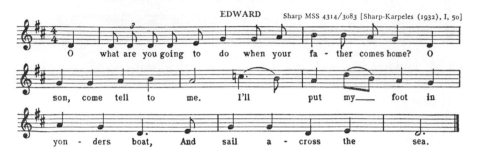

EDWARD   Sharp MSS 4314/3083 [Sharp-Karpeles (1932), I, 50]

O what are you going to do when your fa - ther comes home? O son, come tell to me. I'll put my___ foot in yon - ders boat, And sail a - cross the sea.

The question of relationship between these two ballads opens up a fascinating field for speculation. Both, if not of Scandinavian birth, have important Scandinavian counterparts. Both appear in the Scottish record at approximately the same time. Neither has had currency in England or Ireland. Professor Archer Taylor, in a comparative analysis of all available variants, has shown that the Percy text of "Edward," from the point of view of tradition, is

LIZZIE WAN   Sharp MSS 3838/2810 [Sharp-Karpeles (1932), I, 89]

Fair Lu - cy sit - ting in her fa - ther's___ room, La - ment - ing and a - mak - ing her mourn; And___ in ___ steps her bro - ther James: O___ what's fair Lu - cy done?

spurious and sophisticated.[5] The version next in date is later by more than fifty years in the record, and, although doubtless a good deal closer to tradition, still affected in the dénouement by Percy. The traditional versions of "Edward" do not implicate the mother in her son's guilt, and tell a tasteless story of brother-murder in a fit

---

[5] Archer Taylor, *"Edward" and "Sven i Rosengård"* (1931), especially pp. 26, 38. Cf. also my independent argument to the same effect in the first essay of this collection.

of anger devoid of tragic significance. The brothers fall out about a little bush that might have made a tree, which one of them has untimely cut down. Phillips Barry has suggested that the bush (holly or hazel in the Appalachian variants) is to be interpreted symbolically as a girl. This sort of symbol seems to me—I speak under correction—alien to the popular habit; and "Lizie Wan" shows how unnecessary it was to veil the meaning in such obscurity. Nevertheless, it is natural to suppose that originally the ballad of "Edward" had a more compelling narrative core than appears in extant tradition. And certainly the murder of a sister as a *crime passionel*, or of a brother out of jealous rivalry, would provide a plot sufficiently Aeschylean. It is a fact that some Swedish texts of "Edward" make the sister the victim, whether this mean much or little. "Lizie Wan" is one of four ballads in Child on a similar theme, and its roots are undeniably deep in northern tradition. It might, incidentally, have been expected that a connection would be found between "Edward" and "The Twa Brothers" (no. 49), where the same brother-rivalry and fratricide occur. And in some texts of the latter ballad such a connection is in fact disclosed. (Child no. 49 D, E, F, and G.) But the melodic connections in the latter case do not support the association. Instead, they mainly lie rather with "Little Sir Hugh" (no. 155), and apparently rise from a similar opening of schoolchildren playing ball. But, without being dogmatic, I would only remark further of "Edward" and "Lizie Wan," that if, granting contamination of one ballad by the other, we attempt to establish a priority, the claims of "Lizie Wan" to being more deeply rooted in early Scandinavian lore, and inherently less likely to have derived from "Edward" than the reverse, are claims not to be lightly dismissed.

Another interesting case of possible crossing occurs between "Young Hunting" (no. 68) and "Lady Isabel and the Elf Knight" (no. 4). The melodic tradition of "Young Hunting" is rather perplexed and hard to make out, whilst that of "Lady Isabel" is unusually clear. But a small group of variants of "Young Hunting" makes use of a distinct variety of the "Lady Isabel" tunes, and the texts of this group commence in a very particular way—with the sound of a distant horn, and the conflicting emotions stirred up by that music in the breast of Young Hunting's sweetheart. Elsewhere, the ballad generally opens abruptly with her invitation to come in and stay the night. Now, in the current variants of "Lady Isabel" there is no mention of a horn. But formerly, as in Child's A text and in various Continental analogues, the horn had a most important and necessary function to perform in that ballad. It was elfin music, and it had such power of magic persuasion that before the heroine ever saw the creature who blew it, she was ready to run away with him. No other ballad, I believe, makes such introductory use of a horn except "The Elfin Knight" (no. 2), which Child supposes also affected by "Lady Isabel." The occurrence of the horn in "Young Hunting," then, may be an intrusion from "Lady Isabel" and may have drawn the characteristic tune with it; or the tune may have brought the horn over to the other ballad, from versions of "Lady Isabel" formerly in circulation. It is worth notice, moreover, that both ballads, besides sharing the theme of a sweetheart's killing her lover (albeit for very different reasons), make prominent use of a talking bird. In "Young Hunting," this bird has been understood to be a relic of former belief in metempsychosis, the bird being the soul of the slain lover.[6] It plays a vital and significant role in the narrative. But in "Lady Isabel," the parrot that chatters idly when the heroine comes safely home before the dawning, and has to be bribed to silence with the promise of a cage of ivory and gold, performs no office essential to the plot, and is doubtless an importation. There may be here a borrowing in the opposite direction, underlined perhaps by the similar promise of reward from Young Hunting's mistress, if the bird will not reveal her guilt.[7] However it be, there appears sufficient evidence of a hitherto unnoticed crossing of these ballads in tradition, signalized by the melodic convergence.

Much, again, can be learned about the ways of tradition, both textual and musical, from what has happened within the last three hundred years to the ballad of "Sir Lionel" (no. 18). Back of 1650 lies the earliest known text of this ballad, in the Percy Folio manuscript, a very defective text, without a tune, and not certainly known to have been sung. In spite of serious deficiencies—there are two large lacunae where pages have been torn out of the manu-

[6] L. C. Wimberly, *Folklore in English and Scottish Popular Ballads* (1928), p. 192.
[7] In version E of A. K. Davis, *Traditional Ballads from Virginia* (1928), p. 189, there is an absurd intrusion from "Lady Isabel" into "Young Hunting," stanza 8.

script—this is still our fullest text in narrative content, and a serious treatment of a theme of high romance. Except for a nineteenth-century Scottish text recorded by Christie, all the other versions of this ballad which have been collected, whether from English or American tradition, tend in varying degree toward the farcical. The Percy Folio version is in quatrains, with an interlaced refrain at lines 2 and 4—the refrain, incidentally, echoing a song that has survived in a manuscript of Henry VIII's time.

In the present century, but doubtless going back in family tradition a hundred years or more, there appears in this ballad a marked change of pattern as well as of mood. Instead of the staid refrain of the older form, we find a series of nonsense syllables, fitted to the elaborate eight-phrase scheme already met in "The Twa Sisters." This new (but ancient) pattern is exemplified in a Wiltshire variant, published, without a tune, in 1923:

> Bold Sir Rylas a-hunting went—
> I an dan dilly dan
> Bold Sir Rylas a-hunting went—
> Killy koko an.
> Bold Sir Rylas a-hunting went—
> To kill some game was his intent—
> I an dan dilly dan
> killy koko an.[8]

This, with occasional abridgment, is the nearly universal stanza form of the ballad in current tradition. Now, obviously, there has either been a complete break here with the older tradition, or else the traditional antecedents of the modern ballad are not adequately represented in the examples printed by Child. What has happened to the narrative will support the latter alternative.

Child pointed out that "Sir Lionel" had much in common with the old metrical romance of "Sir Eglamour of Artois." This relationship is clearest in the Percy Folio text. There we have a lady sore beset, whose knight has been slain by a wild boar; a fight between Sir Lionel and the boar (implied, but lost with the leaf or leaves gone from the manuscript); a rencounter between the giant, who owned the boar, and Sir Lionel, in which Sir Lionel is worsted but chivalrously granted a forty-day respite to prepare for a new

---

[8] A. Williams, *Folk Songs of the Upper Thames* (1923), p. 118.

combat; Lionel's return to fight with the giant and rescue the lady; and, finally, in the last portion (again missing, but baldly summarized in Christie's version), the defeat of the giant. All these elements had appeared in the old romance, which, however, Child carefully abstains from calling the original of the ballad.

Now, in the nineteenth-century English versions, the giant's place has been supplied by a "wild woman" whom the hero treats as unmercifully as he had earlier treated the giant. The central incident, however, has become the boar fight. The lady in distress is barely mentioned, and is easily confounded with the wild woman who owns the boar. In the more recently collected versions, she appears only long enough to tell the knight that a blast of his horn will bring on the boar; or (as usually in the American variants) she makes no appearance whatever. The wild woman in some variants does double duty for gentle and savage; but she, like her predecessors, also tends to drop out of the story. What finally remains is the single episode of the boar fight, told now as riotous farce.

At some time in the seventeenth century, apparently early, another ballad on the subject of Sir Eglamore became popularly current, and was perpetuated on broadsides. The first known copy seems to be that in Samuel Rowlands's "The Melancholie Knight," 1615, and Rowlands may have written the ballad. By the last quarter of the seventeenth century it was widely known and was circulating independently of print. It had a catchy tune which went about in variant forms, as popular tunes unshackled by copyright laws will do. One form of the tune—with new words, but identified by its proper name—was printed in Nat. Thompson's *180 Loyal Songs* (1685), page 276, as follows: [9]

SIR EGLAMORE   (N. Thompson, *180 Loyal Songs* [1685], p. 276)

[9] The tune is an analogue of one employed, to judge by its title, with another Child ballad, "The Maid peept out of the window," in Playford, *The English Dancing Master* (1650), p. 42 (cf. Child, no. 276), reprinted by Margaret Dean-Smith (1957), p. 36.

Another was copied into a manuscript of approximately the same time, and now lies in the Edinburgh University Library, hitherto unprinted (MS Dc. 1. 69): [10]

SIR EGLAMORE

(Edinburgh Univ. MS Dc. 1. 69, No. 1 at back of MS)

Sr Eg-la-more that val-iant Knight fa la lan-kee downe dil-ly Hee

tooke upp his sword & hee went to fight fa la And

as hee rode o're Hill & dale all armed with a Coate of Male fa

la la la la la la lan-kee downe dil-ly.

In nearly identical form, this variant later appeared in D'Urfey's *Pills*, with the following text:

> Sir *Eglamore*, that valiant Knight,
>   *Fa la, lanky down dilly;*
> He took up his Sword, and he went to fight,
>   *Fa la, lanky down dilly:*
> And as he rode o'er Hill and Dale,
> All Armed with a Coat of Male,
>   *Fa la la, la la la, lanky down dilly.*
>
> There leap'd a Dragon out of her Den,
> That had slain God knows how many Men;
> But when she saw Sir *Eglamore*,
> Oh that you had but heard her roar!
>
> Then the Trees began to shake,
> Horse did Tremble, Man did quake;
> The Birds betook them all to peeping,
> Oh! 'twould have made one fall a weeping.
>
> But all in vain it was to fear,
> For now they fall to't, fight Dog, fight Bear;
> And to't they go, and soundly fight,
> A live-long day, from Morn till Night.

[10] The time of this tune is equivalent to 6/8; the stemless black notes are twice the length of those with stems.

This Dragon had on a plaguy Hide,
That cou'd the sharpest steel abide;
No Sword cou'd enter her with cuts,
Which vex'd the Knight unto the Guts.

But as in Choler he did burn,
He watch'd the Dragon a great good turn;
For as a Yawning she did fall,
He thrust his Sword up Hilt and all.

Then like a Coward she did fly,
Unto her Den, which was hard by;
And there she lay all Night and roar'd,
The Knight was sorry for his Sword:
But riding away, he cries, I forsake it,
He that will fetch it, let him take it.[11]

Here we have the stanza pattern of the current ballad of "Brangy-well" or "Bangum and the Boar," as "*Sir Lionel*" is called today; and the tunes sung in our century will prove to be variants of the same melodic idea as "Sir Eglamore," with such shortening and rhythmical modification as might be looked for in its translation from country-dance usage to its present solo form. A characteristic example from Kentucky is the following:

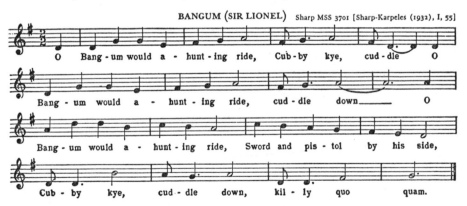

BANGUM (SIR LIONEL)   Sharp MSS 3701 [Sharp-Karpeles (1932), I, 55]

O Bang - um would a - hunt - ing ride, Cub - by kye, cud - dle O
Bang - um would a - hunt - ing ride, cud - dle down_____ O
Bang - um would a - hunt - ing ride, Sword and pis - tol by his side,
Cub - by kye, cud - dle down, kil - ly quo quam.

It is plain, then, that both in spirit, in narrative, and in melodic tradition, the recent forms of "Sir Lionel" are primarily descendants of the "Eglamore" ballad, and only secondarily of the ancient romance ballad. Any who wish for that reason to exclude it from the authentic traditional canon may do so: not I.

[11] D'Urfey, *Pills to Purge Melancholy*, III (1719), 293-294

The foregoing will serve as examples of a common melodic tradition between different ballads, and of characteristic results of such a crossing. What further of the contrary case, where a single ballad is sung to different tunes? One aspect of the problem has, of course, already arisen in this matter of deflecting crosscurrents. But we should like to know more about what might be called the sharp corners in tradition, where tune or text, or both, appear suddenly to have taken a new direction. What is the nature of the prism which must be hypothesized at these nodal points? It is a mechanism that cannot be examined at first hand: we can only deduce it from its effects. But no subject of human inquiry is more open to all the winds of chance than that of folk-song; and it is altogether probable that not one but many prisms have produced these deflections. So that any generalizations are likely at best to account only for a limited group of phenomena.

What, for example, can be deduced from the fact that a ballad is sung in Scotland to one melodic tradition, and in America to another? There are cases of this kind, where no relationship can be discerned between the melodies current or on record in the old world and the new, but where the text is recognizably close. The ballad, we must presume, was brought across the ocean by singers, for the Bell Robertsons who remember only the words are black swans in balladry.[12] And if the tune were dropped overboard on the way, the reasonable inference would be that the ballad came West on paper and not in the head. Then the water barrier, we conclude, is of no real significance: the melodic tradition turned the corner either before or after the ballad crossed the Atlantic. We are thus faced with the original problem: Why is the same ballad, continuously handed on from singer to singer, never heard without its air and committed to paper during such transmission only as an aid to verbal memory—why and how is this ballad found with different tunes?

The conventional explanation would probably be that these songs had been so long in circulation, uncontrolled by an authoritative original version, that the variants had drifted farther and farther apart. The older the song, the wider the differences; so that where we find no traits of resemblance between two or more tunes

---

[12] Bell Robertson was Greig's most generous wellspring of traditional ballads, but tuneless.

of a ballad, we may infer many generations of traditional transmission behind its present state.

To such a conclusion I should myself grant only a tentative and very limited assent, for I do not find that the available evidence at all justifies so sweeping a generalization. There is plenty of evidence, I believe, to support a contrary position: that where a melodic and textual tradition is solidly established, vigorously and continuously alive, its identity will be perpetuated, with a notable consistency in its main outlines, for long periods of time. Such has been the way, for example, with the melodic traditions of "Barbara Allen," and "Lord Lovel," and "Lord Thomas and Fair Eleanor." I do not speak of the texts in these cases, which have been more or less subject to the control of print. Conversely, I believe it sometimes to be an indication of a late start that a ballad displays no dominant melodic tradition. Thus, it strikes me as a suspicious circumstance that "Sir Patrick Spens" (no. 58) shows no such melodic continuity anywhere. It is quite clear that Johnson, when he first printed a tune for this ballad in the *Scots Musical Museum*, knew no traditional setting, for he put it to an unsingable pipe or fiddle tune which has never since been found with it in tradition, although it has been several times reprinted from Johnson. It may, in fact, be a point of real importance that the musical record of this ballad seems to show—I do not positively say it does show, for the variants are not abundant enough for proof—a gradual convergence in the last century and a half. Contrary to what we have been taught to expect, the period of widest diversity here is the earliest, since which time the traditional tunes of the "Spens" ballad have appeared to exhibit a tendency, as yet indistinct and uncertain, to drift toward a relatively similar melodic form. Indeed, I throw it out as an open question whether, in the decline of folksong which we must inevitably expect as more and more of the population becomes corrupted by musical literacy, as it already has been by verbal literacy—for literacy and culture are very different —whether, I say, all folk-music will not evince the same tendency to drift toward a single, universal, indistinguishable, ultimate tune. The one process which seems to be universally operative in the realm of tradition, however it be by fortunate circumstance obscured or delayed, is, alas, no "epic process," but the process of abrasion, which tends always from complex to simple, and more simple, until the iniquity of oblivion, or soon or slow, shall have completed its office.

I believe, none the less, that the natural conservatism of the folk-singer—admittedly very impressive in particular cases—has been greatly exaggerated as a universal phenomenon. It is of course just the cases of extraordinary tenacity which would strike a collector most forcibly, whereas the opposite tendency would be relatively little subject to remark. The evidence, in its total recent bulk, seems to me to point to a greater independence, or potential infidelity to strict tradition, than has heretofore been allowed. The rate of change, involving unconscious, semiconscious, and even willful alteration, may have been considerably more rapid than most students suppose. The coefficient of change—speaking now particularly of consistent and not disruptive change—is the level of intelligence of the folk-singing community, and the liveliness of its artistic sensibility. The higher that level, the more unwilling—indeed, unable—a singer will be to serve merely as a passive transmitter of the songs that he has loved. Those students who have maintained that there was, hundreds of years ago, a creative period of oral tradition, but that since the sixteenth century or thereabouts tradition in balladry has been on the road downhill, have really been saying the same thing. But their view of the matter has been conditioned and limited by the fact that they were looking almost exclusively at the texts. Faced on the one hand with a number of superior early ballad texts, and on the other by the spectacle of increasing dilapidation in the multiplying evidence of the variants collected from recent tradition, their conclusion was in fact almost the only rational one possible. The spread of literacy has drawn off into other channels a large proportion of the creative energy which once went into the ballads. The later generations of ballad singers have for the most part lacked the gifts to do more than perpetuate in a relatively unenlightened fashion the verses they had received, so that, speaking generally, the negative influences of forgetfulness, confused recollection, and imperfect comprehension have been the major influences at work on the ballad texts. But the musical tradition has not been subject to anything like the same rate of decay. Beyond the reach, until very lately, of any sort of written or recorded control, it has persisted, to a surprising degree, in its primitive vitality. That this assertion is hardly open to contradiction is demonstrable in the vast number of beautiful tunes which have been gathered in our own century from illiterate, or nearly illiterate, singers on both sides of the water. It is possible for an uneducated, even a comparatively unintelligent, singer to reach a level of comparatively high musical culture, within the circumscribed limits of traditional song—a power of melodic discrimination, a subtle sense of rhythmical effect, an artistic sensitivity of no mean musical order; to display, in fact, what may fairly be called creative ability, subject again to the unwritten canons of an ancient tradition. I do not mean that many, or perhaps any, of these singers could deliberately create at will a new and original folk-tune. But, in spite of themselves, their musical sensibility and instinctive knowledge of the values they seek inevitably result in constant modification and variation which is effectually creative, or, more strictly, re-creative. They *essentially* remember; and the falling short of exact recollection has, as yet—it may not continue long to be so—been more than compensated by a power of miniature invention sufficient for their habitual needs, and of which they appear but dimly aware. Moreover, what they have in their minds is not a note-for-note accuracy as of a written tune; but rather an ideal melody, or melodic idea, which is responsive to the momentary dictates of feeling or verbal necessity. What else can we conclude from the evidences of constant variation, recorded by meticulous collectors like Sharp, in successive stanzas, or successive renditions, of the same song? Sharp's blind singer, Henry Larcombe, of Haselbury-Plucknett, Somerset, is an extreme case of this re-creative ability. Whenever Sharp asked him to repeat a phrase or a stanza of a song, he got a new variation in return, many of them beautiful, ingenious, and resourceful—and this without the singer's realizing, apparently, that he was not giving what was requested. Joseph Laver of Bridgwater was another singer of the same kind. Now, if any other folk-singer had learned a song from the lips of a singer like these, what else could he possibly have carried away in his memory but the *idea* of a tune, the general pattern or form of it which resides in a more or less constant melodic contour and rhythm? When we are told that a singer hands on his song exactly as he learned it, what other exactness than this is possible to conceive? Since the song was never sung twice in exactly the same way, and since it is humanly impossible for the memory to make an indelible and phonographic record of a single rendition, stanza by stanza, it is obvious that exactitude in this realm bears a very different meaning from what it does when a Schnabel gives us the results of his study of Beethoven's manuscript of a sonata.

Larcombe and Laver are cases at one extreme; but they are not for that reason any the less genuine and authentic folk singers. At the other extreme, and equally genuine and authentic, are the singers with a low coefficient of artistic sensibility, who can neither improvise nor invent, who only dimly remember, and who by dint of desperate effort manage to hang onto a single phrase, or perhaps half a tune, which they repeat at need until so much of the text as they have kept for themselves has been sung through. These, in varying degree, are the singers who most easily get sidetracked onto another tune of which they have a clearer notion; so that, by the hooks and eyes of unconscious suggestion, be it of rhythm, of melodic cadence, or verbal commonplace, a ballad is slowly or rapidly transformed to something other than it was. But these, again, are doubtless most often the deleterious influences: they are in general the disrupters, not the reintegrating and positive forces in traditional transmission. Probably they, in the main, are responsible for the most abrupt and inexplicable departures from established patterns. Their influence must not be minimized, for mediocrity is commoner than talent. Nevertheless, the evidence both of tunes and texts in balladry can lead only to the conclusion that, leavening the undistinguished mass, there have been, even up to our own time, more Larcombes and Lavers than we have any record of; and that, formerly, their verbal counterparts, so to put it, constituted a phenomenon common enough to have molded into familiar forms that body of narrative song, at once naïve and yet capable of the most poignant beauty, which has been enshrined in Child's *English and Scottish Popular Ballads*.

1944

Mrs. Brown and the Ballad

IT was Francis James Child's aim, pursued through the greater part of a scholarly lifetime, to collect and segregate all the genuinely traditional copies of the extant British popular ballads. In the great work which embodies the fruits of his labor, he brands as suspect in varying degree the texts which had received any sort of editing before they reached his hands, and regards as usually most trustworthy those which had been taken down verbatim from the singing of persons who had learned them from others' singing. He was best satisfied when he could discover no evidence, either extrinsic or intrinsic, that a text had had any previous connection with print. In an unbroken oral tradition, he believed, were to be found the specimens of greatest authenticity, because such texts were least likely to have been affected by any sort of deliberate alteration. But the very conditions of such transmission make it, of course, all but impossible to check the accuracy, or fidelity, of the record from stage to stage. For it almost never happens that an interceptor secures successive copies of a ballad in a consecutive line of descent. We only know that changes occur even under ideal conditions, for the existence of variant texts puts the fact beyond dispute. It is the object of the present essay to examine briefly a case which by lucky accident provides more than the usual amount of evidence as to what has happened to ballad texts within a brief span, under very favorable conditions of oral transmission.

One of Child's esteemed sources was an eighteenth-century Scotswoman, Mrs. Brown of Falkland, in Fife, whose importance to the popular ballad may be readily suggested by means of a few figures. Of the nearly three dozen ballad texts which she preserved, Child allowed every one a place in his canon. Four of these are the only extant versions. Twenty others are Child's A, or primary, texts; and four more his B texts. Early in the last century, Scott admitted a dozen of her ballads into his *Minstrelsy;* and Jamieson, skirting Scott's choices, made use of more than a score in his kindred collection of 1806. These are powerful witnesses to the authenticity and value of her records, which offer besides a rare opportunity for the study of variation in traditional balladry.

Anna Gordon Brown was born at Old Machar, Aberdeen, in 1747, and died in the same place, in 1810. Her father, Thomas Gordon, was Professor of Humanity at King's College, Aberdeen; and her husband, the Rev. Andrew Brown, D.D., Aberdeen, was minister at Falkland and later at Tranent. Robert Anderson characterized Mrs. Brown to Bishop Percy in the following highly relevant terms: "Mrs. Brown is fond of ballad poetry, writes verses, and reads everything in the marvellous way. Yet her character places her above the suspicion of literary imposture; but it is wonderful how she should happen to be the depository of so many curious and valuable ballads." [1] The wonder is abated by unpublished letters from her father and herself, which explain that she learned her repertory as a child from the singing of three persons: an aunt, her mother, and an old nurse of the family. The aunt, her mother's sister, was her chief source, and had herself learned these ballads from the singing of countrywomen in the district of Braemar, not far from Balmoral on the River Dee, "a sequestered, romantic pastoral country" where she spent her married life. This lady, Mrs. Farquharson, had had a decent education for her circumstances, and made a respectable marriage. Her father, William Forbes of Disblair, had possessed a music library and musical instruments which together were worth almost as much as all the rest of his property. In speaking of Mrs. Farquharson's songs, Professor Gordon said he was sure that she "invented nor added nothing herself." She had, he said, "a tenacious memory, which retained all the songs she had heard," and her niece, his daughter, was blessed with a memory equally good, and had "almost the whole store of her songs lodged in it." [2]

[1] John Nichols, *Illustrations of the Literary History of the Eighteenth Century . . . ,* VII (1817–1858), 90.
[2] Gordon to A. F. Tytler, 19 January, 1793, transcript in Harvard College Library MS 25241.37.5, fols. 7–8.

Mrs. Brown herself records that in 1783, at the request of William Tytler, she had compiled a manuscript with a large number of her pieces, intending it for him. But when he requested further to have the tunes also recorded, as she writes, "My Father ordered Bob Scott [her nephew, later Professor of Greek at Aberdeen], then a very young boy & a mere novice in musick to try to do it & he & I set to work. but [sic] found the business so crabbed that in order to abridge our labours a little we selected what we thought the best of the Ballads whose tunes being added in the best manner we could were sent" to Mr. Tytler.[3] This was the origin of the two MSS known to Child as the Jamieson-Brown and the William Tytler-Brown MSS: the first with twenty texts and no music, the second, made soon after, containing fifteen texts and tunes. The first, which was later given to Robert Jamieson, eventually found its way to the University of Edinburgh Library among David Laing's papers. The second has vanished, but what we may regard as a very exact transcript in Joseph Ritson's hand was given not long since by Dr. Rosenbach to Harvard [HCL 25241.37.5].[4]

When Walter Scott was beginning to busy himself about the *Minstrelsy*, he applied to Alexander Fraser Tytler, who lent him the William Tytler MS and approached Mrs. Brown afresh in Scott's behalf. The result of his application was a third collection, now called the A. F. Tytler-Brown MS, made in the spring of 1800, and presumably still the property of the Tytler family at Aldourie Castle. This MS contains nine ballads, seven of them new, the other two independent copies of ballads in the Jamieson, but omitted from the William Tytler MS. If Mrs. Brown sent tunes for these nine ballads, as she said she intended to, they were separately transmitted, and have been lost.

Evidences of Mrs. Brown's literary awareness appear in these letters to A. F. Tytler, in a quotation from Ossian, and in her designating certain of her ballads as "not near so ancient" as others. It is pertinent to add that her sense of propriety was much offended by Scott's naming her in print, in his prefatory acknowledgments. These are matters which have a possible bearing on her transmis-

---

[3] Mrs. Brown to A. F. Tytler, 23 December, 1800, tr. in HCL, Child MSS, X, 85.
[4] It has lately been recovered. Cf. *ante*, p. 42. The Ritson transcript is remarkably accurate.

sion of traditional song, which we are now in a position to examine more closely.

The variations that occur between the two MSS of approximately the same date throw valuable light on the degree of fidelity to which Mrs. Brown felt herself committed with regard to a given text. It is unsatisfactory to have to forgo most of the detailed evidence, but any one, I believe, who will take the trouble to collate the texts will find himself in agreement with the following conclusions. We should bear in mind that when Mrs. Brown's second copy was made she had the first one by her, so that any changes must have been deliberately introduced.

Mrs. Brown's alterations are due to five causes: (1) corrections of memory; (2) rationalizing; (3) metrical considerations; (4) regularizing and reducing dialectal features; (5) considerations that may loosely be called aesthetic.

Strikingly little can be laid to the first cause, of memory revisal. "Young Bekie" acquires a couple of additional stanzas, and lines are added here and there in other ballads. There are occasional, but infrequent, shifts in the position of a stanza, which could be owing to the same cause. Such changes usually occur in connection with a sequence involving "incremental repetition." Thus, in "Willy's Lady," the series of proffered gifts in the Jamieson copy stands as *girdle—steed*, but in the William Tytler MS runs *cup—steed—girdle*, with consequent lengthening of the ballad by repetition of the related lines. A clear case of rationalizing occurs in the change of the line "O seven foot he lap a back" to "O seven foot he started back." Changes for the sake of greater metrical smoothness lie on every hand. Thus, "Five hundred pound maid I'll gie to the[e]" becomes "Five hundred pounds I'll gie to thee." The lines

> Then stopped ha they their loud loud sang
> And tane up the still mournin

become

> Soon did they drop the loud, loud sang,
> Took up the still mourning.

The treatment of dialect is not consistent in either MS, but generally dialect is muffled in revision, unless rhyme requires its emphasis. Typical is the change, "An' spear nae leave" to "An' ask nae leave."

By far the majority of changes—and the number can hardly average less than one to a line—can be attributed only to the wish to hand on as attractive a text as possible from the point of view of a reader of taste. To this end, there is continual substitution of one word for another, change of tense, grammatical change, change for elegance, or for logic, even—once or twice—change *pudoris causa*. A few characteristic examples from a single ballad, "Jack the little Scot," are:

> Jamieson-Brown]   O Johney was as brave a knight
> Wm. Tytler-Brown] Johny was as brave a knight

> J-B]   An he's done him to the English court
> WT-B] And he is to the English court

> J-B]   To Johney proves wi child
> WT-B] To Johny grows wi' child

> J-B]   That will rin into fair England
> WT-B] That will gang unto fair England

> J-B]   . . . the king then cried
> WT-B] . . . then cried the king

But the most interesting and significant of such changes have to do with the endings of the ballads. Here there is slight possibility of the differences' being caused by improved recollection. There are five ballads wherein the endings notably differ. Of three of these, Mrs. Brown simply omits the feeble concluding lines. In the other two cases, she rounds off an inconclusive or unclimactic ending with additional lines intended to give force or point. Thus, the final stanza of "Rose the Red and White Lilly" is omitted in the second copy; it is:

> Then out it spake her Rose the red
>   An a hearty laugh laugh she
> I wonder what would our step dame say
>   Gin she this sight did see.

On the other hand, the Jamieson copy of "Kampion" ends thus:

>   An relieved sall she never be
>   Till St Mungo come oer the sea

to which the Tytler copy adds—thereby making a six-line stanza, to which the tune would have to be especially accommodated:

> An' sighing said that weary wight,
> I fear that day I'll never see.

It is, therefore, abundantly clear that for Mrs. Brown there was nothing sacred about the mere words of her ballads. The text which she had drawn out of the stores of her own memory was no more fixed and immutable by virtue of being once transferred to paper than it had been before that irrelevant act occurred. Had some one of Ritson's school of thought—which is to say our current scholarly persuasion—told her that by writing down her ballads she had automatically produced a standard authoritative text, from which henceforth even she herself must not depart by so much as a syllable, unless she could swear that in so doing she was reverting more closely to what she had heard in girlhood—what would have been her amazement! Might she not have retorted that she herself had never in her life heard such a standard text; and that, to cite an analogy, when she told a story on two or three separate occasions she did not think herself obliged, under pain of being considered dishonest, to adhere to a parrotlike repetition of the identical words she had first employed? Had not the person from whom she had received the story done his or her best for it, and should she not do the same? Thus, as clearly appears from her contemporaneous texts of the same ballads, she viewed her proper function as an active participation, not a passive, inert reception as indiscriminately careful to perpetuate blemishes as beauties. Mirror-like perpetuators of tradition have in fact latterly existed, but they must inevitably be either scholars or persons of a very low grade of intelligence. (Parenthetically, it might be remarked that only the former are entirely pleased by the latter, but that not even the latter are quite satisfied with the former.)

If we have correctly described Mrs. Brown's attitude toward her songs as cooperative rather than passive, we have yet to learn what effect might be produced upon her contribution by 'tract of time.' The two ballads of which she made copies nearly a score of years apart provide us with a lucky index of this aspect of individual variation. In these two cases, the later records were made quite independently of the earlier, which in fact she had supposed lost.

The ballads in question are "Lord John and Burd Ellen," previously called "Burd Ellen," and "Love Gregor," which the earlier copy names "Fair Anny." We have, it appears to me, sufficient assurance that Mrs. Brown's remembrance of these ballads had not in the meanwhile become crossed with foreign versions, in that she makes clear to A. F. Tytler, in 1800, that she has not for many years exercised her faculties in this direction, and is now reviving an interest long laid aside.

The amount of change in the first of these ballads is not spectacular, until toward the end. But the divergence between the copies of "Love Gregor" and "Fair Anny," in spite of a close parallelism in line content, is so extreme as to constitute a virtual remaking of the whole ballad. The variations are by no possibility that I can envisage due to imperfect recollection, acting by itself. It is quite clear that Mrs. Brown had a full and accurate recollection of the ballad narrative in all its details. What she apparently did not remember, or care to reproduce, was the exact way in which she had sung the ballad before—the words she had used, the turn of her phrases. She reaches the same points at the same time, but only about a sixth of the lines are even approximately identical. Nothing but a line-for-line comparison can bring home this really startling display of textual fluidity; but we must here be content with a representative extract, stanzas 5 to 9:

Jamieson-Brown	A. F. Tytler-Brown

O gin I had a bony ship
  An men to sail wi me
It's I would gang to my true love
  Since he winna come to me.
	But I will get a bonny boat
	  And I will sail the sea
	For I maun gang to Love Gregor
	  Since he canno come hame to
	    me.

Her fathers gien her a bonny ship
  An sent her to the stran
She's tane her young son in her
    arms
  An turnd her back to the lan.
	O she has gotten a bonny boat
	  And saill'd the sa't sea fame
	She lang'd to see her ain true love
	  Since he could no come hame.

She had na been o' the sea saillin
  About a month or more
Till landed has she her bonny ship
  Near her true loves door.
	O row your boat my mariners
	  And bring me to the land
	For yonder I see my Loves castle
	  Close by the sat sea strand.

[salt]

The night was dark, & the win'
    blew caul
An her love was fast asleep
An the bairn that was in her twa
    arms
Fu sair began to weep.

Long stood she at her true loves
    door
An lang tirl'd at the pin
At length up gat his fa'se mither
Says, Wha's that wou'd be in.

She has ta'en her young son in her
    arms
And to the door shes gone
And lang shes knocked & sair shes
    ca'd
But answer got she none.

O open the door Love Gregor she
    says
O open and let me in
For the wind blaw's thro my yel-
    low hair
And the rain draps oer my skin.

Here are two equally authoritative renditions of the same story. It cannot be maintained that the second is less authentic than the first; indeed, if anything, in the passage quoted the first text seems a little more self-conscious, a shade less natural, than the second. Is it not clear that what Mrs. Brown was trying for in the version of 1800 was, not to recover her own text of 1783, but to recover, or re-create, the ballad itself, the essential, ideal "Lass of Roch Royal," as it exists in solution in the sum of all its traditional variations? In this attempt she produced a new version, one which had not existed before, and in that sense—but that sense alone—quite *un*traditional. It cannot be supposed that this version was any closer to the one she had learned at her aunt's knee than the version she had sung seventeen years earlier. But neither is it to be assumed that the version of 1783 is in any literal sense the exact replica of her aunt's singing. Nor do I believe that there is any need to infer that she had learned two versions of the ballad, one of which she recorded in 1783, the other in 1800. She herself never suggests that she knew more than one. For her, both texts appear to be the identical ballad, which she declares in 1800 she never saw either in print or manuscript, but which she learned as a little girl from hearing it sung, and had carried in her memory all these years.

What was it she had carried in her memory? Not a *text,* but a *ballad:* a fluid entity soluble in the mind, to be concretely realized at will in words and music. When she wrote in 1800 that her nephew had recently been after her in Jamieson's behalf and that by his application her "recollections & faculties" had been aroused,[5]

[5] Letter cited, of 23 December, 1800.

she chose her terms with a clear sense that something more than mere remembering was involved. An exactly analogous case on the musical side has been cited in another connection (essay three *supra*) in Cecil Sharp's experience with his blind singer, Henry Larcombe.[6] What such singers have in mind is a melodic idea, not a note-for-note record; and what any one else will learn from their singing will inevitably be likewise the *idea* of a song, because it is too fluid for any other kind of record to be captured, except by mechanical means.

Thus we begin to understand how much in this traditional art depends upon the instrument of reproduction. But there is another mode of estimating Mrs. Brown's performance, an approach through comparative study of other nearly contemporaneous records of her ballads as they came from different singers. To make such analysis cogent would require a good deal of time and space for the marshaling of details and the weighing of evidence inevitably subjective in greater or less degree. I shall limit myself here to a few unsupported assertions.

First, then, there is no doubt that her ballads, as might have been expected in the light of her origins and background, subsist on a higher than average level of well-bred literacy. This fact is not all to the good. While it generally makes her texts easier and smoother reading, it is not infrequently responsible for the presence of false notes, artificial touches, pretty sentimentalities, and a specious neatness that puts one on guard. Her versions seldom show the gaps and chasms, the rugged and abrupt leaps of narrative which are such characteristic and vivid features of traditional balladry. They show, on the contrary, an expository skill, a faculty of neat transition and summary, which is doubtfully welcome at this stage of art. It is symptomatic, too, that there are almost no real obscurities of phrase or idea, such as often appear in pure oral transmission. There are occasional moral observations and pious reflections, especially at the ends of her ballads, which are little above the broadside level and which jar our sense of fitness. It can hardly be an accident that where the erotic note is bluntly struck in other versions, in Mrs. Brown's it is side-stepped or soft-pedaled. Collateral evidence of a delicate taste is to be seen in the fact that she recalls no ballads which deal with the incest motive, like "Leesome Brand" or

[6] C. J. Sharp, *English Folk-Song: Some Conclusions* (1907), p. 21.

"Lizie Wan"; nor with parricide, like "Edward," nor infanticide,
like "The Cruel Mother"; nor with any vigorous and outspoken
themes of criminal passion, like "Young Hunting." It is striking
that her nearest approach to this sort of thing is "The Bonny
Birdy," a unique counterpart of "Little Musgrave" which plays
down the element of guilty love almost to the vanishing point and
ends with a heavily underlined moral. She pitches for the most part
upon the marvelous, the supernatural, and the sentimentally romantic; and in her appetite for the last she is avid to the point of wholly
uncritical acceptance of the most insipid folly.

All these factors help to define the refracting influences always
at work upon a body of traditional song, even in the presence of a
first-class transmitting instrument. The very finest of such instruments must pass its materials through a filter screen which allows
certain effects to come through directly, but others distorted, or
transmuted; whereas to others it is simply opaque or impervious.
The process is unconscious or instinctive in inverse ratio to the degree of intelligence possessed by the singer. Mrs. Brown was
regarded by Child as one of the best and most authentic of all his
sources, and we have no desire to pull her down from that place of
eminence. But Mrs. Brown, as we have now seen, adopted no passive attitude toward her text: her function was cooperative and re-
creative. In the extent to which, from our point of view, it was successfully so lies the relative excellence of her texts. Confronted by
the evidence of her variations, we can hardly avoid, as it seems to
me, giving her a large proportion of responsibility for the particular form her ballads assumed while they were in her charge. It is
equally certain that she grew up in an environment especially sympathetic and favorable to popular song, and learned her repertory
from sources that differed very little, if at all, from herself. If we
will, we may pass back the credit of her ballads to her aunt, Mrs.
Farquharson, to whom, certainly, all gratitude is due. But we shall
not thereby have altered the nature of the case one whit. There is
no reason for supposing that the ballads were more stable in Mrs.
Farquharson's handling, or that she was less cooperative in her rendition of them, than her niece. We come into contact here with a
vital, active stage of oral tradition. It is creative, or at least re-
creative, and is at a vast remove from the state of mental sleepwalk-
ing in which the older ballads have latterly been perpetuated in one

region or another. At the stage which we are considering, there
was no lack of awareness. There was plenty of quickness of parts
in the eighteenth-century Scot, whether cotter or laird; and nothing is clearer than that popular balladry in that region and time was
as widely practiced, as well understood in its conventions, and as
generally interesting to all levels of the community—from Lady
Wardlaw and Lady Hume to Mrs. Harris's nursemaid, from Lord
Hailes to James Rankin, Peter Buchan's blind beggar—as was, say,
the kindred traditional pastime of country-dancing in seventeenth-
century England. Not all practiced the technique with equal success, it goes without saying; but with whatever degree of success it
was cultivated, it could count on a lively and sympathetic response
among gentle and simple. It was Lady Hume who gave "Young
Waters" to the Foulis brothers to be printed in 1755. It was Lord
Hailes who transmitted to Percy the now famous copies of "Edward" and "Sir Patrick Spens" which appeared a decade later in
the *Reliques*. But it was countless persons, in all walks of life, who
were singing them, shaping and reshaping them more to their liking
as they sang. Eighteenth-century Scotland, there is no doubt at all,
was a nation of ballad singers and ballad lovers. How much earlier
it had been so no one knows; but it is a fact that what we today
know as British balladry at its best is a mass of texts taken down by
interested persons from living Scottish tradition in the latter half of
the eighteenth century, or learned then and transmitted to print or
manuscript early in the following century. It has been estimated
that about 1,000 Scottish texts have been preserved in Child's volumes: and of these almost the whole bulk comes from persons
whose memories reached back into the eighteenth century. Regardless of how deeply the roots penetrate into the soil of the past,
it remains true that the flowers we have bloomed in the age of
Hume and Hailes, of Boswell and Burns: this latter spring is their
season which we know and admire, and which, Robin Hood apart,
gives the dominant tone to Child's whole collection. In the face of
a living and vital tradition, such as is typified by Mrs. Brown, it is
merely silly to speak of the fourteenth or the fifteenth century as
"*The* Golden Age of British Balladry." That may indeed have
been *a* golden age. But it is altogether improbable that "Sir Patrick
Spens," or "Edward," or "Clerk Saunders," or "The Wife of
Usher's Well," were better ballads three or four hundred years ear-

lier than they were when they flowered afresh under the benignant
and vitalizing sun of a later age. Indeed, there is even reason to surmise that Scottish balladry was of comparatively late growth.
There is at least no evidence that it reached its fullest development
much before the eighteenth century, however clear it may be that
with the opening of the nineteenth century it was on the decline.
What I am concerned to insist upon is the fact that in the eighteenth century there was enough vital energy in traditional song to
put forth naturally, as flowers proper to the season, not excavated
fossils, "Sir Patrick Spens," "Mary Hamilton," and the rest. Last
year's blooms are not this year's, though they spring from the same
root. For each season there has to be a fresh re-creative effort; and
in the day of Burns, thanks to a living tradition, as good versions
were burgeoning as perhaps had ever flowered.[7]

If there were occasion, we could find further evidence of a conscious re-creative tradition in the ballad music which has survived.
It is clear, for example, that a four-phrase tune carrying a text in
quatrains, in which the second and fourth lines are refrain, does not
imperceptibly make itself over into an eight-phrase tune carrying a
text in which the first line is thrice repeated, the repetitions being
sandwiched by refrain-lines of a quite different pattern, the whole
concluded by a refrain on the seventh and eight lines. Changes of
this sort are obviously deliberate, not automatic and subconscious.

What is implied by such considerations as the foregoing is a
widening of the meaning of the term Tradition. We must include
in it a much greater allowance for conscious cerebration than we
have been in the habit of doing. Thus, it is clear that a great many
Scottish ballads—and "Edward" is one of the number—were remade in the eighteenth century, not instinctively and unconsciously, but as intelligently and artistically as might be. The
beckoning image of a perfectly pure traditional text which ever
gleams on the ballad-scholar's horizon—a text, that is, over which
the individual transmitters from generation to generation have ex-

[7] Child appears unable to conceive of such vitality in traditional re-creation.
Faced by the discrepancy in Mrs. Brown's two versions of "The Lass of Roch
Royal," he can only suggest that the later, since it is "by no means an imperfectly
remembered version of its predecessor . . . , is to be regarded as a blending of
two independent versions known to Mrs. Brown, which no doubt had much in
common, though not so much as" the version of 1783 and that of 1800 (*English
and Scottish Popular Ballads*, II, 213–214).

erted no conscious control—is nothing but a scholarly mirage. The golden age of balladry, whenever it occurred, was an age when there was a maximum of creative and re-creative energy coursing through the ballads and a minimum of merely passive re-recording. The further into such an active tradition we penetrate, the fainter become the outlines of that "precious specimen of the unspoiled traditional ballad" of which Child was ever in pursuit, unless "unspoiled" and "traditional" be allowed to mean something a good deal more positive than what the terms are generally taken to convey.

Confronted by these considerations, scholars may have recourse to the hypothetical homogeneous community, or society, where all who meddled with ballads were so much alike, so much at one in attitude and outlook, that all the meddling went the same way, so that they finally meddled things into supreme beauty and effectiveness. This is the very ecstasy of meddling. It must have been long ago, because no such homogeneity could be observed in medieval Europe; and after such a triumph as "Edward" or "Spens" or "Usher's Well" had been achieved, there was nothing further to be done but to hand down the miracle in its fragile perfection, unchanged through centuries of oral transmission, until it might haply fall into the hands of a Percy or a Walter Scott, to be placed on display in a literary museum.

But it is, on the contrary, altogether probable that there was good and bad in ballad making from the very beginning. The part which the individual human being was playing in the making of ballads in the fourteenth century was not different in kind from the part played by similar individuals in eighteenth-century Scotland. There were, that is to say, coarse spirits and there were finer spirits, gifted and creative and imaginative singers, and singers uninspired and insensitive. The ballad product mirrored these differences perforce, and in the long run or the short run excellence never survived—unless it was fixed on paper at the lucky moment of its ascendancy. Supreme felicity is inevitably almost nonexistent in balladry; and where it is approached, we may be sure that it has recently been achieved, or re-achieved. Tradition, as Ritson once remarked, "is a species of alchemy that converts gold to lead."

But if any version of a ballad is the net result of the talents and of the shortcomings of the individual singers who have successively

possessed it, it is obvious that we cannot be precise or rigid in defining "pure" tradition. When we try to be, we immediately run
headlong into contradictions. We cannot consistently hold, for example, that Walter Scott's "improvements" of the ballads that
passed through his hands are illegitimate, but that Mrs. Brown's are
not. Let it be objected that Scott's changes were for print, but Mrs.
Brown's were a part of oral tradition: the difference is more apparent than real. In both cases, the changes of which we are aware
were written down. We have, moreover, no knowledge that any
specific text from Mrs. Brown ever passed on into continued oral
circulation. It may have done so, but so may Scott's, if any singer
took it up and launched it on the stream. If such a thing occurred
—and in fact there is reason in Scott's case to believe that it did—
the changes would merely add grist to the traditional mill and be
exposed to the same chances of survival as Mrs. Brown's. In truth,
what Scott did is not different in kind from what every member of
the re-creative ballad-singing tradition had always done or had felt
at liberty to do with these songs, though Scott may have done it
generally with more consideration, and often with more tact, than
most singers could command. Child waxes somewhat indignant
over Scott's independent treatment of his texts, and never fails to
rebuke him and any one else who ventured to change a word. But
had Scott remained anonymous, and had he sung his changes back
into the oral stream instead of fixing them in print, he would have
to be accepted as an unusually gifted, but not less authentic, link in
the ballad tradition. The texts which had passed currently through
his hands would be no more open to the charge of spuriousness
than all the rest which have been altered by unknown hands. Certainly they might conceivably be regarded as uncharacteristic,
either in part or as a whole; but, not to be paradoxical, there is
much more in Child's volumes that is not characteristic of "pure"
tradition than the contrary. In the end it has to be acknowledged
that the changes were introduced, both consciously and unwit-
tingly, both in singing and for print, by *individuals* named and unnamed; and that the only standard of judgment which can be consistently applied is the largely subjective one of the degree of success achieved in the kind attempted. At one end of the scale of taste
and ability is Scott, and at the other end, say, James Rankin of
Tarwathie, or Peter Buchan himself. The mean position is occupied

by numberless singers, unknown, but of whom Mrs. Brown may stand as the type, who took an equally positive and cooperative attitude toward their ballads, but who were not teased by genius or egocentricity into an idiosyncratic contribution, nor betrayed by vulgar and insensitive natures into a debasement of their poetic inheritance.

1945

Folk-Song and the Modes

FOR many years it has been common knowledge that folk-song generally, and Anglo-Celtic folk-song in particular, persists in approximating the tonality of the medieval modes. The understanding of folk-song, therefore, depends in part upon a clear perception of modal functions. For the acquisition of such knowledge there exists an ample literature—large enough, indeed, to embarrass the student whose interest centers rather upon folk-music than upon Greek, or Gregorian, or ecclesiastical polyphonic, or nineteenth-century harmonic practice. Most of the concentrated attention lavished upon the modes within the past century or so has approached them from the historical point of view, and has concerned itself mainly with their development and modification during the thousand years lying, roughly, between A.D. 500–1500. A great part of this learning, enlightening in itself, is yet of very little immediate use to the student of folk-song. I wish to suggest an approach which, so far as I am aware, has not been explored, and which I believe useful for the study in question.

The charts of modal scales to be found in all accounts of the subject, laid out in stepwise ascending sequence, are in accordance with historical exposition and give a lucid and simple picture of the diatonic nature of the system. They obscure, however, instead of revealing, certain features of the scales which are of even greater importance to folk-song. From the point of view of melody, with which alone folk-music is vitally concerned, it is the correspondences and relationships between the modes that really matter. The ascending sequence conceals these correspondences and, though possessed of its own logic, has no melodic significance. A chart, on the contrary, in which all the modes are referred to the same tonic —the term is preferable in this context to *final*—will reveal at a

79

glance the basic melodic distinctions inherent in the different scales, and also their points of likeness. This is true for pentatonic and hexatonic, as well as heptatonic scales. Everyone, in practice, mentally performs such a transposition when he compares variants. Let the pentatonic series, as the briefest example, demonstrate the fact once for all:[1]

Pentatonic Scales on a Common Tonic

The strong difference of mode between these scales will be sensed by every reader; but if the same scales are set down, as they usually are, with tonics on the successive degrees of the series involved, that individual quality will at once be half obliterated:[2]

Pentatonic Scales after Gilchrist and Sharp

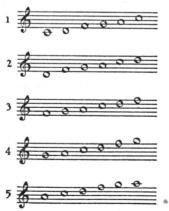

[1] The order of pentatonic scales here adopted will be justified later in this paper.
[2] Cf. A. G. Gilchrist in *Journal of the Folk-Song Society*, IV, 150–153; C. J.

The reason, no doubt, for this diminution of modal impact is that the mind cannot—or does not—immediately divest itself of bondage to the tonic first established, and reads the successive scales with a partial, if involuntary, reference to the original point of departure. Also, the fact that the five-note series is here constructed simply by taking a note away each time from the front and putting it at the back, while the rest of the scale *appears* to remain unchanged, contributes to the same result. It is only when the tonic as originally received is contradicted by an alien system that the mind succeeds in throwing off that tonic's yoke.

These considerations, obviously, are not fundamental, but utilitarian. They have implications, none the less, of far-reaching importance. In the long run, what counts is the sequence of notes that the folk-singer has in his ear, that strike him as familiar and satisfying. For the most part, these must always be the melodic runs he has heard and sung most frequently. When the sequences common to one mode are reemphasized and enforced upon the consciousness by being repeated in other modes, they double and treble their chances of becoming ingrained and habitual patterns in folk-song. Thus, a series of notes that occurs within the Dorian frame deepens its groove when it recurs in the Æolian or Mixolydian schemes. No two modes, of course, are identical along their whole length; but the whole modal system is permeated with partial identities or correspondences. These parallel lines are naturally most noticeable when they run from the tonic to the fifth or from fifth to octave. Confining ourselves for the moment to the simple scale-patterns, we can observe, when we break the octaves into their component pentachords and tetrachords, a succession of such identical sequences between particular modes. These passages, with the aid of constantly changing phrase-finals or cadences, supply the natural bridges from one mode to another, whether heptatonic, hexatonic, or pentatonic, and open the way to the development of new variants of a folk-tune. Especially, perhaps, is it true that this process operates by means of the plagal forms. For every mode in its plagal range is identical with the authentic scale of another mode; but elsewhere only in part.

Somewhere, during the last fifteen hundred years, there is probably set down (although I have not heard of it) an account of so

Sharp and M. Karpeles, *English Folk Songs from the Southern Appalachians*, I (1932), p. xxxii.

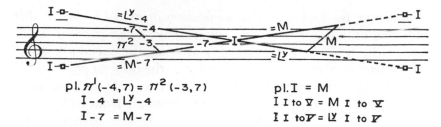

pl. $\pi^1(-4,7) = \pi^2(-3,7)$　　　　pl. I = M
I-4 = L^y-4　　　　　　　　　II to Ⅴ = M I to Ⅴ
I-7 = M-7　　　　　　　　　II to Ⅴ = L^y I to Ⅴ

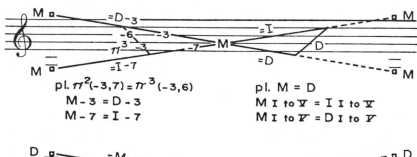

pl. $\pi^2(-3,7) = \pi^3(-3,6)$　　　　pl. M = D
M-3 = D-3　　　　　　　　M I to Ⅴ = I I to Ⅴ
M-7 = I-7　　　　　　　　M I to Ⅴ = D I to Ⅴ

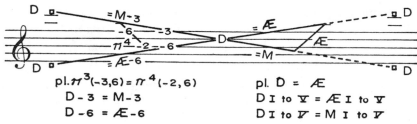

pl. $\pi^3(-3,6) = \pi^4(-2,6)$　　　　pl. D = Æ
D-3 = M-3　　　　　　　　D I to Ⅴ = Æ I to Ⅴ
D-6 = Æ-6　　　　　　　　D I to Ⅴ = M I to Ⅴ

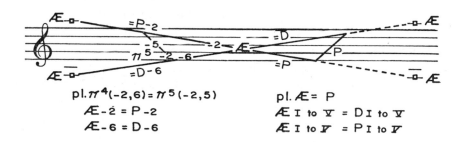

pl. $\pi^4(-2,6) = \pi^5(-2,5)$　　　　pl. Æ = P
Æ-2 = P-2　　　　　　　　Æ I to Ⅴ = D I to Ⅴ
Æ-6 = D-6　　　　　　　　Æ I to Ⅴ = P I to Ⅴ

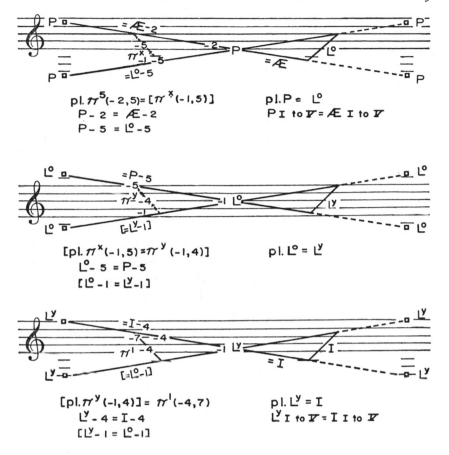

pl. $\pi^5(-2,5)= [\pi^x(-1,5)]$ pl. P = L⁰

P- 2 = Æ-2   P I to V = Æ I to V

P- 5 = L⁰-5

[pl. $\pi^x(-1,5)= \pi^y(-1,4)$]   pl. L⁰ = Lʸ

L⁰- 5 = P-5

[L⁰-1 = Lʸ-1]

[pl. $\pi^y(-1,4)$]= $\pi^1(-4,7)$ pl. Lʸ = I

Lʸ- 4 = I-4   Lʸ I to V = I I to V

[Lʸ-1 = L⁰-1]

obvious a thing as the correspondence of the different modes, apart from and beyond the authentic/hypo relationship.[3] For these correspondences are not accidental: they proceed in accordance with logic and are subject to simple demonstration. The first chart presented will make the matter clear. It should be premised that the right-hand halves of the diagrams are concerned with the full heptatonic scales, the two inner sides of each triangle presenting together the plagal forms, and the third side (toward the right-hand margin of the page) the corresponding authentic scale. The left-hand halves of the diagrams present, in their whole length, the

[3] Professor Manfred Bukofzer later kindly informed me that Glareanus dealt with this matter at some length, but I have neglected to pursue the lead.

hexatonic correspondences; the triangles depict in similar fashion the plagal pentatonic forms and the corresponding authentic pentatonic scales. The legends below the several diagrams summarize the meaning of the pictures. It may be noted further that "I" stands for Ionian, "M" for Mixolydian, etc.; π for pentatonic, to which superior figures are added to distinguish the types. Superior ^{x} and ^{y} with the figure π, designate pentatonic types that are theoretical, because lacking the tonic or keynote. Ionian minus 4 ("I–4") is the Ionian scale without its fourth, and so with the rest. "I$_I$ to v" is that part of the Ionian scale extending upward from tonic to fifth; "I$_I$ to v" is that part extending downward from tonic to lower fifth.

Charts of Modal Correspondences

These correspondences may be stated in another fashion, which will reveal the cyclic organization of the whole system. The following chart, like the first, exposes the points of resemblance between all three kinds of scale. The innermost circle of points, π^i through $[\pi^y]$, comprises the pentatonic scales; the outermost points, I through L^y, represent the heptatonic scales; and the points midway stand for the hexatonic scales. As before, the letters stand for the names of the modes. The index figures numbering the pentatonic scales will be justified below. The figures beneath the letters, preceded by a minus sign, indicate which degree or degrees are absent from the particular scale. The bracketed scales are theoretical, being based upon nonexistent tonics. It will be observed that each pentatonic scale, besides its connection with the pentatonic scales adjacent, bears relation to two hexatonic, and three heptatonic, scales. The hexatonic scales indicate the nature of the bond between each two adjacent heptatonic scales, by showing which note must be removed to produce an identity.

It was allowed at starting that the customary charts of modes have the virtue of clearly revealing the diatonic aspect of the modal system. Owing to psychological factors deeply ingrained in the Western mind, the fifth degree of the scale, both above and below the tonic, is, as every one knows, melodically no less than harmonically the most important point of reference after the tonic. Hence it becomes the most comfortable note for a cadential point. This is but another way of saying that the fifth is to the Western ear the most acceptable and satisfying substitute tonic. But, as we know,

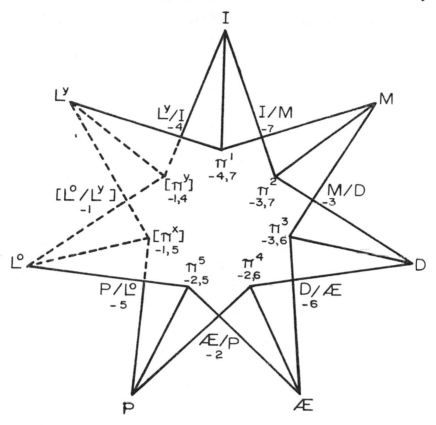

the fifth as tonic generates within the diatonic system its own modal scale and scheme. Thus the connection between two modes of which the tonic of one is a fifth higher—or a fourth lower—than the tonic of the other is felt to be particularly sympathetic. "Alien" systems, as they were earlier called, seem less alien when standing in this plagal relationship to each other.

Now, it will not have escaped attention that the modal patterns that most closely resemble one another when referred to a single tonic—for example, the Ionian and the Mixolydian, the Mixolydian and the Dorian, and so on (each pair having all but one note in common when one scale is superimposed upon the other)—are precisely those modal patterns that stand also in the plagal relation just described. So it comes about that two systems of reference apparently conflicting and contradictory, actually reinforce each other at particular points. The points of connection are apparent on the accompanying charts; and the operation of these interconnections will be clearly evident in the melodic examples to follow.

In the second chart, the Ionian scale has been taken as the starting point because it has been from time immemorial designated as the mode of popular song—the *modus lascivus* of ecclesiastical execration—and because, in bulk, it is by far the predominating mode in the extant folk-song record—at least in British-American tradition. The numbering of the pentatonic scales has been brought into conformity: if π^1 be granted, the rest proceed according to the inner logic of mutual correspondences not arbitrarily imposed. That π^1 *should* be granted precedence seems allowable on natural grounds because (a) it accords with the Ionian and (b) because it is that pentatonic scale which follows the whole-tone intervals as far as possible before introducing a gap.[4] Finally, it may be wise to say that the picture here given neither affirms nor denies an evolutionary development from pentatonic to heptatonic modes, but intends merely to depict their inherent relations.

It remains briefly to suggest the bearing of these interconnections upon the problem of variants in folk-tunes. This question of variants is complicated and obscure, and most of its aspects still await mature examination and analysis. One kind of variation, that of arbitrary and willful substitution of a preference by the folksinger, is, though undoubtedly of much more importance than has hitherto been allowed, by its very nature unamenable to generalization. Next to it would have to be set the class of substitutions that occur as a result of gross or partial lapses of memory, where a singer finds another tune or part of a tune that does well enough for his words, to take the place of what he has wholly or in part forgotten. At some point on a wavering boundary line, this second class passes into a third, of the highest interest and significance to our present concern. Within this field there are of course a number

---

[4] The numbering instituted by Miss Gilchrist in *Journal of the Folk-Song Society*, IV, 150 ff., which begins with the scale here designated π^2 (-3, 7) is based on the fact that Miss Gilchrist, dealing solely with Gaelic melodies, felt that scale to be the primary one for her material. It has no prescriptive right for other areas of song, and on numerical grounds alone, the scale -4, 7 will probably be found to predominate in the proportion in which the Ionian dominates among the heptatonic systems. I am not happy about instigating a renumbering of the pentatonic modes, with its consequent nuisances; but the logic of the change is to me convincing.

of other elements, working simultaneously and exerting their several pressures and influences, all of which together are enough to make impossible any rigorous or "scientific" elaboration of logical conclusions. The question of rhythmical variation alone is a huge one, and such variation undoubtedly affects melodic developments even in their modal aspects. The question of verbal change is another vast field: such change, too, acts upon the field of rhythm, and is acted upon by the latter in turn, and thus, if less directly, has a bearing upon modal change. These are matters that must await their proper time and place for discussion. At present I wish merely to point out in tentative fashion two of the means that naturally operate in producing modal variation.

One of these means, as it appears to me, lies through the chinks of the hexatonic and pentatonic systems. For example, it will not be found, I believe, that an Ionian tune will pass over naturally—and by *naturally* I mean without the singer's conscious volition—into the Æolian camp except by successive stages of translation. This is equivalent to saying that folk-tunes do not ordinarily move directly from major to minor, or the contrary. But it frequently happens that an Ionian tune is found in a Mixolydian form (or vice versa).[5] What I have dubbed the hexatonic chink is in this case, of course, the seventh degree of the scale. Reduce the tune in question to its cognate hexatonic form, without the seventh, and it immediately becomes impossible to tell whether the tune is properly Ionian or Mixolydian. When the absent note is again supplied, therefore, it is as easily filled by the flat (or natural) seventh as by the leading-note. Less often, but yet not infrequently, we shall find both Ionian and Dorian variants of the same tune. In this case, there are two roads of change, a longer and a shorter, one hexatonic, the other pentatonic. That is, the tune may pass into Mixolydian, as we have just seen, and thence, by the same mechanism, through the hexatonic scale that lacks its third, into the Dorian mode. Or, if the Ionian tune be deprived of both its third and seventh—and this is not difficult, since folk-tunes are very often transparently pentatonic in their bony structure—the missing notes may be filled up instead with a minor third and a flatted seventh. In other words, as may be seen at a glance in the second chart above, the tune may

[5] It should be understood that I am generalizing throughout upon the basis of British-American, not Continental, materials.

move thus: I to I/M to M to M/D to D; or it may proceed I to π^2 to D. Obviously, detours are also possible, as I to π^2 to M to M/D to D; or by any other sequence of points lying between these two extremes.

It must be understood that what we are trying to discover here is the norm of variational procedure as it relates to the modes. Very likely, it would be possible to find variants of a tune in Ionian and Æolian forms, without any recorded intermediate stages. In such cases, I think we might plausibly assume either (a) some or all of the intermediate steps, or (b) some extraneous influence.

The following series of variants of the common tune of "Henry Martin" will illustrate the process that has been described. I am *not*, of course, claiming that each successive variant here exhibited arose immediately out of the preceding one; simply that, normally, it may be supposed to have arisen out of one of a kindred sort. The process, of course, will work in either direction, or successively in both; and the home base can be surmised—yet never absolutely established—only where there is a sufficient number of variants to reveal cluster-points with a clear numerical superiority in their favor.

The second, and kindred, avenue of modal change to which I would call attention is that of the plagal correspondences. In the star above, as already noted, if we proceed clockwise around the circumference, every succeeding heptatonic mode is the mode that would be generated by the fifth above, or the fourth below, its predecessor's tonic. Counter-clockwise, obviously, the relationship is reversed: that is, the interval is a fifth down, or a fourth up. These relationships hold equally for the hexatonic series, and for the pentatonic as well.

The evidences of this mechanism that are most easily accessible occur in the Ionian-Mixolydian galaxy. It not seldom happens that variants of a tune will appear in two forms, the one class authentic and the other plagal. Supposing the tune to be originally Ionian, the plagal variant, of course, will still be Ionian. But the latter will be halfway along the road to Mixolydian, for the chances are that the cadence of its first phrase will fall on the note standing a fourth below the tonic. Similarly, the middle cadence will be likely to fall on the fifth of the first-phrase final taken as tonic (i.e., on the second degree of the tune's basic scale), thus indirectly reemphasizing

Henry Martin
1 Major (Ionian), with inflected 4th. Journal of Folk-Song Society IV, 92 [Devonshire, 1908]

2 I/M · ! Barry, Journal of American Folklore, XVIII, 135. [Minnesota, 1904]

3 Mixolydian (but with leading-note once). Sharp MSS 1772. [Somerset, 1908] [6]

4 Mixolydian. Vaughan Williams, Journal of Folk-Song Society IV, 302 [Sussex, 1908]

5 Dorian. Sharp MSS $\frac{551}{622}$. [Somerset, 1905]

6 Æ/D(-6). Sharp MSS $\frac{894}{965}$. [Somerset, 1906]

[6] For permission to quote from the Cecil J. Sharp MSS., I am indebted to Dr. Maud Karpeles, O.B.E.

the lower point of reference. Once that point is established, it will be no surprise to find genuine Mixolydian variants appearing. Subsequently, the new authentic variant may in turn become plagal, in which case the Mixolydian will gravitate towards the Dorian in the same manner, and perhaps later the Dorian towards the Æolian. This force of gravity is so marked, however, that one can frequently see the tune attempting a short cut, especially from the Ionian to the Mixolydian. The drift occurs most readily in an Ionian plagal tune with the fourth phrase repeated, slightly altered, to make a final fifth phrase. The tune may show a marked tendency under these conditions to close on the lower fifth without climbing back again to the original tonic. (Such *fallen closes*, as they may be called, are particularly characteristic of the Appalachian mountain tunes in this country.) Then, if the tune's final be accepted as the genuine tonic, we already have a Mixolydian variant. The two kinds are not always easy to distinguish. The following series of variants of "Lord Thomas and Fair Eleanor" will illustrate what has just been said.

For the sake of clarity, the above tunes have all been referred to a common tonal center; but it will be understood that the principle

Lord Thomas and Fair Eleanor
1 Ionian. Sharp MSS 91/155 [Devon, 1904]

2 Pentatonic, ¬4,7, authentic. Sharp MSS $\frac{3604}{2666}$. [Tennessee, 1917]

3 Pentatonic, -4,7, plagal. Sharp MSS 3219. [North Carolina, 1916]

4 Mixolydian. Broadwood, Journal of Folk-Song Society, V,130 [Hertfordshire, 1914]

5 Pentatonic, -4,7, with fallen close; or -3,7. Sharp MSS 4707 [North Carolina, 1918]

continues to operate, no matter what the pitch of the individual tune. And again, the process may take place in reverse. I do not believe that plagal tunes always develop from authentic ones: it seems to me quite probable, in fact, that plagal tunes are the earlier type; first, because they allowed the primitive singer to stay closer to his tonic while giving him equal melodic liberty; and second, because it is easier for a singer to pitch a plagal tune, the tonic being comfortably in the middle of his range. There is more danger of his not starting an authentic tune low enough; so that the top notes, which usually occur in the second and third phrases, may prove to be out of reach.

One consequence of the foregoing discussion may be mentioned by way of conclusion. Anyone who has attempted to order a large number of variants knows how vexatious and difficult it is to find a logical and consistent method of arrangement. It would appear reasonable, if these remarks find acceptance, to arrange such a series of modal variants in general accordance with the chart of correspondences here indicated. One would logically commence with Lydian (scarcely ever found) and proceed inward along the right arms of each successive star-point from end to end, as the extant variants might permit. Thus: L^y—L^y/I—π^1—I—I/M—π^2—M—M/D—π^3, and so on around the clock. The bimodal cases and other anomalies would fall to be dealt with on their respective merits.

These suggestions are, for the present, tentatively advanced, for they have been tested only to a limited extent. And, clearly, a supplementary method must be employed within the several classes. But, in the field of Anglo-Celtic-American folk-song, at least, the arrangement gives promise of providing a sound and useful rationale of procedure.

1946

Habits of the Ballad as Song

Among educated people, interest in the ballads seems always to have begun apologetically. Sir Philip Sidney confessed his own "barbarousness" at being moved by the old song of Percy and Douglas. Addison was able to avow his liking for the same ballad only by finding analogies in Virgil and Horace. Ambrose Philips introduced his collection of old ballads with facetious condescension—for which he was sufficiently repaid when Pope with solemn irony praised the *Pastorals* of Philips himself for all the wrong reasons.

The charm of artlessness is the virtue that first won approbation for the ballads. These pieces were (in Addison's phrase) "plain simple Copies of Nature," moving in spite of "despicable Simplicity in the Verse" because of their "genuine and unaffected Sentiment." Toward the end of the eighteenth century this appeal was borne out by new theories of the inevitable rightness of primitive impulses—life according to Nature. Thus the prevailing doctrine made the ballads respectable and even admirable. Not long thereafter, thanks particularly to Walter Scott, the rich historical interest of the ballads began to be disclosed, both as a record of earlier belief and as a distorted but influential reflection of actual events. Subsequently, the puzzling connections and analogies with Scandinavian popular poetry began to be explored, and gradually it became apparent that these continental relationships extended in every direction across the whole face of Europe and into Asia.

By the time Grundtvig and Child had finished their labors—that is to say, by the end of the nineteenth century—the study of the popular ballad was accepted nearly everywhere as a highly digni-

The Charles Mills Gayley lecture for 1950.

fied field of research, challenging the best efforts of scholarship by reason of the breadth and variety of learning requisite to its mastery. Child's headnotes in his magnificent edition are universally acclaimed as one of the greatest monuments of the literary scholarship of the last century—staggering in their geographical sweep and historical range.

In the face of Child's peerless knowledge and of his belief that balladry was virtually a closed account, it was not expected that anything of importance would be added henceforward to this branch of learning. Child had sent out circulars to every likely corner, appealing for fresh contributions from oral tradition, and the results were so meager as to discourage further effort in that direction.

It is necessary to observe that Child's labors were the culmination of a long line of studies amateur and professional, almost all of which were singly devoted to the ballad texts. Sidney knew well enough that "Chevy Chase" was a song because he was used to hearing it chanted; but subsequent men of letters usually forgot or ignored the fact. Child felt it to be no part of his proper business to collect and annotate the music. He admitted into his work, however, a list (compiled by another hand) of bibliographical references to the printed records of ballad tunes, and he made provision for a short appendix of tunes from manuscripts that had fallen into his net. Thus was established the custom, which has been continuously followed by Child's successors to the present moment, of full annotation on the textual side and bare reference on the musical side, with at best an appendix of tunes, but with no attempt to relate one tune to another, or to study text and tune as interdependent.[1] The attitude of most of these scholars, to judge by their practice, seems akin to that succinctly put by Calverley:

> I cannot sing the old songs now!
>   It is not that I deem them low;
> 'Tis that I can't remember how
>   They go.

Whether or no this be their dilemma, there has been no method developed in comparative analysis of ballad tunes at all comparable in maturity to what has existed for the better part of a century in

[1] Since this was written, there has been developing a visible tendency to right the balance.

connection with the texts. Thus far, the serious study of ballads, in other words, has advanced always on one and the same leg.

It chanced that, just at the time when Child was carrying to completion what he must naturally have anticipated would be the definitive and terminal account of his subject (since it was to cover the whole surviving record), a generation appeared who were more interested in popular tunes than in popular texts. These enthusiasts made the startling discovery that most of what had hitherto passed in print for popular music bore little resemblance to what the people were actually singing in the thorps and crofts of Britain. What was being sung bore the clear marks of a tradition anterior to the major and minor harmonic habits of the last three centuries. Its melodic outlines were more akin to the modal songs of the Middle Ages, resistant to modern harmonization; and the intonation was almost as reluctant as the bagpipe's to submit to the tempered scale. In face of these discoveries, it was obviously necessary to go to the singers themselves for the truth of tradition, just as Child had tried wherever possible to get behind the printed texts. Therefore, about the turn of the century, a group of devotees banded together to form the English Folk Song Society and set out to collect faithful records from traditional singing. Their success, during the next quarter of a century, surpassed all expectation; and, thereafter, in our own country similar efforts have continued to bring in a harvest of which we do not yet see the end. Ironically enough, search for the music, neglected by Child, has opened the springs of current tradition as he was unable to tap them; so that large numbers of genuine, if often sadly dilapidated, texts have been recovered of the very ballads he was vainly seeking—along with a great deal of other traditional matter from which we may gain further light on the ways of the ballad.

These inquiries, it is clear today, were forwarded at a time when the roots of national culture were being sought out and scrutinized by every Western nation, when racial and national consciousness was particularly acute. They therefore contributed to, and formed a significant part of, a great movement to be remarked by future historians. Among pioneering leaders in the investigation of folksong, Cecil Sharp, for self-dedication, systematic thoroughness, successful collecting, bulk of editorial work, and general influence, occupies the central niche. He is the chief link, as well, between the

English and American activities in this field. His tireless and galvanic efforts on both sides of the Atlantic have proven the most important single force in this half-century's accomplishment.

One result of these investigations has been to establish the fact that the English-speaking peoples are just as genuinely and richly endowed with native musical gifts as their Continental neighbors. In turn, this reassurance has been an element of primary importance in the resurgence of creative energy in English music. Ralph Vaughan Williams, it may be recalled, was one of the earliest members of the Folk Song Society, and is even today [2] president of the International Folk Music Council. The same impulse is being felt at present in American musical composition, as the names of Randall Thompson, Aaron Copland, Henry Cowell, and Virgil Thomson sufficiently testify.

Thus, gradually, the subject of British and American folk music has gained serious attention and respectability. It has acquired an importance equal to that of other branches of folklore and a general interest that bids fair to surpass all the rest. Perhaps we had better admit as well that from this growing favor certain nuisances have ensued. When such an interest arises among groups not originally possessed of it, but able and willing to pay money to gratify it, the paid entertainer is at the door, waiting to capitalize on what has hitherto been a spontaneous and relatively unselfconscious expression of artistic feeling. Audiences, as we know, inevitably corrupt, in that they force the singer to be heedful of *how* as well as *what* he is doing. To be sure, the tendency to professionalize can be observed for almost as long a span as the extant records stretch. The burlesque opening of Chaucer's *Sir Thopas*—"Listeth, Lordes, in good entent, / And I wol telle verrayment / Of mirthe and of solas"—is nothing else but the medieval minstrel's professional knock at the gate, both in its flattery ("Lordes") and in its promise of entertainment. This line passes down through the blackletter broadsides of the sixteenth and seventeenth centuries, beloved of Mopsa and of Pepys; the fly sheets of the eighteenth and nineteenth centuries; on to most of the hillbilly entertainment of platform and radio. The true modern broadside is the phonograph record. The audiences that attend the concertizing of folk-song today are descendants of the people who bought Ambrose Philips'

[2] Dr. Vaughan Williams, O.M., died in 1958.

Collection of Old Ballads two hundred and fifty years ago. And, as a general rule, they are just as much misled by professionalized folk-singers about the genuine qualities of traditional song. By and large, this state of affairs probably does little permanent harm, for in the long run it helps to keep things alive that might otherwise die. Throughout history, folk-song, in spite of continual contamination, has proven almost incorruptible, although never before has corruption had such opportunities, because of identical duplication, to become stereotyped and orthodox. It behooves those at least who know and care for genuine folk-song to insist upon the difference between its imitations and itself. Speaking strictly, a professional folk-singer does not exist: there are folk-singers, and there are professional singers.

By now, after half a century of fairly intensive effort, a good deal is known, or can be discovered, about folk-music. The fashionable interest of the present day, quite properly, welcomes all kinds of it, without much regard to categories. The ballad as a distinctive genre has tended to be reabsorbed into, or reunited with, the great body of traditional music of which it forms a part. Actually, its segregation was a somewhat pedantic and artificial business, convenient for scholars, but resting on no very valid intrinsic distinctions and unknown to the folk-singers themselves. It is ultimately impossible to say where narrative leaves off and lyric begins; and analogous or related tunes are found with all sorts of texts, religious, tragic, ludicrous, narrative, or more purely lyrical. After two or three centuries of interest in ballad texts alone, a wholesale interest in the mass of traditional song has had a salutary tendency to bring into view resemblances and relationships that would otherwise have gone unnoticed, and to throw emphasis upon the fact that words and music belong together, and should be divorced only for laboratory analysis.

We find ourselves today, then, in an advantageous position to begin an intensive study of every extant variety of folk-song, with brighter prospects of success, probably, than ever before. If we choose to commence with the ballad, it is only as a convenient center, with a full realization that we must continually look beyond for additional light. In the time remaining, I should like briefly to survey the materials at our disposal, to suggest the kind of problems which they raise, and to illustrate traditional variation as it affects the melodic patterns of folk-song.

First, then, for the materials, taking the Child ballads as our convenient base. On a rough calculation, the total number of extant musical records, manuscript, printed, and vocal, directly connected with textual variants of Child's popular ballads, or identified by title as belonging to this canon, must be upwards of 5,000. These records provide tunes for slightly more than two-thirds of Child's 305 distinct ballads. For some of the ballads, there is no more than a single record of a tune; for others there are hundreds. An example of the latter class is "Barbara Allan," favorite since at least the Restoration (when Pepys, "in perfect pleasure," heard it sung by his dear Mrs. Knipp), and still probably the most widely sung folksong in our own country today. (Strange that a song about a pair with such an alacrity in dying should have so tenacious a hold on life!)

The total of 5,000 records would include all tunes and tune variants, but of course would exclude identical copies printed one from another or from the same source. This sum, however, could be indefinitely multiplied if we widened our scope on the musical side to take in all variants of these tunes or tune-families regardless of their verbal texts. And a further possible extension would include the records of Continental analogues. Even of the records with ballad texts in English the geographical spread is enormous. It reaches from the Shetlands to California, and no doubt also to New Zealand and Australia and wherever else British folk have settled.

The temporal spread of these records is not at first glance so imposing as the spatial. Whereas the earliest text among Child's ballads, the "Judas," goes back to the mid-thirteenth century, no tune specifically attached in the record by title or accompanying text to any Child ballad is earlier than the beginning of the seventeenth century and probably nine-tenths of the total bulk lie on this side of the year 1900. Yet by the time a folk-song has become genuinely traditional its beginnings are out of sight, and it is very certain that many of our tunes are far more ancient than their earliest date of record. Our temporal range, therefore, may be hesitantly pushed back along a chain of names and resemblances. Thus it is fair to say that the earliest recorded tune of Child no. 1 is to be found with its proper ballad text in D'Urfey's *Pills to Purge Melancholy*, at the beginning of the eighteenth century. But that tune is patently related to "The North-Country Lasse" (alias "I would I were in my own country," or "The Oak and the Ash and the Bonny Ivy Tree"), well known to the latter seventeenth century; and that again is clearly a variant form of "Goddesses" in Playford's *English Dancing Master*, 1650; and this again relates to the Elizabethan tunes set for virginals by both Ralph and Giles Farnaby under the titles "Fayne wolde I wedde" and "Quodling's Delight." There for the moment we may leave it.

On the other hand, conjecture about age from internal evidence deserves little confidence. It is undeniable that an ancient-seeming tune may have acquired its patina through a late singer's unconscious preference for the old melodic habits, and may be antique not in fact but only in style; and that contrariwise a truly ancient tune may have been altered almost beyond recognition by modern harmonic influences. Let anyone try the experiment of singing "Yankee Doodle" with a flatted seventh wherever the leading note occurs and he will know what a folk-singer with an instinctive leaning to the Mixolydian might do to antiquate a modern major tune. For an opposite example: one of the prevalent types of melody in our tradition—found with "Lady Isabel and the Elf-Knight," with "Lord Thomas and Fair Eleanor," and many other ballads—has nothing of an ancient cast about it, being usually a sprightly 6/8 tune in the major; but it can be found latent, almost note for note, in a Gregorian *Sanctus* of the tenth century, in the fourth, or Hypophrygian, mode. Another very common melodic type, omnipresent in the Appalachian region today, is unmistakably the second half of a tune of which the earliest record known at present is to be found in an early seventeenth-century Scottish manuscript for the mandora, where it is called "Lady Cassilles Lilt."

The early records, unfortunately, are often far from dependable. The richest repositories of Elizabethan *popular* music are not vocal but instrumental collections like the Fitzwilliam Book, where the tunes are used as thematic material for keyboard variations. Composers for the virginals sophisticated almost every statement of a tune—frequently even the first—both metrically, phrasally, and in tonality. Elizabethan musicians were fascinated by the kaleidoscopic shifting of modal references; but we can hardly suppose that contemporary folk-singers pursued these refinements when, in our own times, in the face of social and scientific developments that make it impossible to remain unexposed to the current musical environment, the descendants of such singers have persisted in clinging to the stricter medieval modal allegiances. We must believe, therefore, that however close to popular matter they may be, the Elizabethan records are unreliable representatives of genuine folksong. They provide hints that serve to identify a tune in later outcroppings, but not its actual shape in tradition.

Similarly, the seventeenth and early eighteenth centuries are deficient in authentic report. The Playfords' successive publications yield abundant popular tunes, usually in relatively simple forms, but arranged for dancing, and without words. From Child's most fruitful source of texts in this period, the black-letter broadsides, nothing can be gleaned of the music we want. A little later, D'Urfey's miscellaneous collection rescues from oblivion much broadside music, along with tunes composed for the theater and a few traditional ballad tunes; and, thereafter, during the course of the eighteenth century, the song collections, engraved sheets, and ballad operas yield some traditional tunes, and many semi-popular and composed pieces.

At the end of that century comes the first deliberate attempt to record the repertory of a known folk-singer, the famous Mrs. Brown of Falkland, in Scotland. In this case, however, the help at hand was so unskillful and the task proved so difficult that only fifteen tunes were set down, and these in questionable shape. At about the same time, Robert Burns began contributing folk-melodies that he had memorized to James Johnson's *Scots Musical Museum*, an admirable effort toward a national archive of song.

Slender but conscientious additions to the general stock were made from tradition by Charles Kirkpatrick Sharpe, Motherwell, and Kinloch in the early years of the nineteenth century. In the 'forties and 'fifties, William Chappell amassed from printed and manuscript sources the materials of his imposing *Popular Music of the Olden Time*; but, sad to say, he altered his tunes in accordance with nineteenth-century harmonic standards, and preserved very few tunes from tradition. Dean William Christie, twenty-five years later, published *Traditional Ballad Airs*, a large collection drawn from singers in the northeast of Scotland. Christie clearly had access to unparalleled riches in the musical tradition; but he could no more leave things alone than could Bishop Percy before him. He added editorial graces and variational second strains; and moreover cared nothing for an accurate verbal text. What might have been easily the most valuable work of its kind in the century was thus seriously vitiated by its compiler's shortcomings.

In the last quarter of the century, other valuable regional collections appeared: Bruce and Stokoe's *Northumbrian Minstrelsy*, Frank Kidson's *Traditional Tunes* from Yorkshire, the Broadwoods' Sussex songs, Baring-Gould's *Songs of the West*, from Cornwall and Devon. Meanwhile, in Ireland, Bunting, Hudson, Petrie, and Joyce had salvaged, but not published, an enormous number of traditional Irish tunes. With the opening of the twentieth century, there began a new era of systematic and faithful collecting, marked especially by the work of Gavin Greig in Scotland, and of Cecil Sharp in Somerset and in the Appalachians. Together, these two men alone made authentic, personal records of close to 8,000 songs.

In our own country, the formation of regional societies has proceeded apace and has culminated in the establishing of a National Archive at Washington, into which local collections are continually being funneled. This collection will soon become—if it is not already so—the amplest repository of its kind in the Western world. Its phonographic records, of absolute and verifiable authenticity, already number several thousand, and are being made generally accessible in selective albums. Of the Child ballads alone, the checklist of 1940—the latest issued (for folk-song too is dependent on the mood of Congress for financial support)—revealed over 500 variants in the Archive, and in the past decade that number may have been doubled. This means that nearly as many variants of his ballads as Child chose to include from every kind of source are already gathered into the Archive in living, audible form, straight out of the traditional stream.

Surveying the whole scene, therefore, we look out upon a very uneven and surprising terrain. Down to 1900 the records are scanty and spotty and almost everywhere untrustworthy in greater or less degree. Since 1900 they have grown constantly fuller and more precisely accurate and dependable. Whereas Child believed

his ballads to be virtually extinct—a "closed account"—and saw a
vanishing record of which much the more valuable part was the
earlier, we now, for purposes of serious study, see the pyramid of
evidence inverted, its apex buried in the past, and subject only to
casual excavation, while the base lies broad before us, open to
present exploration. As matters stand, the contemporary record is
of greater potential significance than the combined record of previous centuries: first, because we can depend on its fidelity; and second, because only here does it exist in sufficient bulk and density to
justify qualified generalization. I would not belittle the interest and
beauty of many of our early records. But it is simply fact that if as
students we are to deduce and describe underlying laws of devel-
opmental change, we must have abundant and reliable examples
from which to work. And in the English, Scottish, and American
collections of the twentieth century we have three geographically
separate and truly representative masses of evidence, affording a
kind of triangulation on the British tradition as a whole. It is in the
processes of traditional transmission and re-creation, and not in any
mythical parthenogenesis, that the differentiating factors of folk-
song as a distinct type of expression are embedded. It is in the variants alone—words and music—that we can hope to discover the
history and the biological laws of the type.

Variation in folk-song is fascinating from many points of view—
psychological, sociological, and aesthetic. It raises abundant questions of great interest, but full of teasing perplexities. Why is that
certain narrative themes and certain melodic forms come down
through tradition almost straight and relatively stable, while others
lose essential elements and keep nonessentials, flow into divergent
streams and combine with alien matter? How do they achieve patterns of utmost beauty and then dissolve into infelicities without
being quite forgotten? Are the changes controlled by any discerni-
ble laws, or does chance everywhere dominate? If there are laws,
are they applied deliberately, or do they operate involuntarily?
The evolution of the ballad form seems to have obeyed aesthetic
principles: are these lost sight of by the processes of traditional
transmission, or does artistic consideration continue to play its
part? What are the differentiating factors of preference in theme
and melody among distinct racial groups and whence do they
arise? What is the meaning of the periodic shifts that take place on

this basic level of consciousness? Why and how did it happen that so many popular tunes of Elizabethan and Caroline England, for example, took on a 6/8 rhythm, while their melodic descendants in the Appalachians, two and a half centuries later, have stretched out into slow and irregular 3/2 meter, and prefer the gapped scales to the full heptatonic system? To answer such questions as these, we shall need all the lights we can muster, from whatever source.

Moreover, problems of critical method confront us from the start with crucial queries. Basic is the question: What constitutes the identity of a melody? At what point does a melody, by continuous minute changes, cease to be itself, and how far does melodic kinship obtain? The case is far more vexing on the musical than on the textual side. For a story we can usually recognize, even when garbled and distorted, and whatever the words employed, in whatever order. But a tune's identity is intimately involved in the particular succession of notes. Yet we can say we "recognize the tune" when all the notes, or most of them, are different, and even the mode and meter as well. When a Beethoven or a Brahms works out a series of variations, he gives us, first or last, an archetypal statement of the theme. But here, every new variant is an archetype, for there is no authoritative original. Every true folk-singer believes that he has the true original: he sings it and passes it on, as he learned it, without willful change. Yet all the variants differ in some degree from one another. Then what has happened, and how?

Theoretically, it would be possible to take an ordinary ballad tune and, gradually, without any violence or sudden distortion of the melody, alter it note by note into something which by itself could not be recognized as a derivative of the first tune. If such were the normal evolution of folk-tunes, our hope of significant conclusions would be doomed to disappointment. For the casual and fragmentary records with which we have to work never provide long chains of directly connected evidence. Folk-tunes, no doubt, *have* become transformed beyond recognition; but it seems unlikely that changes of the sort suggested are the rule of oral transmission. On the contrary, one of the most striking and wonderful features of these organisms is the way in which, in spite of continual flux, they persist in clinging to some quintessential core of identity. We must then assume some kind of control. In spite of accidental deflections, it appears as if some sort of organic principle of selfhood or inner growth were at work, analogous to that of a biological species, and subject similarly to unpredictable mutation.

Cecil Sharp proposed a threefold hypothesis to account for these phenomena. It was his belief that fresh musical suggestions are continually being thrown off or produced by individual creative impulse within a tradition. These suggestions are as continually being challenged by the instinctive sense of a homogeneous community immersed in the conventions circumscribing traditional melody. Only the suggestions that meet with general acceptance, he thought, have a chance to survive. Thus, the peculiar strength and virtue of folk-song lies in the fact that it has undergone and successfully passed a most exacting kind of communal proving.

In the main, I believe we may tentatively accept this hypothesis, while we qualify it in certain respects. Thus, it does not appear that the process is necessarily a guarantee of strength, unless the tradition is in a vigorous, creative stage of existence. If the instinctive sense or taste of the community were always sound, we should have a sure criterion of adoption. But actually that sense is usually vulnerable to all manner of deleterious suggestions from outside and above, whether from current fashion or from supposed superior taste. Weakness of such a kind will always be present where, as here, values and standards have never been defined and formulated, but rest on instinct and habit. Against such outer influences a tradition cannot be securely insulated. Convention, moreover, being unadventurous by definition, is easily content with mere stereotyped repetition, which in turn gives off impressions ever duller and more blurred. Again and again we see that the perfect form, by some miracle once achieved, is never jealously preserved by the guardian sense of the community. The process of change continues inevitably, like growth and decay in Nature, and "Time that gave doth now his gifts confound." Perfection is no surer of survival than mediocrity, in the popular mind.

From this axiom we might deduce a corollary: that when we find a ballad in a state of supreme effectiveness or felicitous beauty, like "Edward" or "Sir Patrick Spens" in their late eighteenth-century forms, we are not to suppose that it has arrived at that condition centuries earlier and been so preserved in the amber of the folk-memory. On the contrary, if it comes, not from an ex-

humed written record, but directly out of tradition, we may confidently assert that its beauty has been but recently realized. It follows that we shall have to revise our former notions about the
Golden Age of the ballad. Apart from the Robin Hood cycle, it is
untrue, though it has been carelessly said, that the best ballads, in
the sense of the most artistically satisfying, are the oldest. It is one
thing to say that the best ballads are the oldest ones, and another to
say that the best ballad texts are variants of ballads known to be
very old. But I suspect that the distinction has seldom been borne
in mind. In an aesthetic judgment, it is the particular variant, not
the sum total of variants known and unknown, good and bad, that
must constitute the object evaluated. The best ballad, aesthetically,
is the most beautiful variant, not an infelicitous ancestor of such a
variant. And, generally speaking, the best texts in Child's great collection date from near the close of the eighteenth century.

Anyone may declare, if he likes, that the fifteenth century was a
Golden Age of balladry. It may well have been so, for conditions,
so far as we can tell, were favorable. But to support the assertion,
setting inferences aside, three or four Robin Hood ballads, and the
Gest, are all that survive in English. On the other hand, granting
the demonstrable facts of oral transmission,

> When [we] consider everything that grows
> Holds in perfection but a little moment,

and looking at the extant record, we must certainly agree that the
eighteenth century was a Golden Age of balladry. For this assertion we have all the evidence we need. The vitality of tradition, especially Scottish tradition, at that particular time is what gives the
dominant character or tone to Child's whole collection.

Vitality of tradition is to be measured by the amount of re-creative energy flowing into tradition at a particular time or place.
Tradition is not a constant, nor should it be thought of as something strong at the outset and becoming always weaker, like the
diminishing reverberations of a bell. Neither is there any inherent
reason why it should be pictured solely as "the road downhill." No
doubt the historical record will often show it in that light, but it
must have mounted before it started to descend; and again the
image of a living organism suggests itself as a truer analogy. Like
everything subject to growth and decay, it runs an uneven course.

There are fat years and lean years, and after a period of lying fallow, there may be a sudden uprush of vigor, or conversely a decline after unusual activity. There may be enrichments from outside, or new energies released from within, as a tree will grow twice the distance in one year that it grew in another. It has been shown by the French scholar, M. Coirault, how certain songs have passed from Court theatricals late in the sixteenth century into the streets of Paris, then drifted out into the country among the peasantry; been forgotten by the town dwellers meanwhile, and rediscovered a hundred years later by interested musicians; been reintroduced to society and taken up once more as folk-song by sophisticated people; only, perhaps, to go through the whole cycle again. Always there seems to have been this borrowing back and forth, this *va-et-vien* between the country and the town, between the upper and lower levels of society, from the medieval *chansons de toile* downward to the present. In England we see the same process in the adaptations of folk-song introduced into eighteenth-century ballad operas, or the instrumental reworkings of similar tunes in earlier and later periods; and, on the contrary, songs are picked up by collectors from country singers today, that had sunk out of sight since they circulated on Restoration broadsides or in the pages of D'Urfey's *Pills to Purge Melancholy*.

Along with his testimony to the extraordinary retentiveness and accuracy of the folk-memory at its best, Cecil Sharp offered instances of the surprisingly vital re-creativeness of certain individual singers among the folk of Somerset at the opening of the present century. A gifted singer, a blind man named Henry Larcombe, seems hardly ever to have sung two successive stanzas of a song to quite the same notes. He continually altered his phrases, and this not in a pedestrian fashion, but often, as Sharp demonstrates, with a real recasting of the melodic line. The practice was not deliberate. He did it, Sharp declares, without being aware of the difference. When Sharp would ask him to repeat, Larcombe was always ready to oblige—but with a new form of the phrase!

Now, these two impulses, of conservation and of re-creation, are perhaps not so mutually antagonistic as at first they appear. No doubt the proportions of each vary enormously in different individuals and at different times, or we should not have the unevenness of growth and change that we have been remarking. But it is important to realize that they can exist and interact simultaneously in the same individual. We have parallel evidence on the verbal side in the performance of Mrs. Brown, the Scottish singer of the late eighteenth century, who contributed notably to the traditional stores of Jamieson and Walter Scott. At different times, Mrs. Brown gave widely different texts of some of her ballads to these collectors, and did so apparently with no sense of inconsistency or alteration. She was, incidentally, possessed of some education; but for her songs she was undoubtedly drawing entirely on early memories. Her case is exactly analogous to Larcombe's, and to be explained in the same way. These were singers steeped in the traditional idiom, and whatever they sang, judged traditionally, would sound authentic. They were not automatic transmitters, as we ourselves should be, of a standard, received text and tune: they were themselves the living authority, personified embodiments of traditional re-creation. What they carried in their memories was not a fixed, memorized series of words and notes, but the fluid idea of a song which so far as they were concerned had never had any other existence than in the fresh evocations it received from singers like themselves. There was no "authoritative" text or tune to which they might refer for the "correct" reading; but instead, only a narrative idea, a melodic idea, floating in their minds in solution, as it were, until it was crystallized by an act of will. This is tradition at its vital best: a marriage of opposites, an example in miniature of the practice of the ancient rhapsode, half recollection, half improvisation.

The point to be emphasized is that the idea which such singers retained in their minds—whether narrative, melodic, or both—was clear and definite enough to be a positive, controlling, but not constricting force. Within limits they were free: they used the words and notes that occurred to them at the moment, like good raconteurs who re-create their stories at each fresh telling. This kind of invention is too rapid and spontaneous to allow of deliberation. But beyond the traditional boundaries they would not stray. To do so would be a betrayal of their trusteeship, a kind of disloyalty almost unthinkable in the faithful transmitters of these venerable songs.

The nature, the laws, and the operation of this loose kind of restraint—or this restrictive liberty—*laxis immissus habenis*—can of course be studied only in its tangible products, either in the particular successive performances of individual singers, when we are so fortunate as to possess this rarest kind of evidence, or in the commoner yet sadly deficient record, scattered through time and space, to which multitudes have contributed in their turn.

It may perhaps help to give focus to these somewhat discursive remarks if we consider briefly some examples of a typical folktune, or tune-family, with a very long and interesting record in tradition. This family has a far-flung membership that crosses water barriers as wide as the Atlantic, and stretches possibly over eight centuries. Many beautiful melodies appear to belong to it, and it is close to the heart of the British folk-tradition. The names of many individuals within it are thoroughly familiar, but so far as I know there is no family name. The members are mated to all kinds of texts—ballads, carols, love songs, dancing songs, and drinking songs. Variants of the tune are sung to at least a dozen and a half of the Child ballads, and it would be no trick to collect well over a hundred examples of the family. They are found mostly in hexatonic or heptatonic forms. Everywhere they display great reluctance to desert the minor modes, but rare major and Mixolydian examples do occur. To speak more precisely, the majority are in melodic minor or pure Æolian patterns, with the evidence of all the accurately noted recent copies from tradition going to prove that the inflections of the melodic minor copies are editorial, not genuinely traditional readings. (Among the consequences of this fact would be to correct the singing of Ophelia's "How should I your true-love know" by substituting a flat seventh where we habitually employ the leading note.) Very many examples of our family are Dorian / Æolian hexatonics, the sixth being the missing note, the third, of course, being minor. In a fair number of cases, the gap is filled with a raised sixth, making true Dorian variants. Metrically, there is considerable variety: several sorts of duple rhythm, several of triple, and some variants in five-time, some in irregular measures. The bulk of the family is composed of four-phrase tunes. There are a few five-, six-, seven-, and eight-phrase variants, but the majority fall into the non-recurrent phrasal scheme, ABCD. Beyond this point in analytical description it would be tedious to go at present.

The series of musical illustrations here presented comprises a cross section of this single tune-family, ordered not chronologically but according to considerations of structural detail with which I need not trouble my audience.

1. "True Thomas." Walter Scott, *Minstrelsy of the Scottish Border,* IV (1833 ed.), 116.

2. "Geordie." Cecil Sharp MS. no. 1840, from East Coker, Somerset, 1908.

3. "Hind Horn." G. Greig and A. Keith, *Last Leaves of Traditional Ballads and Ballad Airs* (1925), p. 20 (*a*), from New Deer, Aberdeen.

4. "The Lonesome Prairie." C. J. Sharp and M. Karpeles, *English Folksongs from the Southern Appalachians*, II (1932), 237 (*c*), from North Carolina.

5. "Goddesses." J. Playford, *The English Dancing Master* (1650, repr. 1933), p. 52.

6. "A Riddle Wittily Expounded." T. D'Urfey, *Pills to Purge Melancholy*, IV (1719), 129.

7. "Lord Bateman." C. J. Sharp, *One Hundred English Folksongs* (1916), p. 17.

8. "The Carnal and the Crane." E. M. Leather and R. Vaughan Williams, *Twelve Traditional Carols from Herefordshire*, repr. *Oxford Book of Carols* (1927), p. 110.

9. "There is a Fountain." *Oxford Book of Carols*, p. 232, and *Journal of the English Folk Song Society*, II, 133.

10. "Fayne wolde I wedde." R. Farnaby, *Fitzwilliam Virginal Book*, ed. Maitland and Squire, II (1899), 263.

11. "How should I your true-love know?" W. Chappell, *Popular Music*, I (1855), 236, from Miss Field, eighteenth-century stage tradition.

12. "Let all that are to Mirth inclin'd." D. Gilbert, *Some Ancient Christmas Carols* (1822), p. 32.

13. "The Cruel Mother." Johnson, *Scots Musical Museum* (*ca.* 1792), no. 320.

14. "[Coverdale's Carol]." Leather and Williams, *op. cit.*, repr. *Oxford Book of Carols*, p. 260.

15. "King Herod and the Cock." *Oxford Book of Carols*, p. 112, from Worcestershire.

16. "Congaudeat." *Piae Cantiones* (1582), repr. *Oxford Book of Carols*, p. 176.

17. "En gaudeat." A. Gastoué, *Revue du chant grégorien*, XI (September 1902), p. 24, from twelfth century.

18. "Clerk Saunders." G. R. Kinloch, *Ancient Scottish Ballads* (1827), Appendix.

19. "As you came from Walsingham." W. Chappell, *Popular Music* (1855), from (?) W. Barley, *A New Book of Tablature* (1596).

20. "As I walked over London Bridge." R. Vaughan Williams, *Journal of the Folksong Society*, II, 208, from Sussex, 1906.

21. "Searching for Lambs." C. J. Sharp, *One Hundred English Folksongs* (1916), p. 108.

22. "The Cruel Mother." Hammond, *Journal of the English Folk Song Society*, III, 70, from Dorset, 1907.

23. "Go from my Window." W. Chappell, *Popular Music*, I, 142, from tradition, Norwich.

24. "The True Lover's Farewell." Sharp and Karpeles, *op. cit.*, II, 118 (I), from Kentucky, 1917.

25. "Georgie." Vaughan Williams and G. Butterworth, *Journal of the English Folk Song Society*, IV, 332 (1), from Suffolk, 1910.

26. "Captain Wedderburn's Courtship." Greig and Keith, *op. cit.*, p. 36 (1c).

27. "Westron Wynde." Chappell, *op. cit.*, I, 58, from MS. Reg. App. 58, temp. Henry VIII.

Confronted by abundant evidence of this kind, we are driven to conclude that, just as on the textual side there are narrative ideas consisting in a multitude of traditional restatements, the sum of which constitutes a ballad—or better, a ballad-family or species (i.e., Child no. x)—so, on the musical side of folk-song, there are, similarly, melodic ideas, tunes, or tune-families, that have existed for hundreds of years in a parallel state. They are self-perpetuating, and cohere in a multiform unity. Their beginnings are no more to be found than are the beginnings of a biological species. They subsist according to inner principles of organic development and change, and are subject also to accidental mutation. They lend themselves as vehicles for all sorts of texts, but may become allied over long stretches of space and time with particular text-families, changing as the latter change. They are thus deeply involved and interwoven with the world of words, but they have also an independent life. Some day, perhaps, we shall be able to fix the number and character of these archetypes and establish a canon of our melodic tradition.[3]

1950

[3] Some use has been made in this essay, more particularly in the part concerned with conservation and re-creation, of ideas similarly expressed in a paper read on December 28, 1949, before the American Musicological Society in New York City and published in its *Journal*, Vol. III, No. 3 (1950), where also the same musical examples appear.

On the Union of Words and Music
in the "Child" Ballads

THE EXTANT TEXTS of the Child ballads are—in actual record, not in presumptive age—of various dates from the thirteenth century to the present year. From a time earlier than the death of Elizabeth, however, not one text, so far as has been learned, has been preserved together with a tune to which it was sung. In the first third of the seventeenth century, three texts were printed by Thomas Ravenscroft with their tunes.[1] Thereafter, for another century—to 1733—the only Child texts, good, bad, or indifferent that are to be found mated with their tunes are two broadside copies preserved by D'Urfey in various editions of *Wit and Mirth* between 1700–1720;[2] two more in Thomson's *Orpheus Caledonius*, 1725 and 1733;[3] and the sophisticated form, both text and air, of a fifth on engraved sheets of 1711, 1727, and subsequently in collections.[4]

[1] Child no. 26, in T. Ravenscroft, *Melismata* (1611), no. 22; Child no. 112, in *Deuteromelia* (1609), sig. E4; Child no. 284 in the latter, no. 1 of Freemen's Songs, sig. B.

[2] Child no. 1, in ed. of 1719, IV, 130; no. 45 in the same volume, p. 29. D'Urfey also gives no. 112, apparently after Ravenscroft, in III, 37; and a form of no. 164 not accepted by Child, in V, 49. Moreover, he prints pieces related, in one way or another, to nos. 2 (V, 317), 18 (III, 293), 112 (V, 112), 232 (V, 42).

[3] Child no. 181, in 1733, II, 8; no. 215 in 1733, II, 110. Thomson also gives Mallet's version of no. 74 (1725 and 1733, I, 109); Ramsay's version of no. 201 (1725 and 1733, I, 3); Hamilton's version of no. 214 (1733, II, 34); a lyric form of no. 217 (1725 and 1733, I, 18); a tune related to no. 237 with another text (1733, II, 32); the secondary form of no. 279, Appx. (1725 and 1733, I, 95); no. 293 rewritten (1733, II, 95); the song form of no. 204 (Waly, Waly: 1725 and 1733, I, 71).

[4] "William and Margaret," Child no. 74, in Ballads and Broadsides, Brit. Mus. 1876. f. 1, fol. 107. Cf. W. Chappell, *The Antiquary*, January 1880, no. 1, and *Roxburghe Ballads*, III, Appx., pp. 667 ff. Also J. Watts, *Musical Miscellany*, II

Another hundred years, to 1833, yields a better harvest. During that time, more than a hundred different ballads were set down on paper with the tunes to which they were sung; the alternative or variant copies of some of these raise the total by half as much again. The largest single contributor to this sum was *The Scots Musical Museum*, in six volumes published between 1787 and 1803. Of its six hundred songs, thirty-three are Child ballads.[5] Close behind comes Motherwell, with thirty-two.[6] Next stands Mrs. Harris of Fearn, with twenty-three.[7] Then Charles Kirkpatrick Sharpe, with seventeen;[8] Kinloch, with sixteen;[9] Mrs. Brown of Falkland, with fifteen;[10] Alexander Campbell[11] and Sir Walter Scott,[12] with nine each. Although most of these were not published until the

---

(1729), 84; E. F. Rimbault, *Musical Illustrations of Percy's Reliques*, (1850), p. 117.

[5] Child nos. 12 (SMM no. 327); 16 (461); 20 (320); 38 (370); 39 (411); 58 (482); 73 (535); 76 (5); 77 (363); 83 (203); 84 (221); 112 (477); 155 (582); 157 (484); 163 (512); 169 (356); 181 (177, from Thomson?); 191 (303); 192 (579); 200 (181); 209 (346); 215 (525, from Thomson?); 226 (434); 227 (456); 236 (397); 237 (419); 240 (462); 241 (237); 248 (76); 274 (454); 275 (300); 278 (379); 279 (266). Thirteen of these were sent in by Robert Burns. In addition, the collection contains a number of secondary or sophisticated versions: of nos. 12 (502); 74 (536); 92 (115); 106 (89); 196 (286); 201 (128, from Thomson?); 213 (280); 214 (64, from Thomson?); 275 (365, by Burns?); 279 (226); and 293 (445, from Thomson?).

[6] William Motherwell, *Minstrelsy: Ancient and Modern* (1827). The Appendix contains tunes for Child nos. 3, 4, 5, 9, 10, 14, 17, 25, 26, 27, 33, 52, 65, 68 (2 tunes), 69, 81, 83, 88, 99, 114, 155, 156, 182, 204, 208, 217, 233, 243, 254, 281, 289.

[7] Harris MSS., Harvard Coll. Lib., 25241.17. Child nos. 10, 11, 20, 46, 47, 53, 58, 61, 63, 68, 77, 84, 89, 98, 106, 114, 164, 169, 173, 182, 235, 256, 258. These are printed (unfaithfully) in Child's Appendix, V, 411 ff.

[8] Sharpe's tunes are dispersed. Some are in Harvard, and printed in Child's Appendix; tunes to Child nos. 9, 157, 161, 164, 169, 222. Others are in the National Library of Scotland, among the collections of Lady John Scott, MS. 843. Included are tunes for Child nos. 9, 10, 16, 17, 20, 43, 64, 99, 114, 173, 277.

[9] G. R. Kinloch, *Ancient Scottish Ballads* (1827), with an Appendix containing tunes for Child nos. 9, 14, 20, 43, 53, 68, 69, 100, 103, 110, 170, 199, 209, 219, 236, 293.

[10] Mrs. Brown's tunes are preserved in Joseph Ritson's transcript, now Harvard 25241.37.5, of an MS made for William Tytler. They comprise the following Child ballads: nos. 5, 6, 10, 32, 34, 42, 53, 65, 96, 97, 98, 99, 101, 103, 247. The "Abbotsford MS." from which certain tunes in Child's Appendix were printed derives from Mrs. Brown's singing, and duplicates some of the above.

[11] Alexander Campbell, *Albyn's Anthology*, I (1816) and II (1818), containing tunes for Child, nos. 12 (from Scott's daughter Sophia Charlotte), 26, 58 (2 tunes), 86, 185, 186, 187, 293.

[12] Scott's tunes are interspersed through the 1833 edition of the *Minstrelsy*, in 4 vols.: Child nos. 7, 37, 79, 161, 169, 185, 195, 206, 214, transcribed, according to J. G. Lockhart, from MSS in Scott's library. Scott himself professed entire ignorance of music.

second quarter of the nineteenth century or later, we have external evidence that carries them back, in the memory of the singers from whom they were collected, into the eighteenth century.

Since 1833 the record has multiplied almost past numbering, and especially since 1900. The most important names in this accumulation are those of Christie, Baring-Gould, Kidson, Barry, Cecil Sharp, and Gavin Greig. Of the thousands of folk-tunes collected by the last two alone, in England, Scotland, and America, the Child ballad tunes themselves number many hundreds, counting variants. Greig's contribution is around 310.[13] Sharp's is more than three times that number—940.[14] The cooperative efforts of regional societies have also greatly swelled the total.

The whole extant musical record of every kind connected with the Child ballads may easily run above five thousand versions and variants—not, of course, counting mere reprinting or exact duplication.

But the question we are at present facing, of interrelationship between text and tune, strictly considered, greatly reduces the bulk and importance of available evidence before 1900. Looking first at the earliest records: of the three ballads earlier than 1650 that have survived with tunes, one, "John Dory," is given arranged for three voices. If we try to reduce it to a ballad tune, we get various results according to our several notions. We may make a four-, five-, or six-phrase tune out of it, depending on our judgment as to the use and form of the refrain; moreover, the third musical phrase is by no means unambiguous, and the first appears to have an alternate form. Earlier and later copies of the tune all differ. In Ravenscroft's copy of 1609 it has a dancing, 6/8 rhythm; but the drinking song in *Gammer Gurton's Needle* ("I cannot eat but little meat") was set to a version in common time.[15] A character in Fletcher's *The Chances*, however, refers to it as a "warlike tune." The ballad was a favorite in the seventeenth century, but has not been collected from later tradition. If it celebrates events of the French

[13] The Gavin Greig MSS. in King's College Library, Aberdeen, contain 310 tunes for Child ballads, by my count, not including those of his co-worker, Rev. J. B. Duncan.

[14] The Cecil J. Sharp MSS. in Clare College, Cambridge, contain, by my count, 940 Child ballad tunes; but it would be easy to have miscounted.

[15] See W. Chappell, *Popular Music*, I (1855), 67–68, for his reading of "John Dory," and for references and discussion: and *ibid.*, p. 72, for the song from *Gammer Gurton's Needle*.

John's day, as generally claimed, it must have been circulating while Chaucer was alive—and Carew in 1602 refers to it as old; but whether it was sung to an anterior form of the Elizabethan tune, or what such a form would have been, is impossible to guess. The Reading *rota*—of the mid-thirteenth century [16]—would be a nearly contemporary piece with a very homogeneous melodic idea. It must be obvious, however, that the foregoing considerations have deprived us of one third of our evidence about the actual ballad tunes before 1650.

The other two records are not so equivocal. "The Baffled Knight," also 1609, is a gay Mixolydian tune, altogether in keeping with the sense of its words. It is a triple—and tripping—measure, the lyricism of which is reinforced by a two-phrase refrain of "down a down, hey downe derry," making a shapely six-phrase melodic stanza or statement. The third of these ballads is the well-loved "Three Ravens," 1611. As given in Ravenscroft, it needs not have preserved its strictly traditional form. The two-strain melody, while perhaps not too elaborate for pure folk-song, looks rather sophisticated in its handling of the tripartite refrain, each element of which varies in length and character. Modally, also, we should expect a pure Dorian; but the sixth is flatted once, and twice the leading note occurs. These are mildly suspicious particulars. But that a form of this tune was sung traditionally to such a text we have no reason to doubt. A question might be raised about the words of the refrain. It happens that both this song and "The Baffled Knight," so different in temper, make use of the familiar "heigh derry down" syllabics. Now there is perhaps no compelling reason why nonsense syllables, like some modern poems, should not be given whatever interpretation one chooses. But the typical associations of the refrain in question are bold and vigorous, high-spirited, as with "Robin Hood" ballads or "King John and the Abbot." Is the "Three Ravens" refrain a misgrafting or a natural growth? We cannot say. But it has been perpetuated in later tradition.

A full century and more after Ravenscroft, D'Urfey and Wil-

---

[16] Manfred F. Bukofzer, "Sumer is icumen in." University of California Publications in Music, Vol. 2, No. 2 (1944), 79–114. He dates the round between 1310 and 1325. But the late date has been convincingly opposed by B. Schofield, in *The Music Review*, Vol. 9, No. 2 (May 1948), 81–86.

liam Thomson provide us with our next, and still dubious, evidence. Of the four texts admitted by Child from these editors—two from each—the most promising from the point of view of musical authenticity is D'Urfey's copy of "Riddles Wisely Expounded." [17] This has an early look about it, as if it had not long been away from plainsong. It moves from tonic up to fifth and back again, through an undulating succession of even notes, only once as wide apart as a third. How close it is to Gregorian melody may be seen when we compare it note by note with part of the eleventh-century *Sanctus* in the Mass, "Orbis Factor" (Ordinary of the Mass, no. XI):

The primitive freshness of this tune entirely belies the seventeenth-century broadside text to which it is mated. And once again, the text is at variance with the simple pastoral refrain of "Lay the bent to the bonny broom." Far more sophisticated are the others of the group. "King John and the Abbot" [18] is a sturdy tune, thoroughly English, one would guess. Its Mixolydian character is marred by an unfolklike insistence on the leading note. The tunes from Scottish sources are even more elaborate, and have a range much greater than those which have been collected from Scots folk-singers in our day. The tune of "William and Margaret" is certainly popular —a variant of Burns's "Of a' the airts" tune: but the words, made elegant by Mallet or another, tell us nothing about popular singing. "Willy's fair and Willy's rare" has acceptable words and a plain-

[17] Child no. 1, is in D'Urfey, IV (1719), 130.
[18] Child no. 45, is in D'Urfey, IV, (1719), 29.

tive tune which may be tentatively received in spite of its octave-and-a-half range. "The Gaberlunyie Man," however, while a characteristic spirited piece, has a tune that almost demands an instrument, or at least a virtuoso of a folk-singer with a flexible, two-octave range. The text, moreover, itself is relegated by Child to an appendix as being only semi-popular. We approach the close of the eighteenth century, therefore, without a single unchallengeable example of the "Child" ballad as it was sung in its early days by a folk-singer, or even by Sidney's semiprofessional blind crowder, with rough voice and rude style.

So far, I have deliberately left out of account the closely related question of melodic tradition. Just as the textual history of the ballads can be augmented as Child has done by following the written records of various kinds—the folk tale, continental analogues, historical event, and so on—so likewise it is possible to track a tune or melodic idea or pattern back into the past. We may pick up the record of a ballad tune and text in our own century and run down variant forms of the same tune, not related to such a text, in old song-books or manuscripts, native or foreign; and in some cases may reach a date prior to that of any text in Child's canon. There is, besides, a fair number of seventeenth-century musical records, without words, but bearing names that clearly identify them as Child ballad tunes. Or the tunes may acquire different popular names from time to time which can be followed back along a chain of equivalences until we reach a connection with a Child ballad. For example, the early broadsides from which D'Urfey took his copy of "Riddles Wisely Expounded" do not print any music, but direct the ballad to be sung "to the tune of Lay the Bent to the bonny Broom." We have no copy of the tune under that name, but D'Urfey's ballad has it for a refrain line, and D'Urfey's tune is clearly cognate with that of another song popular in the seventeenth century and later, known by various names, such as "At home would I be (in)"--or "I would I were in my own country" or "The North-country Lasse" or "The Northern Lasses Lamentation" or (later) "The Oak and the Ash and the Bonny Ivy Tree." A ballad by Martin Parker, of about 1650,[19] to be sung to this tune, proves the tune's existence at the mid-century. Also, under the name "Goddesses," it appears as a country-dance in the

[19] Cf. W. Chappell, *Popular Music*, II (1859), 456–457.

first edition, 1650, of Playford's *The English Dancing Master*.[20] But in the Elizabethan MSS of pieces for virginals we find the same tune under other titles. It appears twice in the Fitzwilliam Book, once set by R. Farnaby ("Fayne wolde I wedde") and again by Giles Farnaby as "Quodling's Delight." [21] We pick it up earlier on the Continent as a Christmas carol in the Swedish publication, *Piae Cantiones*, by Theodoric Petri of Nyland, 1582.[22] Its Latin text begins, "Congaudeat turba fidelium." But two earlier copies of that same carol have been discovered: one in Paris in an eleventh-century MS, the other in a twelfth-century antiphonary at Apt, near Avignon.[23] The tune of the latter is clearly a simple, plainsong form of the same melody. Naturally, all these permutations and peregrinations have not left the tune unaffected; and what, consequently, we really have to deal with is not so properly a *tune* as a melodic family with a persisting idea—a complex analogous in a musical way to one of Child's ballads in its widest international ramifications, where a germinal idea can be recognized behind all the welter of contradiction and change. It may one day be possible to set up something like a canon of these nuclear melodic ideas in which all genuine folk-song will be comprised. My surmise would be that such a canon would not be very large. The basic types or patterns of melody in the British-American folk-tradition are probably not nearly so numerous—at least as the record has survived—as Child's canon of the text-families. But it is by no means so easy to set up objective criteria of demarcation for tunes as for texts—even though we fully acknowledge the difficulties that beset Child. The mere question: What constitutes identity in ballads? is, in truth, a philosophical—a metaphysical—question, to which Child himself kept making practical, unmetaphysical answers. We need look no further than the variants of Child's no. 1—"Riddles Wisely Expounded"—to realize that undemonstrable assumptions must be nine-tenths of any definition of *A Ballad* in the group sense of the term. The question:

[20] Reprinted in Margaret Dean-Smith's annotated edition of *The English Dancing Master* (London, 1957), p. 44 (original edition, p. 52).

[21] The *Fitzwilliam Virginal Book*, ed. W. Barclay Squire and A. J. Fuller-Maitland, II (1899), 19 and 263.

[22] *Piae Cantiones*, ed. G. R. Woodward (1910), p. 14 [No. x]. The carol is reprinted in the *Oxford Book of Carols* (1927), p. 176.

[23] See A. Gastoué, in *Revue du Chant Grégorien*, XI (September 1902), 24.

What constitutes the identity of a ballad tune? is even thornier, and, for the present, soluble only on practical grounds. Why do we call Child no. 1A*, of *ca.* 1450, and Motherwell's narrativeless 1D and Mrs. Texas Gladden's Virginia copy in the Library of Congress phonograph archive the *same* ballad? [24] Why, only by granting this, that, and the other condition. Similarly, though time be triple, duple, or measureless; though mode be different in each case; though, note for note, there be scarcely a single identical correspondence in the melody, we may say with some practical assurance that the measureless twelfth-century French "En Gaudeat," the sixteenth-century Swedish "Congaudeat" in six-four, the twentieth-century English "King Herod and the Cock" [25] in common time are all the *same* tune. But the *proof* is still to seek: our conviction is perhaps intuitive, like Child's conviction about what was traditional and what untraditional, or that "Henry Martin" was a different ballad from "Sir Andrew Barton" and not, instead, traditionally descended.

In what has been said thus far, there are implicit several inferences. It must be obvious that, however inadvisably, the melodic tradition and the textual tradition of the ballads may be pursued independently and that they are neither coincident nor commensurate with each other. It is always unsafe to ignore the tunes in investigating the textual tradition, and the opposite course is equally mistaken. But in studying the interrelations between ballad texts and tunes, we cannot ignore the fact that close variants of the same tune may be found with a number of other texts of quite diverse sense and spirit. No one would be likely to insist that "Thomas Rymer," "Geordie," "Hind Horn," "The Carnal and the Crane," "The Cruel Mother," "Clerk Saunders," are homogeneous; yet they may all be found in traditional singing mated to members of the same melodic complex. Likewise, there are abundant variants of the ballads of "Lady Isabel and the Elf-Knight," "Lord Thomas and Fair Eleanor," "Sweet William and Fair Margaret," "Lord Lovel," "The Bailiff's Daughter of Islington," "Little Sir Hugh," similarly bound together by a single family of tunes. Moreover, the folk-mind—if the term be allowed—has never distinguished ballad

---

[24] Released in Album no. 1, no. 4A, Library of Congress Archive of American Folk Song.
[25] C. J. Sharp, *English Folk-Carols* (1911), pp. 2–4.

tunes from any other good singing tunes; so that religious songs or
personal love songs without explicit narrative content may employ
the same or kindred airs.

We seem, then, to be precluded from expecting any very intimate or inward correspondences between text and melody in folk-
song. Yet all of us must often have felt, in singing or listening to
some old favorite, whether carol or love lyric or ballad, that it
would be impossible to better its simple, essential rightness. We
make such a judgment on the basis of aesthetic considerations sifted
from a multitude of impressions and associations and purified, as we
hope, by experience and knowledge of good music of many kinds.
But those who for the most part have preserved and transmitted
these songs have done so without benefit of a wide and cultivated
familiarity with the best in lyric expression. We know they have
loved the songs, but of the grounds of their liking, or even of what
for them are the essential components of their artistic impact, we
know very little. We cannot be sure that particular rhythms or
tonalities or melodic patterns or points of verbal style have anything like the same meaning for us as for those to whom we are indebted. It is only when we can examine large masses of authentic
materials that we can begin to be confident that our generalizations
are based not on editorial re-creations or the idiosyncrasies of individual transmitters, but on the genuine habits of folk-singing in a
given time and area of culture. Such a body of evidence has not
existed until recently, and it is therefore from the contemporary
record, in the main, that we may expect the most valuable lights.

Early medieval theorists and their successors were agreed that
semantic value was inherent in the ecclesiastical modes. In such a belief they were, of course, anticipated by the Greeks, though the two
systems differed. Various mnemonic verses, in Latin and other languages, have survived to tell us the mood of each mode and its
effect on the hearer. It cannot be affirmed that there is perfect
accord, but authority tended to perpetuate and reaffirm traditional
opinion in the matter. A set of English verses of Elizabeth's time
defines the modes as follows:

> The first is meeke: deuout to see,
> The second sad: in maiestie.
> The third doth rage: and roughly brayth.
> The fourth doth fawne: and flattry playth,

The fyfth deligth: and laugheth the more,
The sixt bewayleth: it weepeth full sore,
The seuenth tredeth stoute: in froward race,
The eyghte goeth milde: in modest pace.[26]

It will be recalled that the second mode of this system is the Dorian in its plagal range, or Hypodorian. The scale of this mode is identical with the Æolian, except that its tonic is D instead of A. It is therefore the scale of our modern natural minor, which we still think of as "sad" or appropriate to melancholy. But our modern major, strictly speaking, is the equivalent of the sixth, or Hypolydian, mode, which, in the rhyme, "bewayleth and weepeth full sore"—except that the sixth mode again was plagal, with a tonic on F instead of C. In actual practice the Lydian mode, by grace of *musica ficta,* habitually flatted its B and so became identical with the major; and it is the Lydian which is said to laugh and delight. So far, then, we are precariously at one with the theorists in our own feeling.[27]

[26] From Archbishop Matthew Parker's Psalter (1567–1568), as quoted in Morrison Boyd, *Elizabethan Music and Music Criticism* (1940), p. 44.

[27] There is a delightful prose parallel to the above verses in John Dowland's *Andreas Ornithoparcus his Micrologus* (1609), Bk. I, ch. 13, p. 36. In part it reads as follows:

Every mans palate is not delighted with the same meate (as *Pon.* writes in the 16. ch. of his Musick.) but some delight in sharp, some in sweet meates: neither are all mens eares delighted with the same sounds: for some are delighted with the crabbed & courtly wandring of the first *Tone.* Others do affect the hoarse grauitie of the second: others take pleasure in the seuere, & as it were disdainful stalking of the third: others are drawn with the flatring sound of the fourth: others are moued with the modest wantonnes of the fift: others are led with the lamenting voyce of the sixt: others do willingly heare the warlike leapings of the seuenth: others do loue the decent, & as it were, matronall carriage of the eight. . . . The Darian [*sic*] *Moode* is the bestower of wisedome, and causer of chastity. The *Phrygian* causeth wars, and enflameth fury. The *Eolian* doth appease the tempests of the minde, and when it hath appeased them, luls them asleepe. The *Lydian* doth sharpen the wit of the dull, & doth make them that are burdened with earthly desires, to desire heauēly things, an excellēt worker of good things. Yet doth *Plato lib. 3. de Rep.* much reprehend the *Lydian,* both because it is mournful, and also because it is womanish. But he alloweth of the *Dorian,* both because it is manly, & also doth delight valiant men, & is a discouerer of warlike matters. But our men of a more refined time do vse somtime the *Dorian;* somtime the *Phrygian;* somtime the *Lydian;* somtime other Moodes. because they iudge, that according to diuers occasions they are to choose diuers *Moodes.* And that not without cause: for euery habit of the mind is gouerned by songs, (as *Macr.* writeth) for songs make men sleepy, and wakefull, carefull, & merrie, angry, & mercifull, songs do heale diseases, & produce diuers wonderful effects (as saith *Fran. Petrac.*) mouing some to vain mirth, some to a deuout and holy ioy, yea oft-times to godly teares. Of al which I had rather be silent, than to determine

But British-American folk-tradition has preserved much more of a modal sense than has modern harmonic music; and we should like to know whether folk-song has retained modal semantic meaning corresponding to what is alleged for Gregorian music—that folk-song of the church, traditionally transmitted for hundreds of years before it could be accurately written down. Perhaps the only way to get an answer is to collate the general sense of the verbal texts with the modes of their tunes, and so to compile a statistical record. But it might be very difficult to keep the record objective.

The special pitfall to which one is almost fatally liable in such an inquiry is that of *ex post facto* reasoning; finding a beautiful appropriateness in a mating of words and melody, to conclude that accident played little or no part in the result. Shall we say that the wistful melancholy of the Mixolydian tune picked up by Sharp in Somerset as a setting for "The Cruel Mother" is the inspired counterpart of the words? That tune goes as follows: [28]

THE CRUEL MOTHER. From Mrs. Woodberry, Ash Prior, 8/31/07

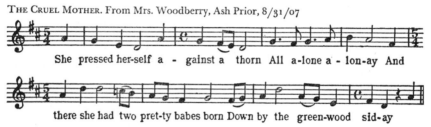

She pressed her-self a - gainst a thorn All a-lone a - lon-ay And
there she had two pret-ty babes born Down by the green-wood sid-ay

Could anything be more fitting? Five days earlier, however, in a village close by, Sharp had collected the following tune with a text of "The Wraggle-taggle Gipsies." [29]

THE WRAGGLE-TAGGLE GIPSIES. From Mr. Geen, Rose Ash, 8/27/07

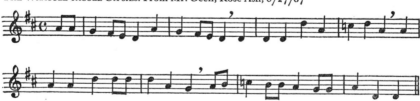

any thing rashly: least I do burthen the wits of children with vnprofitable & vnnecessary precepts. Because whoso in expounding any thing doth poure on more than is needful, increaseth the darknesse, and maketh not the mist thinner, as *Macrobius* saith in the second booke vpon the dreame of Scipio. . . .

[28] Sharp MSS. 1454. The words are from another variant collected by H. E. D. Hammond.

[29] Sharp MSS. 1447.

Modally, the two variants of the tune are identical: but the spirit of
the texts is strikingly different. And if we set beside these a third
variant of the same tune, we shall have further cause for perplexity.
The Æolian mode, our natural minor, is in the Western world melancholy by general agreement. But the now familiar Æolian variant
of "The Wraggle-taggle Gipsies" is a perfect expression of sturdy
defiance and no regrets for outraged convention.

> Oh, what care I for my goose-feather bed,
>   With the sheet turned down so bravely, O?
> For tonight I shall lie 'neath the cold open sky [*or*, sleep in a
>   cold open field]
>   Along with the wraggle-taggle gipsies, O!

This exultant outburst of a newly liberated spirit is admirably
projected by the vigorous Æolian tune: [30]

THE WRAGGLE-TAGGLE GIPSIES. From Mrs. Overd, Langport, 8/4/04

We may, I suppose, conclude that the fluid stuff of folk-melody
lends itself with extraordinary flexibility and sympathy to any
given material. But the more we allow, the more evidence we accu-
mulate, on the score of responsiveness to words, the less we can
genuflect to modal semantics. If a text can subdue a mode to its
own purposes, we shall have to toss out the theorizing of a thousand years—and possibly we should!

A folk-melody or melodic idea nevertheless does appear to transcend any ideational content or meaning. There is striking and
abundant evidence of the persistence of the inner character of melody through all superficial changes. An analysis of nearly three
hundred variants of the tune to which half a dozen favorite ballads
are sung—a melodic idea found with "Lady Isabel and the Elf
Knight," "Lord Thomas and Fair Eleanor," "Sweet William and
Fair Margaret," "Lord Lovel," "The Bailiff's Daughter," "Little

[30] Sharp MSS. 264/373. Printed in C. J. Sharp and C. L. Marson, *Folk Songs
from Somerset* (1904), p. 18, and Sharp, *One Hundred English Folksongs* (1916),
p. 13.

Sir Hugh"—revealed that scarcely a dozen departed from the major scale, and that the features of melodic contour remained remarkably constant to a norm.[31] This is truly a very surprising fact. If we consider that there is nothing objective to hold a folk-tune in line—no authority to controvert individual preference or whim, no individual reading to which to refer as original or authentic, no control over extraneous corrupting influences, or against forgetfulness, no indissoluble bond between text-family and tune-family, no consciously accepted standard of aesthetic judgment or taste—we must wonder at the amazing stability of certain musical ideas. It used to be assumed—and for aught I have seen it still is—that the longer a folk-tune was in circulation, the more widely it departed from its original. But such evidence as I have run across contradicts such an assumption. A tune continuously alive in a flourishing tradition will often be recognizable after centuries of currency. For this reason I am convinced that generalizations arrived at on the basis of recent and reliable evidence are equally true in the main for the traditional song of the preceding four or five centuries.

Yet it is also clear that not all melodic complexes persist with equal stability. Some fluctuate notably in all the particulars that together constitute melodic identity: in mode, meter, and contour. Others cling with almost monotonous fidelity to a normal pattern. The latter way, for example, is the tendency of "Lord Lovel": five phrases, refrain by repetition of last line with short connecting bridge, major tonality minus the seventh, 6/8 meter, middle cadence on v, first-phrase cadence on I, the tune swinging within the authentic octave—first phrase between I and III, second between v and VIII, third between VIII and I, fourth between III and I, fifth between v and I—a shapely stereotype. A merry tune with a lachrymose text. We say "merry"; but why is the dichotomy perpetuated in tradition if the contradiction is perceived by folk-singers? The humble are no enemies to mawkish pathos. How do they experience this tune that so insists on submission to its will? We may be sure there is no conscious desire to counteract or minimize the pathos. If the pathos were false for the singers, the song would cease to be sung.

There are undoubtedly chameleon tunes that lend themselves to

[31] B. H. Bronson, "Melodic Stability in Oral Transmission," *Journal of the International Folk Music Council*, III (1951), 50–55.

lively or plaintive moods with equal readiness. Scotland is rich in these. Such a one is the humorous "I hae laid a herring in saut;— Lass, gin ye lo'e me, tell me now," sometimes called "I canna come ilka day to woo." This is a spirited old air, far from depressing, when sung briskly. But it is also found in slow time with the tender words of "The Bonnie Blinks of Mary's E'e"; [32] and an undeniable cognate of it has been known for at least two hundred and fifty years with the tragic ballad of "Bessy Bell and Mary Gray."

Are we then to conclude that the secret of a tune's character lies, not in its modal cast, but in its tempo? No one would deny, I suppose, that a fast tune accords ill with the spirit of tragedy, though it may portend calamity; but we do not wring sadness out of every tune merely by slowing it down. Such a tune as "Duncan Gray," for example, simply refuses to be solemn; and when it is sung *largo* its mockery is as obvious as Saint-Saëns' in assigning the ballet music from *Faust* to his double-bass elephants.

Tempo is a subject on which there is practically no historical evidence (for folk-song) that is both specific and objective. The sound recordings now being made will, of course, provide a wealth of such evidence henceforward. And they reveal, as we might assume, a great diversity among singers even of the same vicinity. Some singers, as Library of Congress recordings attest, will sing a song with grotesque haste, and others with fantastic deliberation. There seems no reason why wide differences may not always have occurred—except perhaps in work songs or dance songs, where the operation paced the musical accompaniment of it.

We can, however, draw inferences, if with great caution, from metrical signatures and the written record. It becomes evident enough that besides racial preferences—like the French taste for quick and piquantly altered meters, or the German for waltz time, or the Gypsy love of violent contrasts in tempo—there are also regional habits, revealed in large bodies of homogeneous materials. Thus, the drawling style of Appalachian mountain people, with held notes and pauses, has attracted widespread notice, and is evident in the careful record of Sharp and other collectors. It seems probable, also, that there may have been historical shifts of tempo among large groups of singers, either quickening or slowing the habitual pace of singing; though it is doubtless unsafe to make any

[32] G. F. Graham, *The Songs of Scotland*, II (1849), 120–121.

very confident assertions on the point. If we look through the earlier half of Chappell's *Popular Music*, we cannot help noticing the favor shown in Elizabethan days to lilting 6/8 meters—a favor not very conspicuous in the modern equivalents. Yet perhaps we should discount some of this impression on the score of editorial fashions in notation. For example, many tunes appear in 3/4 in Christie and earlier Scottish collections, but relatively few in Greig's careful work around 1900. Greig often uses 4/4 with holds over particular notes; while Sharp, equally conscientious, constantly employs uneven barring. Sharp almost never uses 2/4, but Chappell's nineteenth-century editing often does so. After due reservations, however, we can hardly discredit all evidence of large historical shifts; and these must surely reflect changes in the time spirit, or—as we are learning to call them—shifts of sensibility.

Discussion of tempo and meter passes inevitably into the problems of rhythm. But rhythm is a complicated and difficult subject, even within the relatively simple territory to which at present we are confined. There is room here for little more than one or two suggestions. So far as I have observed, there is no trustworthy evidence, for folk-song, of a general drift in the course of time away from or toward any special rhythm. The alternation of strong and weak syllables in the text, the free admittance of extra unaccented syllables, the perceptible succession of strong and weak stresses (George Stewart's "duple rhythm" of balladry),[33] the compensating pauses at the ends of short lines—these features have been noted everywhere, from beginning to end of the ballad record. Whether as cause or as effect, they are answered in the music wherever it exists for comparison. It is impossible to say, except on theoretical grounds, that the earliest ballad tunes had a triple rhythm. But obviously, accentual verse of iambic or trochaic movement tends to acquire a triple beat as soon as time values are assigned—it is natural to lengthen a musical stress. This is not truly a rhythm in three-time, but more like a dotted duple rhythm, every second initial accent of the bars being stronger than its predecessor. Such a rhythm when slightly speeded up becomes indistinguishable from six-eight time, which in the ballad tunes is quite likely to fall into patterns of alternating quarters and eighths, and, like the

[33] G. R. Stewart, "The Metre of the Popular Ballad," PMLA, XL (1925), 933–962.

slower time, develops a strong dotted duple feeling. Thus, without any effort, these rhythms may be translated into duple rhythms in four-four. It is necessary only to leaf through the pages of Sharp's Appalachian collection to see the same tune appearing in all three ways, and written with signatures of 3/4, 6/8, and 4/4 or common time.

Of late years, thanks particularly to painstaking experts like Percy Grainger and Cecil Sharp, we have been growing more conscious of the rhythmical irregularities of folk-singers. Instead of regarding such things as individual idiosyncrasies to be ignored in notation, careful students now recognize them as vital, energizing characteristics of folk-style. Sharp's pages are full of irregular barring and changes of meter. Noteworthy among the rhythmical schemes appearing in his Somerset collection is a kind of 5/4 time in which bars of 4/4 frequently appear at the middle and final cadences. This rhythm almost never, I believe, appears in Sharp's Appalachian books. What turns up there instead is an irregular 3/2 and 2/2 pattern. I suggest that both the Somerset and Appalachian rhythms are natural extensions of common or duple time. There is a tendency in 4/4 to hold the third quarter, in order, I suppose, to compensate for its relative lack of weight as secondary stress. As soon as this tendency is normalized by the Somerset singers, we find the third beat of a 4/4 bar becoming two beats. The extra beat makes a 5/4 bar, though the rhythm would be more accurately expressed in alternating 2/4 and 3/4 groups. The Appalachian singers exaggerate the same tendency, and normally hold the third beat of a 4/4 bar for three counts instead of two. This gives bars of 6/4 or 3/2. The held note, in turn, with its exaggerated emphasis, now becomes the primary beat in the bar, and as a result we get the highly characteristic rhythmical pattern:

$$\flat \quad \flat \quad \flat \mid \flat. \quad \flat \quad \flat \quad \flat \mid \flat. \quad \text{etc.}$$

The variants of that ubiquitous song, "Barbara Allan," readily illustrate all the stages of this development. Examine, too, in this light variants E to N of "Young Hunting" in Sharp's Appalachian collection, 1932, I, 106–113. But this favorite rhythmical scheme, whether written as 3/4 or as 3/2, is omnipresent in our folk-song, and is not confined to any one region or area.

These observations have been based as far as possible on the record and impression of true traditional singing. So many people are today becoming aware of folk-song through the medium of stage, screen, radio, or phonograph that it is well to insist again and again that most of what they hear is at least as far from genuine folk-singing as the broadsides are from traditional ballads. In strict truth, there is and there can be no such being as a professional folk-singer. A singer who has his livelihood to gain through that medium can never consider the song as an end. He must attract and hold the attention of many people; and inevitably he must become aware of those particular aspects of his songs and of his performance that arouse the liveliest and most immediate response in the majority of his listeners. Inevitably, he will come to emphasize these elements of repertory and of style: so that, the longer he sings, and the greater his success as an entertainer, the farther from genuine folk-singing will be his performance. Of all deleterious influences on folk-song, the most corrosive and deadly is the consciousness of audience appeal.

This is by no means to say that genuine folk-singers do not often bring to their singing a high degree of individuality. But this personal contribution is properly involuntary, inescapable, and below the level of conscious intention. It is an attribute of the song, as in their singing the song exists. A recent collector in Alabama, Byron Arnold, has significantly registered his impressions in this regard. "These songs," he writes, "were sung quietly, naturally, never dramatically, and entirely without the mannerism and clichés of the concert soloist. It was as if each song, as I heard it, was a creation by the singer for the satisfaction of an inner compulsion." [34] Here is a touchstone of genuineness for our native tradition.

The point is stressed because of its bearing on the essential condition of this elusive form of expression. The basic impersonality, the reticent, almost impassive stylistic habit, of the ballad text at its best has been remarked as perhaps its most striking feature by all observant students. This pervasive impersonal quality paradoxically persists in the style of true singing, in spite of and through the piquancy of individual renditions.

Upon reflection, we must perceive that the very idea of narra-

[34] Byron Arnold, *Folksongs of Alabama* (1950), p. vii.

tive, of progress from point to point in a story, is inimical to its statement in identical units of simple melody, repeated as many times as need requires. The melodic form, an integrated succession of a given number of short phrases, has powerfully imposed itself on the verse form, to mutual advantages; but the inherent demands of *narrative* song are for a freer and more dramatic vehicle; and we may therefore perhaps assume the priority of pure lyric in the emergence of genres. Be that as it may, the reading of a single typical ballad text—say, "Sir Patrick Spens" or "Little Musgrave"— would naturally suggest to the nineteenth-century musical imagination something *durchkomponiert*. But clearly, the traditional ballad music operates against narrative effect and acts to reinforce the level impassivity of the characteristic style. And this is a source of its peculiar power. Although it intensifies the emotional (and lyric) effect of the words as they pass, it de-individualizes and objectifies their stated content. It regularizes and levels out the hills and valleys of narrative interest and reduces the varying speeds of travel to its own constant pace.

This neutralizing influence, I suspect, is made more acceptable by the semantic flexibility, already mentioned, of so many of the folk-tunes themselves. It is not merely that a given mode seems adaptable to joy or grief, at will, so that the gamut of emotional possibilities through which a single ballad narrative may run can be accommodated by the same tune. Have we not also a further generalizing factor in the gapped scales so greatly favored in folk-singing communities? Even if we were to allow at their full value the claims of the theorists and grant a particular emotional significance to the Dorian, the Æolian, the Mixolydian, and other modes, it is a fact that each of these modes has a correspondence with two other modes amounting to complete identity except for a single note in the scale. For example, the Mixolydian scale superimposed at the same pitch upon the Ionian or "major" shows no difference in the disposition of full tones and semitones except at its seventh degree. And again, its correspondence with the Dorian scale is identical except for the third. When a tune is built out of the notes held in common between the Ionian and Mixolydian, with the differentiating seventh left out, it is often impossible to say that that tune has more of the feeling of one mode than of the other.

Similarly, when the third is omitted, the tune made out of the notes common to Mixolydian and Dorian may share equally in the character of each of these modes.

These possibilities of interchange are greatly multiplied by the absence of *two* differentiating notes. A tune built on one of the pentatonic scale patterns lays claim to potential relations with three heptatonic modes. Take, for instance, the pentatonic lacking the third and seventh degrees. If both gaps are filled with "major" degrees, the tune becomes Ionian. If both are filled with "minor" degrees, it becomes Dorian. If one gap is filled with a major third, the other with a minor seventh, the tune is Mixolydian, Moreover, if one gap is left unfilled and the other not, the tune falls into one or other of those hexatonic patterns already mentioned as lying neutrally between two heptatonic modes. If neither gap is filled, these relationships remain latent and undefined.

And on the other side it is to be remembered that many heptatonic tunes make slight and unemphatic use of those notes which, if stressed, would give them their essential modal meaning. Many such tunes are already all but pentatonic, the gaps being filled with so little insistence that one is hardly aware of the presence of the fillers. In this way, as the gapped tunes invite connection with heptatonic modes, so the heptatonic tunes likewise go out to meet the hexatonic and pentatonic systems. And thus the areas of common feeling may be broadened and multiplied.[35]

It is a familiar fact that the Scottish folk-tunes have a great predilection for pentatonic scale patterns. And perhaps the strong infusion of Scottish blood in our Southern Highlands helps to account for the frequency with which pentatonic tunes appear in that region. The present point is that an abundance of these gapped scales in our British-American tradition proves them highly congenial, and that a plausible reason for this congeniality may lie in their modal neutrality. I am not accounting for the historical emergence of gapped scales: theorists, I well know, maintain that the gapped

---

[35] I do not mean either to deny or to obscure the truth, already suggested earlier, that each mode has within it a subtle potentiality of varying behavior, according as certain degrees of its scale are rhythmically emphasized, and others minimized, in a particular tune; so that the same mode may express a variety of moods. But here we are considering avenues of mutual interchange through those neutral areas of sentiment and expression where communication is facilitated and fostered: the social rather than the solitary side of modal manners.

scales preceded the heptatonic ones. But it is certain that gapped scales have persisted in our folk-tradition with especial hardihood. And what more probable than that a subconscious recognition of their emotional multivalence has tended to preserve them in areas where a closer definition or delimitation of meaning would militate against the requisite flexibility?

For the dominant impression conveyed by a good folk-song sung in the best traditional style is, it cannot be too strongly insisted, one of genuinely classic impersonality. To this prevailing tone everything contributes. That is why the most brutal and violent, crude and sordid themes, when passed through the crucible of traditional singing, sometimes become, not tolerable merely, but as starkly powerful in their reserve and understatement as all but the very greatest masterpieces of conscious art, and on their own scale of magnitude incomparable. One of the finest illustrations known to me is the rendition on an old Victor phonograph record (No. 35838B) by a folk-singer named B. F. Shelton of a ballad which has a wide oral circulation in this country even today. It is "Pretty Polly"—not a Child ballad, though related in theme to Child's "Young Andrew" (from the Percy Folio), and to numbers 4, 9, and others of the canon. It is a story of love trusting and betrayed. It is known also in eighteenth- and nineteenth-century broadside versions, whence possibly the traditional variants derive—unless perhaps it was the other way round. The copy in question is basically in anapaestic tetrameter rhyming couplets, but the first line of each couplet is repeated in singing—a form not unknown either in Gregorian chant or Negro blues. This repetition—not strictly a refrain but none the less a lyrical element—obviously slows the narrative pace while it intensifies and suspends the conclusion of each successive statement. The added weight would be intolerable if a series of heroic couplets were similarly treated in spoken verse. But here the repetition lends poise and self-control, the dignity of deliberate conformity to a preestablished mould. This sculpturesque effect is perfectly matched by the musical rhetoric, which restates the first phrase at the fifth above, making it the climax of a balanced tripartite structure. As in so many traditional ballads, the narrative commences in the first person and passes to the third when the action becomes too violent for first-personal statement to be endurable. The resulting effect of distancing is comparable to the removal, in a classical drama, of immediate catastrophic action from the stage, and its consequent reduction to a messenger's recital. Within the conventional phraseology, it must not go unremarked how powerfully the stereotyped epithets augment the statuesque impassivity of the narrative by continuing in use beyond the point permitted by verisimilitude. Beginning on a naturalistic level, they acquire in the end a quality of marmoreal, but also dramatic, restraint.

These noteworthy effects, to my mind, produce their due impact on the sensitive ear in spite of all surface crudeness of language, misplaced stanzas, a false sentimental note and intruding morality at the end. They are sustained and made far more impressive by the elemental pentatonic melody and by the characteristic singing, which is of an incantatory masklike aloofness that apparently makes no concessions to ordinary fluctuations of human sympathy or excitement, nor shows any awareness of audience, but tacitly acknowledges, throughout, its allegiance to a higher court, the strangely abstract, impersonal law of tradition.[36]

1952

[36] The recording described has been long out of print and has become a collector's item. It would be meaningless to give the words and the tune on paper here, since the object of the above remarks was to insist that upon the union of the two in living sound, and in a style that cannot otherwise be registered, depends the whole impact and effect of a genuine folk-song.

Two Reviews:

George Pullen Jackson and
the Shaped-Note Spirituals

I

For two decades, with intelligence and devoted enthusiasm, George Pullen Jackson has explored the land he himself discovered, and has earned a secure place among the conquistadors of folk-song. He has changed the map, and he will surely be remembered. His major accomplishment is threefold: he has revealed the presence of a great body of Anglo-American traditional song in a quarter where its existence was quite unsuspected; he has now made it generally accessible, traced its history and described its environmental conditions; and he has put beyond reasonable doubt, with abundant documentary evidence, the fact that the roots of the Negro spiritual lie in this same traditional material.

It is surprising that Cecil Sharp, when he went collecting in the Appalachians in the second decade of our century, entirely missed the folk-character of the religious music. For he, if anyone, was qualified to recognize its affiliations with the traditional secular tunes, and he well knew that texts were not always a sure guide to the nature of their music. When modern street songs, as he observed, got into the mountains, the words were promptly mated to traditional airs. Had he listened with open mind to the religious songs which the people were ready to sing to him, he must have recognized that the same thing had happened here. In fact, Horace Walpole knew the truth a hundred and fifty years earlier. On a visit to Bath, Walpole had the curiosity to attend a service in Lady

Down-East Spirituals and Others. By George Pullen Jackson. J. J. Augustin, Inc., 1943.

Huntingdon's elegant new Methodist chapel and did not fail to note, with agreeable malice, that they "sang hymns to ballad airs." The majority of Sharp's singers were Baptists and Methodists, the very sects which have perpetuated these spirituals; and very often, he writes, "they would give us hymns instead of the secular songs and ballads which we wanted; but that was before we had learned to ask for 'love-songs.' " So "love-songs" he got, except from those whose religious scruples prevented; and from the latter he got nothing, when he might have reaped a further harvest in the only part of the field which Jackson has not yet systematically explored. We should then have had a large body of accurately noted tunes from contemporary tradition to compare with those that Jackson has taken from the old shaped-note books; and should have had valuable light on the degree to which modal features had been edited out of the printed versions.

Jackson's findings have appeared chiefly in a series of books each of which is supplementary to, and to a slight extent corrective of, its predecessor. In the first, *White Spirituals in the Southern Uplands,* 1933, he made a general survey of the field as he then knew it; sketched the bibliographical history of the fasola and seven-shaped-note songbooks; gave much biographical information about the men who carried the movement through the last century in the South; and followed the group-singing tradition down to the present time, as he had come to know it at first hand. He also listed melodically eighty tunes of the most frequent occurrence in the fasola books, and cited a score of parallels both textual and melodic between white and Negro spirituals.

The next portion of his work presents the main bulk, to the number of five hundred and fifty of the religious songs which comprise this field of study. This central portion occupies two books, *Spiritual Folk-Songs of Early America,* 1937, and *Down-East Spirituals and Others,* ready for publication in 1939 but not issued until four years later. It is the last named which gives occasion to the present review; but these two books are really to be regarded as one collection. In a further volume, Jackson completes his historical account in the light of fuller knowledge, and amplifies his study of relationship between white and Negro spirituals.

When he published *Spiritual Folk-Songs,* Jackson had come to recognize his materials as genuine folk-song stemming from British

tradition, but he still regarded them as primarily southern and
Methodist. Further research convinced him—and his evidence is
incontrovertible—that the movement in this country had its beginnings two centuries ago among the Baptists of the Northeastern
States and thereafter proceeded South and Southwest, chiefly
during the nineteenth century, with Methodist assistance. These
conclusions he states succinctly in *Down-East Spirituals*. He declares that about a third of the latter collection is of northeastern
provenience, but adds that the proportion would have been much
greater had he not already printed many songs from southern
sources which could now be located in the northern region. It
would have been desirable to have appended a list of these for the
record's sake; but the matter is perhaps not of essential importance.
In this connection, it is interesting that Jackson has noted "a distinctly stronger trend in the South than in the North toward the
reinstatement, or the preservation, of the modes." But he immediately negates this observation by interpreting the fact as arising
from greater editorial interference in the North, rather than as a
regional difference in the singing tradition. Evidence from recent
collections of secular songs from northern oral tradition would
probably tend to support his interpretation. For the old modalities
have by no means been abandoned in this region, although one has
the impression that gapped scales are of less frequent occurrence
here than in the South.

In his modal identifications, Jackson has adopted the scheme of
Hilton Rufty, who himself has checked the whole work. The
Rufty scheme is based on that of Sharp and Gilchrist. Briefly, it
numbers the pentatonic scales from 1 to 5, and deduces all others,
hexatonic and heptatonic, from these, according to the way in
which the gaps in the pentatonic scales happen to be filled. The
scheme is neat; but, besides the fact that it is based upon an undemonstrable assumption, it has, in the eyes of the present reviewer,
two serious disadvantages. One is that it is cumbersome to use. It
involves the continual use of a chart, for it is practically impossible
to memorize. For example, "mode 2 A + b" necessitates remembering that the tune in question is based on that pentatonic scale which
lacks its second and sixth, but that in this case those two notes are
supplied to complete the heptatonic scale, and supplied by a second
in its natural, not its flatted, position, and by a sixth in its flatted,

not its natural, position. With these data before one, it is still an effort to think the scale through as an organic whole. Moreover, that this kind of thing is difficult to hold in mind is tacitly admitted by the provision of a pair of editorial crutches. One is the notation "heptatonic aeolian," which by itself should be adequate to the occasion, if not tautological; the other is a table of all the degrees of the scale used in the tune: 1 II 3 IV V 6 7—the Arabic figures indicating flatted notes. Everyone conversant with such matters could name the scale Æolian, given its degrees; or list the degrees, given that name: but "2A + b" is inhuman.

There is, however, a second, perhaps even greater, disadvantage: it is that by this scheme each one of the heptatonic modes is split into two or even three kinds, and thrown into different pentatonic systems. Thus, an Æolian tune may belong theoretically to Mode 2, Mode 4, or Mode 5, and similarly the others. That is to say, the notes of its scale remain constant, yet it is to be variously identified by three different names, or numbers, according to particular circumstances. Why? Because if the pentatonic scales are to be the basis of our classification, it then becomes necessary to make a pentatonic tune out of a heptatonic—say an Æolian—one. But since the Æolian scale can be derived from three of the five pentatonic scales, according to whether and in what manner the 2nd and 6th, or the 3rd and 6th, or the 2nd and 5th, are the added notes, we have now to determine which of these combinations is to be supposed to have occurred in each particular instance. The only way to arrive at such a decision is by the often subjective determination of "stronger" and "weaker" notes in the tune in question. It not infrequently happens, from natural shifts of emphasis in successive phrases, that the difference in weight is almost inperceptible; and then we must either flip a coin or abandon the system. Even if the difference be perceptible, is there no element of chance? Can we be certain that that particular tune was ever a pentatonic tune at all, in any valid sense; still more, that it belonged to Mode 2 rather than 4 or 5, or vice versa? If we have a Roman nose, must we be called Italian? In point of fact, it is Æolian, not pentatonic. Or, again, suppose we take an Æolian tune which is adjudged to be a derivative of pentatonic Mode 2. By a little manipulation we may easily contrive to throw somewhat greater emphasis on the second degree and lighten that of the third. The result will be that the analyst will now classify the tune as a derivative of pentatonic Mode 4. Yet we have not had to reduce it to a pentatonic form to bring about the change. Furthermore, all the while it will still have kept its Æolian character; and we are asked to exchange that solid fact for a classification resting on a hypothetical basis which, even if accepted, may involve us in real uncertainties. Unfortunately, after the subjective judgment has been made in the particular case, the result looks deceptively firm, and the modal designations succeed one another, as in this work, with all the gravity of complete assurance. Now, when we remember that the musical notation of a folk-melody is itself nothing more than the veriest rough-and-ready makeshift, leagues distant from an exact and scientific representation of the actual sounds which were sung, the system described above seems a little like putting the finishing touches on the top story before we have built the ground floor. It is, at any rate, too closely analogous to the old logical merry-go-round of the communalists: that is, defining the popular ballad by its communal origins when the communal origins had to be hypothesized for the ballad that was being so defined.

Jackson has classified his materials in three main types, Ballads, Hymns, and Revival Songs. These are useful categories. The ballads are narrative songs, suited for solo singing; the hymns are for congregational singing; the revival songs are of later growth, and developed out of hymns shaken loose in the atmosphere of camp meetings into simpler and freer game-song patterns, with the choral element dominant. It is the last class which especially appealed to the Negroes and contributed most largely to their spirituals; whilst the first shows possibly the most numerous affiliations with secular song. But the hymns are by no means lacking in such associations, and the division here is arbitrary, resting almost solely on a textual basis. It is also probably significant that there is no higher proportion of songs in ballad meter in the first than in the second class. Indeed, the scarcity of the common stanzaic pattern of the ballad (alternating four- and three-stress lines) is a very striking feature of the collection. Where it occurs, it is generally doubled to fit a two-strain tune. This latter procedure is much less frequent among secular ballads, and where it is the rule, as in Dean Christie's collection, is to be regarded with utmost skepticism. It would be interesting to learn whether a similar body of folk-hymns

gathered from oral tradition would be found to have a lower per-
centage of double-strain tunes. Also noteworthy in the present collection is the relatively high frequency of genuine triplicate measures, anapaest or dactyl.

Thus it appears that the ballad tradition and that of the spirituals
are melodically cognate but far from identical. The ballad pattern
is generally simpler and more stereotyped. Jackson has quite properly called attention in his notes to melodic analogues among the
ballads and throughout British folk-song generally. But it does not
follow that the tunes of the spirituals are necessarily and in their
total bulk in a direct line of descent from the ballads and secular
songs, a mere fitting of newly made, pious words to the old tunes.
Rather, they would seem, as far back as we can follow them, to be
drawing on a common melodic stock but combining and recombin-
ing the musical phrases in somewhat different and perhaps slightly
more complex patterns. Because of this fact, Jackson's work is the
more important and indispensable. Had the tunes been taken over
without any sort of modification, it would have seemed virtuous to
restore them wherever possible to their secular associations and to
forget the nonce-connection. Highly as special groups or individuals may prize the pious words, it cannot seriously be maintained
that they have a tithe of the interest or value of the melodies. The
texts are most often on the painful level of individually composed
"vulgar poetry," and have little or no racial purchasing power. To
be sure, a partial exception can be made of the revival songs, which
have fewer ideas and images and are closer to the folk-mind and
utterance.

There can be, on the contrary, no longer any question of the
sterling character of the melodies, and it is unnecessary to argue the
case. For of recent years, thanks in very large part to the pioneering of George Pullen Jackson, they have again been heard far and
wide and have been recognized by good judges everywhere as a
priceless racial heritage. They are, in truth, so steeped in our musical tradition that it is almost impossible to listen to any one of them
without being reminded of other analogous folk-melodies. Since,
moreover, the merit of the Negro spirituals has been a truism for
half a century, it will be hard now to remain skeptical of the
soundness of the melodic stock from which the spirituals have

branched. Nor should it cause rancor anywhere to acknowledge the bond of unity. Rather, give it welcome, and let it stand as a happy augury of the future harmony of our fellow countrymen, black and white.

1944

2

Another Sheaf of White Spirituals, the latest of Professor Jackson's contributions to our knowledge of our national inheritance of religious folk-song, is in some ways the best of the series. It contains all the kinds of song found in the earlier collections (*Spiritual Folk-Songs of Early America,* 1937; *Down-East Spirituals and Others,* 1943), adding fresh examples of the various types—narrative, camp-meeting, and so on, from both "northern" and "southern" sources—and including psalm tunes and fuguing tunes, two classes hitherto omitted. It commences with a group of songs displaying the folk-way of singing, simply but faithfully set down from the rendition of named individuals. There are brief introductory notes to the separate groups; a comprehensive bibliography of (mostly) British and American folk-song that goes much beyond the immediate scope of the collection; and a useful summarizing introduction that briefly sets out in admirably clear focus the historical and geographical position of this music.

An essential part of the apparatus of the book is the annotation accompanying the individual tunes. While obviously intended to be suggestive rather than exhaustive, these notes taken together form a quite impressive body of informed comparative references. Many of the fullest and farthest-reaching of them are from Samuel P. Bayard, whose contribution herein is so considerable as almost to entitle his name to mention on the cover.

It is relevant to inquire for whose benefit such notes as these are compiled, and to what end they lead. For those who come to the book for religious inspiration or to increase their private stock of songs of praise, the notes, we may suspect, will be an encumbrance.

Another Sheaf of White Spirituals. Collected, edited, and illustrated by George Pullen Jackson. University of Florida Press, 1952.

To the church choral directors to whom Charles Seeger, in his provocative preface, recommends the book, the notes will be useless; and it can hardly be supposed that those public school educators whom he also urges to put the book to practical use will have the curiosity (preoccupied as they are) or the time to follow up the clues embedded in the annotation.

For what class of readers, then, it is intended? Surely, not for the musicologists? They are far too busy decoding medieval musical notation, deciphering obscure manuscripts, attributing authorship to anonymous compositions, or strictly meditating the uses of the six-four chord, to cast an eye upon such lowly matter as the musical contents of the present volume.

Nor does it seem likely to find its mark among the social historians, who generally have more direct avenues to their goals than these devious and obscure channels. Something, perhaps, this class of investigator may glean through the direct meaning of words and music together, but little indeed from the notes referring from book to book of a library they neither know nor are likely to have at hand.

And if any such readers should pursue the references, what is it that they might discover? They would find, if they had the musical skill and sensitivity to perceive the facts, that these tunes are made out of phrasal units formed and re-formed by the breath of the generations that utter them, which like clouds or mist are ever and never the same; that the materials of folk-melody over a long stretch of time have been put to a variety of uses, sacred and secular; that this specific melodic shape resembles one that happened to be put down in a book printed, say, in 1719, and that the other resembles some other floating melodic particle that came into the annotator's mind when he confronted it. And if the field of popular song is generally familiar to the reader, he, too, will undoubtedly be able to add here and there references to resemblances that spring to his own mind. It may occur to him that there is no end to this kind of annotation. If multiple reference is the object, he may ask, could not a hundred commentators make a bigger—and therefore a better—pile than one or two experts? And would it not therefore be best for such an enormous collaborative attack to be made on one and the same volume, exhausting all the allusive recollections to be called up by a given body of tunes? And after that, perhaps, upon another, and another? And then, when this were done, would that be the end, or would there be some kind of sense to make of the result? Conceivably, what kind of sense?

If the conclusion should be only what was stated in the beginning—namely, that the materials of folk-melody are common property, to be combined and recombined in ever-shifting ways—to whose advantage or edification does the endless illustration of the axiom operate? Obviously, the knowing annotator achieves a gratifying sense of mastery within his range of familiarity, and this is good for his psyche. The game can be fascinating to those who like to play it. But if the possibilities are pushed to their conceivable limit—if the network of cross-reference he brought to form a thicket of the greatest possible density—will clarification be the end product, or only a patternless complexity like that of the inter-relations of the human generations that begot this melodic flux?

What kind of sense, we repeat, are we pursuing? In his general introduction, Professor Jackson speaks of degrees of connection among tunes: of variants, versions, and tune-families. *Variants* he defines as tunes that differ in unimportant details; *versions* as tunes in which "the differences are more pronounced"; and *tune-families* as melodic groups composed of all recognizable variants and versions "showing merely a general kinship in structure." With definitions so loose as these we can hardly rest satisfied; but, without stopping to quarrel with them, we may ask whether the object is ultimately to relate all tunes to some tune-family or other; and whether, if so, the pressing and immediate point is to agree upon a name for the respective families.

Professor Jackson has found names for his tune-families among "the titles of the songs which seemed to exemplify best the family traits." His names thus derive from the religious categories with which he is most familiar. Barry and Bayard, he remarks, have found secular names, on the same principle, for the same tune-families. Thus, he writes, "my Babe of Bethlehem family is identical with the Bayard-Barry Lazarus group. And to this same group belong probably most of the melodies to which I gave the name the Hallelujah family."

Since neither Barry nor Bayard nor Jackson has objectified his identifications in any abstract characterizations, matters are still, obviously, in a very amorphous and amateurish stage. We can only long for the arrival of some Linnaeus to tell us what defines the Lazarus-Hallelujah-Babe of Bethlehem family, distinguishing it from other tune-families. When is a family a family? Disconcertingly enough, Professor Jackson continues as follows: "My Lord Lovel family . . . Bayard . . . regards . . . not as a family but as a branch of the more comprehensive Lord Randal family. (Bayard prefers to call all these families 'tunes'.) My Roll Jordan family members correspond largely to what Barry and Bayard recognized as another branch of the Lord Randal group and named after the Irish song 'Fainne Geal.' "

The science, then, of categorizing tunes would appear to be still at the stage of choosing favorite names for categories which themselves have not as yet been established as such, either extrinsically or intrinsically, and even before the effort to determine what features separate *any* category from classes larger or smaller. Now, if what Charles Seeger says is true—that our popular music is the main contribution of the New World to the history of Occidental music—it is obviously a task and a duty of sufficient importance to challenge the best efforts of some, at least, of the most highly skilled musicologists to introduce the beginnings of logic and reason into the analysis of this baffling and perplexed area of musical expression. For the significance of the matter in question is by no means limited to present examples: its roots go as deep as those of the people among whom it has been engendered; and itself is the nourishing essential earth from which have sprung, Antaeus-like, all the higher forms of musical art.

1954

The Morphology of the Ballad Tunes:
Variation, Selection, and Continuity

IT WILL be agreed that, apart from aesthetic enjoyment, most of
the attention given to the music of the popular ballad—in
fact, to British-American folk-song generally—has been concerned
with its tendency to alter during the course of transmission.
In his brief but invaluable *Conclusions*, Cecil Sharp gave four
or five times as much space to the discussion of "Variation" as he
did to his other two "principles," of "Continuity" and of "Selection." [1] Phillips Barry devoted much of his attention to the re-
creative properties of oral transmission, and to the tracing of particular melodies or melodic families through their varying appear-
ances in tradition.[2] After Sharp and Barry, most conscientious
writers on the ballad have accepted the importance of "communal
re-creation" as primary in the evolution of the genre; and this term
covers all the processes of change that the ballad undergoes during
its traditional progress. Later research has confined itself all too
singly to the identification of variant forms of the same melody.
Everywhere the interest in variation is paramount.[3]

It is entirely natural that the process of change should have
drawn so much more notice than its opposite. Nevertheless, from
the point of view of tradition, and specifically with regard to the
study of folk-melody, variation is in a sense the negative, not the

---

[1] Cecil J. Sharp, *English Folk-Song: Some Conclusions* (1907, reprinted 1936,
1954; revised edition with Preface by Maud Karpeles, 1965) Chapter III.
[2] See the representative cross section of his work reprinted under the title,
Folk Music in America, edited by George Herzog and Herbert Halpert (National
Service Bureau Publication, 80–5, 1939).
[3] One of the most noteworthy exceptions to this generalization is J. W. Hendren, *A Study of Ballad Rhythm* (1936), which gives a systematic picture of the
varieties of structure of ballad melodies as these affect, and interrelate with,
the metrical and stanzaic patterns of the verse.

positive, side of the problem. The fact was admitted by Sharp himself when he wrote: "Insistence of type must be the rule, and variation the exception." [4] Variation, when subject to no control, can be but the lawless multiplication of diversity. However fascinating the spectacle of mere diversity, it leads us nowhere. Its interest lies wholly in unrelated particulars. If we are to make any sense of variation, we must study its controls, and the controls—if there be any—lie in the opposite principle, of continuity. To devote our efforts to multiplying examples of difference is to discover only the fact of perpetual change—which is axiomatic. But to study the evidences of resistance to change is to pursue law and order, to turn from the disintegrative to the integrative forces.

It is accepted doctrine today that if a tune be left long enough in oral circulation it will in due course alter itself out of recognition. This generalization, unless qualified, would seem to mean that the more a tune is sung, the more unlike itself it becomes. But, obviously, such a paradox will not hold. The way to fix a tune in the folk-memory, as in the individual memory, is to sing it often and to sing it long. If in the course of traditional singing a tune becomes transformed beyond recognition, it will be because extraneous circumstances have too powerfully interfered—not the influences of tradition, truly, but the enemies of such influences. Imperfect recollection, always mildly operative as an instrumentality of traditional change, will, when it reaches the point of actual perplexity or loss of a melodic phrase, become such an enemy. If the tune is flourishing in tradition, the individual's loss will be made good by other singers, and violent change will be corrected. But where, after the lapse of years or exposure to new and untraditional ways, a singer has to restore rather than recall, the probability of major alteration is obviously very great. This, however, is not to be attributed to the action, but rather, to the inaction, of tradition. We cannot, then, believe that a tune truly popular, in all senses of the word, vigorously and continually alive, will be sung into something altogether different. Rather, in spite of incessant slight changes, it will preserve its identity over very long stretches of time. The positive impulse of self-perpetuation, the principle of continuity, will make itself strongly felt, controlling the deviations. Few will deny the existence of such a positive force.

[4] Sharp (1907), p. 16.

In spite of this principle—or rather, by its allowance—variations will continually occur. We may distinguish between "legitimate" and "illegitimate" deviations in tradition—not subtly, but by a crude separation of arbitrary departures (willful substitutions, groping restorations, conscious creations) from such alternative or variant phrasings as are exemplified in successive renderings of a stanza or song by the same singer. The later are "legitimate," and they move within, and activate, the genuinely positive and re-creative part of tradition. They are, we may infer, the all-but-unconscious expression of true musical instinct steeped in traditional habits of melodic thought.

Cecil Sharp's hypothesis of evolutionary development in folk-song imposes upon these phenomena a kind of racial or national instinctive purpose. How firmly or finally he held this theory may be open to question. His introduction modestly states that his views "are advanced, not in any dogmatic spirit, but cautiously and tentatively." [5] His book was written relatively early in his career, when he had done only a quarter of his work and long before he had collected in the Appalachians. But it does not appear that he saw much occasion to alter his theory of evolution. And since his death it has met, I believe, with little or no serious challenge; so that, whatever his final convictions, his three principles of Continuity, Variation, and Selection appear to be well established as orthodox dogma.[6]

Now, the first and second of these principles are facts that have been documented with such frequency as to compel universal assent. But the third principle is of a different order. It stands on no firmer ground than that of plausible hypothesis. Stimulated by the evolutionary thesis, Sharp was naturally led to posit the final element, Selection, in order to complete his analogy. Just as, "in the animal and vegetable worlds, those variations will be preserved, which are of advantage to their possessors in the competition for existence," so, he writes, "in the evolution of folk-tunes . . . the corresponding principle of selection is the taste of the community. Those tune-variations which appeal to the community will be perpetuated as against those which attract the individual only." While, therefore, Continuity is a merely passive agent and Variation an

[5] Sharp (1907), p. viii.
[6] See, for illustration, the General Report of the International Folk Music Council, *Journal*, 5 (1953), 9 ff., *passim*.

ambiguous and irresponsible force for change, whether positive, or neutral, or negative—i.e., toward growth, sterility, or corruption: "the function of the third principle, *Selection*, is to ensure that variation shall, in certain cases, result in organic growth and development."

No one will deny that, as Sharp expresses it, "national peculiarities must ultimately determine the specific characteristics of the folk-songs of the different nations." [7] But does it necessarily follow that, as he says, "the folk-song has derived its communal and racial character solely through the action of the third principle, *Selection?*" [8] When closely scrutinized, the operation of this hypothetical principle is very hard to reduce to credible practice. In the first place, we know from observation that popular taste has in general a very precarious hold on the singing habits of a people wherever it meets with insistent challenge from contrary influences, social or artistic. Its best chance of survival lies in isolated communities, secluded and inaccessible to new fashions. In the second edition of the Appalachian collection, Maud Karpeles wrote, "It is surprising and sad to find how quickly the instinctive culture of the people will seem to disappear when once they have been brought into touch with modern civilization, and how soon they will imitate the manners and become imbued with the tastes of 'polite Society.' " [9] (But, of course, there has always been a "modern civilization": there was never a society that looked only backward.) In the reprint of the same collection, twenty years later, Miss Karpeles records her impressions from a recent visit to the same region, that the incursions of industry, the introduction of roads and radio, are already threatening the extinction of the older traditional singing.[10] The evidence of such effects could be multiplied all over the world today; and, be it said, it is not what one would look for as the result of a controlling national or racial principle, vigilant to conserve what is truly idiomatic, jealous to exclude what is alien to the tradition: "to weigh, sift, and select from the mass of individual suggestions those which most accurately express the popular taste and the popular ideal; to reject the rest; and then, when more vari-

[7] Sharp (1907), p. 29.
[8] *Ibid.*, p. 30.
[9] Cecil J. Sharp, *English Folk Songs from the Southern Appalachians,* Maud Karpeles, ed., I (1932), xvi.
[10] *Ibid.*, ed. 1952, p. xx.

ations are produced, to repeat the process once more, and again once more." [11] It is difficult to see, where theory can be tested by experience, much evidence of "steady growth and development" of an evolutionary sort; or of "a tendency always to approximate to a form which shall be at once congenial to the taste of the community, and expressive of its feelings, aspirations, and ideals": that is, of the exercise of a positive, constructive, "communal choice."

If it be granted that in the widest view such deterioration of tradition as we have indicated is a communal expression of preferences in taste, we shall not thereby, I believe, be brought much closer to Sharp's principle of evolutionary selection. His view is that a whole community, through its component members, exerts a critical judgment in the act of selective preference, preserving only what it approves. The principle acts, or should act, to exclude alien influences, and also to discriminate within the tradition itself.

If we narrow our scrutiny to a flourishing and uncontaminated tradition, insulated from outward attack, and working only within the native products of its own participants, like the majority of Sharp's singers in Somerset, we may still have difficulty in perceiving how the principle operates. Illustrating the principle of Variation, Sharp calls attention to the inspired and creative invention of a number of folk-singers, who could hardly repeat a phrase without altering it in fresh and felicitous ways. To examine the specimens of such variation is to see that they are alternative ways of expressing the same melodic idea. There are abundant examples available for study, and the fact seems proved. Sharp describes his difficulty in catching and fixing these variants as they came from the singer, and says he found that the only feasible procedure was to keep a gifted singer like blind Henry Larcombe singing the same song over and over, for an hour or so at a time. "In this way," he writes, "I have been able to catch and note down those variations which have recurred two or three times, but, of course, I have missed many of those which have appeared but once." Larcombe, he observes, when asked to repeat a phrase, did not realize that he was offering a different form of it when he sang it again; and Sharp significantly declares, "I have never met with a singer who could detect small melodic differences. So long as your tune is, in the main, similar to his, the most musical of folk-singers will declare it

[11] Sharp (1907), p. 31.

to be identical, although the differences may be of considerable importance from a musician's point of view, *e.g.*, a change of mode, or a variation in rhythm." He describes a group of such singers joining the chorus in "Brennan on the Moor," at a village inn, each happily singing his own version of it, "one and all quite oblivious of the cacophony they were producing." These instances are presented by him as typical, not exceptional. But it seems to have escaped attention that they go far to undermine his own hypothesis of Selection. For what he has described is the actual operation of the folk-singing community, both as individual and as group: the individual is unaware of small melodic differences, and the community disregards them even when they are accentuated by simultaneous performance. Sharp's observations were made under relatively ideal conditions: a truly musical singer on the one hand; on the other, an uncontaminated and homogeneous group within a regional tradition. In what sense can it be true that "the suggestions, unconsciously made by" Henry Larcombe, for example, were "tested and weighed by the community, and accepted or rejected by their verdict?" [12]

If these Somerset singers provide, as we believe, a favorable norm for a test of the theory, it will yet surely be allowed that less favorable conditions ordinarily prevail, and that the majority of those who perpetuate traditional songs are not musically gifted, because probably in no time nor place have the musically gifted been in the majority; so that as a rule one could expect still less in the way of minute discrimination. But even if we suppose that elsewhere, in other folk-singing communities, ears have been more acute and critical, able to distinguish small melodic differences, we are still confronted with a nearly insuperable practical difficulty. In the traditional rendition of a folk-song, there is no fixed reading, no absolute norm by which to measure conformity or departure. Within the limits imposed by tradition, every variation evolved spontaneously by such a singer as Larcombe is equally right and good. In order to prefer one to another, they must be severally remembered and compared. Sharp himself, with all his musical quickness and trained powers of discrimination, was unable to keep pace with Larcombe's shifting and liquid rendition, and confesses that he was only able to catch and fix the variations which were recur-

[12] *Ibid.*, pp. 16–21.

rent. Can it then be supposed that the most discriminating members of the folk-singing community would be able to do what Sharp found impossible?

These obstacles to acceptance of the principle of Selection if ever raised have never, so far as I am aware, been squarely faced. Perhaps, indeed, they cannot be surmounted. If so, we shall have to give up the principle and find another explanation for the phenomena it was evoked to cover. For Sharp, its role was a crucial one. Continuity he saw as "a passive rather than an active agent; a condition, not a cause." Variation he read as creative but in itself non-developmental. Variation "creates the material which renders development possible," but leads as readily to "corruption" as to "growth." [13] Selection, the critical element, shaped and moulded the communal form, and determined the direction of traditional change. It was the mainspring of the theory of evolution. We must therefore ask ourselves what would be left if this element were to be withdrawn; and whether anything resembling the situation we know from the surviving records would still be left, if Selection were not assumed. And first of all, we should ask what Variation actually produces or creates. This question can be answered with some assurance.

The variations of individual singers occur within the tradition—that is to say, in a habit of musical thought, the product of minds steeped in an idiomatic continuity. They are in no danger of radical departures from the traditional norm, because such alterations as occur to these minds are confined to the area of legitimate change. These singers are not only creative in variation but also conservative at the same time. The conservative impulse acts before and during the singing, rather than after. We are not to suppose that a great many wildly inventive variations are or ever were being continually thrown out by the singers, only to die and leave no record because the folk-singing community, weighing and testing, rejected them. There was an 'inner check' that prevented what would not be acceptable from coming into being at all.

It is moreover to be kept in mind that the folk-memory does not recall by a note-for-note accuracy, as a solo performer memorizes a Beethoven sonata. Rather, it preserves a melodic idea as an imprecise entity, which it condenses into a fresh particularization with

[13] *Ibid.*, p. 29.

each rendition, even with each new stanza sung. There is no correct form of the tune from which to depart, or to sustain, but only an infinite series of positive realizations of the melodic idea.

Hence, before we subscribe to the hypothetical evolutionary principle, it seems clear that we should try to determine what evidence there is of change that may justly be called evolutionary; and whether or not the changes that occur may be accounted for by the two impulses we already know to be at work—the conservative tendency to transmit unchanged and the opposite impulse to alter: the principles, that is, of Continuity and Variation.

What ideally we would do is to fix the boundaries of change, the limits beyond which traditional variation does not stray, and the habits of that variation as marked by the typical paths it pursues. If we should find that such variational activity as we could observe confined itself in the main to certain well-marked melodic or rhythmic patterns of change, we could be sure that a strong principle of Continuity or stability was at work as a counter-force opposing free variation. If we could determine the relative strength of this counter-force, could measure its success in holding a tune on its traditional track, we should have a gauge that would serve a variety of uses. It would help us to define the norm of traditional variation. We might then say, for example, of particular cases that the centripetal pull never allows the members of a traditional system to swing so wide of their orbits as in this or that instance would appear to have happened; and we might admit or exclude on this basis. With enough evidence, we might discover the points at which the Continuity principle is strongest or most conservative, and where most relaxed: whether there are parts, elements, phrases, features, of a melodic complex, or combinations of elements—as, for example, meter plus contour—that show an especially sturdy resistance to change.

It is only, as it seems to me, by the painstaking collection of factual data from dependable records that we can begin to plot the course, and hence guess at the laws, of the phenomena of melodic tradition. Heretofore, we have proceeded too much upon the basis of theories that rest in turn on a number of 'hunches' about the actual facts. The hunches may be close or wide of the mark, depending on the familiarity of the guesser with a broad field of materials. It is time to seek for sounder foundations.

The facts and generalizations which follow are offered as pointing toward a fuller and more careful examination of a still wider territory. They are based on a restricted class of documentary records. The records range in date from 1600 to the present decade, with much the largest and most dependable portion firmly established in the twentieth century, and deriving in the main from Scotland, England, New England, and the Appalachians. These twentieth-century records alone provide data in sufficient abundance for any halfway-confident generalization. The materials are drawn from the single area of the British-American traditional ballad, as exemplified by F. J. Child's canon of popular ballads in the English tongue. Granted the restrictions of this category, and the large amount of available material outside it: it is yet possible that so much may serve as a sort of pilot project, and that other students may proceed to develop particular areas or categories of folk-song in a similar fashion, and help in turn to compile an exhaustive and universal survey. Within even the present single category, perhaps only two-thirds of the extant material has been subjected to preliminary analysis. This is sufficient for tentative, not final, conclusions. Since the count is not—and for obvious and sufficient reasons cannot possibly be—final, the actual figures are not so important as are the totals and proportions in round numbers. Overwhelming majorities are fairly conclusive, slight numerical superiority is insignificant. The total number of tunes here worked upon and subjected to statistical analysis is about 3450.

Almost any book that attempts to survey the field in broad strokes must sooner or later make assertions that have never been subjected to verification. Thus, a recent and valuable introductory study declares: "Of the modes most frequently found in Anglo-American folk song . . . the Ionian and Æolian are the more common." [14] Now, a statistical count of the ballad tunes shows that about a quarter of the total are strict Ionian tunes—the highest proportion for any single mode—while the Æolian mode comes *ninth* in the list of preferences, with about one-twenty-fourth of the total. Counting hexatonic and pentatonic tunes separately, the *intervening* favorites, in order of popularity, are I/M, with about half as many examples as the Ionian; π^1 (pentatonic lacking 4 and 7) with slightly fewer; Mixolydian, with something more than a third of

[14] Evelyn K. Wells, *The Ballad Tree* (1950), p. 275.

the Ionian total; D/Æ, with approximately a third; Ly/I, with about a fourth; Dorian, with a fifth; M/D, with about a sixth. Other modal proportions follow in the order π^2, π^4, π^3.[15]

The author of another standard work was convinced that the ordinary ballad quatrain "is quite certainly a couplet with seven stresses to the line."[16] He drew assurance from the typical music, citing a "Barbara Allan" variant from Greig's collection,[17] "chosen almost at random," in which the second half of the tune was identical with the first half. Nevertheless, in a phrasal tabulation of 3450 ballad tunes, in which a different letter was assigned to each phrase with a different cadence-note (in order to avoid subjective and fluctuating decisions of underlying identity between phrases that differed in that most important structural particular), the four-phrase tunes of the non-recurrent type ABCD comprised nearly half the sum total of all phrasal schemes together—more than 1600, in fact; while the total of the pattern ABAB adduced by Gerould as typical numbered less than 100. In actual fact, the next most favorite scheme after ABCD is ABCDE, though it comes far short of the other in popularity (less than 250 examples); and the third in line is ABAC (with less than 200). Fourth comes ABCDD (115). Other patterns all fall below a total of 100.

We may, if we choose, be quite specific about a large number of neglected questions of fact relating to the ballad tunes. The examples that follow will give support to this assertion.

About half the tunes are in the *authentic* range: that is, they move between the tonic and its octave above, with perhaps an additional degree or two in either direction. Slightly more than a third are *plagal* tunes, moving between the upper and lower fifth. The remainder are *mixed*, with a range combining the other two in extent. Regional or national counts, however, show some interesting modifications of these totals. Thus, the English tradition displays a considerably larger proportion of authentic tunes—well over half its total; while the Scottish divides almost equally between the authentic and plagal, thus showing a marked liking for a tonal center midway in the tune's range. So strong a tendency appears nowhere

[15] For the designations here employed for the various modal scales, see the fifth essay of this volume.

[16] Gordon H. Gerould, *The Ballad of Tradition* (1932), p. 125.

[17] Gavin Greig, *Last Leaves of Traditional Ballads and Ballad Airs*, Alexander Keith, ed., (1925).

else in the British-American tradition unless in a few parts of the United States (W. S. Central and Pacific regions), where the evidence is too thin for dependability, but where, in the slender total of 87, only 6 tunes are mixed, while plagal tunes predominate over authentic. Psychologically, the effect may be open to question: it might be guessed that authentic tunes are more aspiring, more buoyant than the plagal, since they sustain themselves above their tonal anchorage; and that the Scottish fondness for the plagal range results in a greater weight or sobriety, and tends to the sombre. But this consideration would doubtless be strongly modified by the modal caste, and probably also by the meter, of the individual tunes.

Analysis of the ballad tunes by range yields other interesting facts. While it might be readily anticipated, and is true, that the tonic would be the overwhelming favorite as final, it might not be guessed that the divergences from this norm vary with the range. Thus, of somewhat more than 1700 authentic tunes, while 1500 end on the tonic, more than 100 end on the octave above, carrying buoyancy, one might say, to its logical limit. Among plagal tunes, on the contrary, the urge for a final other than the tonic is not so noticeable. Of a total rather less than 1300, all but about 100 tunes end on the tonic; and here the second choice lies on the lower fifth, but with only 40 examples. After the lower fifth comes the second degree, with 18 occurrences; then 11 on the lower sixth; and thereafter an insignificant scattering. But, looking back at the authentic tunes, we find 27 finals on the upper fifth, 22 on the second, 19 on the third, and 13 on the sixth. (Major tunes with fallen closes on the lower fifth have been regarded in this tabulation as most frequently Mixolydian with final on the true tonic.) The mixed tunes, with negligible exceptions, end almost always on the tonic.

The authentic initial upbeat, so characteristic of our iambic tradition, clearly favors most the tonic; but there are sizable totals also on the fifth, the fourth, and the third, in that order of preference. But the plagal tunes overwhelmingly choose the lower fifth as upbeat, with the tonic as nearest competitor, yet exhibiting less than a third as many occurrences. For the mixed tunes, the order of preference is: lower fifth, tonic, fifth, fourth, and third.

Comparable differences appear in the phrasal cadence-points. For the second phrase—most often the mid-cadence of the tune—

well over half of the authentic tunes cadence on the fifth. Very distant runners-up are the tonic, the octave above, and the second.
Plagal tunes show a more balanced proportion, seeking first the
second degree, next the tonic, next the fifth, and then, with a steep
drop in the total, the lower fifth. The overwhelming favorite of
the mixed tunes is the upper fifth.

Similarly, characteristic differences appear in the other phrases.
Among the authentic tunes, for the first-phrase cadence the tonic is
far in the lead. Much less than half as popular is the fifth. Next,
with a palpable falling-off, is the third; and then, with another
wide interval, the fourth. For the plagal tunes, on the contrary, the
lower fifth is considerably in the lead, though not so disproportion-
ately as is the tonic for the authentic tunes. Next comes the tonic,
among the plagal tunes; and next, the second. It is fairly obvious
that there are artistic impulses of balance and proportion inherent
in these coordinations of first and second cadences; and that they
are the effect neither of blind chance nor of willful experiment. An
interesting fact that begins to emerge from even so limited a comparison as the foregoing, however, is that the basic scaffolding of
the plagal tunes is noticeably less secure, less firmly articulated,
than that of the authentic. It may be that the plagal firmness about
the tonic as final is compensation for the greater malleability of the
structure as a whole. We shall revert to this matter later in our
survey.

It is no secret that Scottish music has a fondness for the gapped
scales. But it is interesting to compare it with the English in this regard. Of pure pentatonic tunes, England shows only 13 out of 733.
Scotland shows 174 out of 877. If we count the hexatonics, we get
the following contrast: for England, 140; for Scotland, 372. Thus,
for Scotland, nearly two-thirds of the total number are gapped; for
England, only about a fifth. Significantly, the Appalachian total of
gapped tunes correspond to the Scottish; but at the same time,
there is in the Appalachians a higher proportion of pentatonics:
above five-sixths as many pentatonics as hexatonics, to slightly over
half as many for Scotland.

If we lump together the scales of all kinds—pentatonics, hexatonics, and heptatonics—and divide these into two groups, arbitrarily separating them between the hexatonic scale with missing third
and with major sixth (M/D) and the pentatonic scale lacking third

and sixth (π^3): we have another interesting point of general comparison. The dividing line is where the scales with predominantly major feeling meet and shade over into those with minor feeling. Let us call the major galaxy Group 1, the minor galaxy Group 2. A regional tabulation yields the following: about one-fifth of the English tunes fall into Group 2; rather less than one-third of the Scottish do so; and rather less than one-fifth of the Appalachian.

A more refined modal count would give the totals for each variety; but the greater proportion of gapped scales in Scotland and the Appalachians must be kept in mind, because they add weight to the one side or the other. Thus, the straight Ionian tunes of England comprise almost half the total; while in Scotland Ionian tunes number slightly more than one-sixth of the total. But Ly/I, π^1, I/M, and π^2 tunes will also strike most listeners as major, and the Scottish totals in these gapped scales together greatly exceed the Scottish Ionian total. The English tunes in the same gapped scales together amount to considerably less than one-third the number of Ionian tunes. Nevertheless, the facts are interesting, and a few of them may find a place here. After the Ionian, the most favored scale in England is the Mixolydian—less than a third as popular; then, with a considerable drop, the hexatonic I/M; next, the Æolian, with only a slight lead over the Dorian. In Scotland, the order of preference is: leading, the hexatonic D/Æ, with the Ionian a close runner-up, then I/M and π^1, some distance behind. The Mixolydian is considerably less favored in Scotland than in England, but M/D, which is practically unknown in England, is found in Scotland nearly as often as is the Mixolydian. Pure Dorian in Scotland is relatively less favored than in England. The order in the Appalachians is: π^1, far in the lead; I/M, at a long interval; I, with another drop; M, at about the same remove, but almost level with π^2; followed by Ly/I and M/D.

A regional breakdown of metrical totals is probably less indicative and less dependable than the previous summary. Much depends on the individual collector's predilections in notation, and even experts differ. For the present, it is not worth while to pursue the analysis beyond the broadest generalizations. The distinction between three-time and two-time, however, may be taken as a relatively reliable mark of difference, reflected in all the records. If we take three and its multiples—e.g., 3/8, 6/8, 9/8, 3/4, 6/4, 3/2—

as varieties of three-time; and 2/8, 4/8, 2/4, 4/4, 2/2, and 4/2 as varieties of two-time, we can make some simple generalizations. (12/8 in this province will fall satisfactorily into 6/8; 5/4 belongs with the instances of mixed timing, not being a steady or regular meter in British tradition.) We find that the proportion of three-time in England is much higher than in Scotland (497 of 773, as against 341 of 877.) Nevertheless, the meter most frequent in the record of the English tradition is 4/4 or common time; as is also true of Scotland. Two-thirds as many of the English tunes have been written as 6/8, and half as many in 3/4. In Scotland, 3/4 has followed 4/4 with a very wide interval between; then 2/4, and then 6/8 close behind. The large count of 2/4 tunes, one suspects, results from personal preferences of editors like Christie, writing in smaller units than do other authorities. Striking in the record as a whole is the very much higher proportion of 6/8 tunes in England than in Scotland—a fact that can hardly be dispelled by means of equivalents. The relatively greater proportion of 3/4 in Scotland will not account for it. 6/8 in England has been felt as a very fitting counterpart to the iambic meter; but the Scots seem not so much to have needed the additional length for the accented syllable, and have chosen subtler ways of accommodating the iambics.

Before the present century, the sporadic appearance of tunes in the record, and the distance of most of our records from actual folk rendition, make a statistical analysis quite undependable. It seems fairly probable that among the earlier records the greater relative proportion of tunes of more than five phrases is due to editorial causes and to the fact that these tunes were being put to instrumental and dance uses. Dean Christie, with his desire to make the Scottish ballads suitable for the drawing-room, regularly cobbled a second strain out of a four-phrase melody.[18] The records of the last sixty years, however, resting mainly on actual folk-singing practice, show a preference of more than five to one for tunes of not more than five phrases. Here also is where the vast bulk of the total record lies. In contrast, the preference in the nineteenth century (before 1890) for short tunes is only two-and-one-half times; for the eighteenth century the balance is cut to the proportion of three to two; and for the seventeenth century, the balance is on the other side, in a proportion of two shorter against three longer

[18] W. Christie, *Traditional Ballad Airs* (1876–1881).

tunes. I doubt that this lengthening as we trace the record back ought to be taken as significant of a trend in folk-singing.

Similarly, a breakdown by date of record of the range employed cannot give us any sure data, nor enable us to trace an evolution one way or the other. It shows authentic tunes in the seventeenth century to be half as numerous as plagal; in the eighteenth century to be more numerous in a proportion of three to two; in the nineteenth, of six to five; and in the twentieth, of seven to five. One might expect to see a greater proportion of tunes in the mixed range where a closer connection with instrumental uses was to be suspected. But the facts here seem to be as follows: in the seventeenth century, a tenth of the total is mixed; in the eighteenth century, a sixth; in the nineteenth, between a fifth and a sixth; and in the twentieth, somewhat less than an eighth.

Rhythmically, three-time in its various meters prevails in the seventeenth century in a proportion of five to one. In the eighteenth century, the proportion is almost equal, but tilts slightly toward three-time. In the nineteenth century, the balance is distinctly on the side of duple time, in a proportion of seven to six. The twentieth century records show a similar proportion—about fourteen duple to thirteen three-time. These are clear cases, ignoring the irregular meters, which only begin to appear in the record with the advent of more scrupulous collectors at the opening of the present century.

Other and more refined analyses of the kind suggested above are obviously possible and in order; but the present purpose is only to point the way to a more meticulous comparative examination of our melodic tradition, so as ultimately to establish its morphology on a sound basis.

The principle of Continuity, the fundamental element in any tradition, is subject everywhere to attack from opposing impulses and influences of many different kinds and of varying force. It is important to recognize that, as it operates in folk-song, it is not a mere inert tenacity resisting change with equal rigidity all along the line, but that it has points of special strength and points of greater and less vulnerability. A comparative study across a wide area of tradition reveals these points of varying stability in an unmistakable fashion. Some of them, like the impulse of melody to assert its tonic as the final of the tune, we already know. But our pursuit of this problem of comparative stability will take us farther than as yet we have ever adventured. To keep the present discussion within bounds, we shall confine our scrutiny mainly to the first two phrases of our ballad tunes. Since more than two-thirds of the total number do not exceed five phrases in length, we shall thus be fixing our limit at the mid-cadence of a large proportion of the tunes here subjected to analysis. But the longer tunes may be left in the count, for they add further evidence of the kind we are seeking. It will be more revealing, however, to consider the authentic and plagal tunes separately, since range is so important an element in the picture of melodic contour. Yet because mixed tunes are in part identical with plagal, and in part with authentic, they may be included in both categories, and will therefore be counted twice.

If we allow that the overwhelming majority of our folk-tunes end on the tonic, it is then true to say that the most stable element of the folk-tune is the final. We may now ask what the next most stable point is. The answer will surely be, the mid-cadence. Surprisingly, however, this is true only of authentic tunes. Over half of these cadence the second phrase on one and the same degree of the scale, and that degree is the fifth. There is no equal to this point in stability (except the final) elsewhere in folk-song. But the point of greatest stability in plagal tunes is not the mid-cadence but the first accented note of the first phrase. Almost precisely half of the plagal tunes agree at this point on the tonic. The point of next greatest stability is the cadence-note of the first phrase of authentic tunes. This is most often the tonic. There is a perceptible decline in firmness here from the consistent strength of the mid-cadence, but little less firmness, even so, than is shown by the strongest point of the plagal tunes. Next in stability comes the penultimate accent of the second phrase of authentic tunes, which is frequently the point at which the cadence-note (held for the length of two stresses) is struck. Next come the first accents of the first and second phrases of authentic tunes; these have almost equal stability, and favor the fifth. They are closely followed in firmness by the cadence-note of the second phrase of plagal tunes and by the second accent of plagal first phrases, which again are almost exactly equal in stability. The cadence prefers the fifth, and the second accent, the tonic. Next follows the first-phrase cadence of plagal tunes (oftenest on the tonic); and next, the second accent of the first phrase of authentic tunes (preferring the fifth). Then comes the first accent of the second phrase of plagal tunes (oftenest the tonic). After this, there begin to appear second choices on accents already mentioned, duly following the order of stability. It will be easier to grasp the sequence if we lay out a table of accents in the first two phrases, indicating with a number the order of stability throughout. It is to be understood that, as between the authentic and plagal tunes, the order is determined relatively, not numerically, since the plagal tunes in sum total number fewer by 450 than the authentic tunes. The order, then, of relative stability stands thus:

	First Phrase				Second Phrase			
	1st Accent	2nd Accent	3rd Accent	4th Accent	1st Accent	2nd Accent	3rd Accent	4th Accent
Authentic	5(17)	13	15	3	6	14	4	1
Plagal	2	8(12)	16	9(11)	10	18	19	7

This table makes it evident that the principle of Continuity operates in a far from simple, straightforward manner. It does not present a uniform, passive resistance to the ever-threatening impulses toward change to which we refer under the collective name of Variation. Rather, it opposes a very uneven strength, a force that alters continually throughout the whole length of the tune. We discover, moreover, that it acts with quite surprisingly divergent habits in the two classes of melody, authentic and plagal; and that the index of stability, so far as our partial analysis reveals it, is markedly higher for authentic than for plagal tunes. If plagal tunes are more vulnerable to influence, it should follow that they have been the readier avenue to traditional change.

The question then arises, whether the factors already touched upon are not in themselves sufficiently complex to account potentially for the phenomena of melodic tradition, without invoking the hypothetical principle of Selection at all. Should we not perhaps conclude instead that the factor of relative stability, which is inherent in the principle of Continuity, itself exercises a flexible control over traditional variation? To the writer it seems probable that this elasticity itself is responsible for (in Sharp's words) "the

moulding of that material, the business of construction, the determination of the form that the building shall take": [19] that, in short,
it performs precisely the functions Sharp attributed to his critical
principle of Selection.

1954

[19] Sharp (1907), p. 29.

About the Most Favorite British Ballads

To TALK briefly about the most familiar ballads in the British-American tradition, it is necessary to make some initial limitations that for many may rob the subject of historical interest. The great bulk of the evidence that shows the ballads to be common is relatively contemporary evidence. We cannot know which ballads were massively current in past ages, since scattered records alone remain to testify to their having been generally known and sung. But for the present century there is factual evidence of widespread dissemination in the multiplicity of variants gathered by many collectors. It follows that we cannot generalize from the inherent appeal of the best of the earlier texts. For it is obvious that out of these narratives has been dropped and lost much that once made them powerful and effective stories. Time has stolen from them the elements of the supernatural, much of the color of scene and sensitiveness of phrase, the right ordering of incident, dramatic suspense, sometimes even the logical relations of the persons concerned. We have, however, no right to assume that because the songs are still popular they are piously remembered today for the sake of what they formerly contained. The contemporary singers, we must believe, are seldom antiquaries: they like and sing the songs for what they are now—the only state, however dilapidated, in which, for the true folk-singer, they exist.

From the evidence, it frequently appears that the element of narrative suspense means next to nothing to these singers. There may in fact be something radically inimical to suspense in the lyrical

This paper was read at the annual meeting of the International Folk Music Council, in Trossingen, Germany, July 25, 1956, and printed in slightly abridged form in JIFMC, IX (1957), pp. 22–27.

conception of balladry itself. Our first example, "Barbara Allan," which leads all the rest in popularity, seems at any rate never to have possessed this ingredient. Barbara's belated remorse may perhaps provide a modicum of surprise. But in almost none of the current variants does her lover put up so much resistance as to offer a word of explanation of the apparent affront with which she sometimes charges him. More often than not, her charge of neglect is also dropped, and her callousness left unexplained. To judge by the briefer variants, the elements with most power of survival in the song, after the seasonal setting of the opening, are the summons to the death-bed, Barbara's languid compliance with it, and the upspringing and intertwining of the symbolic plants from the graves. When, as sometimes happens, the connection between Barbara's death and her desire to atone for her cruelty fails to be made, obviously little remains of genuine narrative. The quality of gnarled old apple trees was what the American poet Carl Sandburg found in this song. But truly, its popularity from the days of Pepys onward to the present, in the face of its undistinguished and unexciting content, its portrayal of unresisting surrender to untoward fortune, is, if we take the song as a fundamental expression of the spirit of the English-speaking people, a phenomenon so strange and mysterious as to deserve prolonged meditation. No love-triangle; no struggle; no complications; no hope; no courage; nothing but passive acceptance: result, the universal favorite! For a contrasting potency, only think of Paolo and Francesca, which has everything that this story lacks. As a national persona, one might justly prefer Werther's Charlotte, who, in Thackeray's well-remembered words,

> having seen [her lover's] body
>   Borne before her on a shutter,
> Like a well-conducted person,
>   Went on cutting bread and butter.

But the contrast between this "wise passiveness" and the violence of the next most popular ballad in the British tradition is extreme. "Lord Thomas and Fair Eleanor" shows no disposition to shy from explosive situation or melodramatic consequence. The delicate beauty of characterization and phrase of the older Scottish version has given way, in the surviving tradition, to headlong provocation of the worst that ungovernable passion can wreak upon its victims.

The three principals are almost equally responsible for the ensuing tragedy. Fair Eleanor comes to the wedding only to taunt the bride for her lack of beauty; Lord Thomas shamefully humiliates his bride both by word and act; the bride stabs her rival as instinctively as a cornered animal would kill its enemy; Lord Thomas retaliates with such brutal frenzy as to dishonor the corpse by kicking (or throwing) the severed head against the wall; and then with equal precipitancy, stabs himself, to make an end of all three. These people are Elizabethan in their lack of emotional restraint. Their story, at least, hangs together better than usual in the folk memory. Its essential parts are seldom lost or confused. The breakneck pace of the narrative is slowed only by the two pauses for maternal advice—wrongly followed by Lord Thomas, wrongly disregarded by Fair Eleanor—and by the repetition, in some copies, of the last line or lines of each stanza by way of refrain. There is a violence even in the extravagance of Eleanor's preparations for the wedding, as if she foresaw that she was playing to the final curtain. The rush of event suffers no real interruption; the temporal sequence is unbroken and straightforward. Here again there is little suspense and little surprise. But it is difficult to find any common ground between this narrative and the other. How could the same people be almost equally fond of these two songs?

"Lord Randal" holds a position of virtually equal security in the folk memory: a place so close to "Lord Thomas" that it would be impossible to say confidently that one was more popular than the other. Here, too, is a story of murderous passion, though in the present case we do not know what has led to the fatal act, which is doubtless more deliberate. But the question of motives is none of the ballad's business; and there is little sign that any singer has ever inquired. What we see clearly is that Lord Randal returns home from a love tryst with an assurance that death is upon him, and that he has been poisoned by his love. The narrative is conducted thenceforward by means of the "legacy" convention; but it would be an unmerited compliment to speak in this case of a "*climax* of relatives*." Which relative comes before which in the distribution of bequests is a matter of complete indifference. The device is not used dramatically, and is only a means of extending the song. The fatal secret is out, at latest, as soon as we learn the nature of Randal's repast in the wildwood. We do not need to be told that his dogs, which shared the leavings, are already dead; and it is not surprising that this detail, as likewise the mother's expressed fears, are often absent from the song as we meet it in tradition. Strictly regarded, the only suspense in the narrative lies in our having to wait through the list of insignificant bequests to learn what is bequeathed to the murderess. Here, one feels, even more than in "Barbara Allan," narrative interest could hardly be more slackly sustained.

The next, and almost equally favorite, ballad in the British-American tradition is one with an enormous range of Continental parallels and a plot of far greater complexity. It is generally, but ineptly, known to English students by Child's title, "Lady Isabel and the Elf Knight," but also by a variety of other names, of which the commonest English one is "The Outlandish Knight." The latent ambiguity of "outlandish" is appropriate to its character. From the current tradition the supernatural element has been eliminated, but an unusually large number of narrative elements survive; and the story has a relatively high degree of suspense and surprise as well as incident. It is noteworthy, however, that in the chances of transmission, the sequence of events is liable to sad deterioration, and that even the characters may be confounded. In cases where the process of dilapidation has made the worst inroads—and such cases are all too numerous—the natural binding force of the plot has been so ineffectual that almost every incident of the story may be found standing alone as the ballad's sole surviving remnant, in spite of its failure to make sense by itself or even to suggest a total meaning. Discounting cases where only the opening survives— which may be due to failure on the collector's part to record the remaining stanzas—a good many examples preserve only the knight's initial promise; a good many, only the injunction to steal the parental treasure and a couple of the best horses; some, only the order to alight, or the command to disrobe; and some, only the bribery of the parrot to silence. Other copies leave crucial gaps in the narrative sequence, or shift the order in confusing ways. The greatest tenacity appears to lie in the first promise, in the injunction to get gold and steeds for the journey, and in the bribery of the talking bird. After these come the parleying over disrobing, the turning of the tables on the villain, and the maid's safe return. The interesting thing is that the song has so often continued to be sung after nearly all narrative meaning has departed. This again would suggest that narrative interest was not essential to survival. In face of the fact that the refrain, when it occurs—and it does so in perhaps only a third of the records—has absolutely no independent interest, being usually a mere repetition of the last line of the stanza: it would be natural to conclude that it was sheer delight in the tune that kept the piece alive. For what else is left?

Much simpler is the next ballad in the series, "The Gypsy Laddie," or "Gypsy Davy," as it is better known in America. Here is a story essentially romantic, without tragic consequences—at least, in recent tradition. The central parts of this song are generally well preserved, and the tale loses little, where it is remembered at all. Seldom forgotten are the following seven elements: the appearance of the gypsies; the lord's return, to find his lady gone; his command to saddle in haste; his riding hither and thither until he finds the lady among the gypsies; his challenging questions; her defiant answers; the contrast between her former state and her lot henceforward. These make a complete narrative; only occasionally is it elaborated with details of her enticement, her thoughts of her children, his commands and threats, and the last farewells. The English forms as a rule have no refrain, but the American are likely to repeat the second half of the stanza or even to add a separable and rather extended jingling refrain that often becomes a full-fledged burden, lending a good deal to the high-spirited lyricism of the song.

Next in line of popularity is "Lord Bateman." Here again we have a simple story rather well preserved in tradition. So consistent is it, in fact, that we must suppose it to have been frequently fortified or refreshed by nineteenth-century broadside printings. What we most often find is the following sequence of incidents: Bateman is seized with a desire to travel to foreign parts; he sails to Turkey, is captured, and put in prison; the jailer's beautiful daughter is interested and liberates him, with a conditional exchange of promises; after a long lapse of time she decides to go in search; arriving at Bateman's palace-gate, she learns from the porter that her love has that day taken a wife; she sends in identifying requests; Bateman impulsively abjures the new alliance and rushes to greet his Turkish flame; the bride is dismissed with a consolation prize, over the protests, frequently, of her indignant mother; and Bateman and his love are united forthwith. The ballad has a strong and consistent (and beautiful) melodic tradition, and habitually no refrain.

Similar generalizations may be made of the last ballad to be mentioned in this list of top favorites: the song called by Child "James Harris, or The Daemon Lover," but generally known today as "The House Carpenter." It is especially popular in America, and in fact has seldom been found of late in the British Isles. Again it is to be suspected that print has contributed to its excellent state of preservation. Almost always present are the opening greetings, with a recapitulation of intervening matters (his loyalty in the face of powerful counter-attractions, her marriage to another man); then his enticements to persuade her to forsake her husband and children; her farewells to the latter; her sudden change of heart after putting to sea; his request for an explanation; her longing for her abandoned babes; the sinking of the ship. In the fuller versions, there is often a moral tag at the end, taken over from the broadside tradition. Like "Bateman," the ballad lacks a refrain but has a strong and fine melodic tradition.

Casting a backward glance, we may ask if there are any obvious features that might help to explain why these particular songs have clung to memory. In the first place, all are motivated by passionate love, though the emotion itself is not the focus of interest. Neither the joys nor the pains of love are of primary concern, but the practical consequences. Love, in fact, is in these songs an illness from which no one recovers. Two of the heroines are, to be sure, left alive after the seizure, but have been carried away by it into what is for them another world. It has no respect for codes of decent behavior; it literally paralyzes moral conventions. The carpenter's wife can bid a tender farewell to her little babes and can bitterly lament her desertion of them, but she could have taken no other course. The gypsy's lady-love is, in the most literal sense, simply spellbound: her former lord, her children, her familiar way of life mean nothing to her any longer. Barbara's lover has no alternative, either; his sickness is fatal, as even she can see: "Young man, I think you're dying." But the disease is infectious; and, after her reckless exposure, *her* death is equally inevitable. We might say, then, that although the so-called supernatural has disappeared from these old pieces, the natural has acquired supernatural potency. We must believe that this is a significant factor in their longevity.

In the second place, these stories are very easily remembered: indeed, with the possible exception of "Lady Isabel," they are nearly impossible to forget. Character, in large part, is reduced to character-in-action, and action, generally speaking, to action-in-crisis. The narrative stream is single; and only in "Lord Thomas" and "The Gypsy Laddie" are more than two persons vitally involved. If the favorite moment of the ballad is, as Gummere taught, the "moment of last suspense," these ballads can hardly be considered characteristic. The rule applies, strictly speaking, only to "Barbara Allan" and to "Lord Randal"; and only in the latter is there evident any wish to prolong that moment by devices of delay or elaboration of its essential statement in dialogue or action. Considerable use is made of the conventions of phrasal repetition as an aid to memory; and the two ballads just mentioned employ in striking degree other formulae as well. In the one case, the chime of the double rhyme on the proper name is like a continuous peal of bells; and in the other, the repetitive interlocking of alternative forms of address—"Lord Randal my son" and "My handsome young man" —together with his reiterated and insistent reply, have established the stanzaic pattern of the Randal ballad with unforgettable uniformity in whatever language it has been found. Only the first half of the first and third lines is new in every stanza; the rest is all repetition. After the series of relatives commences, only the brief and commonplace bequests need be recalled—or invented; the rest runs of its own accord. The task of holding the song in mind could not possibly be made lighter. The structural artifice of this ballad is the most spectacular mnemonic invention in all balladry. "The Maid freed from the Gallows" is perhaps hardly more taxing to the memory; but, with its recurring blocks of identical stanzas, it produces nothing like the same sense of progressive change. ("The Maid," incidentally, comes thirteenth on the list of popular favorites.) A looser and possibly more lyrical form of repetition is exemplified by the syllabic nonsense of the refrain or burden-lines of "Gypsy Davy," which brighten the tone and add gaiety while they relax the strain on recollection. Such are some, at least, of the most obvious and external reasons for the enduring popularity of the ballads in question.

But the ballads are *songs*, not merely spoken narratives; and it remains to inquire very briefly whether the tunes can throw any further light on the question at issue. I shall forgo the temptation to luxuriate in appreciation of the appeal of individual tunes or families of tunes and will confine myself to the statistical analysis of their commonest attributes. My observations are based on an examination of approximately nine hundred variants or, as Dr. Wiora more accurately would denominate them, *Anzeichnungen*, like and unlike, associated with the verbal texts of these seven ballads. I have not proceeded along the lines of an initial subjective grouping or categorizing, but have at the outset approached them as an undifferentiated mass. Of these records, it may be interesting to note, only about seventy were collected before 1900; but these are all I have been able to discover by the most diligent search during twenty years. Approximately one-third of the total number were recorded in Britain; the other two-thirds in America.

I have been led to differentiate between the range of tunes, on the rough distinction of authentic, plagal, and mixed, because of demonstrable differences in the melodic habits of these groups that to me are significant. The authentic tunes outnumber the other two groups combined, in a ratio of about five to four. The plagals outnumber the mixed tunes by about three to one. The over-all proportions are, then, 5:3:1. Roughly three-quarters of each of these classes are four-phrase tunes. The incidence of external refrains is therefore obviously low. More striking is the fact that, according to my count, 536 of the total number of tunes are of the "progressive," or non-recurrent, phrasal type, ABCD. Of these four-phrase tunes, almost all, as would be expected, have their finals on the tonic. The melodic modes are predominantly some form of major. To be more specific, more than half of the authentic tunes are Ionian, Mixolydian, or Ionian/Mixolydian hexatonics. More than half of the mixed tunes are either pentatonic (lacking 4th and 7th), Mixolydian/Dorian hexatonic, or Dorian. More than seventy-five percent of the plagal tunes are pentatonic (lacking 4th and 7th), or Ionian, or Ionian/Mixolydian hexatonics.

Analyzed by meter, nearly half of the authentic tunes show some variety of triple time, most frequently 6/8. More than half of the mixed tunes are in some form of duple time, mainly 4/4. Three-quarters of the plagal tunes are in some form of triple time, most frequently 3/2, 3/4, or 6/8.

It seemed interesting to draw up for each of the three groups a chart of the frequencies with which the accented notes of the first two phrases fell on the various degrees of the scale. The result would constitute an over-all skeletal image, as far as to the mid-cadence, of this large class of ABCD tunes. If we follow the points of highest numerical frequency through the successive stresses of the phrases pictured, we can observe the favorite notes from which and to which the melody swings in its course. Thus, the authentic tunes show, for the first phrase: v (or III), VIII (or v), v (or III), and a cadence on I; and, for the second phrase: v, VIII, v, and v for the mid-cadence—the last two accents being often a held note. Similarly, the mixed tunes show, first, v, VII, v, and I; and, second, v, VII, v, v. And the plagal tunes, finally, show: first, I, III (or I), I (or II), and lower v (or I); and, second, I (or III), v, III, and v (or II). This, it is well to observe, is not the picture of any particular tune, nor even of an archetypical tune, though all the tunes under analysis are of course latent in the chart as a whole.

In spite of all the bewildering individual variety, therefore, we can discern in the scene as a whole some well-marked favorite paths: a greater liking for tunes in the authentic range, for tunes in the major, with four non-repeating phrases and (more often than not) with a triple beat. They end on the tonic, are likely to have a mid-cadence on v, and a first-phrase on I. These facts, based on so large a number of melodies, would have considerable weight in themselves. But besides, we must not forget that they have behind them the force, incalculable but overwhelming, of countless unconscious rejections in their favor of other appeals and possibilities. What makes them extraordinarily interesting, it seems to me, is that we are not here following an arbitrarily chosen and sifted group of kindred or similar tunes, but the *most common* preferences of the *most common* melodic type of the ballads *most commonly* sung throughout the British-American ballad-singing tradition, so far as it has been preserved in accessible records. And this, I cannot but think, has implications aesthetic, musicological, psychological, national, and therefore, ultimately and inevitably, international.

1956

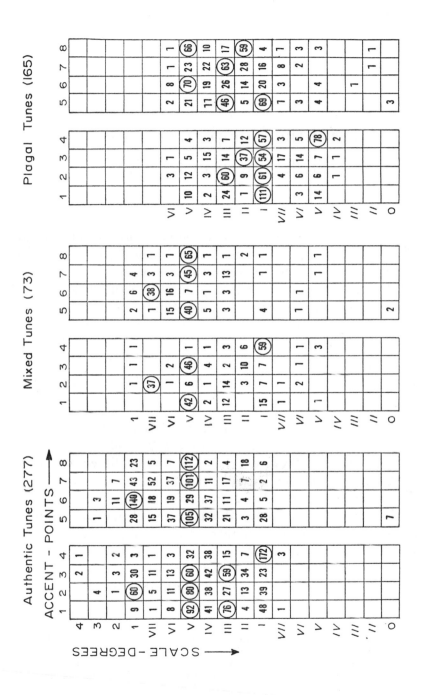

Toward the Comparative Analysis of
British-American Folk-Tunes

THE comparative study of folk-song necessarily involves quantitative as well as qualitative data. Where dependable answers can be reached only by subjecting a large number of items to detailed statistical analysis, machinery makes practicable a variety of frequency tabulations and studies of manifold correlations, and thus invites questions hitherto at once too large and too minute. It hardly needs saying, however, that such procedures are employed to best advantage where the records are both abundant and of comparable homogeneity. The following queries may point to representative uses.

Historical Questions. Are there, in particular eras, predominant phrasal schemes, and if so, what are they? Similarly with refrain schemes? Rhythms and metres? Are there different habits and preferences in melodic range and mode at different periods of history, and what is their relative strength?

Geographical Questions. What are the characteristic differentiae of specific regions? Are there rhythmical preferences? Modal preferences? And to what degree of intensity? Are there other stylistic idiosyncrasies as between localities, subject to objective tests? (National or ethnological implications herein can be developed at will.)

This paper was read at Freiburg, Germany, 23 July 1956, at the Deutsches Volksliedarchiv, to a commission on the comparative study of folk music, under the direction of Walter Wiora and Erich Seemann, in connection with the Ninth Annual Conference of the International Folk Music Council.

Typological Questions.   What are the prevailing melodic forms within a given area of study? Do tunes in a particular mode tend to conform in other respects as well? For example, are there correlations of rhythm and melodic mode? Of phrasal cadences and mode? Are there favorite correspondences between the cadence-notes of different phrases? Between the initial upbeats and other parts of a tune or group of tunes? Are certain phrases of a given body of tunes habitually less stable than others? Are certain accent points of a phrase firmer than others? What are the stigmata that most essentially identify a melodic type?

Obviously, many interconnections are latent among the questions suggested above. The method of recording factual data of various kinds about each tune, by means of code punches on a separate card, provides an extremely flexible means of sorting and re-sorting in a great variety of ways the elements and combinations of elements chosen for investigation, and of tabulating the results with a minimum of effort, a minimum of error, and with maximum speed. Flexibility, accuracy, and speed are the features of this method that especially recommend it.

The summary outline above will have suggested the scope and implications of the method that I shall now attempt to describe as briefly as possible. To advocate the use of machinery in fields of aesthetics is initially and often rightly suspect, since mechanical analysis is notoriously open to abuse. But I am so confident of the potential advantages of this procedure that I shall brave the attendant risks.

The restricted area within which I have worked must be specifically noted because it has largely conditioned the course and direction of my research, posing the particular problems, providing the musical data, and prompting the devising of means to control the material in hand. My special task, undertaken now many years ago, has been to amass and examine comparatively the extant tunes of the Francis James Child canon of British-American popular ballads. Historically considered, the evidence is scanty, and quantitative techniques are not needed to cope with the earlier reaches of the subject. The great bulk of what remains lies on this side of the year 1900; and that fact has led me naturally to focus on questions of typology, and to consider especially the broad variational habits and tendencies of a fairly homogeneous and contemporaneous mass of evidence.

The method which, by a gradual process of experiment, I came to employ has already been described in general terms in the pages of the *Journal of American Folklore*, LXII (1949), 81–86, with a cut showing the layout of the standard and specially adapted IBM cards used for the purpose (Fig. 1). Basically, one of these

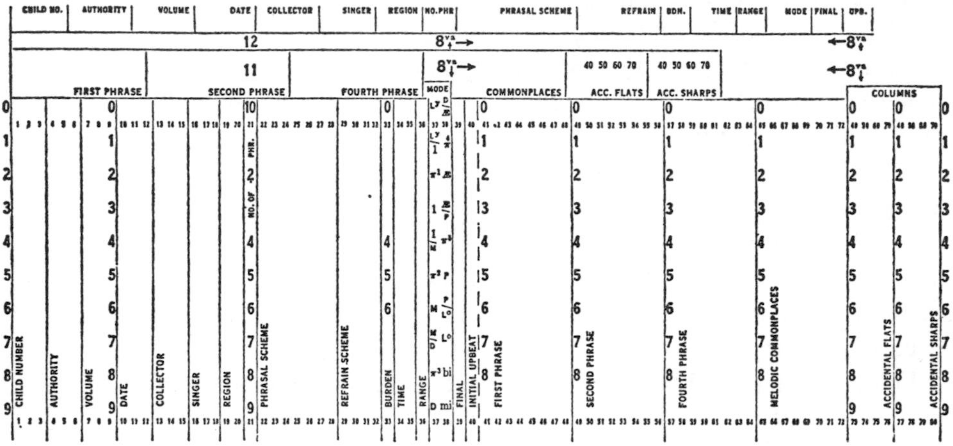

Figure 1

punched cards is equivalent to a sortable linotype slug. "Sortable" is the significant word. When one has assembled a stack of cards, each containing on the same column or columns the desired factual information about one—and only one—specific tune or tune-variant, various ways of sorting for comparative purposes begin at once to suggest themselves.

It was natural to sort my own collection first in the order of the Child canon and, within that numerical order, in such a sequence as had been suggested by the tunes themselves. This was, in fact, the order already imposed on my tune files without benefit of machinery. The data recorded on IBM cards, when transferred to paper as a tabulated list, one line to a tune, fills some sixty 11 × 15 sheets. Two segments of this list are shown on Table I.[1] Since the

[1] Explanation and Tables I through XIV appear on pp. 181–201.

list reflects a conscious, though partial, attempt to bring together melodic variants intrinsically most akin, it should reveal characteristic similarities at a glance. But it seems on examination surprisingly reluctant to do so. Different phrasal schemes, metres, modes, and ranges jostle one another cheek by jowl. It is hard to see any pattern or order in the way the accented notes line up under one another—or, at any rate, an impulse to order seems broken quite as often as it is kept. But, of course, the chance of discontinuity was implicit in the ordering principle. For if the tunes found with the same Child ballad number were unrelated, they would still be ranked next to one another by the numerical control that assembled them in series.

Since mere numerical sequence has thus overridden musical considerations, it must for our needs be supplanted by some scheme that gives superior command to those elements of a tune that essentialize melodic identity. An obvious method promptly suggests itself: let the series of stressed notes, in the order in which they occur, phrase by phrase, be adopted as the relating principle, and follow the line of successive identities as far as it holds. Unluckily, it seldom holds long, and a second control must be found to supplement when it ceases to operate. This further control will probably be a more arbitrary one, as, for instance, starting with the lowest opening notes and gradually ascending the scale. The procedure, then, will present over all a systematic order from low to high, and will show, here and there, clusters of identities where a favorite opening is revealed. Such a method is exhibited in the (A) segment on Table II. This system, in fact, will bring together and instantaneously display the strength of a melodic formula that occurs at the beginning of a tune, as for example the opening on III I III I. The incidence of this formula is common enough to be mentioned by Cecil Sharp as one of the characteristic English melodic figures. (Has it occurred to anyone to wonder why its inverted form, I III I III, or comparably III V III V—both equally natural openings where an upward thrust in the tune is to be expected—are relatively unused?)

As a means of identifying and isolating melodic-rhythmical formulae, this way of sorting offers obvious conveniences. As just described, it gives readiest access to first-phrase formulae. For tracing patterns coming later in the tune, a re-sorting is required, but this presents no difficulties. For, if all the stressed notes of a tune are on the card, any designated segment of it may be made the primary control of the 'sort.' For example, testing in this fashion the strength of the common second-phrase formula, v viii v, one finds upwards of 250 tunes that contain it. The first two phrases of the most familiar form of "The Bailiff's Daughter of Islington" illustrate both of these melodic commonplaces in succession.

In a listing setting forth the simple series of accented notes in a succession of correspondences between tunes, it is striking how soon the lines diverge and how seldom, indeed, there occurs a perfect identity for as long even as four accents running consecutively. All who have worked with the problems of variation in a related body of materials will readily acknowledge that the question of relatedness involves far more than a mere note-for-note or accent-by-accent correspondence. One very soon comes to realize that this is a problem of the utmost subtlety, in which potentially are included all or most of the elements constituting melodic identity; range, melodic and rhythmic mode, number of phrases, patterns of phrasal combinations, refrain schemes, cadence points, and so on to minuter particulars. It therefore becomes desirable to establish, at least tentatively, the relative weight to be allotted to some of these elements. It may well be that herein, with due discrimination, we shall ultimately find the basis of just distinctions between "families" and more inclusive patterns, or "types," of melody.

One way of determining such relative importance is by subjecting a whole mass of undifferentiated materials to synoptic tests, in order to discover the points of most general agreement. In my own investigations—always remembering that I have worked mainly with contemporaneous and relatively homogeneous traditions—I have tended more and more to discount number and scheme of phrases, and metre, and refrain elements as significant factors; but to give added weight to range (broadly distinguished as authentic, plagal, and mixed), and to melodic mode, and to rhythmically determined contour, with special emphasis on phrasal cadence points. In a synoptic view, it was very noticeable that the mass of tunes with which I was concerned exhibited a continually changing strength of agreement at successive points of accent. To chart and count the frequencies of agreement would be to construct a table of relative stabilities existing in the mass. It further became evident that tables separately drawn for the three ranges showed obvious differences. It was thus surprising to discover that, whereas the cadence of the second phrase, usually the mid-cadence, was—except for the final—the most stable point of authentic tunes, it occupied only the sixth place in the comparative stability of plagal tunes, being surpassed by the first, fourth, fifth, second, and third accent points, in the order named. The two ranges, in fact, agreed only once, in that the fourth accent, or first-phrase cadence point, came second in stability for both. The tunes of mixed range proved to correspond in the first two places with the authentic tunes, with the plagal in the third and fourth, with neither in the fifth and sixth, and with the authentic, again, in the seventh and eighth.

If we take these numerical frequencies as indicating common habits or tendencies among the whole mass of undiscriminated British-American melodic material, we may infer that main lines of melodic correspondence would incline to reflect at least partially the emphases of relative stability. By this means we should be provided with a new set of controls in our search for underlying similarities. We should have to keep separate our ranges, since these do not act alike. Next, since modal distinctions are so influential in characterizing a tune, we should probably choose to classify by mode within each range. And then we could set up, as guides in a new sorting, the series of accent points in the order of stability predetermined by our count. We should thus find ourselves taking first the mid-cadence of authentic tunes, sorting all these systematically, say from low to high, or by a less arbitrary sequence if that seemed preferable. Next, we would sort on the first cadence, by the same scheme; and so forth, in the order decided upon. (Cf. Table IIB.) The proof of the effectiveness of our method would become visible if, when we referred to the tunes of which these abstracts are the skeletal outlines, we should find that significantly similar tunes had thereby been brought into a series.

Different systems of control offer different advantages: one system may reveal what another will conceal. It is impossible to achieve every purpose by a single *coup de maître*. If we compare segments of the two kinds of sorting already described, we shall find that they exemplify rival and opposing merits. The earlier and simpler, for instance, will disregard the importance of the second cadence, because few tunes run parallel as far as their eighth accent. On the other hand, the second method will ignore the formulae so sharply focused by the first. Again, the first scheme, not respecting melodic mode, will leap the barriers of major and minor scales, to reveal the kinship of variants arbitrarily separated by the other scheme. But the latter may disclose a series of subtler connections ignored or obscured by the first.

Other factors, obviously, may be brought in at will as controls, up to the limits of what may be registered on the cards; and correlations of all kinds—of length, of date, or region, of mode, of metre, of phrasal scheme—can be carried out with a minimum of trouble. Illustrations of the two kinds of sorting suggested above may be studied in Tables III and IV, which exhibit the series of tunes (omitting duplicates) assembled and listed, identified and analyzed, in parts (A) and (B) of Table II.

In a search for broad analytical characterizations of the melodic tendencies of the whole mass of British-American ballad tunes, it seemed worthwhile to make a number of frequency counts to determine the favored degrees of the scale at each accent point, as far as to the mid-cadence of four-phrase tunes. In this inquiry, for the sake of comparative exactness, I limited myself to tunes having the same relative length of phrase—i.e., the same number of accents per phrase. These I divided into the classes of authentic, mixed, and plagal; and then subdivided into modal groups, isolating each modal pattern, heptatonic, hexatonic, or pentatonic, of each variety, in a group by itself. The frequency counts displayed some interesting contrasts between groups, as a glance at the charts in Tables V, VI, VII, and VIII will prove. It is very noticeable that the authentic classes appear more consistent than either the mixed or the plagal, and that, of the authentic groups, the second phrase is steadier than the first. Moreover, the authentic tunes incline to use a wider span in the single phrase than do the mixed or plagal tunes. Thus, the latter two kinds tend to cluster more thickly within limits of a third or a second than a fifth; and the mixed tunes go less often to the octave than to the seventh, in the second phrase.

These charts, surely, are interesting and revealing of habitual preferences. But they may also mislead. They should not be read as the typical paths of the actual modal melodies studied, for, in the majority of cases, the sum of frequencies at any one accent point falling above and below the most favored single degree (circled in the charts) is greater than the number falling *upon* that degree. From this fact it must follow that any single tune has a greater likelihood of choosing some other note for its next accent than of conforming to the majority. But that is conspicuously not true of the pentatonic tunes lacking III and VII in the authentic range, nor of the Mixolydian/Dorian tunes in the mixed range.

To attain a clearer idea of the inner dynamics of these melodies, we must inquire into what actually happens to those particular, favored accent notes when they pass to the next accented position. For example, how many tunes, we may ask, having their first accent on the fifth degree will remain there at the second accent; and how many will rise from that point, how high, and how many fall, how low? Another set of charts will make it easier to see what is involved.

We can take the commonest cluster points at each accent, tabulate the movement thence by correlating with the next accent, and thereby calculate the upward and downward thrust of these tunes at each particular stage of their progress to the mid-cadence; or estimate the force of inertia—in other words, the stability—when they repeat the same note. These impulses can be represented in simple graphs like those of Tables IX and X, where the figures within the left-hand loops are the numbers of cases that fall at the next accent on the successive degrees below the starting point; those within the right-hand loops, the numbers of cases that ascend; and the figures unenclosed, the numbers that remain stationary. A series of such charts would prove how variable are these inner dynamics at different points and from different degrees of the scale. [*Note.* The impulse from one point to the next might be expressed mathematically in the formula

$$M = \frac{n: (x-y)}{N}$$

wherein: M stands for Motion; N stands for the total number of cases on a particular degree of the scale; n for the number remaining stationary; x for the sum—a + b + c . . .—of the number moving to degrees above the starting point; and y for the sum—r + s + t . . .—of the number moving to degrees below.]

Another, more complex but also livelier, way of exhibiting these forces, the thrusts and counter-thrusts of the tunes in their mass effects, is displayed in the composite Tables XI to XIV, where motion up and down is shown by the arrows that scatter from a center on successive accents to various degrees at each subsequent accent as far as the mid-cadence.

To sum up: in the most general view, the scene which we have been surveying appears to exhibit the following large outlines. In the first phrase, authentic tunes of the Ly/I, first pentatonic, I, I/M, M, D, D/Æ, fourth pentatonic, Æ, and Æ/P modes agree with Æ tunes of the mixed range and fourth pentatonic tunes of the plagal range, in a liking for the i to v pentachord. D/Æ mixed, and M/D plagal, tunes use the octave from lower to upper v in the first phrase. First pentatonic plagals, and mixed tunes of the Ly/I, first pentatonic, I, I/M, and M systems are inclined to limit themselves in the first phrase to the trichord i-iii, or often, lower vii to iii. In the second phrase, authentic tunes of nearly all modes, and mixed I, I/M, and second pentatonic tunes show a strong preference for the span iv or v to viii; while the pentachord i to v is again favored by mixed tunes of the D/Æ, fourth pentatonic, and Æ modes, and plagal tunes of the I/M, second pentatonic, M, third pentatonic, D/Æ, and Æ modes. Such are the most prominent comparative likenesses revealed by the evidence at my disposal.

But the focus of this brief statement is not so much on any conclusions that may have been reached with regard to the specific material of my study as upon the possibilities of this method in the further comparative investigation of folk-tunes by other students of the subject. It is, I believe, only by means of a great many careful studies of particular areas of folk-music that we shall be enabled to give sure answers to such questions as were suggested at the opening of this paper, and thereafter to achieve a connected picture and, like dependable cartographers, to fill in the outlines of this *terra paene incognita.*

1956

EXPLANATION

The explanatory notes to Table I will serve equally well for Table II. It should be observed that there has been a shift of order among the elements tabulated. In the upper list (A), it will be seen that all the tunes, in spite of variety in upbeats, have the same pattern of accented notes in the opening phrase. In the lower list (B), all have the same range (authentic); all have the same mode (3 is for Ionian); all have the same note at the mid-cadence (V); at the first cadence point (I); and at the first accented note (I). Thereafter, they differ in varying degrees from one another, showing most similarity at the next-to-last accented note of the second phrase. List (A) corresponds to the tunes on Table III. List (B) corresponds to Table IV.

Child no.: the numerical sequence of the ballads in Child's canon of *The English and Scottish Popular Ballads.*

Authority: the initials of the nominal editor of a collection, or an arbitrary designation. Joint editorship is indicated by single initials with a gap between. E.g., cjs: Cecil James Sharp; c.g: Gardner and Chickering; PB: Phillips Barry; bes: Barry, Eckstorm, and Smyth; alc: Library of Congress Archive of Folk Music.

Medium: nature of the record, as: v: live recording (voice); s: manuscript; assume printed record unless otherwise stated.

Date: since no records antedate A.D. 1000, three digits suffice to indicate the century, decade, and year. A blank indicates ignorance of the exact date.

Collector: the first three letters of the collector's family name.

Singer: the first three letters of the singer's family name.

Region: expressed in an arbitrary system of geographical symbols: 1 is England; 2 is Scotland; 3 is Ireland; 20 is Canada; 21–29 are the census area divisions of the U.S.A. (e.g., 21 is New England; 22 is Middle Atlantic States, 23 is East North Central States, etc.)

No. of phr.: number of phrases in the tune, up to nine, continued by an alphabetical series, e.g., A is 10, B is 11, etc.

Phrasal schemes: not followed after 8. The first, a, is always assumed.

Refrain scheme: the lines of the stanza at which refrain elements occur.

Burden: separable choral or refrain element with independent or stanzaic melodic vehicle.

Time: predominant metre, as: 44 is common time, etc. x4 is an uncertain number of units to the bar, taking a quarter note as the unit. 12/8 is registered as 6/8 in fact; but above nine the parts may be given alphabetical symbols, and then 12/8 would be C8.

Range: registered in three symbols, A for authentic, M for mixed, P for plagal.

Mode: to each of the typical scales, heptatonic, hexatonic, and pentatonic, is assigned a number on one or the other of two columns. Thus, 5 in the left-hand column is the pentatonic lacking its third and seventh; 3 in the same column is the Ionian or major scale; 9 in the same column is for the Dorian; 2 in the right-hand column is the Æolian; o in the same is D/Æ hexatonic.

Final: degrees of the scale are numbered upward from tonic, i.e., 1 to 7. The upper octave uses letters from the front of the alphabet, A,B,C. . . . The lower octave, counting upward, uses the letters J to P, for lower tonic to lower VII. Accidentals are cued in at the end of the card. The system automatically transposes all keys to a single tonic, and, as indicated, allows the coding of three octaves.

First (second, fourth) Phrase: the accented notes of the phrase, essential for comparison. The fourth phrase is not registered unless it carries the mid-cadence of a "two-strain" tune. Notes sustained through two accents at the cadence are set down twice.

Table I

Child Ballad-Tunes, Sorted Numerically, with Selected Data. (Extract)

Child No.	Authority	Medium	Volume	Date	Collector	Singer	Region	No. of Phrases	Phrasal Scheme	Refrain Scheme	Burden	Time	Range	Mode	Final	Upbeat	First Phrase	Second Phrase	Fourth Phrase
93	C G			939	CHI	RIL	23	4	BCD		0	44	A	5	1	1	144W4	A455	
93	JFD		1	932	KAR		20	2	B		0	34	A	3	1	1	55BA	5651	
93	JFD		1	932	KAR		20	2	B		0	34	A	8	1	7	B552	5331	
93	VR		1	946	RAN	CAR	27	4	BAC		0	34	A	3	A	5	5365	4263	
93	PB	V		93	BAR	HAR	21	4	BCD		0	34	A	3	3	1	1521	2255	
93	WC		1	876	CHR		2	4	BCB		0	34	A	9	1	P	111A	5211	
93	CJS	S		909	SHA	EMM	1	4	BAB		0	34	P	9	1	N	1635	3P31	
93	JFS		2	905	WIL	CHI	1	2	B		0	34	P	0	1	1	3135	3131	
93	ABS	S		62	BLA		2	4	BCD		0	34	M	2	1	1	3254	5P31	
93	JFS		1	902	BRO	WHI	1	4	ABC		0	44	A	3	1	1	23554311	22454311	
93	JFS		1	902	BRO	WHI	1	4	ABC		0	44	A	3	1	2	23544311	22454411	
94	RAS		2	820	SMI		2	8	BABCDAB		0	44	A	0	A	C	A54A	ACAA	ACAA
95	B W			916	WYM		26	A	BCDABAB		0	24	P	4	1	3	330N	5555	3411
95	ESB			929	HER	MAC	21	4	BCD		0	68	A	6	1	5	3AACA5	7655544	
283	ESB			929	BAR	YOU	21	6	ABCDE	56	0	24	A	9	1	5	5315	5315	
283	N F			937	FLA	EDW	21	5	BBCD	5	0	24	M	2	1	N	1313	1355	
283	JFS		2	906	WIL	AND	1	8	ABCDEDF	5678	0	24	A	2	1	5	3115	3115	A545
283	CJS	S		910	SHA	HUG	1	6	BCDEF	56	0	34	P	3	1	N	11MN	10P1	
283	JFS		2	906	WIL		1	4	BCD		0	68	A	6	1	5	1541	4475	
283	CS			927	SAN	FOR	23	5	BCDE	5	0	68	P	0	1	N	134P	1314	
283	JFS		2	906	WIL	WHI	1	4	BCD		0	68	A	2	1	3	5521	4721	
284	TR			609	RAV		1	5	BCDB	5	0	34	A	3	1	5	66A5	4211	
284	WC		1	855	PLA	686	1	6	BCDBB	56	0	68	A	3	1	5	66A5	4211	
284	WC		1	855	RIT	783	1	4	BCD		0	44	A	3	A	5	566A	1441	
285	ALC	V		941	LOM	GRO	21	4	BAC	24	0	44	P	6	1	6	542N	5452	
285	SBG	S		88	GOU		1	4	BCD	24	0	44	A	2	1	4	A555	4121	
285	CJS		4	908	SHA	LAV	1	4	BCD	24	0	68	P	0	1	N	1311	5415	
285	JAF		18	905	BAR	MAY	11	4	BCD	24	0	44	P	9	1	P	32P2NN	N51355	
285	CJS	S		916	SHA	WHE	22	4	BCD	24	0	68	P	0	1	1	N32N	N515	
285	WBW			927	WHA		1	4	BCD	24	0	68	P	0	1	N	N32N	N515	
285	ALC	V		93	ROB	GRA	29	4	BCD	24	0	44	P	0	1	1	N13P	N514W1	
285	B F			931	FLA	DEL	21	4	BCD	24	0	44	P	6	1	N	N12N	5212	

Table II

(A) Child Ballad-Tunes, Sorted by First- and Second-Phrase Accents, in Order of Actual Occurrence. (Extract)

Child No.	Authority	Medium	Volume	Collector	Date	Singer	No. of Phrases	Phrasal Scheme	Upbeat	First Phrase	Second Phrase	Final	Range	Mode	Time	Burden	Refrain Scheme	Region
79	AKD			FAU	9 29	SPR	4	ABCD	P	1551	1A61	1	<A2	π9	34	0		25
43	JFS		4	WIL	9 10	POW	4	BCD	N	1551	5A5	1	<A7	P1	24	0		1
200	CJS		1	SHA	9 32	HEN	5	BACC		1551	1545	1	<A2	π7	66	0		21
200	JAF	18		BAR	9 05	FLI	4	BCD		1551	1545	1	<A2	A3	24	0		24
76	VR		1	RAN	9 46	ONE	4	BCD	N	1551	1552	1	<M7		44	0		25
243	CJS		1	SHA	9 32	SHE	4	BCD		1551	5555	1	<A3		44	0		21
53	PBS						BS		1551	1585	1	<A3		44	0		23
200	MOE			EDD	9 39	HOB	BCDABCD		0	1551	1665	1	<A3		24	0		24
200	CS			TOL	9 27	SCH	4	BCD		1551	1665	1	<A3		44	0		24
76	VR		1	RAN	9 46	MCC	4	BCD		1551	3144	1	<A3	P4	24	0		25
155	CJS		1	SHA	18	OO	4	AC	0	1551	3555	1	3		44	0		1
200	SBGS			BUS	8 88	PAR	8	BCDABCD		1551	3575	1	M2	9	68	0		1
200	SBGS			BUS	8 88	PAR	8	BCDABCD		1551	3575	1						
237	GG			GRE	9 25	JOH	4	BCD		1551	3PP		P4	0	44	0		1
250	SBGS			BRO	8 94	BUR	4	BCD		1551	4555	1	<A6		34	0		1
4	CJS		1	SHA	9 32	MOO	5	BCDD	N	1551	4655	1	<A6	M3	32	0	5	25

(B) Child Ballad-Tunes, Sorted by Range, Melodic Mode, First- and Second-Phrase Accents in Order of Relative Stability. (Extract)

Child No.	Authority	Medium	Volume	Collector	Date	Singer	No. of Phrases	Phrasal Scheme	Upbeat	First Phrase	Second Phrase	Final	Range	Mode	Time	Burden	Refrain Scheme	Region
269	CJS		1	SHA	9 32	MEL	8	CDEBCD	1	153	16A55	1	A3		22	4		26
93	PBV			BAR	9 3	HAR	4	BCD	1	1521	12255	3	A3		34	0		21
293	DS			SCA	9 37	GIB	8	BCDEFCD	4	1531	16655	A	A3		74	0		25
75	PBS			BAR	9 07	WAL	4	BCA	1	121	5255	1	A3		68	0		21
4	JFS			BRO	9 10	FLE	4	BCD	1	1541	16255	1	A3		44	0		1
4	CJS			SHA	9 08	JAR	4	BCD	1	1541	16B55	1	A3		68	0		24
243	VR		1	RAN	9 46	ING	4	BCD	1	1531	15A55	1	A3		24	0		24
85	JAF	32		RIC	9 19	FOG	4	BCD	5	1141	13A55	1	A3		34	0		25
43	JAF	64		HUB	9 51	HUB	4	BCD	1	1521	1755	1	A3		44	0	5	20
100	MO			MAN	9 33	WAL	5	BCDD	1	1531	A755	1	A3		24	4		23
200	MOE			EDD	9 39	HOB	BCDABCD		0	1551	1665							

Table III

Sorted on Accents 1, 2, 3, 4 (on I V V I)

"The Three Little Babes". Davis, 1929, p. 576. Virginia March, 1915   Child No. 79

"A Wager, a Wager". Vaughan Williams, JFSS, IV, 114 (5). Herefordshire, 1910   Child No. 43

"Edward". Sharp & Karpeles, 1932, 1, 47 (B). N. Carolina, 1916   Child No. 13

"Gypsy Davie". Barry, JAF, XVIII, 194 (E). Rhode Island, Apr. 7, 1904   Child No. 200

Child No. 76

"Oh, Who Will Shoe That Pretty Little Foot". Randolph, 1946, 1, 121(H). Missouri, 1941

Child No. 243

"The Daemon Lover". Sharp & Karpeles, 1932, 1, 248(D). N. Carolina. Aug. 29, 1916

Child No. 53

"Lord Bateman". Barry MS Bk. 1, No. 53 C, Harvard. Massachusetts, July 2, 1907

"Gypsy Davy". Eddy, 1939, p. 68 (B). Ohio, n. d.

Child No. 200

"Oh, Who Will Shoe," etc. Randolph, 1946, 1, 117(D). Missouri, April 19, '34   Child No. 76

"Sir Hugh". Sharp MSS 4749/3308, Clare Coll. N. Carolina, Oct. 3, 1918   Child No. 155

Child No. 200

"The Gipsy Countess". Baring-Gould MS No. 50 (1), Plymouth. Devon, Dec., 1888

Child No. 237

"The Duke of Gordon's Daughters". Greig & Keith, 1925, p. 189 (1a). Aberdeen, n.d.

"Henry Martin". Broadwood, JFSS, 1, 162. Sussex, 1893   Child No. 250

"Lady Isabel and the Elf Knight". Sharp & Karpeles, 1932, 1, 7 (C). Georgia, May 1, 1910

Child No. 4

Table IV

Sorted on A - Range Ionian Mode, Accents 8, 4, 1, 7 (on V I I V)

"The Mermaid". Sharp & Karpeles, 1932, 1, 291 (A). Kentucky, Oct. 2, 1917   Child No. 289

CHORUS

"Lamkin". Barry Dictaphone No. 91, tr. Bayard, Harvard MS, p. 24. Maine, n. d.   Child No. 93

"John over the Hazel Green". Scarborough, 1937, p. 415. Virginia, n. d.   Child No. 293

"Lord Lovell", Barry MS Bk. IV, No. 295, Harvard. Maine, Sept. 4, 1907   Child No. 75

"The Outlandish Knight". Broadwood, JFSS, IV, 119 (3). Devon, 1893   Child No. 4

"The Outlandish Knight". Sharp MS 1557. Somerset, Jan. 7, 1908   Child No. 4

"The House Carpenter". Randolph, 1946, 1, 176 (O). Missouri, Sept. 4, 1941   Child No. 243

"Johnnie Collins". A. D. Richardson, JAF, XXXII, 500. W. Virginia, 1918   Child No. 85

"The Broomfield Hill". L. A. Hubbard, JAF, LXIV, 42. Utah, learned ca. 1871 Child No. 43

Child No. 100

"Young Barbour". Greenleaf & Mansfield, 1933, p. 30 (B). Newfoundland, 1929

"Gypsy Davy". Eddy, 1939, p. 68 (B). Ohio, n. d.   Child No. 200

CHORUS

Table V

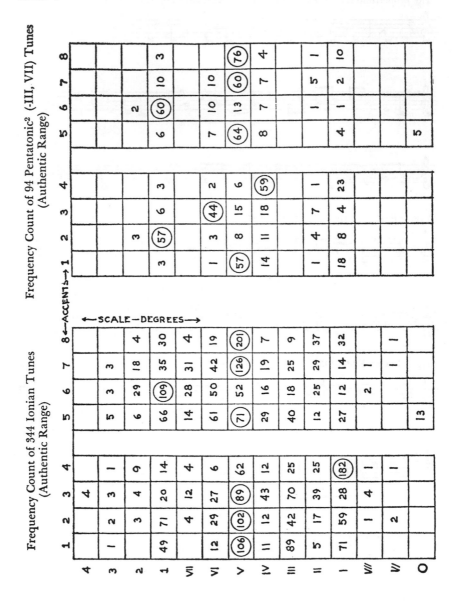

Table VI

Frequency Count of 63 Æolian Tunes (Authentic Range)

Accents	O	V	VI	VII	I	II	III	IV	V	VI	VII	1	2	3
1				1	12		(19)	3	16	4	2	6		
2					14	2	8	5	(21)	1	4	7		1
3					6	2	(21)	9	13		5	4	1	
4				2	(29)	4	3	5	14		2	3		1
5	6				5	8	7		(15)	6	4	12		
6	1				6	1	9	5	10	4	12	(14)		1
7	2				3	7	2	11	(17)	3	11	7		
8				1	11	6	4	4	(30)	1	6			

←SCALE DEGREES→   8←ACCENTS→1

Frequency Count of 45 Mixolydian Tunes (Mixed Range)

Accents	O	V	VI	VII	I	II	III	IV	V	VI	VII	1	2	3
1		3	2		(17)	2	9	2	9	1				
2					(19)	5	5	3	7	1	4	1		
3			2		(13)	8	6	4	5	2	4	1		
4		8	3	2	(14)	5	2	1	5	2	2	1		
5	6		2		4	2	2	5	(10)	3	6	5		
6	1		1		5	2	5	7	(10)	3	9	2		
7			2		6	2	1	10	(14)	4	3	3		
8	1		2		9	3	2	5	(19)	1	2	1		

Table VII

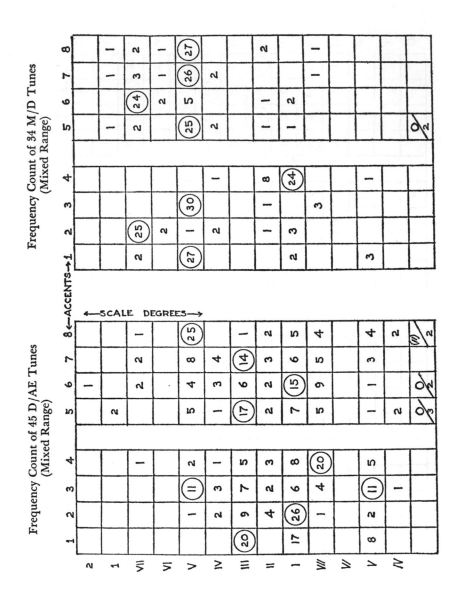

Table VIII

Frequency Count of 303 Ionian Tunes
(Plagal Range)

Scale-degrees	1	2	3	4	5	6	7	8
VII								
VI		1	3	1	4	10	11	4
V	16	19	25	31	41	47	36	45
IV	5	7	24	5	31	42	24	12
III	32	55	35	20	53	(54)	49	26
II	3	36	65	57	32	46	(86)	(106)
I	(197)	(112)	(92)	61	(104)	50	38	48
VII		18	24	5	5	21	27	3
VI	1	28	20	17	5	10	11	6
V	40	25	10	(113)	10	17	17	49
IV			2	1	1		1	2
III	6	1	2	1	4	1	2	1
II							1	1
O	3				13	4		

Frequency Count of III D/AE Tunes
(Plagal Range)

Scale-degrees	1	2	3	4	5	6	7	8
VII			2					
VI								
V	3	1	7	3	8	(39)	12	18
IV		6	6	8	2	14	17	(37)
III	36	33	(31)	5	(45)	27	(34)	5
II		10	7	4	5	6	15	14
I	(53)	(47)	27	27	27	5	15	29
VII	2	3	17	21	8	9	11	5
VI								
V	17	11	9	(30)	12	11	4	2
IV			5	11			2	
III								
II								
O	4							

←ACCENTS→ ; ←SCALE—DEGREES→

Table IX

Frequency Count of Most Favoured Degrees at Points of Regular Accent, outlining First Phrase. Combined Authentic Ly/I, Pentatonic[1] I/M, and Mixolydian Tunes (Total 578)

ACCENT 1 → ACCENT 2

	V/	V//	I	II	III	IV	V	VI	VII	1	2	3
1 (66)			1				13	13	2)	12	(7	18
V (147)			13	7	3	5)	45	(11	4	59		
IV (44)			13	3	3)	15	(9	1				
III (152)			38	13)	47	(4	42	5	1	2		
I (127)			12	(4	17	23	61	7	1	2		

ACCENT 2 → ACCENT 3

	V/	V//	I	II	III	IV	V	VI	VII	1	2	3
1 (83)					4	3	29	23	11)	10	(2	1
VI (41)				3	2	2	23)	5		(5	1	
V (183)			8	24	32	36)	34	(22	5	16	3	3
IV (49)		1	10	12	7)	5	(9	3	2			
III (75)			13	23)	14	(9	13	3				
I (80)	1)		3	(5	29	22	15		1	4		

ACCENT 3 → ACCENT 4

	V/	V//	I	II	III	IV	V	VI	VII	1	2	3
1 (61)			1		1	5	23	7	1)	5	(18	
VI (58)			5	2	9	11	24)	3		(3	1	
V (135)			59	12	20	7)	30	(1		6		
IV (80)		1	48	10	3)	7	(7	1	2	1		
III (97)		1	69	6)	10	(1	9	1				
II (71)		3	49)	5	(5		7	2				
I (39)			32	(1	5		1					

Table X

Frequency Count of Most Favoured Degrees at Points of Regular Accent, from First to Second Phrasal Cadence. Combined Plagal Ly/I, Pentatonic[1], I/M, and Pentatonic[2] Tunes (Total 414)

←ACCENT 4 / ACCENT 5→	*III*	*IV*	*V*	*VI*	*VII*	I	II	III	IV	V	VI	VII
V(31)						14		1	3	5	5	5
III(36)			1			15	4	6	1	5	1	1
II(49)				1		25	6	7	1	5	1	
I(100)			3	1		31	17	20	5	15	3	
VI(53)			9	3	2	26	6	4		1		
V(129)	1		7	1	1	54	2	30	3	24	1	

←ACCENT 5 / ACCENT 6→	*III*	*IV*	*V*	*VI*	*VII*	I	II	III	IV	V	VI	VII
V(59)						5	8	20	7	11	7	
III(76)			2	2	2	7	14	13	4	28	4	
II(35)			5	2		3	8	10		7		
I(167)	3		1	10	4	47	25	46	5	23	2	1

←ACCENT 6 / ACCENT 7→	*III*	*IV*	*V*	*VI*	*VII*	I	II	III	IV	V	VI	VII
V(84)						6	33	21	6	13	5	
III(101)				5		17	35	17	2	22	4	
II(66)			8	5		13	18	16	1	5		
I(76)			8	6	2	19	17	7	5	10	2	

←ACCENT 7 / ACCENT 8→	*III*	*IV*	*V*	*VI*	*VII*	I	II	III	IV	V	VI	VII
V(65)						2	6	5	1	49	2	
III(77)						21	17	22		17		
II(121)			3	3		14	93	1		6	1	
I(73)			8	6		39	4	12		3	1	
VI(25)			4	10		8	3					

Table XI

Motion-Chart, showing Relative Force of Impulses Up and Down from Successive Accents of 344 Ionian Tunes, Authentic Range (Partial Data). **Highest Frequencies at each Accent-Point Correlated with Following Stress**

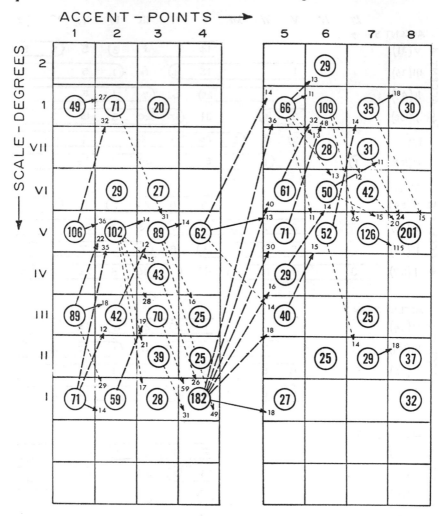

Table XII

Motion-Chart, showing Relative Force of Impulses Up and Down from Successive
Accents of 303 Ionian Tunes, Plagal Range (Partial Data). Highest Frequencies
at each Accent Correlated with Following Stress

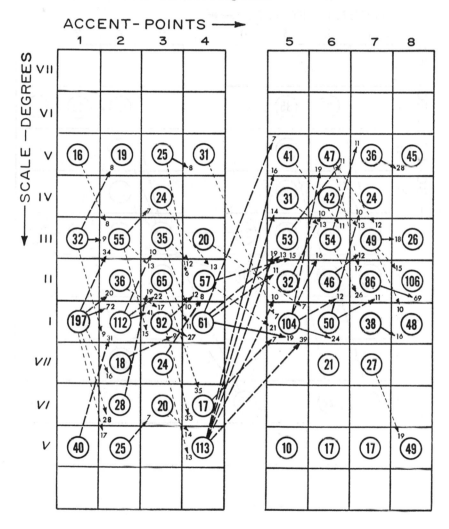

Table XIII

Motion-Charts, showing Relative Force of Impulses Up and Down from Successive Accents of 227 Pentatonic[2], M/D, Pentatonic[3] Tunes, Authentic Range (Partial Data). Highest Frequencies at each Accent Correlated with Following Stress

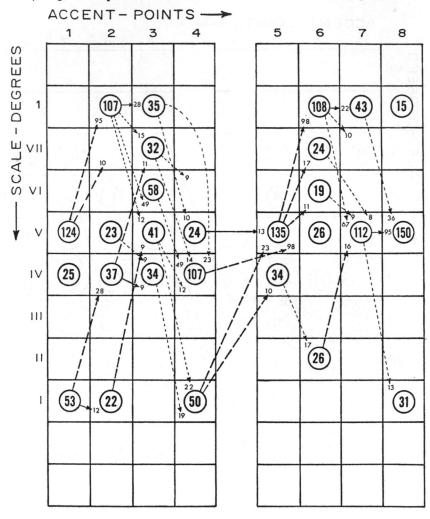

Table XIV

Motion-Chart, showing Relative Force of Impulses Up and Down from Successive Accents of 414 Ly/I, Pentatonic[1], I/M, Pentatonic[2] Tunes, Plagal Range (Partial Data). Highest Frequencies at each Accent Correlated with Following Stress

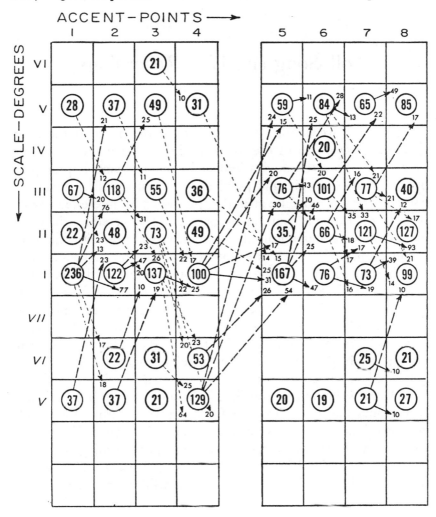

Folk-Song and Live Recordings

WHETHER we like it or not, we are in the midst of the most active eruption of the folk-song impulse that the world has ever seen. It is a thoroughly self-conscious movement, prompted by religious, economic, and political ideas that are the matrices of contemporary democratic attitudes; promoted by interested parties who see their own account in its spread; and powered by the techniques of mass communication, the influences of publicity, and capital investment. Formerly a spontaneous diversion of people with little business, it has become the absorbing, determined concern of people with big business. The size of the commercial market, the vastness of the potential audience, is a most surprising new phenomenon which has opened attractive prospects of fame and fortune to many aspirants with the requisite talents. The concert platform, the nightclub, the stage, the cinema, television, radio, the phonograph, all offer tempting media for the exploitation of suitable knowledge, skill, and personality. Folk-song has probably always been vulnerable to employment for doctrinal or professional ends but these influences formerly were local and casual and relatively momentary. It remains to be proved whether anything like folk-song as it has existed in the past, an instinctive expression of the free artistic impulse in man, as natural as wildflowers, will survive its mass transplantation: whether, bought in packages like seeds from the dealer's catalogues, it can take root in its new surroundings as other than a standardized product to be had at a set price, with or without benefit of Burbank. To answer this question is beyond my powers of extrapolative prediction. If folk-song can con-

This paper was read at a meeting of the California Folklore Society, at Stanford University, on April 12, 1957.

tinue, as in former uncommercial habitats, to serve as a touchstone of our common humanity, calling us to re-collect ourselves—as a norm by which to measure our aberrations and idiosyncracies, our frenetic or perverse invocatory solicitations of our private egoisms —we may face the future with hope and patience.

For the moment, we must limit our attention to one aspect of the larger problem: the effect on folk-song and folk-singing of the phonograph record industry, its perils and its opportunities. Although but a part, this is yet a crucial part, of the total picture, for several reasons.

The live recording stands in very much the same relation to the music of the folk-song as formerly the old broadsides stood to the text. The broadside, when it took up a traditional song, affected it in important ways, as we all are aware. First, it made it audience-conscious. Being directed to readers rather more than to hearers, it tended to divorce the words from the tunes, to give separate and independent status to the text as a verse narrative. Because the readers were, at least in verbal habits, a more sophisticated class, the text at once became more self-conscious. It began to cultivate the clichés of written speech at the level of vulgar art, and introduced urban attitudes and values. It smoothed out the irregularities of rhythm and statement; filled up gaps in the narrative and made the transitions explicit; rationalized events with inexpensive mortar of epithet and commentary; instead of ignoring, addressed itself overtly to an audience of whose emotional responses it was consciously solicitous. It invited attention as entertainment, and thus divided author and reader, or, in other terms, performer and hearer. It provided a static text that could be accurately memorized and repeated verbatim, and stultified the old re-creative habit of oral transmission.

All this the phonograph record now does, too, but in a more compelling, more insinuating way. Whereas different readers gave different emphasis and different intonation to the words of a broadside in reading or singing, and so preserved the vestiges of individual rendering, the hundreds, or thousands, who today buy a favorite record all hear, over and over, the same voice, the identical emphasis and inflection at every step of the way, in an eternally fixed and unchanging repetition down to the last nuance and breathing. The single rendition becomes the Law, and the more appealingly the song is sung, the more completely is the process of learning it likely to be limited to an effort toward faithful imitation, in large effects and in the smallest detail. This normalizing process, moreover, is reinforced by the contemporary all-but-universal habit—at least on records—of singing to instrumental accompaniment. It is demonstrable that accompaniment, for ease of coordination, tends to confirm a melodic norm, and a relatively unvarying phrasal repetition. This is noticeable when even the same singer performs the same song, at different times, with and without accompaniment. An important consideration, this, in the vitality of folk-singing as a living experience, since as every one knows who has listened much to the untrained country singer, the minute and generally unconscious but continual variations from stanza to stanza of a single rendition are a major factor in sustaining interest and keeping so diminutive a musical vehicle, so frequently repeated, from going stale on the ear. In natural folk-singing, these slight variations, perceived in the total effect even when not consciously registered by the attention, are largely dictated by those verbal inequalities which the professionalizing of folk-song tends of its own accord to reduce and minimize or eliminate.

Another inevitable result of the commercial exploitation of folk-song is the shortening of texts. There are no long ballads to be heard in professional performances, either in concert—where audience sophistication is assumed, or in radio—where time is calculated to the split second, or on records—even LP's, where the number and variety of songs on a single surface is a persuasive factor in appeal to buyers. The effect of this tendency on our total impression of folk-song is in the long run transforming and potentially profound. We think of folk-song as a moment's monument, the briefest of lyrical utterances, and consequently too light for a tragic impact. Tragedy requires a little time to work its effects; here there is at most only time for a poignant heart-throb. To be sure, we have all *read* the longer tragic ballads, and as readers we remember how impressive some of them are. But very few of us have ever heard a single one sung through in our whole lives. Eleven or so stanzas of "Sir Patrick Spens" are long enough for most listeners when sung. The thirty to forty of "Lord Thomas and Fair Annet" are something we are not likely to hear. And the seventy stanzas of "The Battle of Otterburn" are probably to most of us inconceivable. Yet that was the song that stirred Sir Philip Sidney's heart more than a trumpet, "though *sung* but by some blind crowder." I say, therefore, that we shall probably never experience the full, hypnotically gripping impact of a long tragic ballad when sung. And I say that whether or not many of us regard this as a deprivation, our conception of the range of possibilities in this kind is patently inadequate, calculated even by the evidence extant. And I say, further, that a mental attitude is being fostered by current conditions which would make a revival of the extended ballads intolerable and which, every day, works for further abridgment and a sense in ourselves of the propriety of such curtailment.

In this connection I am reminded of some unpremeditated remarks made by one of the best of our American professionalized folk-singers, Jean Ritchie, at a conference two summers ago at Harvard. (Parenthetically, in the interests of clarity and economy of statement, I should like here to plead for the introduction of a new word into our folkloristic vocabulary. We need a simple term for those who make a vocation of folk-song, who are to all intents a professional class of vocal artists that use folk-songs as their subject matter; as contrasted to those who have disinterestedly kept them in memory as part of their social inheritance, and who sing them only for their own sake. Without any pejorative intent— because the second category may pass over into the first without any disgrace—I think the professionals are "folk-songers," as contrasted with the traditional "folk-singers.") Since I had something to do with the programming of the conference, I asked Miss Ritchie in advance to sing as many of the Child ballads as she could find room for in her evening of folk-song. When she came to introducing the first one, she said, in her informal way, that she seldom had occasion to sing one of the old ballads like "Annie of Lochroyan," because two minutes was the utmost limit for radio songs, and that she only ventured now because we were an audience of "experts" and this was being done by my particular request on my students' behalf; but that we could go to sleep if we chose, and anybody listening over the air could twist his dials. She was quite apologetic; and at the second instance she said, hesitantly, "I don't know whether I should subject you to another Child ballad right now—maybe it's all right—I guess we might's well get it over with." The song was "Little Musgrove" (27 stanzas), and I was interested to note that the applause was long and enthusiastic. (It goes without saying that "Little Musgrove," reduced to a radio-song outline, would have made no impact at all, tragic, or comic—or even salacious. Miss Ritchie sang it through without accompaniment, at an even pace, with no rhetorical highlighting nor any theatricality whatsoever.) Yet later, toward the close of the program, she remarked: "There's a whole lot of things I haven't got to yet, but it's all the fault of those old Child ballads—they take so long."

A final point to be noted is that live recordings, preserving the song as it was sung, entire, and carrying it to the ends of the earth, have at one fell swoop obliterated the usefulness of studying local traditions and habits of melodic transmission. When it has become easier for a singer to sit in his own room in California and learn a song from an Orkney Islander than to go across the street and learn one from a descendant of the 49'ers, it is folly to waste time any longer over questions of who learned what from where. The matter is not worth pursuing, if nothing is to be learned except the single fact. I heard of a devoted research man who traveled at considerable trouble and expense, and with the best recording equipment obtainable, to a remote and unplumbed region in the Southwest, and spent months tracking down and recording the folk-songs of the district, only to discover, upon returning home and recovering from his exertions, that much of what he had gathered had been learned from recent Eastern radio broadcasts.

But it would be ridiculous, however real and menacing the perils of commercial dissemination, to claim that the effects were only evil, and it is time to count some of the gains. It is obvious, from the start, that people by the thousands are regaining possession of a vast inheritance which they value and which was fast disappearing from contemporary life and indeed all but lost to multitudes. Regardless of quality, regardless of the dubious authenticity of perhaps the greater portion, the popular dissemination of folk-song among a whole society fractured by industrial conditions and the artificial compartmentalization of modern life may help in some small degree to re-create that medieval community in which, they tell us, the ballads were born and wherein they throve. It seems likely that, for the first time in many generations, there have again arisen the conditions in which a sound and valid taste founded on tested experience *can* evolve. For abundance and variety are the essential prerequisites of discriminating comparisons and just preferences. And only an uncritical appetite among masses of people can create a commercial market huge enough to tolerate the indulgence of selective tastes. Within the current welter of commercial folk-song have already emerged a handful of firms, and a considerable number of "folk-songers," who appreciate the special, inherent values of the genuinely popular; and we may hope for more as the scope and range of the market is explored and clarified and proved. Moses Asch, with Folkways, is a pioneer, and firms like Stinson, and Elektra, and Riverside have been putting intelligent and yeomanly effort into the guidance of public taste; while their best singers, such as Ewan MacColl, Jeannie Robertson, Margaret Barry, A. L. Lloyd, the late Leadbelly, Pete and Peggy Seeger, Jean Ritchie, stand in need neither of defense nor special pleading. With this leadership, we may anticipate the gradual abating of the medley type of record and the increase of homogeneous collections.

Thanks to the encouragement of many small successes, Kenneth Goldstein and Riverside have recently issued the boldest single venture yet in their eight double-sided LP set of Child ballads, sung unaccompanied by Ewan MacColl and A. L. Lloyd. It is not, I think, an exaggeration to declare that this is the most important event in the field since the publication of Sharp and Karpeles' Southern Appalachian collection.[1] It may be short of ideal that eighty-odd ballads are sung by only two persons, but in spite of their professional status, both of these men, in their very different styles, carry conviction. Lloyd, although he has learned most of his songs from print, sounds more folklike; but MacColl is rooted in a strong family tradition, and wins our fullest assent.

The length of many of these versions as sung by MacColl and Lloyd is a new experience, and as such it prompts reconsideration of ballad-form by bringing into sharp focus questions hitherto unasked or but dimly perceived. For one thing, it shows that the ideal musical structure is inevitably a non-recurrent phrasal pattern for the quatrain. Repetition is an important part of the ballad's effect,

[1] The date of these remarks is to be kept in mind.

but internal repetition within so short a unit tends toward a monotonous extreme. The phrasal scheme ABAB doubles the number of
repeated melodic statements from, let us say, forty to eighty, and at
the same time doubles the *frequency* of repetition. ABBA is less insistent, and is intrinsically more shapely and artful. It is the favorite
Irish "Come-all-ye" pattern, and sustains very well a short song.
But both it and ABCA have the disadvantage of doubling the phrasal
beginning and ending of a repeated tune: that is, A B B A A B B A A B B A;
or A B C A A B C A A B C A, etc. Whereas, ABCD allows the maximum
variation and widest phrasal spacing within the recurrent unit, separating every phrasal repetition by the tune's whole length. How
important this is can be seen in MacColl's "Gil Morris," which
would be less of a *tour de force* and much more satisfying if the
tune were not shaped on an identical mid- and final cadence. If,
moreover, the non-recurrent pattern is so built that the tune's final
calls us back to the beginning, we have in this circularity the maximum continuity combined with the greatest variety possible. Such
a tune is MacColl's "Lang Johnny More," where a major four-
phrase tune begins on the tonic and ends on the second degree.

The influence of ballad music on ballad-form has never been
sufficiently explored, perhaps in part because of students' lack of
opportunities to hear and ponder the whole range of effects. Listening to these longer British ballads, we can make a beginning. It
becomes apparent that laws of natural selection have been operat-
ing here for a long time. It is clearly the music that has dictated,
and probably created, the rhetorical and syntactical habit of the
ballad's textual line, which must be seized auditorially as a musical
phrase; and of the tactics of the stanzaic statement, which ought
not to overrun the tune. Mid-cadence and final cadence are virtually musical rhyme, and, in the vast majority of cases, chime on the
dominant and tonic. Think, for examples, of "Barbara Allan" in
most of its musical forms. Such a correspondence, reinforced by
the mid-cadence and final pauses, makes accompanying verbal
rhyme almost inevitable.

Again, the music has governed the strategy of dialogue in the
typical ballads. It has determined that speakers should ordinarily be
given a whole tune's length to themselves. Splitting the tune among
different speakers is likely to confuse. When it *is* done, it comes
easier if a refrain-line occurs between the first and second speeches;

and, certainly, to split a single phrase of the tune between speakers is almost never possible. The refrain-line in such cases is best unrelated to the narrative path; is preferably aphoristic or syllabic—so as to sharpen the break. The very idea of refrain is, of course, musical in origin, and its types must accord with the scheme of the tune. When the refrain is internal, it is a further concession by the narrative to lyricism; when the refrain is external, the tune fixes the shape it must take and keep. Controlling the speakers in melodic blocks makes for simple confrontations of balanced proportions, of question and answer, of agreement and disagreement, of formulaic reply, and discourages all subtlety and indirection. Innuendo and irony do not flourish under these conditions. Thus, for example, in MacColl's impassive traditional singing of "Thomas the Rhymer," when the Queen of Elfland guerdons Thomas with the "tongue that can never lee," his mordant protest, tactless in the extreme, is simply swallowed up by being couched in the same vehicle and voice as the Queen's offer. The quasi-statuesque aloofness of traditional rendition subdues slight inflections or modulations of idea: irony of statement gains no foothold; a more flexible medium would be requisite. Such subtleties, consequently, do not survive in oral transmission: the ballad text simply *loses what doesn't sing*, and one may suspect the magic finger of Walter Scott in the stanzas occasioning these comments. (This song MacColl learned, both words and tune, from the *Minstrelsy*.)

> Syne they cam' to a garden green,
> And she pu'd an apple frae a tree:
> "Tak' this for thy wages, True Thomas,
> It will gi' ye the tongue that can never lee."
>
> "My tongue's my ain," True Thomas said,
> "A guidly gift ye wad gie to me!
> I neither dought to buy or sell,
> At fair or tryst where I may be.
>
> "I dought neither speak to prince or peer,
> Nor ask grace from fair ladye."
> "Now hold thy peace," the lady said,
> "For as I say, so must it be!"

Another example of melodic domination can be cited from the breathtaking ballad of abduction, "Eppie Morrie":

They've taken Eppie Morrie, then,
And a horse they've bound her on,
And they ha' rid to the minister's hoose
As fast as horse could gang, could gang,
As fast as horse could gang.

Then Willie's ta'en his pistol oot
And set it to the minister's breist:
"O, marry me, marry me, minister,
Or else I'll be your priest, your priest,
Or else I'll be your priest."

Willie's ironic threat is lost in the singing, and the mere listener is sure to miss the point.

In such ways as these, the ballad music has exerted its ineluctable and unremitting influence on the ballad words, on the ballad rhetoric, on the ballad style, on the *dramatis personae* of balladry, their range and complexity of character and habit of expression. As primary condition and chief limiting factor of the ballads' existence, it is the music that has always, both directly and indirectly, been shaping and defining and setting bounds and rendering inimitable this *genre* of popular art. With the multiplication and ensuing study of such living records as are now technologically possible and commercially feasible, the integrity of the ballad-form may begin to be understood.

1957

Two Reviews:

Frank Brown and North Carolina Folklore

I

THIS huge work, of which three closely-printed volumes of
over 700 pages apiece now loom before us, with four more
close behind, is surely the most imposing monument ever erected in
this country to the common memory of the people of any single
State. Whether North Carolina has a more capacious memory than
do other parts of the nation is an open question. But that it so appears is due to the prolonged interest, energy, effort, and persistence
of one man, to whom also the volumes stand as a memorial. Frank
Clyde Brown is said never to have relinquished any piece of tradition that came within his grasp. But neither did he ever relinquish
the aim of housing his verbal antiquities, properly ordered and la-
beled, in a commodious and durable museum. The joys of the
chase, however, were far more exhilarating to him than the quieter
satisfactions of taxidermy; and he consequently found it easy to go
on convincing himself that he had not yet multiplied and diversi-
fied his specimens to the point where the next operation was justifi-
able. He put off or resisted the more clamorous members of the
North Carolina Folklore Society, hot for tangible evidence of its
activity; and he continued to try the patience of his most devoted
co-workers and backers, many of whom would quite naturally
have rejoiced to see their own contributions in a book before their
eyesight failed. Some he evaded, some he silenced, and some he out-
lived: and the collection went on growing.

The Frank C. Brown Collection of North Carolina Folklore. Volumes I, II,
and III. Edited by Newman Ivey White, Paull F. Baum, and Associate Editors.
Duke University Press, 1952.

Perhaps in the end it was better so. There are those who collect Old Masters and New; others who gather in *meubles;* still others who amass great libraries: but it can seldom happen that the giants of collecting live to see their efforts fixed for final advantageous display—still less to devote their own powers to that secondary enterprise. That were for them to write *finis* to a passion, to put up a mausoleum over a dead love. There is an equable distribution of talents in this world, as between the acquisitive and the expository.

Certainly, no collector could have hoped for better fortune in the choice of editorial executors who would realize his life's dream. The list of editors in charge of this enterprise is a roster of the most distinguished living experts in their several fields. Organized and brought within sight of the goal by the general editor of Brown's own choosing, the late and lamented Newman I. White, and carried through by Paull F. Baum, the work has enlisted the knowledge and skill of Archer Taylor, Stith Thompson, Henry M. Belden, Arthur P. Hudson, G. P. Wilson, B. J. Whiting, and Paul G. Brewster in the volumes already issued, and the remaining volumes are in the authoritative hands of Jan P. Schinhan and Wayland D. Hand. Under such auspices, treatment commensurate with the magnitude of the archive was assured.

And what, then, is Folklore? Giants, we suspect, are naturally inclined to be omnivorous. Frank Brown's rule, clearly, was for inclusion, not exclusion. He accepted whatever resembled the sort of thing he sought: at a later stage the winnowing fan could blow away the chaff. And to some extent it has done so, though by some editors it seems to have been wielded with less fervor than by others. The difficulty was that without the masterful sanction of Brown himself, no one wished to step in and impose rigidly strict standards that were possibly out of accord with the original purpose. Hence it may occasionally be felt that the contents of any portion of the work can hardly correspond with what the editor in charge might have included, had he himself compiled as well as annotated the collection. Rather than reject absolutely, the tendency consequently has been to admit with an editorial caveat.

One might therefore complain that, as it now stands in print, the collection is possibly larger than it ought to have been allowed to be—that in spite of initial reductions it might still be called Materials for a Collection of Folklore rather than the simon-pure article.

Thus, for example, Archer Taylor admits a large number of punning questions into the Riddle section, but writes in his introductory note that these are not true riddles—though they pass current. Thus, too, under Beliefs and Customs, for an amusing
instance, we learn that children are told that the doctor keeps
babies in his saddlebags. Is this a true "belief," or a grown-up's ingenious evasion? Did it ever have roots in folk-superstition, like the
old-world feeling about the stork? But it might catch on and be repeated by other sorely pressed parents, and it might be believed by
the child. Is it then a popular belief or custom? Then what is "popular"?

On this question, Professor Baum has an explicit comment.
" 'Popular,' " he writes, "means both originating with the unlet-
tered folk and also acquired or adopted by them. It means both
what belongs to them and what is suited to their taste and finds
favor with them." Hence it comes about that, generally speaking, it
would be difficult to educe from the contents of these volumes any
but the very broadest and loosest definition of the term "Folklore."
The question comes into sharpest focus in connection with the
songs. So far as concerns admission into the collection, no discrimination exists here as between ancient traditional ballads, recent
topical songs, parlor songs, broadsides from the "vulgar" press,
music-hall songs, or pieces like Harry McCarthy's "The Bonny
Blue Flag," a Secessionist song written and dated early in 1861. No
basic distinction is made between "folk-song" and any sort of song
that has enjoyed a wide popular appeal in its day, with slight control by the printed original. In many instances, the author has been
identified in the notes, as in the case of Rednap Howell's "Regulator" songs (1765–71)—historically as interesting, truly, as anything in the whole work. Perhaps Professor Hudson's view of the
matter may be gathered from his introduction to the Satirical
Songs: "Up-to-date means of rapid communication simply acceler-
ate the process by which a song of individual authorship in the old
days gradually became the possession of a group, next [of] a neigh-
borhood, and finally a region or even a nation, somewhere along
the line becoming a genuine folk-song." Perhaps this is ultimately
the only defensible position: but if so, we have come a long way
from the classical criteria of immemorial antiquity and anonymity.
And it must be confessed that one feels a certain reluctance about

including a dozen sadly garbled versions of "Danny Deever" or O. W. Holmes's "Ballad of an Oysterman" in a collection entitled "Folklore," on the sole ground that they have been liked well enough to be memorized and orally transmitted. If rapid communication is to be allowed to take the place of time in dispersal, and imperfect recollection to do duty for anonymity, it will at this cheap rate be an easy matter to compile thesauri of "folklore" until the presses fall. Characteristic effects of oral communication these things no doubt exemplify; but can we afford to dispense with every other requirement? This is too close to the familiar undergraduate proposal, "Let's make it a Tradition!" Surely it is time now to strive for tighter definitions.

But these are perennial dilemmas, upon which many a good scholar has been impaled, and no simple solution is yet in sight. Meanwhile, the positive virtues of the present work compel our admiration. Professor Hudson has had the difficult task of editing the native American songs; and his introductory notes, whether short or long, are models of informative and scholarly comment, of tact, discretion, and proportion, perfectly pitched whether grave or gay. Professor Belden's notes, covering the older ballads and songs —those most clearly of British descent—are done perhaps with less obvious enjoyment, and are less discursive; but they are packed with condensed bibliographical and other information, and survey a very wide area in space and time.

Between them, these two editors account for nearly a thousand songs and ballads with multiple variants. Their work fills the second and third volumes before us and may be considered the most important part of the archive. Among the older pieces here represented are no fewer than fifty of the ballads that Harvard's Child admitted into the genuine canon of traditional balladry—a very impressive number indeed to be found within the boundaries of a single state: unequaled, in fact, save by Virginia and Maine. One of them, as it happens, appears to be a fragment of "Robin Hood and Guy of Gisborne," a ballad never before picked up in tradition, and hitherto known only in a mid-seventeenth-century English form, from the famous Percy Folio. To be sure, it survives here in a most dilapidated state, and is hardly more than a doggerel summary of the central incident. But this cannot have derived from the folio version; and the thought of this piece drifting and sifting down from one singer to another, from the late middle ages, its life a perpetual hostage to fortune; crossing the Atlantic perhaps 200 years or more ago and lasting on in memory until the opening of the First World War: all this staggers the imagination. How to account for such tenacity of life? But the case is not unique; and those best acquainted with tradition will be the readiest to believe that the piece may well be a purely oral legacy from the immemorial past.

One cannot but note with acute regret, while acknowledging the practical expediency of the editorial decision, how much the collection loses of fresh and living interest by reserving the tunes for separate treatment in a volume of their own. There is only too much precedent for this truly crippling procedure. Any one who has ever read through a volume of mediocre verses divorced from the music to which they were intended to be sung is familiar with the stultifying effect of that separation. One is left with a flat, insipid impression from which, even with the aid of historical notes and the best will in the world, one can scarcely be roused. But where *folk-songs* are divorced from their airs, the offense is still graver, for it not only bores but falsifies too. The vital existence of a folk-song or ballad depends on its tune. If it were not sung, it would die and be forgotten. Singing affects its tone and temper, mitigates its crudity of language and rhyme, softens and dignifies its violence or brutality, lends it poise and regularity of utterance: in a word, transfigures it. It is impossible to exaggerate the injury which loss of the tune entails. Granted, there are fewer ballad collections with tunes than without. We are so familiar with these that we tend to accept the method as conventional. But we should only put up with them *faute de mieux*. In the present collection, hundreds of songs were recorded *with their tunes*, and there was no insurmountable reason or necessity to put asunder what the people have joined. This was an error so serious, in my view of the case, as hardly to admit of extenuation.

In the face of this deprivation, which can only partially be repaired by the appearance of Volume IV, many readers will find most amusement in the varied content of the first volume, which contains children's games and their accompanying rhymes; folkcustoms and remedies or preventives and traditional household beliefs and superstitions; riddles and puzzles; proverbs (with an extended and valuable as well as delightful essay on the subject by Professor Whiting, and nearly one hundred pages of examples with parallel references); a fascinating glossary of folk-speech filling another hundred pages, enriched with an extraordinary series of early historical precedents; and a considerable collection of tales and legends. Here is such a treasury of fascinating, picturesque, surprising, and entertaining matter as will prove well-nigh inexhaustible for bedside reading. Here we may gather such practical hints as that to place a rattlesnake's rattle in a violin will improve its tone. Or that if you leave the water running from the faucet while peeling onions, the eyes will not water. Or that if you are given to headaches and afraid of being *puny-turned*, it will be advisable to let your head get soaked by the first rain in May. Or that a one-legged man had better dance away from the fire. . . . Need we go on? Scrap the television set and buy this book!

1953

2

SURVEYING the former volumes of this massive collection, I had occasion to lament the fact that the tunes of the ballads and songs had not been printed with their texts. All that could be done to remedy that situation has now been done, and the volume before us, *The Music of the Ballads*, is the first of two which will contain all musical records, whether manuscript or phonographic, that could be salvaged from what was gathered by Professor Frank C. Brown and his associates of the North Carolina Folklore Society during thirty years of activity. These records amount to more than 1250 tunes, of which the part now published, the music of the ballads, comprises 517 tunes. The horrendous prefatory tale of the musical editor's difficulties and vexations will daunt all but the stoutest aspirants to succession and fully accounts for the lapse of time—six years—between this volume and Volume II, its textual companion. But it must be testified in Professor Jan P. Schinhan's honor that he has triumphed mightily over all physical obstacles. The clarity and meticulous accuracy of his transcriptions everywhere reveal the hand not merely of an expert but also of one who has taken extraordinary pains. If there are mechanical errors in these 400 pages of musical print, they will not be discovered by the casual eye.

There are tunes here for some forty of the Child ballads, besides a handful of secondary forms, and for many numbers a quantity of

The Frank C. Brown Collection of North Carolina Folklore. Volume IV. *The Music of the Ballads.* Edited by Jan Philip Schinhan. Duke University Press, 1957.

variants—eighteen, for example, of "Barbara Allan." In addition, there are tunes for 100 old narrative songs chiefly of English provenience, of three dozen widely known American, half that number of North Carolinian, and two dozen miscellaneous additional ballads. Professor Schinhan has also supplied a twenty-page critical introduction on questions of musical analysis, and two appendices containing elaborate statistical tables of various musicological data.

One stanza is usually printed with the notes, and occasionally a whole new text; but most of the verbal record is preserved in Volume II, to which this fourth volume is supplementary and corrective, so that they must be read together. The tunes themselves are a rich harvest, the special features of which the editor often illuminates with analytical comment. The most interesting tunes generally belong to the earlier tradition. Here, as elsewhere, they have clung with surprising tenacity to their immemorial, pre-harmonic character and modal scales. A striking fact is the numerical superiority of plagal tunes (3 to 1) in this collection. The high incidence of tunes in gapped scales, particularly pentatonics, is noteworthy throughout the Appalachians, and very evident here; and this feature of the melodic tradition is obviously being perpetuated in the later songs, where the proportion of heptachordal tunes is not perceptibly larger than before. The trait does not derive from the English, but points to the indelible strain of Scottish, or northern, tradition that yet stamps the region. It is altogether fortunate, however, that so much was saved from the earlier decades of the century; for what roads and radio have done to the ancestral memory is not cheerful news, and it is idle to hope for the preservation of local melodic habits in the face of these powerful and pervasive influences.

Professor Schinhan's book is the first extended effort we have seen in this country to go beyond the mere identification of scale in the analysis of Anglo-American folk-song. This is tantamount to saying—and the point must be stressed—that the conventions and rules of procedure in such analysis are yet to be fixed and agreed upon; and that Professor Schinhan's methodology, if it stand the test of general convenience, may become a norm for subsequent works in this field—reinforced as it soon will be by the companion volume of music for the North Carolina folk songs. It is thus of considerable importance to recognize the gravity of the present occasion. We shall put our observations so far as possible in the form of queries.

The musical analysis of individual tunes, as here conducted, consists usually of six parts. The elements are as follows: (1) scale, (2) range, (3) tonal center, (4) structure (i.e., phrasal scheme), (5) final, (6) relative emphasis on notes employed. In addition, there are notations on "melodic relationship." The last may be dismissed with a word. No hypothesis of traditional stability or variation is suggested by calling attention to occasional likenesses either in the tune as a whole or in particular parts of it.

The first element taken seriously is the matter of scales and modes. Professor Schinhan, for reasons undisclosed, *in practice* reserves the term "mode" for the five pentatonic scales, assigning the number 1 to that which lacks the third and seventh of the diatonic system; 11 to that lacking the second and sixth; 111 to that without its fourth and seventh; 1v to that without its third and sixth; and v to that without its second and fifth. The questions here to be asked are: Why limit the term "mode," contrary to all historical precedent, to the pentatonic system? and why begin the numerical series with that particular scale here selected for pentatonic 1 rather than with one of the others? Are these not both undefended, arbitrary editorial decisions, which need reasoned justification?

Professor Schinhan separates tunes lacking one degree of the diatonic seven into two classes: hexachordal and hexatonic. Either class may be plagal or authentic in range. In the hexachordal tunes, counting upward from the tonic, six adjacent notes of the diatonic scale must be present somewhere in the tune. But, since the tune may cover more than an octave in range, one or more of these notes may be borrowed editorially from the upper or lower octave to complete the tally. Thus there may be immediate gaps in the series as actually employed. But so long as the note entirely missing is the seventh, and whether or not the third is major or minor, Professor Schinhan will call the tune hexachordal. On the contrary, if a tune fails to use the second, third, fourth, or sixth, it will be called hexatonic, even though its tonal complement contains a run of six consecutive notes and no more—say, from the lower v to 111 above the tonic. Question: is this distinction between hexatonic and hexachordal as significant as the fact that the range of the tune lies within a sixth or not; or that the third, when it is present, is major or minor? These latter facts are not recorded by the editor. Or, again, is it consistent to reserve the term *heptachordal* for major (or Ionian) tunes alone, and deny it to Mixolydian, Dorian, Æolian, or Phrygian scales (supposing the last should occur)? All the latter are equally heptachordal but are never called so here.

Professor Schinhan always carefully records the fact that a given tune is plagal but is not concerned with whether, besides descending to the lower fifth, it also rises to the octave. In the latter case its range, of course, is as truly authentic as plagal. Would it not be preferable, as more accurate, to specify a third class of tunes with this wider, mixed, range?

The editor, anxious to avoid harmonic implications, eschews the terms "keynote" and "tonic," employing instead "tonal center." When the tonal center, in his judgment, is not the final note, he calls the tune "circular." Here we run head-on into problems the complexity of which is scarcely hinted by Professor Schinhan. The simplest question that springs to mind: Why must every tune that ends off its tonic be a circular tune? A tune, to be sure, of which the last notes are contrived not for conclusion, but to lead without a pause back into the first notes again (as in the Elizabethan "Peg o'Ramsey"), is undeniably a circular tune. But many of the tunes so denominated here have none of this feeling. Their conclusions are intended to *conclude*. While they may sound somewhat strange to ears unused to this music, they are entirely satisfying to the traditional mountain singers, as their frequency attests, and they soon grow quite acceptable to a mere outsider. They are, in fact, no more "circular" than many a ballad tune that ends on its proper tonic, with a first phrase deliberately avoiding that note. Often, indeed, the "circularity" of these tunes that end off the tonic is further suppressed by a first phrase stressing the actual final as a phrasal anchor conditioning the tune from the start. In the commonest cases of this kind—the tunes superficially major but with a final on v below the putative tonic—it is really a highly subjective decision that an editor must make. In spite of his determination to stay clear of the modern major/minor "infection," as he dubs it, Professor Schinhan seems in these cases always to catch the virus he warns against, and to decide for the major instead of the Mixolydian tonic. In view of the widespread regional tradition, this reviewer, at any rate, would reverse the editorial decision in perhaps four out of five cases. The question is, then: Which is preferable, to adopt the regional idiom as normal meaning, or to import a standard sense from an alien context?

In his desire to reduce his structural analyses to the simplest terms, Professor Schinhan has read the tunes wherever he could as composed of two or three phrases, each indicated by a letter, and followed by the number of bars in each. Frequently, he gives alternative schemes, one twice the length of the other. Thus, for example: "a a^1 a^2 a^3 (2,2,2,2) = a a^1 (4,4,)." Here, again, we are in a highly subjective area. The matter really demands musical illustration for fair discussion. But it must be insisted that in so minute a form, small differences are important. Phrasal cadence-points are essential elements in comparative analysis. The chief differences between a, a^1, a^2, et cetera, frequently lie in the phrasal endings, which this manner of denoting tends to minimize. Especially subjective, moreover, is the judgment of how big a difference must exist between a and a^1 to transform a^1 to b. Thus, it might easily happen that by another analyst Professor Schinhan's a a^1 would be set down as abcd. It should be steadily kept in mind that text and tune are intimately related, and that a sound analysis must keep both factors in view. The structural analysis of the first tune in the book is "a a^1 (4,4)." The stanza carried by this tune is printed thus:

> As I went through Wichander's town,
>   Arose Mary in time!
> I threw my specs to a certain young woman [i.e., respects?]
>   And told her she could be a true lover of mine.

Here is a sufficiently normal ballad quatrain, with internal refrain elements at lines 2 and 4. Is it desirable to ignore the abrupt shifts of the text—which may be reemphasized in performance by alternations of solo and choral singing, and even by altered steps in dancing—and to take the first two phrases as a single musical unit (denoted a), and the third and fourth as the same unit but varied (a^1)? Does this not falsify the living reality of the song? In recognition of the different cadences of phrases 2 and 4, would it not for comparative uses be better to analyze the tune as abac? But whether or no, can it be justly said that the analyses of musical structure here given, and statistically tabulated in an appendix, provide us with much solid ground for comparison in wider contexts of folk-song?

With a diligence that can only excite admiration, Professor Schinhan has compiled an appendix containing individual tables of the notes used in every song, arranged on a staff at the pitch at which the song is printed, and with the relative frequencies of every note numerically evaluated beneath. This is a meticulousness much in excess of anything commonly to be encountered, though the same editor has formerly employed it in ethnomusicological studies, and even more elaborately. The questions which the appendix raises in the reviewer's mind do not impugn the solidity of the achievement but are directed toward its potential utility. Again for comparative purposes, it would advantageous to transpose the tunes to a common tonal center, which could be indicated by a white note in the scalic series. Tunes of the same modal scheme could thus be compared, authentics and plagals separately or together. The question of relative emphasis of different degrees in the tunes is more problematical. The practice here employed, of counting all frequencies in aggregate totals of sixteenths, is valid only for each tune separately. Its comparative utility is quite doubtful except as between tunes in the same metre and number of phrases, and only after they have been reduced to the same tonal center. A four-phrase tune in 6/8 time (like no. 52) gives only about half the numerical count of a tune of the same length in 6/4 (like no. 54). If, then, the tables cannot as they stand be safely used in comparative studies, why not employ the basic metrical unit of the tune in question as the unit of measurement? Thus, a tune in 2/2 time will take a half-note as its integer; in 4/4, a quarter-note; in 6/8, an eighth-note; each being given a value of 1. Then, if comparisons were tried, the relative weight of emphasis in tunes of different metres could be estimated more justly. And since different editors may express the same tune in different time-signatures, proportions over all would not be falsified.

Our reservations as to methodology, however, do not in the least detract from the importance of this work. As a faithful record of what was sung in the Southern Highlands in the earlier twentieth century, it is probably the last major contribution to be expected. With the Sharp-Karpeles Appalachian collection, it constitutes a primary document the historical value of which can only increase with age. As a scholarly discharge of the difficult and complex responsibilities of so significant an undertaking, Professor Schinhan's editorial work leaves his competitors far behind: he has done a truly outstanding job.

1958

"All This for a Song?"

WHEN Good Queen Bess, in her large wisdom, ordered Lord
Burleigh to give the poet Spenser £100 for his excellent
verses, Burleigh is said to have exclaimed in protest, "What! all this
for a song?" It can be inferred from the late files of the *Congressional Record* that a similar view is alive today in certain quarters.
During the 1961 debates on the National Defense Education Act,
an amendment was introduced in the House, "that no part of the
appropriations . . . shall be available for fellowships in the humanities and social sciences field." Earlier, word had reached the
press that part of the fellowship funds would be allocated to the
study of folklore and "other things like that"; and the bad publicity that followed had so alarmed the committee that already they
had cut the funds by a million dollars before bringing up the bill
for debate. Congress was mollified by this evidence of discretion;
but anxiety was not entirely dispelled.

I know of no reason [declared the mover of the amendment] why
under the National Defense Education Act there should be studies
of . . . English folklore, and American folklore. What is the difference
between English and American folklore? I will be pleased to have any
member of the committee tell me the difference and why we should
be providing fellowships under the National Defense Act to study
folklore, jazz, the theater, and so forth. [*Congressional Record*, 87th
Cong., 1st Sess., p. 8268. House Debate, 17 May 1961.]

The cash value of *The Faerie Queene* or of *Henry V* would, it
may readily be granted, puzzle anyone to establish. As a prudent
treasurer, Burleigh saw no need to lay out any of the national

This paper was read at the Semicentennial Exercises of Rice University,
Houston, Texas, on October 11, 1962.

wealth in the encouragement of poetry and drama, whatever his private liking for a song or a play. The congressman, in turn, whether or not he got satisfaction from speaking the tongue that Shakespeare spoke, saw the matter in the same light, although as a realist he might set a high value on a Broadway success. But, contemporary with Burleigh, there was one who saw things in truer perspective, who wrote with proud eloquence:

> And who in time knowes whither we may vent
> The treasure of our tongue, to what strange shores
> This gaine of our best glorie shall be sent
> T'inrich unknowing nations with our stores? . . .
> What powres it shall bring in, what spirits command,
> What thoughts let out, what humors keep restrain'd:
> What mischiefe it may powrefully withstand,
> And what faire ends may thereby be attain'd? [1]

The odd thing is that neither Burleigh nor the congressman could see these products as national assets, nor was able to imagine any connection they might have with their country's interests at home or abroad. For the practical and utilitarian value to a nation of the theater, jazz, or songs is so much easier to demonstrate than is their absolute value. Indeed, their worth as propaganda is so obvious that folklore in one or more of its manifestations—song, dance, dress, or other handicrafts—is exploited to the utmost by countries behind the Iron Curtain. Certainly, Russian ballet has been one of their most positively ingratiating and valid exports to foreign parts; and it can be argued that Louis Armstrong and Benny Goodman have been two of our most successful ambassadors. Is there any nearer way of allaying suspicion, banishing rancor between peoples, reaffirming the common ties of humanity, and building mutual trust than by sharing popular entertainment together? "No man," Dr. Johnson sagely observed, "is a hypocrite in his pleasures." And when beauty joins pleasure to excite admiration, how much the better! Can we neglect to foster such useful intermediaries of understanding?

Fortunately, the humanities do not have to be vindicated here, in an assembly committed to their recognition, on an occasion so memorably auspicious. If I have raised the issue in a defensive way, it is only because I am concerned with them primarily in one of

[1] Samuel Daniel, *Musophilus* (1599), lines 939–968.

their humblest walks, and intend to plead that even there they are worthy of serious and prolonged investigation.

Our civilization has become so deeply committed to print for the normal conveyance of its ideas that we tend to ignore the subtler influences of hearsay in our lives. But the latter can be of great importance, and it is the more necessary to be awake to this fact because of their relative obscurity. The persistence of oral tradition in a literate, cosmopolitan, urban society, or any segment of it such as the present company, is worth investigation. What sorts of lore —limericks, songs, stories, proverbs, superstitions, games, social conventions—are conveyed habitually in speech from person to person, generation to generation, and at what ages, in what contexts: these form a study richly contributory to a knowledge of our communal living. Even limiting ourselves to songs, we can find matter to occupy us for a long time.

Folk-song, to be sure, is a warmly human, natural, and lovable phenomenon, and there can be no complaint against those who wish only to keep it alive and to put it to its natural uses: to dance or to work to it, to express their feelings of joy or love or sadness through it. But because it *is* so spontaneous and universal, it deserves serious attention. There are a hundred ways of approaching it: through social studies of family tradition, or the way of life of its bearers—in the woods, on the plains, on ships, on trains, in the mines; of its regional or geographical dissemination; of its persistence through time as fragmentary history by, and of, the generations; of its disclosure of national character; of its psychological significance in choice of subject matter, character prototypes, themes continually reformulated; of its accepted conventions in the telling of stories; of its deeply rooted preferences in the patterns of melody.

There must be few among you who are not familiar with half a dozen of those British-American ballads of which there are records as far back as the seventeenth century and which may very likely be a good deal older than the earliest records. They are so rooted in our tradition that the same acquaintance could be assumed almost anywhere in the country. Any similar gathering would know "Barbara Allan" from childhood and probably, under varying names, a handful of such songs—perhaps "Lord Thomas and Fair Eleanor," "Lady Isabel and the Elf-Knight," "Lord Lovel," "The

Two Sisters," "The Gypsy Davy," or "Lord Randal"—not learned from books but from other singers. If only we could immediately pool all the versions of these which are known to the present company, we should have in our hands the materials of a very interesting research project. The factors, thus visibly exemplified, of stability and variation, perpetually at odds, would yield fascinating data.

Variation-form in Western composed music has been intensively studied. Yet, although everyone would admit its importance in the ceaseless fluctuation of traditional text and tune, one finds little or no discussion of variation as a phenomenon in folk-song. Narrative change has received attention, and verbal change has been noticed incidentally. But musicology in this country is too young a science to have condescended to scrutinize folk-song, and melodic change here has gone unanalyzed. Obviously, text and tune are interdependent, exercising mutual influences. But, when we analyze, variational effects, musical and verbal, have to be separately described. The *story* of a ballad identifies itself almost automatically, given a number of exemplars. But we cannot go far in studying a *melodic* theme without beginning to wonder about its identity. What *is* a tune, in fact? Does a series of notes in common time constitute the same tune as a similar series in another meter? Are the tunes of "Dixie" or "Yankee Doodle" the same tunes if sung in the minor as in the major? Yes, we might say, if you allow that one is incorrect. In this case there is an established norm. But what if none exists? Is a tune with phrases repeating, as ABAB, the same with similar phrases in the order ABBA? Can a tune ranging from its lower to upper dominant (or fifth) keep its identity when, with requisite adjustments, it is stated in a form ranging from tonic to upper octave?

A composer, working in variation forms, will put a theme through all sorts of gymnastics. He states his point of departure, and his object is to excite and sustain our interest by ingenious and imaginative transformations of the melodic idea. Since the norm is fixed, he can invent with the utmost freedom, altering one element after another at pleasure. In folk-song the situation is very different. True, most of the kinds of variation appear in miniature—as figuration, ornament, changes of cadence, dynamics, mode, pitch, rhythm; suppression of phrase, contraction or expansion; and so on. But these variations have occurred, in the chances of oral tradition, without reference to one another, and mostly without conscious intent—indeed, usually in spite of it. For the traditional folksinger, no archetype exists except the one he learned, the one in his head. There is and can be no true original of a genuine folk-song. The beginning is out of sight and, if the original survived, it would be only as another version, unauthoritative and without control over the derivatives that are perpetuating it. What, then, constitutes a folk-song's essential identity? Of what is each statement of its tune a variation? Can we say that its identity lies in the sum of persistent resemblances to apparently kindred tunes? That may not carry us far, but, as with the study of other living species of which the prototypes have disappeared, it must force us to comparisons.

Comparisons are not necessarily odious—indeed, they can be fascinating—but they are burdensome, time-consuming, and full of vexation when they are not superficial. Because we have no archetype to start from, we must begin with a miscellaneous gathering of tunes, collected, with whatever diligence, at the mercy of chance; each one differing from every other at least in minute particulars and therefore unique, but having enough in common to strike us as varying forms of the same melodic idea. What we are pursuing is the precise objective nature of that sensed community.

How shall we start comparing if we do not know that any one characteristic is more symptomatic than any other? If we start with tunes that look alike in their opening notes, we find them wandering apart as they proceed. Or we find more similarity in the *second* phrase of others—or the third—or the fourth—than in the first. Some tunes whose melodic lines are nearly alike may be in quite different meters: 4/4, 6/8, 3/2. Shall we discount on the side of meter or of line? Some tunes have four phrases, some five, some six, some eight. Should this fact be counted essential? The tunes appear in different modes, different scales: how much weight does this deserve in analysis? The difficulty is to set things in order of importance.

In each phrase, the notes that carry metrical emphasis seem more indicative of the melodic line than the notes between stresses. This fact is encouraging, for it suggests the possibility of skeletal abridgment, a shorthand of the tune that may avoid a note-by-note comparison, without too serious a loss. Perhaps, then, at certain points, as the end of a phrase, the shape of the tune is more dependent than elsewhere on the particular note that occupies that position. In this case, phrasal cadences in relation to one another will be significant factors. Close comparison begins to bring out other diagnostic elements: how high the tune rises above its tonic, how far it falls below, within what portion of its range it is comfortably at home, and where, throughout the tune, characteristic phenomena occur. Particular features may not always seem of equal weight. Meter, though never to be ignored, seems less individualizing than might have been anticipated, but sometimes a typical rhythmic habit can be highly indicative.

Very significant is the question as to which notes of the diatonic series are employed by a tune, for these establish its modal character. In our British-American songs the occurrence of chromaticism is a suspicious circumstance. I do not mean microtonal shading, or a singer's intonation. In our older tradition, there is no modulation of the familiar harmonic kind; and it follows that every note has a meaningful, implicit reference to the tonic—most often the final note—of the tune. We testify instinctively to the tonic's latent power by our surprise when a tune ends on another note. Equally significant, in our tradition, is the *absence* of a note or notes from the diatonic octave. Many of our Appalachian tunes, in the veins of which flows a deal of Scottish blood, lack one, and more often two, notes of the scale; and of course the position of these gaps, in relation to the tonic, is as important melodically as, in other tunes, is the *presence* of the particular notes that fill them.

The melodic benefits of folk-song stemming from these simple but numerous differences are greater than its harmonic deprivations. For, besides the four favorite (seven possible) heptatonic modes, our tunes may make use of six hextonic and five pentatonic modal patterns, each of which to a sensitive ear has its own distinctive capabilities. Our folk-song, this amounts to saying, is closer to the medieval *variety* than to the modern *simplicity* of major and minor with chromatic blurring, repeated at differing pitches. And something of that ancient feeling, and emotional response, for modality must have filtered down in a tradition that still prefers these patterns to the familiar sun and shade of today's major and minor. It is not a question of merely pedantic interest, for those persistent, instinctive reactions must antedate and underlie all the

quaint theorizing that runs from Plato down almost to the eighteenth century in music of the Western world.

How specific the semantic meaning of the modes was felt to be
in an ordered universe where every note of the terrestrial diatonic
scale had its counterpart above in the planetary spheres, and where
these influences, still echoing adjectivally as martial, mercurial,
saturnine, or venereal, were palpable on earth in humors, bodily
organs, in days of the week, hours of the day, so that the whole
universal system may be said to have been full of sympathetic vi-
brations and celestial overtones—how specific may be readily illustrated in a quotation, contemporary with Shakespeare, and useful
to today's professors of musical therapy:

The Dorian *Moode* [writes Dowland, the great lutenist] is the
bestower of wisedome, and causer of chastity. The *Phrygian* causeth
wars, and enflameth fury. The *Eolian* doth appease the tempests of the
minde, and when it hath appeased them lulls them asleepe. The *Lydian*
doth sharpen the wit of the dull, & doth make them that are burdened
with earthly desires, to desire heavenly things. . . . Every habit of the
mind is governed by songs.[2]

If we are to keep track of all these data in a large, comparative
study, we shall find ourselves staggering under a load of statistics so
multifarious as to be quite unmanageable and indeed discouraging.
For we may want to take out and study in various correlations any
of the elements or factors noted in our search for norms. It seems
time, therefore, to cast about for some means of controlling the
oppressive mass of detail. In this extremity, it naturally occurs to
us to inquire of those electronic robots, clothed in power and
magic, which speak with sibylline utterance in our day and which
can answer the hardest questions in the twinkling of an eye. Might
they not be entreated on our behalf to idle away a vacant moment
in aesthetic relaxation? After all, we shall not need the thunder and
lightning of the greater gods. All we ask at present are a little
counting and a few correlated statistics. A mere "drudging goblin"
would almost do our business.

Looking intently at the familiar IBM card (Fig. 1, *A*) with a
hopeful eye, it dawns upon us that those serried ranks of figures on
dress parade can just as well stand for the degrees of a musical oc-

---

[2] For a diagram expressing modal relationships, see the fifth essay of this
collection.

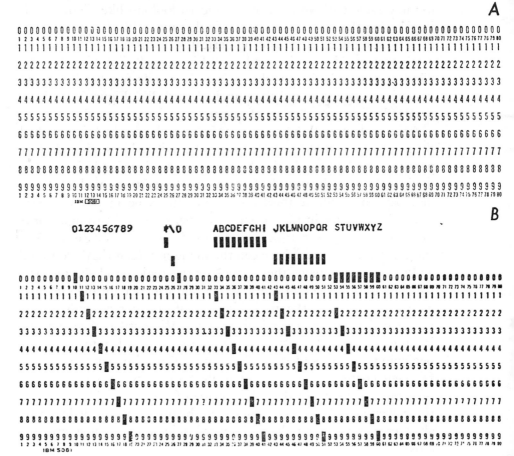

FIG. I

tave as for less Pythagorean entities. Since with a double punch to the column they translate into letters, we could use the first eight letters of the alphabet, if we wished, for a higher octave, and the middle series for a lower (Fig. 1, *B*). Three octaves would more than cover the vocal range we need. Taking only the stressed notes, of which in a typical tune in our folk tradition there are normally four to a phrase, we could register the skeletal outline of eight such phrases on less than half the length of a card. Elsewhere a punch could indicate which modal scale was being employed, and space could be saved for noting accidental sharps or flats. The rest of the card could be given over to whatever data we thought important to tabulate. With some initial experiment, we might come to the Oracle with an interpretative card looking like Figure 2, *A*. Registering the desired data for a single tune, with the punches interpreted in alphabetical and numerical symbols, we should have a result that could be easily read, as in Figure 2, *B*. But of course the Sibyl understands the punches as readily as our familiar letter and numerical languages, and the punched card, like Figure 2, *C*, is all she needs to answer the sort of questions we have in mind.

Armed, then, with a pack of cards on each of which is punched the information about a single tune to be collated in statistical comparisons, we approach the Sacred Grove. Once admitted, and doffing our sandals, we ask the Priest such questions as the following: Say, an it please thee, how many tunes lie in the authentic range, how many in the plagal, how many extend through both? How many share the same melodic mode, and which are they? Is there a correspondence between the mode in which they are found and the region whence they came? or the region and the metrical pattern? Pray collect all tunes with a mid-cadence on the same degree and say what the probability is of the corresponding first phrase cadencing on a particular degree. We entreat thee, arrange in order the linear identities of tunes, by accented notes from the beginning, as far as identity goes; and tell us also where the most frequent correspondences lie over all. So may we learn the points of greatest stability in that ideal image of the tune which exists in the collective mind of the singers, and begin thence to deduce that abstract copy, or paradigm, "toward which the whole creation moves."

It could not be that the god would send us away empty-handed. We emerge, in fact, with a pile of folded sheets in exchange for our cards. What is stamped on the sheets might look like the specimen shown in Figure 3, the order from left to right being arbitrarily determined. The order downward answers also to a series of factors of predetermined, graduated importance.

Supposing, to give specific illustrative point to our generalizations, we had elected to focus on that most familiar of all ballads in English, "Barbara Allan." Supernatural assistance has not, alas! enabled us to anticipate and analyze the versions of the present company. Instead, we have been obliged to scour through libraries, comb collections, both printed and manuscript, of various dates, and transcribe phonographic recordings of sundry kinds, in order

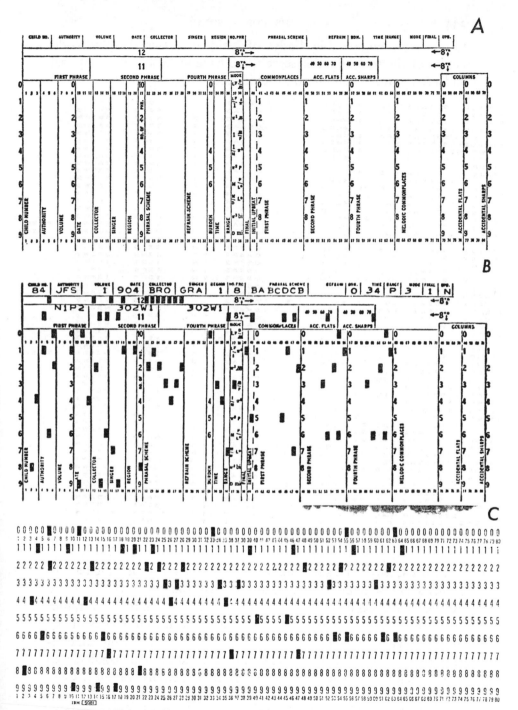

FIG. 2

to amass a comparable body of evidence—two hundred–odd copies of the song. By this search, we have at least added a spatial and a temporal dimension to the evidence.

```
84CJSS   904GHA  PAL   1  48CD          066A3  1 1      1551    6A7W5
84CJSS   906SHA  LOC   1  48CD          054A3  1 5      A6A6    AB7W5
84CJSS   907SHA  LOC   1  48CD          054A3  1 5      A6A6    AB7W5
84CJSS   906SHA  STO   1  48CD          054A3  1 1      3211    6A7W5
84CJSS   906SHA  GRA   1  48CD          054A3  1 1      3411    3A7W5
84 WC    2859CHA       1  48CD          054A3  1 1      3441    6A7W5
84EFR    850RIM        1  48CD          034A3  1 1      3531    3A7W5
94 CF    65              48CD           034A3  1 1      3531    3A7W5
84CJSS   921SHA  RIC   1  48CD          034A3  1 5      3541    6A7W5
84JIF    1904FOX  CAR  3  48CD          068A3  1 1      3531    6B7W5
84WRM    928MAC  LAN  20  48CD          044A3  1 1      3631    4A7W5
84CJSS   918SHA  MAC  25  48AC          032A4  1 5      6543    322W1
84JFS    7924CLA  CRE  1  48CD          032A4  1 1  3152W1     4465
84CJSS   908SHA  SAY  1  48CD           054P1  1 N      11PN    333W2
84 PBS   91 BAR  COB  21  48AC          044P1  1 5      311N    122W3
84 RS    928SMI  COM  25  88ABCDC8      034A5  1 O      1425    652W1    652W1
84JFG    1904BRO  GRA  1  88ABCDC8      034P3  1 N      N1P2    302W1    302W1
84JFS    1904BRO  VAI  1  58CDE   5     034P3  1 N      102N    P33W2
84CJSS   906SHA  CHA  1  48CD           054P3  1 N      3310    153W2
84 PBV   91 BAR  WIL  21  48CD          044P3  1 1      33NN    343W2
84 FK    891KID  WAR  1  68CDCD   56    034P3  1 N      1321    15PW2
84 FK    891KID  HOL  1  48CD           034P3  1 N      13P4    13PW2
84 PBV   93 BAR  HAR  21  48CD          034P3  1 N      13P4    13PW2
84 CS    927SAN  DAV  29  48CD          068P3  1 N      13P4    13PW2
84CJSS   906SHA  STO  1  48AC           068P3  1 N      121N    53PW2
84CJSS   905SHA  DUR  1  58CDE    5     054P3  1 N      1300    22PW2
84EHL    939LIN  HAR  21  48CD          044P3  1 3      332N    N54W3
84CJSS   907SHA  CHA  1  48CD           054P3  1 N      3310    165W3
84 PQS   906GRA  HOR  1  48AC           0X8P4  1 5      6311    633W2
84MOE    939EDD  HOU  23  48CD          034P4  1 N      131N    514W2
84CJS    1932SHA  SLO  26  48CD         032P  O 1 1     1541    141W3
84CJS    1932SHA  HEN  26  48CD         032P  1 1 1     1551    141W3
84 GQ    925GRE  QUI  2  88ABCDA8       044A9  A C      5355    535WA    535WA
84PWJ    912JOY       2  48CD           044A9  1 5      3131    535WA
84 GQ    925DUN  GIL  2  48CD           034P9  1 1      3541    P21N
84 GQ    925GRE  JOM  2  48CD           044A  O A 7     ACD8    AA5WA
84 JJ    3790JOM      2  48AB           044A  O A 5     AC7D    AC5WA
84 CQ    925DUN  GIL  2  48AB           044P  O 1 N     1N32    1NPW1
04 WC    1876CHR      2  48CD           034P  O 1 1     3131    3534
04 WC    1876CHR      2  68AC           034A  2 1 3     5A57    5AAW5
84 WC    1876CHR      2  68CDCD   56    044A  2 A 5     AC88    AC5WA
84BNE    13935BAR  FRE  21  48AC        034P  8 1 2     2NON    N3NW1
84 DS    937SCA  CAL  25  48CD          034A3  1 5      5AA4    5AAW5
84 PBS   907BAR  CLA  22  4ABC          044A6  1 5      5AA5    5AA5
84AKD    929STO  DAV  25  6ABCBC   56   044A1  1 5      6663    6663
84 VR    1946RAN  MCC  24  4ABA         032P  1 1 P     1441    1441
84 VR    1946RAN  MCD  24  4ABC         024P  O N N     1431    143W1
84MOE    939EDD  DAR  23  48CD          044A7  1 4      5A75    5A7W6
84HMB    9408EL  CHA  24  4A8C          034A7  1 4      5AA5    5AAW5
84HMB    9408EL  CAS  24  5ABCC    5    044A7  1 4      5AA5    5AAW5
84JHC    925COX  BAR  25  4ABC          044A7  1 5      5AA5    5AA5
84AKD    929DAV       25  4ABC          044A7  1 5      5AA5    5AA5
84CJSS   917SHA  SLO  26  48CD          044M7  1 5      5751    5755
84JAF    22002BAR  HAL  22  48CD        034A7  1 4      45A74   45A7W5
84CJSS   917SHA  TOW  26  48CD          044A7  1 4      5AA4    5AA5
```

FIG. 3

In brief, what the sibylline leaves seem to say—for oracular responses are seldom crystal clear—is that the tunes of "Barbara Allan," with negligible anomalies excepted, fall into four rather unequal groups, members of which are found on both sides of the Atlantic with varying frequency. One class is mainly English, consistently major and heptatonic, and divided about equally between the authentic and plagal ranges (Fig. 4, A^1). Many variants, especially in southwestern England, lean to 5/4 time (Fig. 4, A^2). The over-all shape of examples in the authentic range is from tonic to

FIG. 4

dominant and back to tonic in the first phrase; rising in the second phrase to the octave, but falling back from the seventh degree to the fifth for a middle cadence. The melodic curve of the third phrase is often rather like the second; and the fourth resembles the first, but seldom closely, so that the phrasal scheme is generally ABCD.

Another class is mainly Scottish, with a darker modal cast, from Dorian to Æolian (Fig. 4, *B*). It favors common time, often commencing with a dotted meter; and it typically rises at the middle and final cadences from the lower fifth or flat seventh to the tonic.

A third class, which includes many American variants, is habitually in that pentatonic scale which lacks the fourth and seventh degrees (Fig. 4, *C*). Its members are mostly plagal tunes, frequently in 3/4 or 3/2 time. Its most consistent features are a rather chaconne-like rhythm, and a middle cadence with a feminine ending that rises like a query from the major third to the fifth degree. The query is answered in the musical rhyme of the final cadence, typically from lower sixth to tonic.

The fourth class is composed almost entirely of American variants of a tune that goes back at least to the seventeenth century. Whether its origins are Scottish, Irish, or English is uncertain. Its usual form nowadays is only the second half of the ancient double-strain tune; and the final makes a rather dubious tonic without the missing half to rationalize it (Fig. 4, *D*). The middle cadence of the remaining half commonly falls from the octave or seventh to the fifth. This class is composed mostly of pentatonic tunes lacking their third and sixth, but there are also a good many hexatonic variants lacking only their third. Over all, the first and third classes have perhaps a good deal in common, while the Scottish, or second group, is the most distinct—though it has affiliations with other songs than the "Barbara Allan" tribe. The fourth class, too, is of frequent occurrence in other connections.

But we must not forget that "Barbara Allan" is a song; and all this while the words have been left languishing. Returning, then, to the text, we may ask first whether the welter of change, "each way in move," shows any traces of a *current* of tradition; and whether, against "the everlasting wash of air" and the ever present erosive action of forgetfulness, which alters while it gradually obliterates, there stand out harder substances that resist destruction, or if perhaps there may even be re-creative forces at work.

At the start, the name of the place where the action occurs has clung in memory with surprising tenacity. "Scarlet Town," which is not to be found on any map, and which may even be an inspired corruption of a known locality, has stood firm in the popular imagination. Reading (town), for which it might once have been a punning substitute, has not been taken up, nor has London, though they both occur sporadically. But place has often thinned to vaguenesses like "in the town," "in the west country," or "way down South"; and where the localizing impulse has grown so weak, it has tended to drop out, usually taking with it the line which emphasizes Barbara's local potency: "made *every* youth cry wellaway."

Two contrasting seasons for the central event have made strong claims to permanent acceptance: autumn and spring. Autumn, the time when green or yellow leaves were falling, was the choice of the first surviving Scottish version, of the early eighteenth century. Whether the Scots have a special weakness for the pathetic fallacy has not been determined. Burns, we recall, protested its absence:

> Ye banks and braes o' bonnie Doon,
> How can ye bloom sae fresh and fair?
> How can ye chant, ye little birds,
> And I sae weary fu' o' care!

At any rate, the opposite choice has been greatly preferred, perhaps because it sharpens the pathos, the poignancy, of the death of young lovers:

> All in the merry month of May,
> When green buds they were swelling.

Analysts suggest that the reason most suicides occur in fine weather is because of the clash between that and the private unhappiness.

The lover's name has never been felt to matter: it could be Green, Gray, Grame, Groves; and Jimmy, Willie, Sweet William, or just nothing at all. But Allan in some form has clung through thick and thin, being built into rhymes and echoed in the melodic cadences. Better rhyming has sometimes prompted "Ellen"; and

thereupon the first name may become an epithet, "barbarous." But
that word is rather too literary, and Barbara has generally held her
ground.

The reproachful death bells have seldom been forgotten, even in
regions where one may suppose bells to be rare; and sometimes, to
clinch their message, they have stirred up a chorus of birds to the
same import. But when even the birds say "Hard-hearted Barbara
Ellen," bells are no longer needed, and sometimes are forgotten.

To make a good ending, Barbara's remorse and death used, as the
earlier texts indicate, to be judged sufficient. But not latterly: familiar formulas from other songs have suggested themselves, and the
conclusion is drawn out at length. Barbara orders her mother to
make her bed, her father to dig her grave; if Jimmie dies as it might
be today, she dies as it might be tomorrow, of love in the one case,
in the other of sorrow. They are buried in churchyard and choir,
respectively, and the old favorite rose-and-briar ending, symbolic
or, as some say, metempsychotic, is appended. Frequently the
metaphor fades, and the briar springs from Willie, the rose from
Barbara. What matters is that they twine in a true-love knot.

A fact that seems to have escaped attention is the very interesting metamorphosis which has befallen Barbara herself in her lifetime. Tradition has gradually transformed her, subtly but surely,
without much conscious assistance from anyone. This characteristic process is worth a closer look.

The first known reference to the song's existence is in Pepys's
diary, January 2, 1666, when, at end of a very long day, that indefatigable man hurries off in the evening to my Lord Bruncker's,
where he finds a numerous company—"but, above all, my dear
Mrs. Knipp, with whom I sang, and in perfect pleasure I was to
hear her sing, and especially her little Scotch song of 'Barbary
Allen.' " How much older the song may be we cannot surely say,
but the frequent mention of old songs, like "Greensleeves," in earlier literature makes the lack of a single casual Elizabethan allusion
to Barbara an argument for a mid-seventeenth-century origin.
Pepys calls it a Scottish song, and Mrs. Knipp, like Maxine Sullivan
some years later, may have picked it up and given it an urban currency by singing it on the stage. It has even been wildly conjectured that the song was a covert attack on Barbara Villiers,
Countess of Castlemaine. We have no Scottish text so early; no re-

corded tune in Scotland for another century, in England for two
centuries. But an English broadside text was printed in London in
Pepys's own day, and its most salient features—with powerful assistance from Percy's *Reliques*, a work continually reprinted after
1765—have been perpetuated in the traditional memory. "Barbara
Allen's Cruelty," it was called, and unexplained cruelty was her
chief characteristic trait. It has been a main business of tradition to
rationalize this quality and explain it away. In the broadside, when
the young man's servant comes to summon her, she ruthlessly replies:

> If death be printed in his face,
>   And sorrow's in him dwelling,
> Then little better shall he be
>   For bonny Barbara Allen.

This *anticipative* obduracy, inessential to the narrative, has disappeared from the popular mind, though her reluctant and tardy arrival is remembered:

> So slowly, slowly she got up,
>   And so slowly she came to him,
> And all she said when she came there,
>   "Young man, I think you are a dying."

In the broadside, his appeal for her pity is met by the retort:

> "If on your death-bed you be lying,
>   What is that to Barbara Allen?
> I cannot keep you from your death;
>   So farewell," said Barbara Allen.

So stony a heart was too much for the popular sensibility, which
went to work on motivation. In the earliest Scottish copy, printed
about fifty years later, in Ramsay's *Tea Table Miscellany*, and also
reprinted by Percy, she is not cold but bitterly resentful:

> "O the better for me ye's never be
>   Tho your heart's blood were a spilling.
>
> "O dinna ye mind, young man," said she,
>   "When ye was in the tavern a drinking,
> That ye made the healths gae round and round,
>   And slighted Barbara Allen?"

In the Scottish copy, he has no reply, but turns his face to the wall
with a kind adieu. She leaves the deathbed with visible reluctance

and a parting sigh, and goes home to announce her imminent death.

Not so the early broadside. Walking "on a day," Barbara hears the death bell, turns round to see the funeral procession, orders the corpse to be set down, and takes a long look, all the while loudly laughing. Again the popular mind has recoiled, and in copy after American copy, we find verses like these:

> The more she looked, the more she grieved,
>   She busted out to crying.
> "I might have saved this young man's life
>   And kept him from hard dying."

Sometimes self-reproach changes even to self-exculpation:

> "Oh mother dear, you caused all this;
>   You would not let me have him."

Thus, little by little, and partly through mere abridgment and condensation, a kindlier, more sympathetic image has been wrought in tradition. If Barbara was once a "real person," as Phillips Barry believed that she must have been, she has certainly mellowed with age!

"Barbara Allan" is unquestionably and by all odds the best known, most favorite traditional ballad among English-speaking peoples in the twentieth, and like enough the nineteenth, century. This is a curious fact, and one not very easy to explain. By ordinary standards, one must acknowledge that the story has few of the elements that make a smash hit. The action is far from violent; there is little suspense in it, and a minimum of surprise. The "hero" —if he may so be called—is pallid in every sense: he is acted upon, and hardly acts at all—unless to throw up the sponge in round one constitutes an act. For although he pleads he is misunderstood in some variants, far more of them have no trace of his defense; yet the song flourishes. There is no love triangle, no defiance of conventional morality, no struggle, no complication, no delay. Where is the heroic spirit of the common man, the indomitable will to live, come what may? Here is neither hope nor courage: only abject surrender. As the first choice of the English-speaking peoples, it is a strange phenomenon.

The psychological problem—and I think it is a real one—must be consigned to the experts. But before we leave it, we may remind

ourselves that the idea of love as a destructive power has been a potent concept for almost as long as the records of Western civilization can be traced. By the ancients it was looked upon as a seizure,
a calamity, a madness; and the lover's madness was a disease also
well known to the Middle Ages. In all early literature, as in the best
loved ballads, love is an illness from which few or none recover.
Because of it, Barbara's lover is doomed. Her own observation is as
clinical as cruel: "Young man, I think you're dying." But what she
does not as yet realize is that the disease is infectious. After her rash
exposure, *her* death is almost equally predictable, and imminent.
She can do nothing to avert it: Love strikes unerringly where he
will, and "caught is proud and caught is debonair." "But these are
all lies," protests Rosalind cynically: "Men have died from time to
time, and worms have eaten them, but not for love." It may be true
—but we wish they had! Truly, we wish they had. The ideal of a
love so complete and entire as to be essential to the continuance of
life is a conceptual archetype persisting through the ages, through
all literature, the greatest—and the least. While we scorn the spine-
lessness of Barbara's lover, some ray of this compelling magic
touches him and transfigures him at last; and Barbara herself is re-
deemed by the *Liebestod*.

To descend to more humdrum matters. I think we may lay it
down as axiomatic that whatever is under no external necessity to
be remembered will be forgotten if it is possible to forget it. Survival depends partly on ease of recollection. In this sense, "Barbara
Allan" is an extremely memorable song. It is next to impossible to
get the narrative twisted. There are but two characters, and they
are at once delineated by word and act in crisis. The heroine's
name is not only unforgettable by virtue of syntactical management
but itself serves as a mnemonic for the stanzaic rimes, calling back
the successive phases of the narrative: dwelling, swelling, telling,
knelling; while the double rime is its own reminding device, requir-
ing special heed and a matching musical cadence to parallel and
reinforce it.

So we return once more to the tunes, which are the vital element
in which the story exists—the air it breathes, and the breath of its
life. We find, when we extend our correlation of the tunes to a
comparative analysis of the whole body of most common and typical British-American folk-tunes, that those of "Barbara Allan," in

spite of superficial differences and casual exceptions or anomalies, fall into the central norm of our tradition.[3] They act as we should expect them to do, and require no extra will-to-remember. They end on the tonic, their mid-cadences are usually at the fifth. Their rhythms are simple and familiar. Their length is the common four-phrase length; their phrasal patterns are habitually progressive, ABCD; and in their individual shapes the phrases are typical. Their ranges stay within normal bounds; their melodic modes are among the commonest: major or near-major pentatonics, or (for Scotland) Dorian/Æolian.

These normal likings gain their importance from being so widespread and universal in our traditional culture. Things need not have gone this way; they might have turned out otherwise. To make these the prevailing patterns, there had to be an infinite number of rejections, conscious or instinctive, or alternative choices or different appeals. Thus, in the long course of time, racial music traditions tend to establish their idiosyncratic distinctions and habitual characters. The psychological and aesthetic implications of these musical facts are far-reaching and profound. When someone asks, why all this fuss and bother, this endless trouble and expenditure of time on an old song, the answer is: because this old song, in its mere, sheer *commonness*, strikes to our very roots. There is no obligation on these old things to survive. They have lived on in the minds and hearts of countless men and women, untainted by compulsion, for the purest and most disinterested reason possible to be conceived: because they have continued to give joy and solace, on the basic levels of artistic experience, to generation after generation of our humankind. "The proper study of mankind is man"; and so long as this precept remains valid, folk-song will continue to be an important subject for human inquiry.[4]

[3] For a frequency chart, see essay ten of this collection.

[4] What is said above of "Barbara Allen" echoes and expands the summary statement on this ballad in the author's *Traditional Tunes of the Child Ballads*, II (1962), 321. Figure 5 was printed in the *Journal of the International Folk Music Council*, IX (1957), 27.

Latterly, "Barbara Allen" has been the subject of two weighty musicological studies: by Charles Seeger, in *Selected Reports*, a Publication of the Institute of Ethnomusicology, UCLA (1966), pp. 120–167; and by Mieczyslaw Kolinski, in *Ethnomusicology*, Vol. XII, no. 2 (May 1968), pp. 208–218; and Vol. XIII, no. 1 (Jan., 1969), pp. 1–73.

Folk-Song in the United States, 1910—1960:
Reflections from a Student's Corner

AS I WRITE the title, I am frightened at my temerity, and hasten to warn the reader that he will be disappointed if he expects the following brief remarks to cover much of so enormous and bewilderingly diverse a territory. Lack of knowledge, sympathy, time, and space forbids discussion here of many fascinating fields of inquiry, such as the aboriginal songs of American Indian tribes; the songs of various ethnic groups that have settled with their budget of traditional music: Spanish in the Southwest, Creole and "Cajun" beside the Gulf of Mexico, Norwegian in the North Central States, German in Pennsylvania, Jewish in some of the large cities eastern and western; Negro throughout the deep South, with a permeating national—even international—influence on popular music everywhere, vocal and instrumental, in Spirituals, Blues, and the various styles of jazz. I shall be concerned with the English-speaking tradition, but even here I can say little or nothing of the songs belonging to special kinds of labor—to sailors, lumbermen, miners, railroaders, cowboys—or of the recently developing songs of social protest; or of prison-songs; or of religious sects like the Amish, Mormons, and Shakers. The revolution that has occurred within a single area, that of British-American folk-song, is sufficiently striking and important to occupy us fully. To follow its course for the past half-century is like tracing a stream from its high-withdrawn springs to their gradual confluence into a channel, widening into a lake, then pouring down a succession of cataracts, and finally sweeping along with the power of a wide river put to multifarious commercial uses before it empties itself into the estranging, undifferentiated ocean. Distinctions are already disappearing, and this water can never recover its earlier clarity nor revert to its source.

There is irony in the fact that academics were, in this country, responsible for the beginnings of what we now perceive as a mass phenomenon of our mid-century. They could never have imagined what forces their inquisitive probing would release. They were not seeking to revitalize the past, except as antiquaries in search of ancient remains. The greatest American student of popular verse, Professor Francis James Child of Harvard, patterning his work upon Svend Grundtvig's labors on Danish balladry, thought of his own research as primarily a salvaging operation, to rescue all that remained in English of an all-but-defunct *genre*, for the historical record. To him, the music that had once given the ballads wings was of such slight importance that it could safely be neglected, though he was glad to have a feather, for a keepsake, when it floated to his desk. Mutual relations between text and tune as formative process were undocumented and beyond reach; but the text could be studied by itself.

When the American Folklore Society was founded, in 1888, Part V of Child's great *English and Scottish Popular Ballads*, carrying the work to its halfway point (through no. 155), had just appeared; and it was by natural right that he was elected first President of the Society. Already, before the outbreak of the Civil War, his earlier collection had established his authority in this field; and under his leadership, with the dynamic support of W. W. Newell and an enthusiastic band of eager young scholars like G. L. Kittredge and F. N. Robinson, the Society took vigorous life. In the 'nineties and the first decade of the new century, branches sprang up in many parts of the country: in Boston, Philadelphia, New Orleans, Hampton (Virginia), Baltimore, Washington, Cincinnati, Berkeley, Buffalo; in Wisconsin, Tennessee, Arizona, Missouri, Iowa, Texas; and within the second decade other productive regional groups, in Illinois, Kentucky, North and South Carolina, Nebraska, Virginia, Oklahoma, West Virginia—some of them dying down, to be reborn in later years. In the late 'twenties and during the 'thirties a dozen more commenced, some of them, notably the Folk Song Society of the North-East and the Southeastern Folklore Society, among the most vigorous and fruitful of all. California, New York (revived), and New Jersey came later still.[1] Like their parent, few of these paid any special attention to American folk-music. But the interest excited by Child's ballad collection persisted, and the effort to find new variants of the "Child Ballads" in their own localities stimulated the amassing of regional folk-song archives.

Some of this effort was surprisingly successful, coming as it did in the wake of Child's defeated attempts to collect significant new ballad texts from oral sources in America. Always the greatest successes occurred where the contagious enthusiasm of a devoted leader—nearly always a professor with magnetic personal appeal—sparked the interest of numerous persons with special opportunities, energy, or freedom to explore the regional byways. Many whose useful activity was thus stimulated were schoolmistresses. Some of the most successful were people in search of a hobby, with little scholarly background but needing to be reassured that what they were doing was potentially valuable and respected by the learned. Some of the most effective leaders, like Kittredge of Harvard, C. Alphonso Smith of Virginia, J. H. Cox of West Virginia, Reed Smith of South Carolina, H. M. Belden of Missouri, did little or no collecting but gave encouragement and prestige; others, like Phillips Barry of Cambridge, John Lomax of Texas, Frank C. Brown of North Carolina, Dorothy Scarborough of Columbia, and Helen Hartness Flanders of Vermont, did a considerable amount of field work as well as lecturing and writing. Some astute devotees, like Cox and Brown, became permanent secretaries and archivists of societies, and they guarded the growing stores with an eye to future publication. As a whole, the widespread development of unsubsidized interest and effort proceeded with close affiliation to universities. From its start, the connections were literary; not anthropological, not sociological, and not musical. But the scholarly leaders had the good sense to insist upon records as accurate and full as the case permitted, and this meant that the musical account gradually and inevitably accumulated along with the textual one, though never in equal degree.

[1] Cf. Wayland D. Hand, "North American Folklore Societies: A Survey." *Journal of American Folklore* (1943), pp. 161–191; and the same author's "North American Folklore Societies: A Supplement." *Journal of American Folklore* (1946), pp. 477–494. These articles contain brief historical sketches of the individual societies by present or former officers.

There was one exception to the general inattention to the music of folk-song among these pioneers and that was Phillips Barry. Barry was a man of ranging interests which he did not manage to bring under perfect control; but there was little question that what commanded his deepest sympathy was the music of the ballads, and he devoted much of his very considerable energy to it. Barry was probably self-taught in music, and his theory outran his expert knowledge; but he insisted on the essential importance of the ballad tunes, on the fact that it was *song* that must be captured, not just a text, and that traditional lines of transmission were also a significant factor in the entity to be studied. The soundness of these precepts would be seen when in due time *British Ballads from Maine* appeared (1929), edited by Barry and collectors Fannie Eckstorm and Mary W. Smyth, with the tunes accurately noted by George Herzog, a musical anthropologist in the Hornbostel tradition and friend of Bela Bartók. This was the first American collection in which critical attention was paid to the individual ballads as folk-*songs* existing in a socio-historical milieu, a family tradition, words and music combined. Barry was also a pioneer in the use of a dictaphone in collecting, though he does not seem to have relied heavily upon it, nor to have transcribed many of the songs he recorded on wax cylinders—perhaps because of the clumsiness of the apparatus and the risk of destroying the records by repeated playing.

W. W. Newell had published a small collection of children's songs, with some music, in the early 'eighties (twice reprinted), and John Lomax in 1910 brought out a volume of cowboy songs with a handful of tunes. He, too, used a phonograph in collecting. There had been publication of "Slave Songs" in the 'sixties, and the spirituals of the Fisk "Jubilee Singers" had reached 130,000 copies before 1890; but apart from such special categories there was almost no publication of true folk-song before the First World War in the U.S.A.

All the while, however, since the founding of the parent folklore society, the reservoir of the regional chapters was filling by slow degrees, and a climate of favorable interest was forming. Now, in the War decade, and in part probably stimulated by the upsurgence of patriotic feeling local as well as national, there was (we see now in retrospect) a spectacular burst of activity, particularly in the Southern Appalachian region. The Societies of Virginia and

North Carolina were almost a twin birth; Kentucky came slightly
earlier and South Carolina slightly later; Tennessee, though
founded in 1900, had a more tenuous hold on life. These bodies
awoke to the realization that their rugged and inaccessible hill
country was a mine of tradition, generations deep: an undisturbed
deposit of English and Scottish folkways, folk-speech, and folk-
song incomparably rich. This discovery proved a tremendous spur
to activity, and many enthusiastic amateurs went busily to the
work of collecting. Among the minerals they sought, versions of
the Child ballads occupied the place of highest esteem in the growing archives. At the same time, by a miracle of good luck, a spotlight was thrown upon the interest and value of the music, through
the excitement aroused by the opportune visits of the great English
collector, Cecil J. Sharp, in 1916, 1917, and 1918.

Just at the end of the 'nineties, shortly after Child's death, the
English Folk Song Society was founded by a group of enthusiasts
with an orientation quite the opposite of Child's. Where his interest
had been textual and antiquarian, theirs was musical and focused in
contemporary survivals. Their primary materials were in the memories and on the lips of living singers in village and field. They dis-
trusted the meagre and imperfect records of what had hitherto
passed for English popular song, and dedicated their efforts to the
accurate recovery of the actual singing tradition of English "folk."
With the excitement of explorers, the zeal of missionaries, and the
creative appreciation of composers—which several of them out-
standingly were—they discovered and made known through their
Journal in the years before the War a whole new world of song.
Among them all, by virtue of his devotion, untiring energy, and
success in collecting and publicizing, Sharp was preeminently the
leader of this distinguished company of pioneers. When he came to
the Appalachians, it was with a record of vast achievement, familiar subject matter, assured and rigorous habits of procedure in collecting, technical skill and patriotic self-dedication—for he came in
search of *English* folk-song and was only extending the range of
his earlier work. In the course of his three visits, amounting in all to
only forty-six weeks of active collecting, he captured the astound-
ing number of 1612 tunes from nearly three hundred singers, taking down the tunes by hand without mechanical aids. The total
was almost as large as that which he had amassed in a decade of

intermittent collecting at home: larger than his Somerset gathering in the years 1903–1907, from which he had extracted and published with his own piano accompaniments the five-volumed series of *Folk Songs from Somerset*, three sets of Novello's series for schools, a number of the *Journal* (1905), and upon which was based his too brief treatise, *English Folk Song: Some Conclusions*, 1907. Now, with characteristic energy, Sharp at once set about making his fresh findings known and, with Olive Dame Campbell, wife of the Director of the Southern Highland Division of the Russell Sage Foundation, from whom he had learned about these songs, brought out after his first (nine-week) visit a volume containing 122 texts and 323 tunes, with a valuable Introduction in which he described the country and its people, the scales and the style of singing employed, the presumed ethnological background of the singers, and ended with a ringing declaration "of the supreme cultural value of an inherited tradition" even in the absence of formal school education; and of the importance of the folk-arts of a nation as the wellspring of all artistic endeavor. "It is my sober belief," he wrote, "that if a young composer were to master the contents of this book, study and assimilate each tune with its variants, he would acquire just the kind of education that he needs, and one far better suited to his requirements than he would obtain from the ordinary conservatoire or college of music." [2]

This was a clarion call that could hardly be ignored, and it chimed well with the prevalent spirit of the day. The slow ripening of the previvous quarter-century, the dispersed efforts of individuals, now began to appear in printed form. Kittredge gathered a number of the pieces that had been sent him by various collectors and printed them in the *Journal of American Folklore* in 1917. Josephine McGill published *Folk-Songs of the Kentucky Mountains* in the same year. Loraine Wyman and Howard Brockway published *Lonesome Tunes* in 1916, and *Twenty Kentucky Mountain Songs* in 1920. A. T. Davison and T. Surette edited a selection of folk-songs for schools in 1917, and the Texas Folklore Society commenced its long series of miscellaneous publications in book

---

[2] *English Folk Songs from the Southern Appalachians*, collected by Olive Dame Campbell and Cecil J. Sharp (1917). The Introduction was reprinted in the second edition, edited by Maud Karpeles, 2 volumes (1932), I, pp. xxi–xxxvii. Quotation from this edition, p. xxxv.

form in 1916. It is symptomatic that three of the presidents of the American Folklore Society in this period had a predominant interest in folk-song: H. M. Belden, J. A. Lomax, and Marius Barbeau (still actively concerned with French-Canadian song). *Songs from the Hills of Vermont,* by E. B. Sturgis and R. Hughes, appeared in 1919, closing the decade's accomplishment.

The tide of publication was still growing in the 'twenties, which saw twice as many books as did the previous decade, expanding in range of interest and regional scope. There were songs of sailormen, lumberjacks, Negroes, and several very important regional collections, three of the most noteworthy being J. H. Cox's *Folk Songs of the South,* 1925, a product of the West Virginia Society's efforts; *Traditional Ballads of Virginia,* 1929, edited for the Virginia Society by A. K. Davis, Jr., and entirely composed of Child ballads; and *British Ballads from Maine,* 1929, already mentioned and also composed entirely of Child ballads. In 1930, the Folk-Song Society of the North-East, galvanized by Phillips Barry, began its significant annual issuance of a valuable *Bulletin,* regrettably terminated after eight years, upon the death of two mainstays of the Editorial Board. Among other collections were W. R. Mackenzie's *Ballads and Sea Songs from Nova Scotia,* 1928, and the influential and widely popular *American Songbag,* 1927, edited without much of a scholarly conscience by the poet Carl Sandburg.

But the great decade in rediscovery of traditional American song was that of the 'thirties. The record of the 'twenties was probably doubled, and at least a dozen compilations of major importance saw the light. First of all, and without question the foremost contribution to the study of British-American folk-song, was the revised, amplified, two-volume collection of Sharp's *English Folk Songs from the Southern Appalachians,* edited by Maud Karpeles in 1932. This work contained 968 tunes to 274 ballads and songs— something short of two-thirds of Sharp's total American harvest— each faithfully dated, attributed to singer and place, and analyzed as to scale. If all other records were destroyed, this one would provide a truly representative record of the unspoiled traditional state of British-American folk-song in the first quarter of the twentieth century, before the days of radio and phonograph and the other encroachments of modern living. The decade also witnessed publication of the accumulating collections of various groups, as of

Tennessee, Indiana (P. G. Brewster), and Missouri (H. M. Belden); and of the persistent and continuous industry of individuals, such as Mellinger E. Henry in the Southern Highlands, Elizabeth B. Greenleaf and Grace Y. Mansfield in Newfoundland, Maud Karpeles in the same province, Helen Creighton in Nova Scotia, John and Alan Lomax, Vance Randolph in the Ozarks, Emelyn E. Gardner and Geraldine J. Chickering in Michigan, Mrs. Flanders and others in Vermont, Mary O. Eddy in Ohio, Dorothy Scarborough in the Appalachians; and the commencement of the valuable *Southern Folklore Quarterly* for the Folklore Society of the South-East. George Pullen Jackson found a rich, special vein in the early "shaped-note" hymnals of the Southern Baptists, who still maintain their century-old spiritual singing tradition.

The same decade of the 'thirties has another significant claim to remembrance in the fact that much important field collecting was being done with or without recording machines, not to be transcribed for printing until much later. This is true, for example, of the valuable and meticulous collections of Winston Wilkinson in Virginia, most of which are regrettably not even yet available in published form. The same may be said of a large portion of L. W. Chappell's collections, whose labors are generally known only through his slim but worthwhile *Folk Songs of Roanoke and the Albemarle*, 1939, and his study of a single song, *John Henry*, 1933. The important field work of A. K. Davis in the Virginia Highlands, done in the middle 'thirties, has only lately, in part, seen the light, in his *More Traditional Ballads of Virginia*, 1960. Mrs. Flanders was busy augmenting her large archive of New England folk-song, not to appear until the 'fifties, and still in course of publication (*Ballads Migrant in New England*, 1953; *Ancient Ballads Traditionally Sung in New England*, 1960—[3]). Vance Randolph was compiling his great Ozark collection, to be published in four volumes between 1946–1950. Most impressive of all, Frank C. Brown was amassing his vast North Carolina stores, begun in 1913 with the help of wax cylinders, and greatly increased on the musical side by summer field trips in the late 'thirties: riches that have only very lately been revealed in the fourth and fifth volumes of *North Carolina Folklore* (1957, 1962), under the painstaking and scholarly editing of J. P. Schinhan, the first musicologist to devote a

[3] Completed in 1964, in four volumes.

major effort to such a task in this country. The texts of these songs had already appeared some years earlier, skillfully edited by H. M. Belden and A. P. Hudson; the latter of whom was also busy in the 'thirties with his own collection, *Folk-Songs of Mississippi*, 1936, unfortunately devoid of music except in a meagre mimeographed pamphlet issued by the National Service Bureau in 1937, soon after unobtainable. Three other publications of a relatively late date but of an earlier, scholarly, habit deserve to be mentioned here, all published in 1950: A. C. Morris' *Folk-Songs of Florida*, Byron Arnold's *Folk Songs of Alabama*, and W. A. Owen's *Texas Folk Songs*.

It is to be observed that all nor nearly all of the activity thus far reviewed was the direct outgrowth of academic impetus in the Folklore Societies; that the work brought forth was responsibly edited by persons with scholarly training for a public friendly to learning; and published usually by university presses. There is perhaps a paradoxical element in this situation; and it was always the dearest wish of Cecil Sharp and his friends to "give back the songs to the people to whom they belonged"—not only to the few who had previously known and preserved them but to the many—in fact, every one—whose proper national heritage they were. The way of restoration, however, was to prove more circuitous than by the simple acts of publishing and re-learning; and in the terms in which it was offered, the gift seems to have been repudiated by the public at large. During the years since the end of the Second World War, folk-song has been adapted to commercial uses, and the transformation is a tidal wave that has swept away the old landmarks. The manner in which this has come about is stranger than fiction.

Even in the first two decades of the century, there were a few, as we have noticed, who were eager to preserve the actual sound of the voices, and who were willing to go to the effort of carting their cumbersome recording machines on expeditions, or of inducing the singers to come to the machines and sing into them. As the machines were improved, they were more frequently used. Phonograph companies saw an opportunity here, and a considerable number of untrained, country singers were recorded in the middle 'twenties, to make discs of their familiar songs for limited commercial sale. The results were classified as "race" records, and sold

mainly in the South. They were not usually listed in the big national catalogues of the record companies; but among them were
interesting versions of genuine traditional folk-song, very charac-
teristically sung. Some of these singers began to acquire a wider
reputation and adopted a variety of aliases to evade the efforts of
recording companies to monopolize their services. Thus they considerably increased the poor pay they got from a single company.
The "folk festivals" which were organized with increasing frequency in the 'thirties (and which are still in vogue) were natural
outlets for such talent. Songs were exchanged and recorded at
these gatherings, and reputations were made and confirmed. Small
bands of singers and instrumentalists began to spring up and acquire followers and imitators. Besides appearing at dances and social and political rallies, they were heard over the radio; and more
and more their records were heard. The folk-songs which they arranged and adapted and performed became "hits" of the day, and
were sold as sheet music and phonographic records in increasing numbers. Individual singers, Burl Ives, Pete Seeger, Josh White,
Harry Belafonte, and others with great personal appeal, achieved
fabulous peaks of national fame. Many so-called folk-singers today
make a more than comfortable income. To produce this result, a
calculated and complex system has developed, with a multitude of
people performing specialized functions, each of them receiving a
proportion of the earnings. In order to make certain that every one
gets his share, two organizations, ASCAP (American Society of
Composers, Authors, and Publishers), and BMI (Broadcast Music
Incorporated) were developed to safeguard their members' interests. Part of their business is to keep a record of sales and performances of whatever kind and collect the claims.

The sums involved can be very large. It is possible for a "hit"
which has been successfully promoted by all the devices of modern
publicity to reach a sale of 1,000,000 phonograph copies. Another
10,000 copies may be sold as sheet music. The copyright owner
can collect $20,000 from these, and performances and foreign
rights may net him another $5–10,000. It is said (on hearsay) that
the first dozen "Sing-Along" record albums made by "Mitch"
Miller, a current leader of television and other programs the purpose of which is to get audiences to learn and sing the songs while
they are being played, netted upwards of $25,000,000. So many

persons can be involved in the success that it is very difficult to say who is responsible, or who deserves credit and reward. Suppose a commercially-minded collector sees possibilities in a song he has obtained from a traditional folk-singer. He may alter it somewhat before he consults an "A and R" (artist and repertoire) man. The latter's business is to know what singer is best suited to exploit the song. A chosen singer (usually with his supporting group, vocal or instrumental) makes a taped studio recording, which is taken to a publisher. The publisher requires assurance of a contract for a commercial recording before he will consent to publish the song in sheet music. When the record has been made, it is played on radio programs consisting of the latest hits. The man who plays the records also announces them and may talk about the song and the singers; and he too will develop a following that respects his opinions on these matters. He is known as a disc jockey ("deejay") and his power to influence the fortunes of a song can be very considerable. A song performed by one of the idols of the day in his characteristic fashion, or by a popular group like the Kingston Trio, tends to become identified with the singer or group, and this increases its sales and its popularity.[4]

In this multifaced development there is a great deal that is scarcely relevant to our present concern. In the early 'thirties and later 'forties, the songfests or "hootenannies," as they came to be called, engendered the excitement and sympathetic fervor, and some of the purposiveness, of a "brave new world," in social and political attitudes. It must be obvious that most of those who flocked to the meetings, joined in "audience participation" on the choruses, followed the named singers, learned the songs, and bought the hits as the records appeared, were young people. The movement, in so far as it achieves definition, has shown traits analogous to the European Jugendbewegung in the days of the Wandervögel prior to the First World War and after. In the United States a similar restlessness is visible today, with the musical manifestations that in one sort or another appear to be the natural attendants of social disturbance. "Die Gedanken sind frei"; but in song they are shared even with strangers; and the parting song of

[4] Cf. Sigmund Spaeth, *A History of Popular Music in America* (1948); Ray M. Lawless, *Folksingers and Folksongs in America* (1960); Oscar Brand, *The Ballad Mongers* (1962).

many a "hootenanny" has been "So long, it's been good to know you," one of the inventions of the militant folk-singer Woody Guthrie.

The attitude of these *esprits forts* is of course inimical to tradition. Their music need not be traditional but nevertheless much of it demonstrably has had roots in, or affiliations with, folk-song. As one successful producer-performer put it recently, they think of the traditional material as the ore out of which they can make something of their own, something expressive of current ideas and emotions. What has been described, however, is what is known to the younger generation as "folk-song." It is the kind of thing they have grown up with, and in the mass they do not in fact know anything else by that name. They associate it naturally with professional entertainment, platform performance, paying audiences, and mass communication. They have started practicing on banjos and guitars and other, stranger, instruments, improvised or exotic, in the hope, if they have enough original talent and skill and personal appeal, of winning themselves acclaim and "big" money. They learn by copying successful singers and performers; and, as they acquire knowledge, they go back to the collections of genuine folk-song gathered by "pedants" and "purists", in search of *vehicles* by means of which to launch their own professional careers. There is money, too, in the publication of fresh collections cannily gathered in whatsoever way, adapted, altered, edited, and sometimes composed by well-known and knowledgeable stars in the "Folk-Song" firmament. Lip service is paid to "authenticity" but there is seldom very scrupulous regard to the significance of the term, and the new collections are *always copyrighted*. What is authentic consists mainly, perhaps, in the genuinely personal and unique style of performance which they receive.

It was the conviction of Cecil Sharp, Vaughan Williams, Holst, and their fellows that what was most precious about folk-song was its very *im*personality, its idiom of nationality divested of all idiosyncrasies of individuals, which was the effect of oral tradition. This process, which molded while it preserved a song, gave it the stamp of community approval, its weather-beaten quality, as of something that had been there for a long time, and of which generations of common descent had been fond. They regarded it, therefore, as a primary duty not to change a note of what they recorded from native singing, and were certain that the aesthetic as well as scientific value of their contribution lay in this absolute fidelity to tradition. Their faith was that from these national well-springs of song, become once again familiar and habitual from childhood, English music would have a rebirth. In the persons of such composers as Delius and Vaughan Williams, the hope was literally realized.

Apart from the living and ever-fresh beauty of many of the songs, there is a valid interest in studying the ways of traditional, not arbirary, change. There is a fascination in seeing how, for centuries, a folk-tune has preserved its identity; and an equal fascination in studying the never-ending succession of continual, minute changes occurring within a tradition carried by singers concerned to preserve it, concerned to do no more than remember and repeat the old songs they have loved. To try to determine the unconsciously operative principles in accordance with which such changes take place is to raise significant questions, with implications of interest to students of many disciplines.

By reason of scientific discoveries, and notably by the invention of magnetic tape for recording and reproducing sound, it has recently become possible to preserve and repeat for analysis or other reasons a more exact duplication of folk-singing than could ever previously be achieved. Not merely the general outline now can be set down but every slightest change throughout the whole length of a many-stanzaed ballad. Not even a Bartók or a Sharp could capture more than a few such variations in a single hearing under normal conditions. We have thus acquired unprecedented advantages for accurate research.

Ironically, this ideal potentiality appears to have arrived just too late. The reasons for this pessimistic view, I think, are primarily two, and they are interconnected. The invention of radio, television, and, to a lesser extent, of the older phonograph has brought worldwide resources of entertainment into the most inaccessible parts of the country. This has, on the one hand, reduced the need of isolated folk to draw from their traditional supplies for relaxation and delight. They can afford to forget the old songs. But they can also learn new ones from across the world as easily as across the hollow. Already, stories are in circulation of collectors spending months on research fellowships in the back country with a tape re-

corder, gathering the repertory of the region's singers, and returning home only to find, on analyzing their treasure trove, that much
of it had been learned from the airwaves. Thus, almost overnight,
the regional and family traditions are being obliterated. The mass
media, while they frustrate geographical distinctions, also take
away the personal desire to cherish and preserve a tribal inheritance
of song, such as that of the Ritchie family in Kentucky, or Mrs.
Carrie Grover's in Maine, or the Harmons in Tennessee.

The other chief destroyer of traditional transmission, as I see the
situation, is Copyright, which in its turn is a by-product of the
commercialization of folk-song. The recent sudden potentiality of
folk-song as a money-maker, and the large sums invested in the industrial development of it, have led to its being jealously guarded
as a property, to be possessed or transferred or restricted at will.
This has a fatal effect on traditional change because it sets a pre-
mium on deliberate, judicious, unacknowledged alteration. A version of an old ballad, for example, which has been copyrighted in
that form, must be perceptibly different from the form in which it
had been published elsewhere, to avoid the risk of a suit. But both
of these copyrighted forms will be claimed—or proclaimed—to be
"traditional," which in part they are. And in part the copyright of
both is truly justified, for indeed there is originality in both—an
originality quite destructive of genuine traditional values. The new
generation sees nothing paradoxical about an "original" folk-song;
and an aspirant to folk-singing laurels will modestly deprecate his
own performance as that of a "rank amateur."

In view of these developments, it seems unreasonable to expect
anything in the foreseeable future which can be justly regarded as
traditional, in the traditional meaning of the term as used in the
context of our discussion. For the materials of any serious study of
our traditional folk-song, we must return to our older anthologies,
or to collections made, if not actually published or issued, before
the Second World War.

1964

Fractures in Tradition among
the "Child" Ballads

ABSOLUTE tradition, if there were such a thing, would act like Newton's first law of motion: it would proceed through time like a body falling through space, in the same direction without change. For tradition does not act upon itself. If it be conceived as a force, it is conservative, not variational. We all know, however, that it does not and cannot exist in a vacuum. It influences, and is affected by, circumstances outside itself with which it comes into proximity. Thus, in its normal condition, it undergoes perpetual alteration. By its own nature it resists change and yields reluctantly, whether like the dial's hand it "steals from its figure and no pace perceived," or by gross and violent influence is suddenly or swiftly transformed. Every student of folk-song has noticed extreme alterations, which are too palpable to escape remark. They are so common, in fact, that they seem an inseparable element of tradition. It is therefore well to insist that they are not, properly regarded, traditional at all but anti-traditional. Such phenomena may more accurately be called fractures of tradition, some major, some minor. It may be clarifying to examine a few cases where evidence is unusually indicative.

Let us start with that very obvious kind of fracture, the irrational collocation of text and refrain. A highly characteristic example is to be found in Child no. 2, "The Elfin Knight." This ballad makes its first recorded appearance on a solitary black-letter broadside copy of about 1670, now in the Pepysian library at Cambridge. The heading reads: "A proper new ballad entituled The Wind hath blown my Plaid away, or, A Discourse betwixt a young

man [*sic*, but probably a printer's error for *woman*] and the Elphin
Knight." The copy is bound with Blind Harry's *Wallace* printed
at Edinburgh, 1673; but although there are in the ballad a few
Scottish words, the piece has obviously passed through English
hands—the printer's place is not revealed. There is no indication of
the tune; but Child's B text, which is close, and perhaps mainly derivative, is directed to go to its own "proper tune." Since the ballad
is here called "The Wind hath blawn my Plaid awa," this must also
be the tune's title as well. There is a burden of four lines, presumably to be repeated with each stanza, as follows (A):

> My plaid awa, my plaid awa,
> And ore the hill and far awa.
> And far awa to Norrowa,
> My plaid shall not be blown awa.

The text of the ballad proper commences thus:

> The elphin knight sits on yon hill,
>   Ba, ba, ba, lilli ba
> He blaws his horn both lowd and shril.
>   The wind hath blown my plaid awa
>
> He blowes it east, he blowes it west,
> He blowes it where he lyketh best.
>
> "I wish that horn were in my kist,
>   Yea, and the knight in my armes two."
>
> She had no sooner these words said,
> When that the knight came to her bed.
>
> "Thou art over young a maid," quoth he,
> "Married with me thou il wouldst be."
>
> "I have a sister younger than I,
>   And she was married yesterday."
>
> "Married with me if thou wouldst be,
>   A courtesie thou must do to me.
>
> "For thou must shape a sark to me,
>   Without any cut or heme," quoth he.
>
> "Thou must shape it knife-and-sheerlesse,
>   And also sue it needle-threedlesse."

Presumably the intercalated refrain-lines are to be sung unchanged; of course the tune requires their repetition.

Without the testimony of the tune, however, we do not know how to read the first refrain-line. The other (second) refrain-line gives a norm, tetrameter iambic. But the first, "Ba, ba, ba, lilli ba," has only six, instead of eight syllables, and the accents are uncertain. The scansion would be settled instantly by the tune, but not the meaning of the line, if it had a meaning. Supposing it were meant to suggest the horns of elfland (whence the knight fetched his instrument), we should then know how they sounded. By the merest chance, a traditional version of this ballad was sung in West Newton, Massachusetts, about 1870, to a pentatonic tune with a hornlike second phrase containing the same number of syllables, thus:

Blow blow blow ye winds blow

It may be only a coincidence; but since the version is traditional, it is at least a curious coincidence. When we find in Scottish tradition, in the first decade of the present century, a form of the ballad to another tune but with twelve stanzas of the earliest text still recognizable, and with refrain-lines almost identical, we begin to suspect a persistent continuity, viz.:

Ba ba ba lee-lie ba

But the sense remains obscure. This, we remember, is a riddling ballad, in which the adversary imposes an impossible task on the maid as a precondition of marriage. This she counters by setting equally impossible prior requirements to his. Let the wind blow as it may, the situation is unaltered. The broadside demi-poet felt the need of a conclusion, and invented a silly *non sequitur* that further perplexes matters:

> (He) "I'l not quite my plaid for my life;
> It haps my seven bairns and my wife."
> The wind shall not blow my plaid awa

(She) "My maidenhead I'l then keep still,
        Let the elphin knight do what he will."
        The wind's not blown my plaid awa

Since somebody's plaid had already been blown awa by the end of the first stanza, we are not enlightened by this nonsense.

Burden, title, and refrain all indicate that the blowing away of the plaid is a central fact. But mere common sense prompts the conviction that originally neither refrain nor burden had anything to do with this ballad. No one, making a song on the riddling theme, could have thought up the refrain on rational grounds, or have supposed it appropriate. How, then, did it get in?

How else than because there was already a familiar tune that went to those words, and because, when this tune was borrowed for a fresh occasion, the refrain stuck fast? Actually, toward the end of the seventeenth century, versions of a tune turn up in manuscript and print under the alternative names, "My Plaid awa," "The Wind hath blawn my Plaid awa," and "Oure the Hills and far awa." We now recall that John Gay adroitly appropriated the tune for his new and favorite song in *The Beggar's Opera*, "Were I laid on Greenland's Coast," and most of us have learned it latterly, not from tradition but from the popularity of the play. But it is a fact, nevertheless, that no version of "The Elphin Knight" yet collected from traditional singing, or found in manuscript or book, has been mated to this familiar tune. Greig's "Laird o' Elfin," 1908, was sung to a quite different tune, though the refrain may have been caught up from print. Which suggests that the anonymous adaptor of 1670 met with some resistance to his effort to force tradition to turn a corner.[1] The tune went on its way alone.

That is not to claim, however, that in the history of this ballad, tradition has not been sharply deflected from time to time. In America, the sort of fun latent in "ba lilli ba" has been exploited in a series of nonsense refrains supplely responsive to interplay between notes and syllables. Thus, a Texas version transfers its refrain to the second half of a four-phrase tune in quick 4/4 time:

        Madam, will you make me a cambric shirt
        With not one stitch of needle work?

[1] Lately found is a version recorded in Perthshire, 1956, containing the refrain-lines, "Blow, blow, blow the wind, blow," "And the wearie wind blows my plaidie awa." Hamish Henderson and Francis Collinson, "New Child Ballad Variants," in *Scottish Studies*, Vol. 9 (1965), p. 5.

> Keedle up a keedle up a turp turp tay,
> Tum a lum a do, castle on my nay.

A Maine version, also in quick time, extends its tune to five phrases, keeping the second line for refrain, but adding an extra refrain-line at the end.

> I want you to make me a cambric shirt,
> Fum a lum a link, sup a loo my nee,
> With neither seam or needle work.
> Redio tedio, toddle bod bedio,
> Fum a lum a link, sup a loo my nee.

Another Maine version, agreeing as to time and number of phrases, cuts the fifth phrase to half-length:

> Oh say, do you know the way to Selin?
> Hickalack, tickalack, farmalack a day
> Remember me to a young lady therein.
> Hickalack, tickalack, farmalack a day,
>   Just below my knee.

This seems an amusing rationalization of "sup a loo my nee," but, apart from the last phrase, there is little resemblance in the tunes. There is a Vermont version, likewise in five phrases; but the metre is now 6/8, and the ballad thereby catches more of the lilt of a children's game-song: along with its remaining dignity it has given up its danger. It is all a fantastic jest (as, indeed, the New England versions mainly are):

> "Oh where are you going?" "I'm going to Lynn."
> Fellow ma la cus lomely.
> "Give my respects to the lady therein,"
> Ma ke ta lo, ke ta lo, tam pa lo, tam pa lo,
> Fellow ma la cus lomely.

But so long ago, probably, as the mid-eighteenth century, a more significant corner had been turned: an arbitrary mutation, as yet unexplained, in the plant, which took traditional root and ever since has been the sturdiest shoot of the tree. *Natura non facit saltum* is a rule that should be assumed wherever possible; but it is impossible to see how any scheme so far mentioned could in itself by *gradual* modification have led to the pattern that has achieved dominance: that of a quatrain wherein the second and fourth lines are given over to a refrain scheme of which the second has reference to natural phenomena—e.g. "Savoury sage rosemary and thyme," or some formula analogous in sound or sense—and of which the fourth contains the idea, and usually the verbal phrase, of "true lover of mine." The tune-variants of this stem are most frequently in a major tonality, and almost always in a compound duple, or 6/8, metre. So far as concerns the text proper of the ballad, there is relatively little change: that is, the tasks set by the opponents are of the same order as before, and recognizable in their mutations. The *idea* of the ballad is consistent, but also consistent in having given up the feeling of a supernatural threat of dire consequence, or as containing aught of greater import than the winning of a wit-contest of which the object is to outdo the opponent in extravagant demands. Solutions are not in question: the riddles cannot be resolved. The game is played for fun. This decline of faith in supernatural potency is of course a familiar feature of traditional balladry in latter-day currency, gradual and pervasive; or like the friction of the atmosphere on a falling body.

Lucy Broadwood's suggestion that herbs, and so forth, with magical properties may serve in these refrains as charms against the forces of evil [2] is a pertinent reminder of earlier superstitions, but by itself it can hardly carry this form of the ballad back to such an era of belief; and it is clear that since both parties employ the same charm, it no longer performs a primitive function in the song. The meaning had been forgotten before the ballad acquired its present shape.

The melodic scheme is kin to surviving Elizabethan tunes like "Hanskin" and "Jog on, jog on," but the "true lover of mine" refrain cannot be followed so far back. The least taxing hypothesis is that at some point in the not very distant past the riddling contest was taken over for use in a rudimentary sort of domestic drama or game-song. Baring-Gould in fact has noted that his A version was sent him out of Cornwall as a piece "enacted in farm houses." Beyond recognizing that when this event first occurred there was a real fracture or turning point in the traditional transmission of the ballad, and that the new form gradually gained ascendancy and wide dissemination, we have little to add. It has been found in England north and south, in Ireland, in many parts of the United States and Canada, as far west as British Columbia and California.

[2] *Journal of the Folk Song Society*, Vol. III, p. 14.

The latest form of the song seems to reflect an equally abrupt transformation of pattern and a further decline in complexity. This is the pattern called "An Acre of Land," found in various southern counties in our own century, and now widely known in Vaughan Williams's delightful choral setting. There is only one speaker; the impossibilities are narrated by him as accomplished fact; there is no challenge; the true lover is sacrificed for more vegetation. The refrain-lines, phrases two and four, now approximate: "Sing ivy, sing ivy," and "Sing holly go whistle and ivy," or "A bunch of green holly and ivy." The conjunction of holly and ivy is certainly old but its appearance here could have been adapted from the familiar carol on the subject, and need not argue age in this style of our ballad, considering how much has been lost here that still survives in the rest. Obviously, the special appeal of this shape is to the imagination of children, or children at heart. The dramatic function, the challenge of impossible tasks assigned under peril, has melted into simple assertion of diminutive achievement—

> I reaped it with my little pen-knife . . .
> I stowed it in a mouse's hole. . . .

The devil—for the Elphin Knight suggested deviltry—has lost his terrors: the world is a safer place, and nothing is impossible for little folk.

Very similar, apparently, to the "plaid awa" burden of Child no. 2A must be the case of no. 178A, "Edom o Gordon, or Captain Car" (Ker). It is the earliest known text of this tragic ballad. There is no refrain proper to the ballad, but a burden reads as follows:

> Syck, sike, and to-towe sike,
>   And sike and like to die;
> The sikest nighte that euer I abode,
>   God lorde haue mercy on me!

Apart from the mood of distress, this burden has little to do with our ballad. Doubtless, it properly belonged to a pestilence song, something like Nashe's:

> The plague full swift goes by,
> I am sick, I must die—
>   Lord, have mercy on us!

There is a once famous Elizabethan tune called the "Sick Tune," and this may be the one in question here. But the rhythm of the first and last lines suits better the second, or burden, half of the ubiquitous and still popular "Greensleeves." There can be little doubt, at any rate, that when the "sick" burden was attached to the ballad, the tune of it was that to which the ballad was supposed to be sung. This again, therefore, indicates a fracture in tradition, though again, so far as the record tells, the break was knitted up, for the burden does not appear later.

We may, I think, safely assume that where a tune comes in like this from an alien quarter, it does so only when it accords metrically. There is little reason to suppose that a text will modify a tune in important ways, though in small and inconstant details it may produce alteration, within the phrasal line. There is always the chance of a lapse of memory, producing irregularities in the text, and thereby in the tune, either by shortening or lengthening. But the tune itself, on the contrary, is more potent, for good or ill. Where a tune gives over parts of its length to a constant and rhythmically idiosyncratic refrain, or where a tune exceeds the normal quatrain pattern and runs to seven or eight phrases with melodic unity not merely repetitional (as five- or six-phrase tunes usually are), there we shall be most apt to find genuine breaches and new directions in traditional transmission.

The preceding remarks may be illustrated by the ballad of "The Two Sisters" (Child no. 10). The A text, from broadsides of the mid-seventeenth century, divides its four-beat couplets with a refrain-line that recurs on alternate phrases of the tune. Typical is the fifth stanza:

> Somtymes she sanke, somtymes she swam,
>   With a hie downe downe a downe-a
> Until she came unto the mill-dam.
>   With a hy downe downe a downe-a.

No one, I believe, would propose that the refrain *preceded* the tune. It is there because the tune needed it, and it would doubtless be found that musically those two phrases were balancing counterparts, with rhyming feminine cadences, such as we see in "Barbara Allen," for a familiar example. The tune, in other words, not the text, has given its formal structure to the ballad. The intercalation of the refrain has also compelled a syntax in lines one and three such as would sustain these lines as separable units of thought.

We cannot say that this was the earliest of our ballad's schemes, for in other ways to be mentioned later, Child A appears distorted from tradition. Whether it was simply made over into English from Scots is also impossible to determine. But at any rate it has the stanzaic pattern of the commonest Scottish form, which, however, has other refrain-lines, namely (most often), "Binnorie, O Binnorie" and "By the bonnie mill-dams of Binnorie." The tune used in the North is quite consistent, and recognizable from the end of the eighteenth century into the present. Greig found many variants in the decade before the First World War. Perhaps it should not be claimed, since the stanza-pattern remains the same, that there was a real break here in tradition. But at about the same time and place where we encounter the *Binnorie* style, the redoubtable Mrs. Brown, Jamieson's and Tytler's most valued informant, sang a more elaborate form of the ballad, a two-strain, seven- (or eight-) phrase piece set down too inexpertly to be very sure about. This introduces refrain elements at the second, fourth, and seventh (and eighth) phrases. The new refrain-lines are (2) "Edinbrough, Edinbrough"; (4) "Stirling for aye"; and (7) [or (7) and (8)] "Bonny St. Johnston stands upon Tay." (It is probably best to reckon the last line as two phrases.) Unquestionably this embodies a different and more elaborate musical vehicle, with a tripartite refrain. There is no reason to suppose that it is endemic here, and it will be found to recur in a closely similar form in Motherwell's "Lady Maisry." The refrain elements, featuring place-names, have no logical connection with the ballad's proper text. We have every reason, therefore, to regard this as a genuine fracture in tradition. And again, the guilt must lie with the tune. It is unlikely that Mrs. Brown imposed the change, since C. K. Sharpe's mother taught him a variant with the same refrain and a similar but more comfortable form of the tune. But, however it got into circulation, it has continued so until our own time and been given official sanction in Diack's *New Scottish Orpheus* between the Wars.

A third strain in the morphological history of this ballad makes its first appearance about a century ago in England and has been overwhelmingly the dominant form of the ballad in America: more than fifty variants of it have been recorded in our own century.

The copies collected in England, though older, could be counted on the fingers of one hand. Formally, this style is not unlike the Edinburgh-Stirling one just described, with a tripartite refrain. But the spirit is completely transformed. Instead of the predominantly minor and soberly duple-metred Scottish tunes, this Anglo-American branch is in a rollicking 6/8, most often in a major tonality and refusing to take itself seriously, regardless of tragic implications. It seems made to be sung in a happy dance, and the refrain elements, though sometimes obscure, seem to confirm the connection, as for instance: "Bow down, bow down," "Bow and balance to me," and "I'll be true, true to my love, If my love will be true to me." It is fairly certain that it started somewhere in England—the first known copy is from the Vale of the White Horse, in Berkshire; but the Appalachians made it their own, and it has been collected in New England, and has spread west and south. Again the agent of transfiguration seems to have been the tune—the tune responding to a mood of high and carefree jocularity. Or, to put it the other way round, this change of mood has supplied a new function for the ballad, and the different need has given rise to a more suitable melodic vehicle. "Why should a man whose blood is warm within/ Sit like his grandsire carved in alabaster?"

We may therefore surmise that another, and possibly very potent, cause of fracture is social attitude. Now, the outcome of a shift of attitude toward the subject matter of a ballad can be called loosely parody, and a number of varieties of parody may be distinguished. One kind we have already seen in the A version of Child no. 10, found on a number of broadsides. This can be considered a sort of burlesque. Since burlesque normally consists of exaggeration, it will be likely to stay sufficiently close to the original to make the contrast vividly part of the fun. It can be regarded as a kind of practical joke at the expense of an original on which it is patterned. It need not, therefore, and commonly will not, change the scheme, and the tune can be left unchanged. The text will be pushed to ridiculous extremes. Thus:

> What did he doe with her nose-ridge?
>   With a hie downe down a downe-a
> Unto his violl he made him a bridge.
>   With a hy downe downe a downe-a . . . .

What did he doe with her two shinnes?
With a hie downe down a downe-a
Unto the violl they danc'd Moll Syms.
With a hy downe downe a downe-a . . . .

Of course, it by no means goes without saying that the author of
a burlesque despises or dislikes the object of his sport. But he must
be so far detached from it in spirit as to be willing to see its tragedy
or high romance travestied from time to time without psychic re-
coil. Such psychic detachment is alien to tradition, which typically
accepts without criticism what it passes on. An instructive example
of the process of alienation is "Sir Lionel" (Child no. 18). This serious romantic ballad survives sporadically into the present century. But a burlesque of the theme, "Sir Eglamore," with a catchy
tune, achieved wide currency in the seventeenth century—more,
probably, because of tune than words—and this rollicking piece,
centering on a fight with a wild boar, broke away from its model
to achieve independence. The serious piece wilted away, to be supplanted by the vigorous upstart, which, as "Bangum and the Boar,"
has been giving delight to young and old in our own time over a
wide territory, English and American. Such an event will happen,
presumably, when the original is lost sight of. The process can be
seen again in Child no. 26, where—until the late resurrection of the
Elizabethan "The Three Ravens"—the old tragic forms have been
driven into hiding by popular versions of the "Crow Song." In
most of the latter, all semblance of former narrative has disappeared, whilst the crows, in caucus, discuss their next meal. The
stanzaic patterns of these textual degenerates follow the tunes, of
which the majority are familiar in other connections and borrowed
for the nonce. We may conjecture that a similar cycle has occurred
in the case of "The Whummil Bore" (no. 27) and "Kempy Kay"
(no. 33), where, however, the originals vanished without being recorded, and only the mockeries have survived. It is probably significant that a palpable number of the earlier Child ballads on romance themes have left no singing tradition behind them.

Another kind of parody is evident in ballads that have undergone change for the benefit of a particular and more restricted public, that of the very young. Here, again, we do not often have
enough evidence to establish the prehistory with confidence. The

purpose of the remaking is not mockery or ridicule but the reduction of a tragic theme to accord with an audience yet unacquainted
with grief in the deeper sense. Pathos may be the result, as in the
very clear case of "The Croodlin Dow," an egregious re-creation of
"Lord Randal" for the nursery. Or the remaking may go in the
opposite direction of nonsensical comedy, as can be seen in that
other branch of "Lord Randal" derivatives, widely familiar as
"Billy Boy" or "My Boy Tammy." The expansibility of this style,
and its more adult implications, have given it a further range, and
we find it also as a game-song and even as a shanty. Or again, it is
tempting to speculate on the earlier history of that most delectable
—"sparkling," Child calls it—of fairy ballads, "The Wee Wee
Man" (no. 38). If this be a remaking of more ambitious materials—
Child points to a fourteenth-century analogue—it is too perfect in
its present state to wish it other than what we have left from David
Herd's manuscripts, however incomplete.

Another sort of parody appears to come into being for reasons
more functional than the above. Instances have already appeared in
Child no. 2 and no. 10. In the case of no. 2, it is clear that there was
a need for a sort of home theatricals, in which a sharing of responsibilities among the group required an equal division, with a leader
on each side, one a boy, the other a girl; and that the mutual challenge of the tasks set by the principals, interrupted by the choral
lines sung by the group, provided a satisfactory resolution of the
need, in which all could engage. Thus, in Baring-Gould's Cornish
version A:

         (He) Thou must buy me, my lady, a cambrick shirt
        (Cho)   Whilst every grove rings with a merry antine
         (He) And stitch it without any needle work
        (Cho)   O and then thou shalt be a true lover of mine.

         (She) Or ever I do these two and three
        (Cho)   Whilst every grove rings &c.
         (She) I will set of tasks as many to thee
        (Cho)   O and then shall I be a true lover of thine.

         (She) Thou must buy for me an acre of land
        (Cho)   Whilst every grove rings &c.
         (She) Between the salt ocean and the yellow sand
        (Cho)   O and then thou shalt be a true lover of mine.

Whether or not there was any motion or dancing during this simple confrontation, we can be sure that there was when "The Two Sisters" was sung and danced in the Kentucky mountains. The words of the refrain partly spell out the action of the two sides:

> There lived an old lord by the northern sea,
> Bowee down,
> There lived an old lord by the northern sea,
> Bow and balance to me.
> There lived an old lord by the northern sea,
> And he had daughters one, two, three,
> I'll be true to my love
> If my love will be true to me.

It is very clear that the participants here are not anxious to tell a tragic story, whether of the supernatural or the natural. Their minds are on the immediate social scene, to which they have compelled an old and familiar ballad to do submission. They have found a spacious and subservient lilting tune, customarily in 6/8 time, with plenty of repeated lines so as neither to overcharge the memory nor to end too soon; and the social orientation, irrelevant to the narrative, is carried home in the concluding phrases of each stanza:

> I'll be true to my love
> If my love'll be true to me—

a proposition that is void of embarrassment and supplies an easy retreat. All this has come about in a perfectly natural, simple way; and although the fracture of the old tragic tradition is patent, there is no sense of an individual's having imposed his will on the majority. All comes about by mutual accommodation.

Once again, we feel certain that the sense and mood of the community has collaborated in this departure from an older norm. This is how the group felt about the song: this is the way they all wanted to sing it, to put it to use. But there is another way, less drastic than this, that is no doubt quietly operative most of the time. When a song grows old, although it may still be loved, it comes to seem outmoded; and there is an unexpressed but pervasive pressure to update it. The old allusions, credulities, and patterns of thought grow unfamiliar and fail to satisfy; and a more modern version is invented—whether swiftly or by degrees is unimportant and generally cannot be determined. In some such fashion, we find that "Henry Martin" has taken the place of "Sir Andrew Barton." We cannot be sure about the details of transition, or even guess how many contributors brought about the change. But enough of the old is embedded in the new to convince us that there was no sudden or violent alteration, and that parody is hardly the word to describe it. It is more like the unconscious changes in habits of speech and pronunciation, of manners, of familiar reference, of shifting preoccupations, than a desire to have done with old fashions and introduce novelties. Captain Charles Stewart seems a more natural figure than my lord Charles Howard, and King George than King Henry; but historical accuracy is not in question, and the spirit of the piece is relatively unchanged. But it is undeniable that over all the dress has been transformed. To see this, we need only set the courtliness of the Percy Folio's opening stanzas beside a recent version:

> As itt beffell in midsumer-time,
>   When burds singe sweetlye on euery tree,
> Our noble king, King Henery the Eighth,
>   Ouer the riuer of Thames past hee.
>
> Hee was no sooner ouer the riuer,
>   Downe in a fforrest to take the ayre,
> But eighty merchants of London cittye
>   Came kneeling before King Henery there.
>
> *   *   *   *   *   *
>
> There lived three brothers in merry Scotland,
>   In Scotland there lived brothers three,
> And they did cast lots to see which of them should go,
>   should go,
> For to turn robber all on the salt sea.

We lack the intervening links but we can hardly doubt that the chain was continuous, although the ends do not match.

It should be possible to distinguish between this sort of change and the more abrupt kind of updating generally called "secondary" in composition. I should prefer to keep the latter term for a more professional re-handling that smacks of the broadside poet. Although there might be dispute in particular cases, the latter kind does not seem to have grown out of the earlier by any traditional or gradual transformation, by functional adaptation, by humorous parody or mockery, but rather out of an individual desire to make a new and up-to-date song on an old theme. Such a case would be "The Dragoon and the Lady," on the pattern of "The Douglas Tragedy" or "Erlinton" (Child nos. 7 and 8), or "The Sea Captain" or "The Maid on the Shore," based on the idea of "The Broomfield Hill" (no. 43), or "Katie Morey" on the theme of "The Baffled Knight" (no. 112). It might also be argued that kindred cases of this impulse are to be found in the effort now and then appearing to encapsule an old song in a ballad narrative. An example would be "Captain Wedderburn's Courtship" (no. 46), which incorporates the ancient song of "My love gave me a cherry," appearing as early as the fifteenth century in the Sloane MS. 2593. Another is "Jamie Douglas" (no. 204), which contains "O Waly, waly, up the bank." A third is, possibly, "The Broom of Cowdenknows" (no. 217), which seems somehow interconnected with an early song on the "The bonny Broome."

Such evidence as has been brought forward in the foregoing remarks—and of course it could be multiplied abundantly—is merely symptomatic of the forces and processes that have been operative in the traditional field. The question remains to be asked whether the conditions under which folk-song flourishes today have significantly altered matters. Is not what is going on in the way of change just what has always gone on, although doubtless accelerated by facility of communication? Is there any need to be concerned, and if we were, what happened to King Canute, the first named balladeer? Since we can do nothing to prevent, shall we not welcome?

Accept we must, like it or not. But, if concerned with traditional values, we should try to be clear as to where those values lie. And a good deal of what is happening to folk-song today, good or bad, never happened before because it was physically impossible. It is now possible to hear a song repeated as often as one likes, without a single change of note, tempo, intonation, timbre, phrasing, or even breathing. And this identical rendition can be, and is, often experienced by hundreds of thousands of other ears, scattered all over the globe and attached to memorizing brains. It is now possible for thousands in front of a television screen to watch the singer, as closely as one might a beetle under a microscopic lens, while he renders, item by item, the data of his performance. It is now possible for the identical singing of a song to be learned by persons on opposite sides of the earth, within the interval of a fortnight or a month. Songs thus cast abroad are inevitably associated with the voice, the personality, and one particular way of singing. That it will be stellar is assured by all the skills, artistic and mechanical, that expertise can devise to enhance the production. But *optimi corruptio pessima*. In so far as it touches folk-song, it is deleterious: instead of impersonality, it exploits the celebrity; its fixative control, exerted with maximum impact and regulated by punitive copyright, acts like a straitjacket on traditional freedoms and by the same token compels extreme departures from traditional norms. Fractures of tradition are by definition anti-traditional; and if they are established as a norm in themselves, what is there left to differentiate folk-song from any other kind of individual artistic effort in lyrical composition, provided it be sufficiently simple in structure and sentiment? The old autochthonous bases are gone, the matted roots that characterize like a thousand-year-old olive grove are torn loose and flung far and wide. When the old values are dispersed and rendered inoperative and ineffectual, were it not better to encourage the young proponents of a self-styled folk-song which they make up as they go? They obviously speak with conviction to and for their own generation: let them see how far their voices can carry.

1966

Cecil Sharp and Folk-Song

SWEPT by the force of contemporary example into the folk-song current, the younger half of our population must think of it first as a form of social activity. There is little occasion for them to give a thought to it as an historical phenomenon, or to trouble themselves about the beginnings of the movement of which they are a part. Yet this movement is so young that its pioneers are within living memory; its transformations have been so extreme that the values attached to it at the opening of the century can hardly be said to motivate any of those who give their energies and time to the practice and promotion of folk-song as we move into the closing third. A few comparisons may help us to sharpen our sense of values, and the appearance of *Cecil Sharp: His Life and Work* by Maud Karpeles [1] gives us a timely occasion to review the scene.

The differences between then and now are physical, sociological, and psychological. Among the physical differences, the most potent lie in the development and exploitation of tape, disc, and radio. Magnetic tape has made it possible to record instantaneously, and with utmost fidelity, all the nuances of individual renditions—to "freeze" a particular performance for unlimited repetition and exact memorization. Disc can saturate demand, local or international, for a favorite version of a song by a popular voice, girdling the globe within a measurably short time so that China and Peru, if they choose, may learn the same song from the same source, on a single singing, multiplied thousands of times. Television may *introduce* such an influence, reinforced by visual appeal, and create a

[1] The University of Chicago Press, Chicago; and Routledge and Kegan Paul Ltd., London. 1967.

celebrity overnight; radio may perpetuate it by free circulation. The effect on other singers may be to stultify individual variation, just as an orchestra will not depart from the written score. Or repetition *ad nauseam* may drive less docile spirits to creative invention and the radical remodeling of traditional norms. In the latter case, of course, tradition, in the sense of communal expression, recreation, preference, has died of a surfeit. In the former case a local or regional idiom tends to become universalized and no longer distinctive.

Sociologically, folk-singing today has developed an orientation primarily purposive. The purpose may be merely to generate a feeling of fellowship—"togetherness"—in a gathering collected for group expression, or it may be to promote or oppose an idea or a cause, some program specific or general. Although the old stark and tragic narrative ballads have not lost their hold on the average hearer, the later, programmatic songs have more in common with the old broadsides expressing a *parti pris* for a kindred-minded audience, sharing political or class attitudes more or less clearly defined—the sort of subjects formerly felt to be basically alien to the impersonality of folk-tradition.

Psychologically, the motivation of folk-singing has moved in the direction of professionalism. The spotlight in folk clubs and festivals favors the exploitation of "personalities" and the display of skills vocal and instrumental; of ingenious, witty, and original invention; of public performances amplified electronically and highlighted by the self-magnifying devices of platform appearance. As the economic rewards of success increase with personal reputation, folk-singers work harder and longer at perfecting their private talents and become fulltime members of the entertainment business. Thus the characteristic anonymity of folk-singing at the beginning of the century has in the span of a lifetime turned inside out and become the very opposite of what it used to be.

On the musical side, folk-song collecting of a serious and systematic kind in the United States was at first an unimportant byproduct of the regional folklore societies that sprang up in the 1890's and in the first decade of our century in the wake of the formation of the American Folklore Society. But it took root only after Cecil Sharp's visits to the Appalachians during World War I. By that time Sharp had finished the greater part of his song collecting at home—mainly in Somerset. He had published several volumes of songs together with piano accompaniments, and several more volumes of folk-dances. It is surprising to realize that he was in his middle forties before he heard a genuine folk-song sung by a native singer in a natural, unself-conscious rural setting. Previously, enough sporadic interest had been generated here and there in England by a few scattered publications of songs from oral tradition gathered by Bruce and Stokoe and Miss Mason in Northumbria, Kidson in Yorkshire, Baring-Gould in Devon, and Lucy Broadwood in Sussex, to lead to the establishing of the Folk-Song Society in 1898. By the close of 1902, more than one hundred songs and variants had been contributed to the first four parts of the Society's *Journal*, but the Society was far from active.

Late in the summer of 1903 Sharp paid a visit to his old friend, the Reverend Charles Marson, in the village of Hambridge, Somerset, in the hope of finding songs. Sitting in the vicarage garden, he heard the gardener, John England, singing "The Seeds of Love" to himself as he mowed the lawn. He took down the notes, later got the words from John England, and then, abetted by Father Marson, set out to scour the vicinity for more songs. Before Sharp's holiday ended, the two enthusiastic collectors had flushed about forty folk-songs from hiding places round about. Sharp was so stirred by these discoveries that he delivered a well-attended lecture, with musical illustrations, on his findings before the end of November. Of the excitement and droll adventures of these first years of exploration and discovery in a musical New-found-land, Maud Karpeles gives many delightful glimpses in her biography. Father Marson, who collaborated with Sharp in the first three volumes of the promptly appearing *Folk-Songs from Somerset*, reflects their surprise in the preface:

The folk-song is like the duck-billed platypus [Marson and Sharp had become acquainted in Australia, where both of them spent several years] in this particular, you can live for years within a few yards of it and never suspect its existence. . . . Eight years of constant residence in the small village of Hambridge . . . had left [me] in Stygian ignorance of the wealth of art which that village contained.

Another companion of Sharp's early expeditions exclaims with evocative nostalgia: ". . . the early freshness and expectant adventure of those primitive bicycling forays into unexplored regions where even a scarecrow in a cornfield might be expected to burst into unaccompanied song!" Sharp himself, on another occasion, recounts the following incident:

One singer in Langport could only sing a song when she was ironing, while another woman in the same court sang best on washing-day! . . . I was in her wash-house sitting on an inverted tub, notebook in hand, while my hostess officiated at the copper, singing the while. Several neighbours congregated at the door to watch the strange proceedings. In one of the intervals between the songs one of the women remarked, "You be going to make a deal o' money out o' this, sir?" My embarrassment was relieved by the singer at the wash-tub, who came to my assistance and said, "Oh! it's only 'is 'obby." "Ah! well," commented the first speaker, "we do all 'ave our vailin's."

Sharp was very soon set upon two objects as major aims in life. One was to spread the gospel of true folk-song throughout the length and breadth of England, to return to Englishmen everywhere their native heritage, to brand as forever false the slander often mouthed by Continental musicians against his country, "Das Land ohne Musik!" He was convinced that when every child of whatever class of society had repossessed his birthright of folk-song, a new and native race of composers—not aping foreign rules or nourished in the schools of the Continent (though his own eldest children were baptized Iseult and Tristan!), but steeped in their own natural idiom—would spring up and reestablish a great English musical tradition, lost since the German and Italian invasion after the death of Purcell. To this end, after 1910 he gave up his regular job at the Conservatory and devoted his whole time and energy for the rest of his life to the strenuous but precarious activity of recovering whatever he could of England's native music and by every means at his disposal—publication, lecture, and demonstration—of making it everywhere familiar. Through his tireless devotion and indefatigable crusading, he became, as his fellow-collector Greig, in Scotland, wrote with strict accuracy, "the greatest dynamic in the folk-song world."

Sharp had no doubts of the sterling worth of what he was finding. To begin with, he had the testimony of his own taste, tact, and musical discrimination—an inner conviction that grew stronger as his knowledge widened and deepened. But also he had what must have been powerfully reassuring: the continual evidence, immediate and instinctive, on the basic level of simple human response, that the singers loved these songs for some essential value without any thought of self. The quality of this experience, both on the part of singer and collector, is well illustrated by a representative anecdote:

Cecil Sharp had heard that a song which he had not hitherto recorded was known in an out-of-the-way corner of England. Accordingly he rushed off to secure it. On arriving at the place he was told there was only one person who knew it and this was an aged woman. On [reaching] her cottage he found she had gone out to work in the fields. After much difficulty he discovered her, engaged in gathering stones off the land. The day was bleak and there was a cutting wind; when the old woman heard Cecil Sharp's inquiry, she replied that she knew the song. "Shall I sing it to you?" she said; and raising her old weather-worn face to his, taking the lapels of his coat in her hands, and closing her eyes, she sang . . . in her quavering yet beautiful voice, while he rapidly made notes. When the song was finished, she gazed into his eyes in a sort of ecstasy, and, in perfect detachment from herself, exclaimed, "Isn't it lovely!"

Two things followed for Sharp from this conviction of value: First, that it was of the utmost importance, even a sacred trust, to be the faithful transmitter of this heritage to others, ultimately to posterity. And second, to try to discover the secret of its peculiar virtue. The many volumes of his handwritten transcripts in Clare College, Cambridge, untouched by the effort to improve, bear eloquent witness to his conscientious discharge of the primary responsibility. His straightforward, unpretentious little treatise, *English Folk-Song: Some Conclusions*, contains his fullest written attempt to account for the secret.

Although appreciative of the characteristic merits of folk-poetry at its best, Sharp felt that by his own day it had passed the stage when it was often to be found in that state. He believed that for the truth of the record and for historical reasons it ought faithfully to be preserved in its current condition, whatever the imperfections. But he set no superstitious value on corrupt and fragmentary texts, because he did not believe that the words contained the treasure. Other things being equal, however, he preferred to print an accurate text rather than one that was prettified or scrubbed up to shine in company.

On the music, however, he did set a value that some would call superstitious, and his reasons go to the heart of the whole question. A folk-tune—at least of the sort favored in the Western world—is not too complex a structure for the idea of it to be carried in many minds and memories. Unfixed though it be in a single authorized form, after many repetitions the *idea*, in spite of incessant minute alteration, persists in recognizable identity. It may be perpetuated spatially and temporally, that is to say, widely disseminated and passed down from generation to generation. Sharp and his contemporaries observed that many of the folk-tunes they were recovering from traditional singers preserved, despite continual change in detail, modal habits that had been given up by professional composers very long ago. Pondering this fact, one could say that tradition is old-fashioned and reluctant to change. And this is true. Another word for it is *conservative*.

There is a positive side to conservatism: it may contain and project valued preferences chosen from among various alternatives. Thus, considering the interests of pure melody, or unaccompanied tune, the sacrifice of the diatonic modal scales to harmonic developments was an impoverishment. Where the melodic line, therefore, the tune phrase by phrase, is still primary, there is the best artistic justification for clinging to modal distinctions. It is possible for a stable, homogeneous society to preserve these patterns over long periods of time. Sharp believed that this modal habit, among many characterizing traits of the music he was collecting and studying, was evidence of a whole people's instinctive feeling for melody, the expression of deep-lying artistic preferences held in common. He thought it worthy of veneration, not merely because its products were so beautiful, but also because it was communal and fundamental, not the momentary invention of individual idiosyncrasy. As a stream running over a sandy bed is gradually strained and purified, so a tune in passing through many relatively kindred recollections loses the particular marks of individual minds, and becomes the clarified melodic expression of the race. Sharp rationalized the evolution of such a tune into the principles of Continuity, Variation, and Selection. The first is the relatively faithful transfer from memory to memory of a tune by oral transmission; the second is the inevitable counter-force of individual centrifugal departures from stereotypical reproduction; the third is the straining off of idiosyncrasies by the unconscious action of communal taste. Setting so high a valuation on the part which the larger community played in this evolutionary process, Sharp felt it to be of the utmost importance to differentiate between products of individual composition widely favored by popular acclaim and products of racial composition in this evolutionary sense.

This conviction brought Sharp into head-on collision with the dominant authorities of his day, who, not recognizing the distinction in kind that he was making, were ready to settle for the superficial sort of popularity that results in what was hitherto known as "national song," and which they were recommending to be taught in elementary schools as wholesomely propaedeutic. And of course it is clear that he would regard as entirely irrelevant to his deepest concern most of what passes today under the general name of folk-song. In the Appalachians at the time of his visits, Sharp found his ideal singing community, almost a laboratory demonstration, to validate his faith; nowhere has he formulated his belief more forcefully and eloquently than in the Introduction to the first edition (reprinted in 1932 and 1952 with the enlarged edition) of his and Maud Karpeles' *English Folk Songs from the Southern Appalachians* under the subheading "The Cultural Significance of Tradition." Anyone who doubts the solidity of his convictions, or the serious importance of the subject for the artistic well-being of the nation, should reread those pages. Concern for national well-being is always and inevitably concern for the future; Sharp justly, therefore, points his remarks emphatically toward the education of the young. The measure of the civilization to which at any given moment man has attained is the success of his efforts to express himself, Sharp declares.

The process is a cumulative one, the children of each generation receiving from their fathers that which, with certain modifications and additions of their own, they bequeath to their children. . . . Nations pass through different phases, and . . . their artistic output varies in character and quality from period to period. . . . [But] the form of expression remains fundamentally true to one type, and that the national type. And this national type is always to be found in its purest, as well as in its most stable and permanent form, in the folk-arts of a nation.

Although this theory of nationalism in art is now very generally accepted, the fact that it is based upon the intimate relationship which the art of the folk must always bear to that of the self-conscious, cultivated, and trained individual artist is too often overlooked. . . . We

talk glibly of the creative musician, but however clever and inspired he
may be, he cannot, magician-like, produce music out of nothing. . . .
The value of such songs as these as material [for the young composer
and] for the general education of the young cannot be overestimated.
For, if education is to be cultural and not merely utilitarian, if its aim
is to produce men and women capable, not only of earning a living, but
of holding a dignified and worthy position upon an equality with the
most cultivated of their generation, it will be necessary to pay at least
as much attention to the training and development of the emotional,
spiritual, and imaginative faculties as to those of the intellect. And this,
of course, can be achieved only by the early cultivation of some form
of artistic expression, such as singing, which . . . seems of all the arts
to be the most natural and the most suitable one for the young. Moreover, remembering that the primary purpose of education is to place
the children of the present generation in possession of the cultural
achievements of the past, so that they may as quickly as possible enter
into their racial inheritance, what better form of music or of literature
can we give them than the folk-songs and folk-ballads of the race to
which they belong, of the nation whose language they speak? To deny
them these is to cut them off from the past and to rob them of that
which is theirs by right of birth.

There is no space here to go into Sharp's prolonged and strenuous efforts to recover, to describe accurately, and to hand on in
authentic form the folk-dances of his country, or to recapitulate
the battles fought to establish the revival on a ground of truth, nor
does it seem so immediately relevant to what is taking place today.
Maud Karpeles, who was more fully involved in both these cru-
sades than any one else alive has given a straightforward, un-
adorned, and dependable history of these events and the issues at
stake. She reprints as an appendix Fox Strangways' eloquent tribute
to Sharp's life and achievement; in it he declares:

He believed that all men have something of the artist in them, and
that to "lead that out" is an "education" worthy the name. He believed
that when we say all souls are equal in the sight of God, it is not a
mere theory for Sundays but a truth to be lived. . . . He was more,
then, than a musician. He was an artist in humanity and a patriot.

In her own admirably unimpassioned Epilogue, Maud Karpeles
justly says:

Reviewing Cecil Sharp's work in retrospect, one cannot but marvel
at what he achieved in a comparatively short space of time—a period of
twenty-one years. . . . Collecting, writing, teaching and organizing:

had he been engaged in only one or two of these activities it would still have been a full life. . . .

Many have remembered him as a delightful companion with interests ranging far beyond his particular subjects; others have been attracted by the gaiety which permeated his being, despite—or perhaps because of—his intense seriousness of purpose; while others were drawn to him because of the fundamental serenity of his nature which, born of conviction and single-mindedness, remained unruffled by surface waves of irritability. But it was above all his love for and his understanding of his fellow-creatures which endeared him both to those who knew him in person and to those who knew him only through his work. . . . Cecil Sharp understood the human significance of the songs and dances he had gathered and through them he gave us the means of realizing more fully the possibilities of our own natures. . . . And in the story of his life we see the complete integration of his faith and his works.

In truth, as G. L. Kittredge wrote of Sharp's predecessor and fellow laborer in a kindred field, Francis James Child: "In all ways he lived worthily, and he died having attained worthy ends."

1968

"Of Ballads, Songs, and Snatches"

I

THE SUBJECT I ask your company in pursuing is one that in
its total extent could engulf many lifetimes: the mutual relations of words and music. My immediate interest is the intercon-
nection of folk, or popular, music and the development and practice of lyric verse-forms. More particularly, I wish to consider the
hypothetical and actual influence of simple tunes on song texts, to
inquire whether they may not have exerted, over the centuries of
western European culture, a shaping force and control on the
structural patterns of lyric texts.

I am well aware that, if adopted as a governing hypothesis, this
may strike many as fanatically perverse, like Oliver Goldsmith's
persuasion that, in chewing, a man moves his upper jaw rather than
his lower. It will be declared at once—and even by composers,
whom one might hope to enlist for vanity's sake—that the opposite
direction is the normal one. It will be pointed out—what cannot be
denied—that thousands of lyrics have been made for no tune, and
with no thought of a tune. It will be insisted that in fact the commonest stimulus to musical composition in song-form is the prior
existence of a fine text. Can there be any sense in not assuming
what seems so natural, that verbal patterns have been worked out
by those whose first concern is with words and their ways, without
the leading or interference of another medium? In the face of ob-
jections so palpable and immediate, it will be necessary to raise
more fundamental considerations, and tack about if we are to make
any headway against so loud a wind.

This paper, abridged, was read at the English Institute, meeting in New York,
September 1967.

What happens on the basic level, we may ask, when words and music meet? Is there any way to determine preeminence or authority? The difference is, I suppose, one of degree rather than outright opposition. Both have a temporal, both an accentual, interest: verse, with us, puts a stronger insistence on stress; music lays more importance on duration. Since words can be set to music, or music to words, we can start from either side.

Suppose, for the sake of discussion, we assume the priority of words. Keeping everything as simple as possible, let us start with a verbal statement chosen at random, with its own natural stresses. I take a letter from the unanswered pile on my desk, and read the first sentence:

"It is time to remind you that the annual dues are now payable."

How shall we most simply and easily turn this into song? For a start, we might look for a metrical scheme into which the line will naturally fall. We may have to exaggerate or minimize some accents; and it may be best for the present purpose to divide into phrasal groups, perhaps leaving something over for another line. The rhetorical pauses come after *you* and *dues*. Holding off the concluding three words for the nonce, we begin to sense a rhythm in:

It is tíme to remínd you that the ánnual dúes . . .

The *you* strikes us as hypermetrical: it asks perhaps for special emphasis, with a shortening of subsequent unaccented syllables:

It is tíme | to remínd | ‸ yóu ‸ | that the án- | nual | dúes . . .

This is more satisfying than:

It is tíme | to remínd | you thát | the án- | nual dúes . . .

But we might well prefer a triple rhythm like:

The point to be observed is that, however we proceed, we have to make concessions to quantitative, i. e. musical, emphasis. Following the last lead, we might, with a timid impulse toward lyric, conclude in the same metre with another line:

Are now   pay-a-ble ,   pay-a-ble   now

which would equalize the two parts of the statement, achieve a balance, and give it a lift. Thus, for a try:

Time to   re- mind you that   an - nu -al   dues , my love,

are now   pay- a -ble ,   pay - a - ble   now.

So, by a natural impulsion, we arrive at two regular musical phrases of equal length, each with four primary pulses; in this case, four bars in ¾ time. For reasons of musical logic, they imply two previous balancing phrases of the same length, with a mid-cadence contrasting with, but looking forward to, the final tonic. The well-known Elizabethan folk-tune, "Callino Casturame," of course supplies the missing phrases. What I wish to emphasize here is the structural whole, of four equal phrases, each four pulses long, and falling into two balanced halves. These are musical facts, to which the text (so far as it exists) has readily conformed, however unlikely it seemed.

There may probably be physiological reasons for so universal and apparently instinctive a feeling in Western culture for four underlying pulse-beats as the normal length of a simple melodic phrase. I am speaking here of foundations, below metrical varieties and despite interruptions and irregularities (often piquant in folk-music) which occur ofttimes because of the particular activity, game, dance-punctuation, work-signal, shortness of breath, playful emphasis, or singer's idiosyncrasy. I speak of that underlying beat which includes the rests as integral factors, and brings together metres superficially diverse: like

Hárk! hárk! the dógs do bárk!

and

Aetérne rérum cónditór

and

Blest bé the tíe that bí-yínds

and

Flow gently, sweet Afton, among thy green braes

and

Crás amét qui núnq'm amávit, *etc.*
(which has its melodic twin in Beethoven's setting of Schiller's
"Ode to Joy" in the Ninth Symphony)

and

Súmer ís icúmen ín

and

It wás a lóver ánd his láss

and

The king sits in Dunfermline toun

All these fulfill the rhythmic and durational limitation specified.
Someone has said that the rhythm of Nature is duple; and of course
duplicity can be multiplied or subdivided to any desired extent.
Triple time is latently duple, as is plain when it receives an extra
push. For witness, a name for 6/8 is "compound *duple* time." But
why the four-pulse length should be so widely accepted as a norm
is beyond my power to explain on any rational ground. When, in
the fourth century, St. Ambrose wrote his hymns in four-lined
stanzas, of iambic dimeter, or octosyllabics, thereby setting a pattern for hymnology that would last for all the centuries to follow,
he must have done so, not by way of innovation, but on the contrary, to take advantage, for a simple flock, of the familiar accentual verse models of the people; much as the Methodists did in the
eighteenth century. It has even been conjectured that, apart from
possible Syrian influences from earlier Jewish tradition, Ambrose
adapted his melodies from Italian folk-song. And it is, I believe,
generally agreed that the primordial popular verse of the Romans
was accentual. The quantitative classical tradition was a sophisticated interlude, a complication but hardly a denial of this inherited
racial instinct for recurrent stress patterns. The classical system,
though (thanks to the supreme genius of its masters) it left indel-

ible marks on Western poetry, was too subtle and difficult to survive in common use, and was already beginning to give way by St.
Ambrose's time. The ease of the relapse is readily illustrated in the
anachronistic but conveniently familiar example of Horace's Sap-
phic ode, "Integer vitae," turned into duple metre as a student
song.

This four-pulse length of melodic phrase goes far beyond the
limits of the merely popular, moreover, and in fact is basic to most
melody even down through the classical age of music into the nineteenth century. The diatonic scale itself yields to it. Give a heavy
stress to each note of the octave, up or down, and you have two
four-beat phrases. A classic example is Mozart's "Variations on a
Theme from Gluck's 'Pilgrims of Mecca' ": basically a descending
major scale in duple time, the first phrase from the upper tonic to
the dominant, four bars, the second from the subdominant to the
tonic, four bars. A second example, backed by all the time-honored
authority of a ground-bass, eight bars long, is the Canon of Pachelbel, a descending octave, recently orchestrated by Karl Münch-
inger. A final and spectacular use of the octave as a four-pulse
thematic statement is Haydn's trio of the *Menuetto* of Quartet
No. 80, Opus 76, No. 6 in E$\flat$ (1797).

To resume our discussion of the relative authority of music and
words, and assuming again the primacy of words, let us take a
meeting—a mating, rather—wherein there is genius at work on
both sides. Our example is the famous pair of heroic couplets from
Pope's "Summer," set by Händel in his opera *Semele:*

> Where'er you walk, cool gales shall fan the glade,
> Trees, where you sit, shall crowd into a shade;
> Where'er you tread, the blushing flow'rs shall rise,
> And all things flourish where you turn your eyes.

In their play of vowels, their adjustment of pause, their management of phrasal balance and contrast, these lines are a miracle of
art, the wonder of which increases the longer they are studied.

But they do not affect us as truly lyrical. How is Händel to turn
them into song? It would be otiose to attempt a full account. For a
relevant start, however: he settles upon a four-pulse length of
melodic phrase. This requires that the iambic pentameters be cut in
two, and that the two parts be somehow equalized in the musical
handling. Carried on, this will result in a four-phrase strophe, with

a rhyme coming at the ends of the second and fourth lines, emphasized by the cadences on the rhyme-words. But Händel repeats the
second line like a refrain, to new phrases, building an ampler stanza
six lines long and sinking to the lower dominant on the last note.
There is a superb logic about the structure: the skeletal form of the
second, fourth, and sixth phrases will show how firm it is:

$$(2)\ e^b\ c\ A\quad (4)\ d\ b^b\ G\quad (6)\ A\ G\ F$$

Not content, however, to leave it at this, he now proceeds to take
the same words through another six-phrase strophe, extended to
seven by a florid melisma on the word "shade," and returning to
cadence on the tonic. It is unnecessary to follow him into the relative minor with the second couplet, heightened and again elaborated by textual repetitions into seven phrases, and then into the
concluding *da capo*. Without expatiating on the pictorial subleties
and further complexities of the aria, it must be obvious that the
music has taken command and imposed on the text its own laws, its
elevated emotional rhetoric, its own stately pace of delivery, its intensity of feeling, its power of exalting the whole statement to a
supernal level, where the poetic metaphors seem to exist as merely
the unexaggerated description of a normal condition of being. It is
as if the meaning of the sentiment were only now fully revealed.
And thus much for music's potential in relation to words.

II

Turning now to the long historical panorama, we must collect
most of our earlier evidence from the Christian Church. Two conspicuous and perennial features of the picture are: the impulse to
enrich and enhance the service of worship by means of music, and
the tendency to intermix the secular with the sacred. The first of
these was for a thousand years a sort of perpetual tug-of-war, sheer
musical exuberance straining always to take the bit in its teeth and
achieve more importance, more prominence, more striking effects.
Spreading from particular points in the service of the Mass, the
practice of "troping" gradually punctuated most parts of the lit-
urgy with increasingly florid and elaborate, relatively independent
ornamentation. *Tropos* in Greek means properly melody, not text;
and this is significant of the priority of the lyrical impulse prompting these outbursts of song. The supposed maker of the oldest ex-

tant tropes, Tuotilo of St. Gall, was also an instrumentalist, it is worth noting; and in the fact that the music antedated words some authorities find evidence that instrumental music played a part in the emergence of the tropes. These began probably well before the eighth century, but it was then that they fully flowered. Starting as extensions or additions to existent chants, they had no texts and were at first vocalizations of increasingly elaborate melismata on a particular word or words. The most notable case, and one of far-reaching importance, is the Alleluia, the last syllable of which took off on a long and independent flight of lyricism (described by St. Augustine as "a *song* of joy without words" and called the *Jubilus*). One might compare it to the classical cadenza. These flights had to be learned traditionally, in the absence of precise notation, and if you tried to memorize note for note the "mouth-music" of an Irish folk-singer—who also is instrumentalizing in his own traditional way—you would see how difficult the task was. Someone had the idea of attaching words to make it easier. Notker Balbulus, a monk of St. Gall, is credited with first coping effectively with the problem. He provided Latin texts, in unmetred and unrhymed prose, matching a syllable to each separate note. Sometimes these were given the French name of "proses"; and the melodies, with words, acquired the name "sequences"—they *followed* after the Alleluia. The sequences grew more formal and more regular. Examples of about the beginning of the tenth century show a series of paired strophes, each of two phrases, the second of each pair exactly matching its fellow in number of syllables, but with other words. We assume that half the choir sang one strophe, and was answered on the same melody by the other. But the melody was not absolutely constant from pair to pair: in minor respects it varied. Each pair, however, would combine in a structure of ABAB; and the cadences of all the B phrases remained constant throughout, but not those of the A phrases. This is tantamount, musically speaking, to identical rhyme on every second phrase. There were also a brief introductory and a closing clause, each single, and sung by the full choir, The texts were biblical in inspiration, sometimes based on a psalm. Recollecting the final vowel of Allelui*a,* whence the sequences derived, Notker and other early makers ended each phrase with -*a,* approximating assonance.

By the time of Adam of St. Victor (twelfth century), through gradual, successive steps, the sequences had progressed to the point of exact regularity, most often in trochaic metre, strophe and antistrophe rhyming on the last line, the other lines rhyming in couplets or triplets. This is a form of the metre of the *Pervigilium Veneris*, the old *versus popularis*, with the first member doubled or trebled with rhyme, 88(8)7 88(8)7; and the shorter members rhyming together. By this time, also, appear evidences of that too seldom recorded goliardic spirit in burlesques of known sequences like "Verbum bonum et suave," "Vinum bonum cum sapore/Bibit abbas cum priore/Et conventus de pejore/Bibit cum tristitia." It may be noted here that the sequence and the *estampie*, a danceform, are both constructed on the binary principle of repetition with different endings. By this date, also, it has become clear that no valid distinction can be made between the forms of religious and Latin secular songs, in metre, rhyme, or stanza patterns, or in melodic types; and Latin and vernacular are closely allied. The *Carmina Burana* can show parallels to all the liturgical structures in song. The same tune, for example, is recognizable in Vatican and Monte Cassino MS copies of "O Roma Nobilis" and with "O admirabile Veneris Idolum" in the Cambridge Book. Notation so early is uncertain, but Westrup reads it as trochaic four-pulse phrases in 6/8, the even lines on a single rhyme. Interesting, too, is the fact that Horace's *Ode* IV, 11, is found set to the hymn-tune, in sapphics, of "Ut queant laxis," which gave Guido of Arezzo the idea of the Gamut and system of tonic *sol-fa*.

Evidence toward similar conclusions is to be found in the history of the *conductus*. These melodies were independent of plainchant, and more movable than the sequences from place to place, though they appeared normally on processional occasions. Like the sequences, they were optional, but could be transferred from function to function in the same feast. They were strophic in form, usually repeating but sometimes with progressive repetition or even changing melodically. The music was more elaborate, and contrasted sharply with the syllabic sections before and after, containing long melismata. It was at first monodic but by the beginning of the twelfth century had become polyphonic, with two or even three upper parts above the tenor. These upper voices move in step with the tenor, which is not in long notes like organum or plainchant tenors. Full-fledged by the thirteenth century, the conductus contained *caudae*, which for the most part lack words and may either have been vocalized or played by instruments. The lowest voices have a lively and fresh melodic interest. Indeed, Dom Anselm Hughes has suggested that the *caudae* may be an unexplored mine of medieval folk-dance and song tunes. Again, the absence of words suggests an instrumental background in their development, and of course signalizes the musical, as opposed to verbal, inspiration.

A comparable development took place more or less concurrently in *organum*. With the contrapuntal and harmonic aspects of organa we are not at present concerned, but only with their implications for popular development. Simply put, organum is a plainsong melody, the *tenor*, in long notes, above which a second voice, the *duplum*, vocalizes in quicker notes.

Certain intermittent sections of the organa broke the monotony with a conspicuous contrast of movement. The stricter metre was like a parenthesis in the unmeasured organum enclosing it. Here the lower voice quickened and the upper grew regular. These sections were called *clausulae*, and their significance is great because they contain the germ out of which came the *motet*. Next, a *triplum* was added, and eventually—and much favored in England—a *quadruplum*. When the *triplum* appears, it is obvious that measure is required to keep the two upper voices together in consonance. Now, these upper parts were of course not built, as was the tenor, on a prescribed theme, and could develop with independent invention. This they proceeded to do, to a point where they parted company with the basic plainsong, although keeping their own accord, much like the *caudae* of conductus. A very large number of *clausulae* was produced, and over a hundred are still extant; some eighty of these, we are told, are already motets. Originally, the upper voices had no words, but texts were added in due course, Latin at first, then French in place of Latin, then French for top voice and Latin for the middle. The French texts were undisguisedly secular, treating mainly of sexual love. A technique arose of interchanging the musical phrases between the parts, which led to canon—e.g. "Sumer is icumen in." In this development, it must be evident that the gradual synchronization from unmeasured to measured time, and the coordination of parts in concerted singing was a function of pure musical necessity, and had nothing to do with verbal needs. When two or three different languages were sung simultaneously, clearly structural unity and phrasal proportion depended on musical control. The point to be observed is that even in the Church, where one would assume the dominance of extra-musical considerations and liturgical texts, all the parts of the Service that led to lyrical development—tropes and sequences, *conductus* and *caudae*, *clausulae* building up to the motet—were wordless at the start, and vocalized; then acquired syllables for pre-existent melodic structures; then grew progressively regular and strict by the increasingly compelling musical logic of vocal combination, in phrase-length, metre, and cadence. In other words, liturgical song-types—including chant, which, however, cannot be discussed here—are largely owing to the leading of musical rule, and not the other way round.

The motet form, in its far-reaching variety, its long history, the greatness and profusion of its outstanding monuments, is a subject for many volumes, and does not belong in a discussion of monodic song, although it incorporates abundant examples of borrowed melody, including many popular tunes or tune-fragments, as well as liturgical thematic material. A very large proportion, Dom Anselm Hughes says, of the surviving music between the mid-thirteenth and early fifteenth century is motet music. The form takes in much church polyphony, even parts of the Ordinary of the Mass and the Proper; [1] secular songs of celebration and festivity, ceremonial occasion, and love; and continues in unbroken development on into the great age of polyphony, with Machaut, Dunstable, the Netherland School, the Tudor composers, Tallis and Fayrfax, on to Byrd and Palestrina at the end of the sixteenth century

---

[1] *A propos*, it might be to such a context that the beguiled girl refers in her complaint (early fifteenth century):

Jankin at the Sanctus
Craketh a merye note . . .
Jankin craketh notes
An hundred on a knot,
And yit he hacketh hem smallere
Than wortes to the pot,
Kyrieleison . . .
Benedicamus Domino,
Christ fro shame me shilde:
Deo gracias, therto—
Alas! I go with childe,
Kyrieleyson.

and the beginning of the monodic reaction. It demonstrates super-abundantly how close musically were sacred and secular during all that time. But any soundly representative collection of texts, such as R. T. Davies' *Medieval English Lyrics*, displays in little the literary side of the same truth. In the Middle Ages, Hughes has said, the dichotomy between sacred and secular was unknown, and while we might not go so far, the fact is nearly demonstrable so far as music is concerned. Hughes calls to witness the "story of the motets", and "such things as the 'sacred' words written for 'Sumer is icumen in.' " [2] It is well remembered that in the MS of the latter are inscribed the words of an alternative Latin text, "Perspice Christicola," for the benefit of those who needed it most. But it has not been observed, to my knowledge, that the pious task was left unfinished. The two singers who are told off to sing the "foot," or continuous ground, of the piece are not instructed what words, if any, to supply in place of "Sing cuccu nu, sing cuccu"! An impish monastic jape?

We know that the Bishop of Ossory, early in the fourteenth century, disapproving of the insinuation of love lyrics into the sacred precincts, provided his clerics with Latin godly texts—some sixty in number—to be sung to the self-same popular tunes. Unfortunately, the tunes were not recorded, being hard to forget. One of them, it is sad to learn, belonged to the teasing "Maiden in the mor lay," for which alone we would readily give his three-score improvements. On the contrary side, the eleventh century Christmas sequence "Laetabundus," was often imitated and adapted for secular uses, and the double refrain incorporated wholesale. The English version of mid-fifteenth century is a close enough paraphrase for it to be sung to the same music—another way in which tunes exert their influence on the metrical patterns of texts. Other instances are Chaucer's clergeon's favorite, "Angelus ad Virginem"; and Fortunatus' "Crux Fidelis." A later example, Jean Tisserand's "O filii et filiae," at first a trope to "Benedicamus Domino," shares its tune with May Day carols, from which, indeed, it may well have borrowed it: "En revenant dedans les champs" is one; another is "Mois de Mai qu'est arrivé, c'est aujourd'hui qu'il faut chanter." These I believe are still current.

[2] *New Oxford History of Music*, Vol. II. *Early Medieval Music up to 1300*, ed. by Dom Anselm Hughes (1954), 403.

III

Another confluence of sacred and secular, learned and popular, a treasure-trove of monody that we could never have imagined would have survived in such quantity, is the rich hoard of troubadour and trouvère songs, some 250 melodies of the former, 1400 of the latter, and hundreds more texts, dating between the end of the eleventh and the early fourteenth centuries. The notation of these is sufficiently exact as to pitch to show the melodic line; but the rhythm is unregistered and problematic.

Careful scholars have shown where the roots of this fascinating breed of singers lie, and whither their influence was carried. It is significant that most of the song-tunes of Guillaume IX, the earliest of the school, have been traced to *conductus caudae* from Limoges. Westrup notices the kinship of Bernard de Ventadorn's well-known song of the lark, "Quan vei l'aloete," to the Kyrie melody "Cum Jubilo." But it transmigrated into other songs, both French and Latin, with new texts. A good deal of evidence, both specific and general, could be compiled from the work of troubadours and trouvères and their followers in other countries, of ecclesiastical influence on their music. But the interconnections of Church music and folk-music are so frequent and close that the two sources of influence are hardly to be separated. Fétis and Julien Tiersot both call attention to the deposit of pagan festivals—May Day, Midwinter, Midsummer—in Christian feasts. "There is reason," writes one authority, (Colles' edition of Grove, s.v. *Song*), "to believe that some melodies, or fragments of melodies, of Celtic origin have been preserved from the days before Christianity was introduced into France. . . . from the eleventh century onwards popular songs are to be found in the vulgar tongue side by side with the Latin canticles." The troubadours, trouvères, and Minnesinger reach down into this intermixture everywhere. In their rhyming stanzas, their fondness for refrain, their repetitions of musical phrases, their general preference for the Ionian or major tonality, they show their popular inheritance. To quote Grove again: "The most numerous (of the trouvères' songs) are *pastourelles*, and the songs written to accompany various kinds of dances. The latter, which always have a refrain, have a special importance in the history both of literature and of music, since it was from them that the fixed forms of song, such as the *ballade* and the *rondeau* were developed." (Grove, s.v. *Trouvères*). And Westrup: "The refrain may recur at the beginning (as in the virelai), in the middle, or at the end of successive verses, or within a single verse. It may consist of a single word, a series of conventional and virtually meaningless syllables, or an extended phrase. It is closely associated with dancing and clearly has a primitive origin." [3] Westrup quotes the melody of a Provençal *rondeau* (not common in the South) employed elsewhere for a Latin text on the Assumption of the Virgin, and also made into a thirteenth-century motet, "Tuit cil qui sunt enamourat"; and another trouvère *rondeau*, "En ma dame a mis mon cuer," the refrain of which occurs in a Latin *rondeau*, "Veni, Sancte Spiritus" (p. 246). [4] Many refrains may have been commonly available as tags in popular use: they often reappear in motets, between which and the trouvères' songs there is frequent interchange. Westrup finds an analogue of Walther von der Vogelweide's "Nu alerst leb'ich mich werde" in the Easter sequence, "Victimae paschali laudes"; and I have myself wondered whether it was fantasy to find here in Wipo's tune, the oldest sequence still in use, an ancestor of the popular Elizabethan ballad-tune, "Packington's Pound"—irrelevant as that may seem. But Westrup points to Neidhart von Reuental, a contemporary of Walther's, as the clearest illustration of "the frank simplicity of traditional melody" among these singers, citing his spring song, "Winder wie ist nu dein Kraft," structured ABA in twelve four-beat phrases, of which the closely rhymed stanzaic pattern looks more complicated than it actually is. But again, the trouvère tunes of the *lais*, paralleled by the German *Leich*(*en*), seem equally simple, if not simpler, composed as they are of short sections loosely strung together, capable of a shift of order, and recurrent; four-stress lines sung syllable-to-note, using a fairly common stock of melodic formulae emphasizing the major triad. The melodic lines of "In dulci jubilo" or in fact, of "Sumer is icumen in," are of the same type. They are close to dance-tunes, like *estampie*.

The trouvère Gautier de Coincy took over secular tunes of other singers like Blondel de Nesle and remade them into songs in honor of the Virgin, encouraging the compilation of some 400 sacred songs on the *trouvère* model by King Alfonso X of Spain—

---

[3] *Ibid.*, p. 241.
[4] *Ibid.*, pp. 245–246.

the English Edward I's brother-in-law—collected as the *Cantigas de Santa Maria*. Like the *virelais*, they have refrains at the beginning and end of the stanzas, with *overt* and *clos* cadences.

There are no surviving troubadour songs of Italy, though they were known and admired. The nearest approach to them is found in the *Laudi Spirituali*, vernacular hymns of the thirteenth and fourteenth centuries, structured like *virelais*, with refrain, verse, refrain, and displaying the same religious and secular influences. The verse was three four-stress rhyming lines, with a final line rhyming with the two-line refrain.

On the whole, at a broad guess, the troubadour schools and their offshoots were a good deal less inventive in their music than in their texts, although in the latter, too, they were not so much innovators as skillful craftsmen, intricately refining respected formulae, sometimes with an esoteric rhetoricism.

There was a continual interchange between these monodists and the motet composers, although the former did not write motets. The outstanding exception was Adam de la Hale, one of the latest and most versatile of the lot. He composed motets and much else, including, of course, the pastoral operetta, *Le Jeu de Robin et de Marion*, 1285. By virtue of the last, he is claimed as the first anthologist of French folk-tunes, since some authorities think that he strung together popular melodies current in his day, just as John Gay was to do, four and a half centuries later, in England. "Robin m'aime" is still traditionally sung.

In Germany, the influence of Volkslied is omnipresent, and impossible to escape. Symptomatic of the regard in which it was held, collections begin to appear as early as the fourteenth century, with the *Limburger Chronik* and the *Locheimer Liederbuch*. The polyphonists made constant use of it in their sacred works. For a conspicuous instance, Heinrich von Lauffenberg, in the fifteenth century, systematically set his religious compositions to secular tunes, making frequent use of the popular Tage- and Wächterlieder. At the Reformation, the practice became still commoner. More than half the melodies in the chorale books were folk-tunes. The reformers naturally wanted the congregations to unite in the hymn-singing, and therefore chose familiar melodies, and, moreover, preferred the vernacular to the Latin texts. For example, the old song "Innsbruck, ich muss dich lassen," which had been set polyphonically by Isaak in 1475, was now adapted for choral use by

Hasse, with a sacred text, "O Welt, ich muss dich lassen." Since 1633, as an evening hymn, "Nun ruhen alle Wälder" (P. Gerhardt), it has been a constant favorite in Lutheran churches. Again, Bach's Passion tune, "O Haupt voll Blut und Wunden," was originally a secular song, "Mein Gmüt ist mir verwirrt." Many other similar cases are cited by F. M. Böhme in his *Altdeutsches Liederbuch*, 1877. (*L'homme armé*, on the contrary, wherever it started, achieved international celebrity by the distinction of the settings it received at the hands of a series of brilliant composers, from Dufay to Carissimi).

In the fifteenth and sixteenth centuries, polyphony was supreme; but, on the popular level, this was very probably the time when many of the folk-carols and traditional ballads, known to us today, took recognizable shape, though unfortunately little of the early music was set down for our profit. In the mid-sixteenth century, Clément Marot deliberately laid hold of popular French and Flemish songs for the setting of his collection of psalms. In 1561 Tylman Susato published his *Souterliedekens*, consisting of portions of the Psalms in the rhymed French version, set unchanged to popular song-tunes of his day. But a hundred years earlier the Rederykers, a belated variety of Dutch Meistersinger, had taken hold of the rough and realistic secular songs of the time, and, while retaining the tunes, had substituted either new religious texts or had carefully adapted and altered the popular ones to give them serious meaning. Relations between Britain and the Netherlands were good in the sixteenth century; and it may have been these examples that prompted pious Scots to put out about the same date "Ane Buke of Gude and Godlie Ballatis, changeit out of prophane Sangis in godlie Sangis for avoyding of sin and harlatrie" (1567). Regrettably, this collection lacks its music.

So far as concerns England, one cannot look into the typical collections leading into the Elizabethan renascence—say *The Paradise of Dainty Devices* (1567), *The Gorgeous Gallery of Gallant Inventions* (1578), not to speak of Tottel's *Miscellany* (1557), without realizing that the sixteenth-century world, even before the great efflorescence, was full of popular song, ballad measures, tunes, old and tried patterns, music to sing, to work, to play to, to moralize with. These things pop out on all sides, in pamphlets, broadsides, anthologies, plays like *Ralph Roister Doister*, Wager's *The Longer Thou Livest*, *Love's Labour's Lost*, *Twelfth Night*,

Hamlet, The Winter's Tale, The Knight of the Burning Pestle:
songs and snatches either traditional or so close to traditional that
one cannot be sure whether they were picked up or invented for
the occasion.

IV

When, after three centuries at the flood, the tide of polyphony began to recede, the reaction did not proceed without bearing traces
of the past. The fashion of madrigals, spreading from Italy in the
mid-sixteenth century, though social, kept the contrapuntal habit
which minimized the importance of words; and in the new keyboard music the folk-tunes were mainly a thematic springboard for
elaborate technical virtuosity. Their identity was certainly no more
sacrosanct than fragments of plainchant had been, long before. But
their simple being was omnipresent and familiar. Recall came upon
the hint and entire statement was unnecessary. There is a rare example of the same sort in one of Dowland's songs, where, in the
refrain of "Can she excuse my wrongs" (I, 5), the lute accompaniment introduces the folk-tune "Shall I go walk the woods so
wild?" Ballets, with their *fa-la* refrains or choruses, were of course
closer to the dance and popular in structure.

The great outpouring of Elizabethan and Jacobean lutenist ayres
is a most interesting phenomenon, displaying the divergent impulses of a critical quarter-century. Although employing texts of
the highest lyrical quality, and for the most part of regular metrical
and stanzaic patterns, there is in the music seldom a tame submission to a merely verbal reading.

The question naturally arises, especially in the case of a
composer-poet like Campian, whether the music was set to words
or the words to music, or whether they were twinborn. Confident
answers, I think, can often be given in particular cases.

Take for example, Dowland's Book I, Song 11. The opening
lines *read* thus:

> Cóme away, cóme, sweet lóve!
>   The gólden mórning bréaks.
> All the earth, all the air
>   Of love and pleasure speaks.
> Téach thine árms then tò embráce,
>   Aǹd swèet rósy líps to kíss,
>   and mix our souls in mutual bliss.

The first four lines would seem to be three-stress lines, typically iambic, as in line two, "The golden morning breaks." The next three are four-stress troches: as in "Teach thine arms then to embrace." The music, however, follows another pattern:

And   sweet   ro ——————— sy lips to kiss

Since the musical phrasing, with the initial 4/4 accents, exactly repeated, followed by the triple rhythm, is precisely duplicated in the *following* stanzas of text, we have to suppose that the poet had this tune in mind: for such a metrical scheme would not have been suggested by the words themselves.

A similar instance appears in a better-known song, "Come again! Sweet love doth now invite." After three lines in regular iambic trimeter, there is a rhyming iambic pentameter couplet, of which the first line, which has its exact parallel in the next stanza, is comprised of five monosyllabic infinitives, "to see, to hear, to touch, to kiss, to die"; these have their counterpart in the musical phrase, which ascends one step at a time, with the stress coming *on a rest* before each sign of the infinitive. Another signal of the music's authority is the exclamatory opening of the strophe, which has no logical nor metrical unity with the following line in three of the song's six stanzas. How should we scan the "Come again" when followed by iambic trimeters? The answer lies in the music, which supplies the missing first beat by an opening chord in the lute accompaniment, and allows three full beats to the accented syllable of *again*. Obviously, music prompted the words: x̄ "Cóme agáin! x x̄ Sweet lóve doth nów invíte," and so forth. Another song of

Dowland's that cannot be read with any assurance as a verbal text
is Book II, Song 13, of which stanza one is as follows:

> Now cease, my wandring eyes
>   Strange beauties to admire.
> In change least comfort lies,
>   Long joys yield long desires.
>   One faith, one love
> Makes our frail pleasures eternal, and in sweetness prove
>   New hopes, new joys
> Are still with sorrow declining unto deep annoys.

Without the music, any metrical interpretation of the last four
lines is simply idiosyncratic.

Dowland's most famous song, "Lacrimae," or "Flow my Tears,"
is a more egregious example of the same kind. The latter three-
fifths of it, in spite of rhymes on the alternate lines, is hardly more
than cadenced prose of varying phrase-lengths.

> Never may my woes be relievèd,
>   Since pity is fled;
> And tears and sighs and groans my weary days
>   Of all joys have deprivèd.
> From the highest spire of contentment
>   My fortune is thrown;
> And fear and grief and pain for my deserts
>   are my hopes, since hope is gone.
> Hark! you shadows that in darkness dwell,
>   learn to contemn light.
> Happy, happy they that in hell
>   feel not the world's despite.
>
> Dowland, Book II, Song 2

Another song, Book 1 Song 5, is so clearly ordered by the musical (alternation of) timing that the text is forced into its service:

Can   she excuse my   wrongs   with Virtue's   cloak?
ONE   2   3 | ONE-2 &| THREE   1 |TWO   3 | ONE-2-3
   Shall I   call her good   when   she   proves   unkind?
   ONE 2   AND 3 & | ONE-2 | THREE 1 | TWO   3 | ONE-2-3
Are those clear   fires   which   vanish   into   smoke?
ONE   2   3 | ONE-2 & | THREE 1 | TWO 3 | ONE-2-3
   Must I praise   the leaves   where no   fruit I   find?
   ONE 2 AND-3   & |ONE-2 |THREE 1| TWO   3 | ONE-2-3
No, no: where shadows   do for bodies stand,
ONE 2   3 | ONE 2   AND3 & |ONE-2 3 | ONE-2-3

Thou mayst   be   abused   if   thy sight   be dim;
ONE   2   AND-3 &| ONE-2 | THREE 1 | TWO   3 | ONE-2-3
Cold love is like to words written on sand,
Or to bubbles which on the water swim.

Wilt   thou be   thus   abused   still,
ONE-2   &   3 | ONE-2 3 | ONE-2-3 | ONE 2 3
    Seeing that she will right thee never?
If   thou   canst   not   o'er-come   her   will
ONE-2 3 | ONE   2   3 | ONE-2 | THREE-1 | TWO
    Thy love will be thus fruitless ever.

Another song of Dowland's, although closely bound to a constant strophic pattern, is so lyrical that we must suppose its inspiration to be purely musical. With or without the repetitions, it is unlikely that any poet working with words alone, would devise such a stanza. The song is the 15th in Book 1, "Wilt thou, Unkind." Take the third stanza as typical:

> If no delays can move thee,
> Life shall die, death shall live
> Still to love thee,
> Still to love thee.
>
> Refrain: Farewell! Farewell!
> But yet or e'er I part, O cruel,
> Kiss me sweet, kiss me sweet,
> Sweet, my jewel!

Examples of this kind raise at least a strong probability that Dowland was himself the author of a number of his texts. Obviously, here we are at the opposite pole from folk-song; but the tunes still have the whip hand.

Interesting from another point of view are the abundant ayres in which, so to put it, we find evidence of cross-purposes between words and music. This characteristic has for us today a special appeal. It introduces tension, and nowadays we tend to decry anything lacking visible or audible tension; although between the Elizabethans and ourselves there was a long span during which this feature was perhaps the chief barrier to the enjoyment of the lutenists' songs.

Examples of the trait are readily found. There is among composers of Dowland's calibre and of his contrapuntal background a manifest reluctance to take orders from a four-square stanzaic or rhythmic pattern. Dowland's well-known "Now, O now, I needs must part" will serve as an illustration:

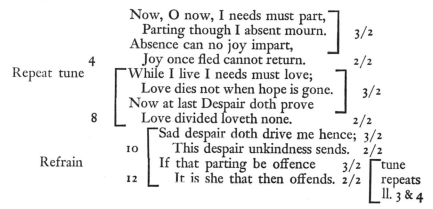

> Now, O now, I needs must part,⌉
> Parting though I absent mourn. ⎬ 3/2
> Absence can no joy impart, ⌋
> Joy once fled cannot return. 2/2
> Repeat tune 4
> ⌈While I live I needs must love; ⌉
> Love dies not when hope is gone. ⎬ 3/2
> Now at last Despair doth prove ⌋
> 8 Love divided loveth none. 2/2
> ⌈Sad despair doth drive me hence; 3/2
> 10 This despair unkindness sends. 2/2
> Refrain If that parting be offence 3/2 ⌈tune
> 12 It is she that then offends. 2/2 ⎢repeats
> ⌊ll. 3 & 4

There is no reason, on its face, why this shouldn't be read as trochaic tetrameter throughout. But Dowland singles out the fourth, eighth, tenth and twelfth lines and imposes upon them a contrasting duple metre which crosses the triple rhythm of the whole song:

ONE -two three,   ONE-two   three, etc; then:
ONE   two THREE   one   TWO three ONE two three.

This is not a matter of bringing out the natural emphasis of the words. He might with equal propriety have given the same rhythm to any other line or lines of the song. But, clearly, he wished to relieve the monotony which threatened in the opening lines.

It is instructive in this connection to compare with Dowland's the work of Campian. The latter was a supreme literary artist and a composer as well. If we examine his songs to learn which of his talents came foremost, or whether both combined in a simultaneous inspiration, we must, I believe, conclude that he was first a poet. He was a subtle metrist, with a sensitivity refined by his study of classical metres and close attention to syllabic values, to the relative weight of consonantal and vowal lengths. Witness his justly famous, and exquisite, "Rose-cheekt Laura." He enjoyed varying his metrical feet as well as the line lengths within his stanza patterns, and this kind of surface variety is conspicuous throughout his work. It tends to lead him towards the underlining, or illustra-

tion, of his metrical effects by his music, and it is usually clear that
the primary stimulus is verbal. The tunes are not likely to reveal
what is not already expressed in the text. Typical are lines like:

> Love me or not, love her I must, or die.
> Leave me or not, follow her needs must I.
> (Book IV, Song 10)

Or, a particularly felicitous and subtle example:

> Kind are her answers,
> But her performance keeps no day;
> Breaks time, as dancers,
> From their own music when they stray.
> All her free favours
> And smooth words wing my hopes in vain.
> O did ever voice so sweet but only feign?
> Can true love yield such delay,
> Converting joy to pain?

But Campian is also capable of the kind of musical independence
that we saw in Dowland. A good instance of this is the following
song, from Book II, Song 20:

> Her rosy cheeks, her ever-smiling eyes,
> Are spheres and beds where love in triumph lies.
> Her rubine lips, when they their pearl unlock,
> Make them seem as they did rise
> All out of one smooth coral rock.
> O that of other creatures' store I knew
> More worthy and more rare;
> For these are old, and she so new,
> That her to them none should compare.

There is no difficulty nor visible ambiguity here in the scansion: it
is impossible to go wrong. But when we turn to the music we find
that Campian has given it a triple rhythm that quite contraverts
what the text had determined. Dogged subservience to it would result, for example, in the second line's being read:

> Áre spheres and / béds where love / ín triumph / líes

Similar conflict arises in lines 3, 5, 6, 7, 8. The accompaniment is
persistently triple. But of course, the voice line takes its own road
and gives due emphasis to the right words. This seems enough to
prove that Campian did not compose words and music by a single
act of creation but *seriatim,* in that order. The pendulum does not

swing in two rhythms at the same time. And the firmness and clarity of his stanzaic patterns raise none of the doubts characteristic of some of Dowland's finest songs when read. His texts always make their own metrical sense, and must have come separately to birth.

V

It is safe to say that by the beginning of the seventeenth century most of the stanzaic patterns practicable for lyrical use had long since been thought of—many of them certainly as early as the days of the trouvères. The idea of conflict between musical and metrical patterns could either be welcomed and elaborated, or reacted against. To be exploited, at least two voices were essential, and in monodic song the accompanying instrument(s) provided the opposition.

To be resisted, the simple, transparent models of folk-song needed to be reinstated. These had not been forgotten: they were everywhere known and familiar, to be sung, whistled, danced to, worked to, and played. By a paradox of language, they were classic; and the course of song as the century progressed reflects a reversion in their direction by those lyricists and composers who valued form. The sophisticated songwriters of the mid-century, the Laweses, Lanier, Wilson, and their sort, chose uncomplicated and lucid stanzaic schemes to set; and the new intellectual school of poets, in contrast, drifted away from the idea of music. But, just as the earlier *composers* had challenged the *verbal* metrics in their settings, accepting the forms but introducing counter-rhythms, so now the metaphysicals accepted the time-honored outward shape of conventional lyric patterns but subverted them. Liberated from subservience to melody, they flouted the traditional equation of units of thought to line-length. They paid nominal respect to form by metre and syllabic count, rhyme and stanza scheme; but they wrote for the eye, and only partially for the ear. Their preoccupations were not primarily lyrical, and it is no accident that so relatively few of their short pieces were set. What could a composer of melody do for *them?* How could a maker of airs have matched a typical, superficially regular, stanza like this of Herbert's?

> Who would have thought my shrivel'd heart
> Could have recover'd greennesse? It was gone
> Quite under ground; as flowers depart

    To see their mother-root, when they have blown;
        Where they together
        All the hard weather,
    Dead to the world, keep house unknown.
                              ("The Flower")

Or this, from Traherne's "Solitude":

        Nor could I ghess
    What kind of thing I long'd for: But that I
        Did somwhat lack of Blessedness,
            Beside the Earth and Sky,
                I plainly found;
        It griev'd me much, I felt a Wound
    Perplex me sore; yet what my Store should be
    I did not know, nothing would shew to me.

Even when there is, later on, some return to the lyric mode, as in
Waller's famous and successful "Song," the complicated syntax
with two subordinate clauses before the thought is completed,
would prevent its being grasped in singing, and proves how lyric
and tune have become alienated:

        Goe lovely Rose,
    Tell her / that wastes her time and me, /
        That now she knowes,
    / When I resemble her to thee /
    How sweet and faire she seems to be.

This school, incidentally, might boast Marianne Moore as one of its
latest practitioners—strict syllabic count, rhyme, varying length of
line, stanzaic pattern exactly repeated, utterly unsingable; the
whole prose statement poured time after time into a container fan-
tastically irrelevant to the natural shape of the content. We are reminded of the syllable-counting of the earliest prose sequences of
the Alleluia.

    Herrick has been called (by Swinburne) the greatest lyric poet
in the language; but again it is not accidental that none of his most
characteristic pieces has been set to music. Lawes attempted a bare
handful, but almost all of his choices are in octosyllabic couplets.
The reason is obvious. The exquisite artistry of Herrick must be
seen on the page to be appreciated, even though he exploits rhyme
for all it is worth. He writes for the eye; and many of his happiest
effects cannot be fully expressed in sound. A number of them
when read aloud turn into heroic couplets with internal rhyme. He
plays with the iambic pentameter very ingeniously, dividing it into

unequal lines, with a rhyme on the first foot or the second, the
third, and even, I think, the fourth. For example:

> Though clock, }
> To tell how night draws hence, I've none, }
> A cock }
> I have to sing how day draws on. }
> ("His Grange," *Muses Library*, no. 726)

> Love, I have broke }
> Thy yoke, }
> The neck is free; }
> But when I'm next }
> Love-vexed, }
> Then shackle me. }
> ("Upon Love," no. 460)

> { Both you two have
> { Relation to the grave:
> And where }
> The funeral-trump sounds, you are there. }
> { I shall be made,
> { Ere long, a fleeting shade:
> Pray, come }
> And do some honour to my tomb. }
> ("To The Yew & Cypress," no. 280)

Another exquisite example:

> A funeral stone, }
> Or verse I covet none, }
> But only crave }
> Of you that I may have }
> A sacred laurel springing from my grave:
> Which being seen, }
> Blest with perpetual green }
> May grow to be }
> Not so much call'd a tree }
> As the eternal monument of me.
> ("To Laurels," no. 89)

Once more:

> Behold this living stone }
> I rear for me, }
> Ne'er to be thrown }
> Down, envious Time, by thee. }
> ("His Poetry his Pillar," no. 211)

In these examples, Herrick counts powerfully on the time-interval that the eye takes to move back and down from the end of the line to the beginning of the next, and on the emphatic length imposed by the rhyme on the last word. There is a psychological illusion of greater duration than can be sustained in an oral rendition—at least without affectation.

With the Restoration, if not before, sets in the overwhelming *flood* of songs written to preexistent popular tunes. It is in spate for 200 years—if indeed it should ever subside. One has only to mention the successive waves: Political and topical broadsides by the hundreds, separately issued day by day and sometimes gathered up in collections like D'Urfey's *Pills*; ballad operas, again containing hundreds of familiar tunes, with fresh words; Methodist and Dissenters' hymns, all written to musical pattern, so as to allow for interchange of tune.

I shall pass by all these with the bare notice of their substantial weight in our hypothetical scale; and I shall forgo discussion of the potent influence of popular ballad forms on the course of "literary" verse in the Romantic Revival. Others have treated the subject better than I can do.[5] I would merely insist on the immemorial role played by the music in fixing these traditional patterns of rhythm, rhyme, and rhetoric on the mind's ear; so that, in abstract, melody is always present, regardless of whether or not a particular tune is in question. I wish to come at once to the demonstrative case of Robert Burns.

VI

It may be necessary to insist that Burns had, if not a professional, then an expert and sufficient musical knowledge and training. Actually, although he must have written down many a tune, Johnson and Thomson, his printers of music, apparently made no effort to save his manuscript; or if they did, all but a page seems to have vanished. But the single page shows a bold and workmanlike hand, by no means unpractised in setting down notes; and we know, too, that Burns had some skill on the violin. His library of eighteenth-century Scots song-books was fairly complete, and his heavily an-

---

[5] E.g., cf. Josephine Miles, *Eras and Modes in English Poetry* (1957), ch. 6; "The Romantic Mode," *English Literary History*, Vol. XX, No. 1 (1953); Anne H. Ehrenpreis, *The Literary Ballad* (1966).

notated set of the *Caledonian Pocket Companion* is extant and very revealing. He himself declared that he knew more Scots airs, both printed and unprinted, than any other living man. He sent quantities of these to his printers, along with the sets of words, old or new, that went with them; and according to J. C. Dick, who made a careful study, he contributed "at least" 235 songs written by himself to old tunes, for inclusion in the *Scots Musical Museum*.

His inspiration in song-making was self-declared to be musical. He thus describes his own practice in composition: "These old Scottish airs are so nobly sentimental that, when one would compose for them, to *south* the tune, as our Scotch phrase is, over and over, is the readiest way to catch the inspiration."[6] Elsewhere, more particularly, he writes: "until I am compleat master of a tune, in my own singing . . . I never can compose for it. —My way is: I consider the poetic Sentiment correspondent to my idea of the musical expression; then chuse my theme; begin one Stanza . . . humming every now and then the air with the verses I have framed."[7] In his correspondence with Johnson and with Thomson, both of whom had a better opinion of their own musical competence than rightly belonged to them, Burns was forced to give frequent instruction on the merits, the suitability, and the just treatment of individual tunes; and it is obvious that he had a nice discrimination in, and subtle perception of, points which would go unnoticed by the majority of hearers. "There is a certain irregularity in the Old Scotch Songs," he notes at one point, "a redundancy of syllables . . . which glides in, most melodiously with the respective tunes to which they are set. . . . This particularly is the case with all those airs which end with a hypermetrical syllable."[8] Talking of rhyme elsewhere, he remarks, "it might be possible for a Scotch poet, with a nice judicious ear, to set compositions to many of our most favourite airs, independent of rhyme altogether."[9]

It might be worth while to ask oneself, starting with the assumed priority of the music, as formerly we began by assuming the priority of words, just what and how much help a lyric poet like Burns

[6] *Commonplace Book* (1782), p. 52, quoted by J. C. Dick (ed.), in *Notes on Scottish Song*, by Robert Burns (1908), p. xli.
[7] *Works*, VI, 274, quoted by Dick, *loc. cit.*
[8] Dick (1908), p. xxxiii, quoting from Burns's *Commonplace Book*.
[9] Dick, *loc. cit.*

might conceivably extract from his racial melodic tradition, setting aside for the nonce any consciousness he might have of a *literary* tradition. What is there implicit in a folk-tune to further the construction of a lyric text?

A folk-tune is brief enough to be readily grasped and remembered as a whole: it has an inner unity that makes it *shapely* to the ear and mind. Hence, it is individual, recognizable, and welcome on repetition. As a temporal event, or succession of notes, it consists of a little pathway through a sonic landscape; so that as we proceed we recognize its topography: the setting forth, the approach to a turning point, a moment of heightened interest, a pause of retrospection or anticipation, a homecoming. It falls naturally into related and relatively equal, self-defining stages of its whole extent, revealing balance, contrast, and decision. The balance normally relies on approximately the same number of stresses in corresponding phrases; the contrast (also an aspect of balance) usually on tonal sequence and management; the decision appears in cadential statement and held, or repeating, notes, like direction signs. Because the tune is seized as a whole, and because its several parts have these mutual references, we gain already the suggestion of stanzas of a certain pattern and identical length. Since the cadence-points of the component phrases get their weight and meaning from their relative emphasis and relation to the tonic, they inherently prompt corresponding verbal emphases, of rhyme or pause. By their perceptible division or separation, they exert, moreover, a pressure on the accompanying verbal grouping, so that the total syntactical and rhetorical structure is palpably affected, and restricted, by their influence.

Because the constant repetition of the tune encloses these units of verbal statement within equal divisions, the instinctive and natural verbal counterpart of a folk-tune is the varied expression of a dominant emotion or idea in successive illustrations, rather than free narrative development. Thus, for example:

    (a) O, wert thou in the cauld blast
          On yonder lea, on yonder lea,
       My plaidie to the angry airt,
          I'd shelter thee, I'd shelter thee;

    (b) *Or* did Misfortunes bitter storms
          Around thee blaw, around thee blaw,

Thy bield should be my bosom,
To share it a', to share it a'.

    (c) *Or* were I in the wildest waste,
        Sae black and bare, sae black and bare,
    The desart were a paradise,
        If thou wert there, if thou wert there;

    (d) *Or* were I monarch o' the globe,
        Wi' thee to reign, wi' thee to reign,
    The brightest jewel in my crown
    Wad be my queen, wad be my queen.

Besides the four-pulse line-length, which always overrides the metre, whether iambic, trochaic, dactylic, anapaestic, spondaic, alternating tetrameters and trimeters (*versus popularis*) or what not; and besides the traditional syllabic or semi-syllabic adjustment of words to notes: what else may we find in this song that seems the clear dower of the music? The clausal correspondence with the musical phrase is obvious; all the lines are end-stopped except the first, fifth, and next-to-last. These are all unrhymed, but even in these the line is thought-contained and does not wait for completion to be understood by itself. Further, the repeated half-lines are not for sense but for lyrical emphasis, the obvious counterparts of the melodic rhetoric: *on yonder lea, on yonder lea* is the kind of repetition that is not self-prompted, but suggested by the contour of the tune. The rhymes, also, occurring on the even lines, chime with the articulating cadence-points, the signal-points, of the tune. In other words, the tune has instigated both rhyme and refrain. The dotted metre of the tune, moreover, matched by the syllabic correspondence of the words, may be held responsible also for Burns's rhythm, since the tune came first. (Incidentally, this particular tune, earlier called "Lenox Love to Blantyre," has another claim to remembrance, for after it was named a famous Historic House in East Lothian, "Lenoxlove," which may be visited today.)

Burns's metres, of course, invariably accord in their considerable variety with the tunes that gave rise to them:

In 4/4,

        Duncan Gray cam here to woo,
        Ha, ha, the wooing o't!

In 6/8,

> Her daddie forbad, her minnie forbad;
> Forbidden she wadna be . . .
> The long lad they ca' Jumpin John
> Beguil'd the bonie lassie.

In 6/8 again,

> Bitter in dool, I lickit my winnins
> O' marrying Bess, to gie her a slave;
> Blest be the hour she cool'd in her linens,
> And blythe be the bird that sings on her grave.

In 3/4

> Flow gently, sweet Afton, among thy green braes.

In 4/4,

> Lándlădў, coúnt the láwin,
> The dáy is near the dáwin;
> Ye're á' blind drunk, bóys,
> And I'm but jólly foú.

Cho.
> Héy tútti, táiti,
> Hów tútti, táiti,
> Héy tútti, táiti,
> Wha's foú nów?

This last is an illustration of Burns's unerring sense of the capabilities of instrumental dance-tunes in altered metres and speeds for use in other moods; for, of course, given a bold, marching 2/4 tempo, the same tune inspired his immortal "Scots, wha hae." He wrote at length to Thomson on the tune, in part as follows:

My dear Sir,—You know that my pretensions to musical taste are merely a few of nature's instincts, untaught and untutored by art. For this reason, many musical compositions, particularly where much of the merit lies in counterpoint, however they may transport and ravish the ears of you connoisseurs, affect my simple lug no otherwise than merely as melodious din. On the other hand, by way of amends, I am delighted with many little melodies, which the learned musician despises as silly and insipid. I do not know whether the old air *Hey, tutti, taitie* may rank among this number; but well I know that with Fraser's hautboy, it has often filled my eyes with tears. There is a tradition which I have met with . . . that it was Robert Bruce's march at the battle of Bannockburn . . . . I shewed the air to Urbani, who was highly pleased with it and begged me make soft verses for it;

but . . . . I am afraid that the air is not what will entitle it to a place in your elegant selection.[10]

Burns's premonitions were justified in the event. Thomson liked his song but not the tune, and suggested many changes, actually only filler, watering it down to suit a tune with a different metre, which put Burns's back up till he refused to have anything further to do with it. In the altered form Thomson published it three years after Burns's death; but lived himself to regret the act, and restored the original on demand.

Of Burns's adaptations, which are abundant and equally inspired, and of which "Green grow the rashes, O" would provide an example for long discourse, there is no room to speak here. The upshot of the matter is that without the familiar knowledge of anything except his own native traditional song, Burns, with his genius, could have derived therefrom every formal element of his technique as a lyric poet: stanza pattern, length of line, metrical disposition, placement of rhyme, clausal strategy, sequence of thoughts and ordering of expressive emotion. Of course, he did study and learn the English literary lyric. Where it coincided with his own tradition, he did not reject it. But he *followed* his own: he had the Scots tunes in his mind and heart, and the words that went with them.

Where did they come from? Follow them back, from generation to generation, as far as they can be traced, and they are not appreciably different. The Scots songs to be found in D'Urfey, Ramsay, the *Orpheus Caledonius*, in the early eighteenth century, are recognizably cut from the same bolt. The Leyden, the Blaikie, the Guthrie tune-manuscripts of the late seventeenth, are of similar stuff, though they lack the words. The early seventeenth-century MSS, the Skene, Straloch, and Rowallan, except where they borrow English art-songs, are akin in content and nature. Moving back into the sixteenth century, we find traces of the same popular tradition behind the "Gude and Godly Ballatis," however manhandled. For testimony:

> All my luve, leave me not,
> Leave me not, leave me not,
> All my luve, leave me not
> Thus mine alone,

[10] Quoted by J. C. Dick, *The Songs of Robert Burns* (1903), p. 448.

> With ane burden on my back,
> I may not bear it, I am so waik,
> Luve, this burden fra me tak
>   Or ellis I am gone.

As pure literary invention, this is inconceivable: it cries aloud for
the tune that gave rise to it.

Beside the radiant example of Burns, all others are by comparison "Meaner beauties of the night." Tom Moore's is an exactly
comparable case: in fact, the *Irish Melodies* were modeled on
George Thomson's Scottish collection. His songs were precisely
tailored to specific tunes, to which he helped himself freely from
Bunting's volumes of 1796 and 1807. His success was spectacular
and for his contemporary audiences absolute, promoted as it was
by his very attractive concertizing. Most unlike Burns, who would
not take money for his songs, Moore grew rich on his: his rewards
rose to the height of £1300 per published song. Today, they are
out of print, and his superheated Ossianic sentiment seems so out of
phase with an age of ironic disillusion that it is unlikely we shall see
any serious effort to reinstate him. He was a far less careful and
loving workman than Burns and, though facile and clever, he committed some serious offences against the shape and scansion of the
Irish melodies to which he was so deeply obliged.

It would be pleasant to pursue the influences of traditional melody upon lyricists of the nineteenth and early twentieth centuries,
but time runs out. Who taught Meredith the lilting music, which
must be chanted with full time-values, or else ruined, of "Love in
the Valley": eight-stress lines, but really four plus four?

Under yónder béech-trée, / síngle ón the greénswárd,
Coúched with her árms x / behínd her gólden héad, x
Knées and trésses fólded / to slíp and rípple ídly,
Lies mý yoúng lóve, / sleéping ín the sháde. x

Housman, of course, is unthinkable without the old homespun patterns upon which to exercise his sombre petit point. One might
have expected to find much to our use in De La Mare, with his
early musical training, his fine and subtle ear, and exquisite sense of
time. But he is above the level at which we are aiming here, and his
best effects are themselves wayward music:

> Whence else upwelled—strange, sweet, yet ominous—
> That / moment of happiness, / and then was gone?

Nimbler than air-borne music, heart may call
A speechless music to the inward ear . . .
Yet nought that listening could make more clear.

Much more deeply embedded in the common stuff of familiar song was Yeats, with his love of balladry and his ongoing, additive style, always preferring the simple, coordinating connectives to logical, conditional, subordinating, or complicating ones: *and*, not *though*. And often and often, refrains: repetitions for their own singing sake, or repetitions incremental.

> She carries in the dishes,
> And lays them in a row,
> To an isle in the water
> With her would I go.
>
> She carries in the candles,
> And lights the curtained room,
> Shy in the doorway,
> And shy in the gloom
>   ("To an Isle in the Water.")

That is the ageless note. And, at a deeper level, with the personifying instinct of the ballad, and with refrain:

> 'Three dear things that women know,'
> *Sang a bone upon the shore;*
> 'A man if I but held him so
> When my body was alive
> Found all the pleasure that life gave':
> *A bone wave-whitened and dried in the wind.*
>   ("Three Things.")

And now, if any think these leaves, flotsam lifted from off the stream of Time, only an ill-assorted random skimming of old snatches adrift, let him take them as talismanic reminders. As Johnson said, men more frequently require to be reminded than informed.

1967

Index

By Janet M. James

Accompaniment, effect on tune, 204
"Acre of Land, An," 263
Adam de la Hale, 295
Addison, Joseph, 92
"Admiral Benbow," 25-27, 28-29, 32
"Admiral Byng and Brave West," 27-28, 33
"Aikendrum," 33
Alfonso X, King of Spain, *Cantigas de Santa Maria*, 292-293
Ambrose, Saint, 285
American Folklore Society, 244-245, 249, 274
American Society of Composers, Authors, and Publishers (ASCAP), 252
Anderson, Robert, 65
"Angelus ad Virginem," 292
"Annie of Lochroyan," 205
Armstrong, Louis, 225
Arnold, Byron, *Folksongs of Alabama*, 128, 251
"Arraignment of the Divel for stealing away President Bradshaw," 33-34, 35
"As I walked over London Bridge," 110
"As you came from Walsingham," 110
Asch, Moses, 207
"At home I would be (in)," 117
Augustine, Saint, 288
Authentic range. *See* Tunes
Authenticity: of texts 64; of folk-song performances, 206; sought by professional folk-singers, 254

Bach, Johann Sebastian, "O Haupt voll Blut und Wunden," 296
"Baffled Knight, The," 115, 271

"Bailiff's Daughter of Islington, The," 119, 123, 176
Balfour, Colonel D., *Ancient Orkney Melodies*, 33
"Ballad of an Oysterman." *See* Holmes, O. W.
Ballade, 294
Ballads without tunes, 59-60
Ballets (song form), 297
"Bangum and the Boar," 58, 267
Baptists, 134, 135
"Barbara Allan," 33, 60, 97, 127, 153, 163-164, 168, 208, 218, 226; textual and melodic variation in, 232-242
"Barbara Allen's Cruelty," 239
Barbeau, Marius, 249
Baring-Gould, Sabine, 114, 262, 275
Barry, Margaret, 207
Barry, Phillips, 53, 114, 142, 144, 240, 245-246, 249; *British Ballads from Maine*, 246, 249
"Battle of Copenhagen, The," 28
"Battle of Otterburn, The," 205
"Battle of the Baltic, The," 28
Baum, Paull F., 212, 213
Bayard, Samuel P., 140, 142
Beaumont and Fletcher, *The Knight of the Burning Pestle*, 297
Bedford's *Excellency of Divine Musick*, 32
Belafonte, Harry, 252
Belden, Henry M., 212-214, 245, 249, 250, 251
Benbow, Admiral John. *See* Admiral Benbow
"Benedicamus Domino," 292
Bernard de Ventadour, 293

315

"Bessy Bell and Mary Gray," 125
"Billy Boy," 268
"Binnorie," 44-45, 48, 265
Blaikie MSS., 311
Blind Harry, *Wallace*, 258
Blondel de Nesle, 294
Böhme, F. M., *Altdeutsches Lieder-buch*, 296
"Bonnie Annie," 44
"Bonnie Blinks of Mary's E'e, The," 125
"Bonny Birdy, The," 73
"Bonny Blue Flag, The," 213
"Bonny Broome, The," 271
"Brangywell," 58
"Brennan on the Moor," 149
Brewster, Paul G., 212, 250
Broadcast Music Incorporated (BMI), 252
Broadwood, John, *Sussex Songs*, 100
Broadwood, Lucy, *Sussex Songs*, 100, 275
Brockway, Howard. *See* Wyman, Loraine
"Broom of Cowdenknows, The," 271
"Broomfield Hill, The," 191, 271
Brown, Mrs. Anna Gordon, of Falkland: as source of ballads, 42-44, 48, 64-78, 99, 106, 113, 265; biographical sketch, 65-66
Brown, Frank Clyde, 211-212, 217, 245; Collection, 211-223, 250
Bruce, J. C. and J. Stokoe, *Northumbrian Minstrelsy*, 100, 275
Buchan, Peter, 77
Bukofzer, Professor Manfred, 83n., 115n.
Bunting, Edward, collection of Irish folk-songs, 100, 312
"Burd Ellen," 70
Burlesque. *See* Parodies of ballads; "Sequences"
Burns, Robert, 32-33, 99, 113n., 306-312
Byng, Admiral John. *See* "Admiral Byng and Brave West"

Cadence. *See* Tunes
Caledonian Pocket Companion, 307
"Callino Casturame," 284
Calverley, Charles Stuart, 93
Campbell, Alexander, 113
Campbell, Olive Dame, 248
Campbell, Thomas, 28
Campian, Thomas, 297, 301-303; "Rose-cheekt Laura," 301-302

"Captain Kidd," 24-33 *passim*
"Captain Wedderburn's Courtship," 109-110, 271
"Carnal and the Crane, The," 109, 119
Carmina Burana, 289
Caudae, 290, 291, 293
Chambers, Robert, 4-5
Chappell, Louis W.: Collection, 250; *Folks Songs of Roanoke and the Albemarle* and *John Henry*, 250
Chappell, William, 26-28; *Popular Music of the Olden Time*, 26, 99, 126
Chaucer, Geoffrey, "Sir Thopas," 50, 95
"Chevy Chase," 92, 93
Chickering, Geraldine C. *See* Gardner, Emelyn
Child, Francis James, 4-14 *passim*, 40, 44-45, 54-56, 64, 75-77, 92-94, 100-101, 116-118, 214, 244-245, 281; *The English And Scottish Popular Ballads*, 53, 63, 74, 244-245
"Chimney Sweep," 23, 28, 32
Christie, Dean William, 99-100, 114, 126, 157; *Traditional Ballad Airs*, 27-28, 99-100, 137
Circular tunes, 220
Clausulae, 290, 292
"Clerk Colvill," 42-43
"Clerk Saunders," 74, 109-110, 119
Climax of relatives. *See* Narrative
Coirault, Patrice, 105
Collinson, Francis M. *See* Henderson, Hamish
"Coming Down," 25
Commercialism, effect on folk-song and folk-singers, 95-96, 128, 251-256, 273, 274; deleterious effects of, 202-206, 271-272
"Common metre" CM, 38-39
"Communal origins" theory, 39-40, 76; instance of communal change, 269
"Ane Compendius Buik of Godly and Spirituall Sangis Collectit out of sundrye partes of the Scripture," ed. A. F. Mitchell, 35-36, 296, 311
Complaynt of Scotlande, The, 36
Computers, use in ballad study, 173-174, 230-233
Conductus, 289-290, 291, 293
"Congaudeat turba fidelium." *See* Petri, Theodoric
Congressional Record, 224
Conservatism of tradition, 60-61, 150-151, 278; importance of tune in, 166-167, 169. *See also* Traditional process

Continuity (Sharp's principle), 144, 146, 150, 151, 158, 160, 278
Contrapuntal music, 297
Conventional formulae. *See* Narrative
Copland, Aaron, 95
Copyright, 254, 256
"Coverdale's Carol," 109-110
Cowell, Henry, 95
Cox, J. H., 245; *Folk Songs of the South*, 249
Creativity of ballad singers, 61-62, 67, 69-72, 76, 104-106, 148-150, 203; communal action in (re-)creation of songs 61, 144, 148-149, 269
Creighton, Helen, 250
"Croodlin Dow, The," 268
"Crow Song," 267
"Cruel Mother, The," 73, 109-110, 119, 122-123
"Crux Fidelis." *See* Fortunatus
"Cum Jubilo," 293

"Daemon Lover, The" 186
Dalrymple, Sir David. *See* Hailes, Lord
Dancing, ballads adapted to, 266, 269
Daniel Samuel, *Musophilus*, 225
"Danny Deever," 214
Dating: texts, 112-117; tunes, 117-124, 157-158
Davidson, A. T., 248
"Davie," 3, 9, 12-13
Davies, R. T., *Medieval English Lyrics*, 292
Davis, Arthur K., *More Traditional Ballads*, 250; *Traditional Ballads from Virginia*, 249
De La Mare, Walter, 312-313
Delius, Frederick, 255
Diack, John Michael, *New Scottish Orpheus*, 265
Dick, J. C., ed., *The Songs of Robert Burns*, 307, 311
"Diggers." *See* Winstanley, William
"Dixie," 227
"Douglas Tragedy, The," 271
Dowland, John, 297-303; *Andreas Ornithoparcus his Micrologus*, 121n-122n; on moods of modes, 230; "Can she excuse my wrongs," 297; "Come again! Sweet love doth now invite," 298; "Lacrimae" or "Flow my Tears," 299-300; "Wilt thou, Unkind," 300; "Now, O now, I needs must part," 301
"Dragoon and the Lady, The," 271

"Duke of Gordon's Daughters, The," 187
"Duncan Gray," 125
Duplum (in *organum*), 290
D'Urfey, Thomas, *Pills*, 23, 28, 57-58, 98, 99, 105, 112, 115, 116, 117, 306, 311

"Earl Brand," 44
Eckstorm, Fannie, 246
Editing texts for print, 68, 77, 157
"Edom o' Gordon," 4, 263-264
Eddy, Mary O., 250
"Edward," 73, 185; age and authenticity of Percy's version, 1-17, 52, 74-76, 103-104; Appalachian version, 12-14, 53
"Elfin Knight, The," 53, 257-263, 268
"En ma dame a mis mon cuer," 294
"En revenant dedans les champs," 292
England, John, 275
English Folk Song Society, 94-95; and *Journal*, 98, 247-248, 275
Entertainment and entertainers, 253, 255; attitude toward ballads, 274. *See also* Commercialism
"Eppie Morrie," 209-210
"Erlinton," 271
"Essex's Last Good-Night," 35
Estampie (dance form), 289, 294
Evolution (Sharp's theory), 146-147, 151, 279-280

"Fair Anny," 70
"Fair Flower of Northumberland," 10
"False Knight upon the Road, The," 40
Farnaby, Giles, 98, 118
Farnaby, Ralph, "Fayne wolde I wedde," 98, 109-110, 118
Farquharson, Mrs., 65, 71, 73
Fétis, Francois-Joseph, 293
Fisk "Jubilee Singers," 246
Fitzwilliam Virginal Book, 98, 118
Flanders, Helen Hartness, 245, 250; *Ballads Migrant in New England* and *Ancient Ballads Traditionally Sung in New England*, 250
Fletcher, John, *The Chances*, 114
Fortunatus, "Crux Fidelis," 292
"Folk festivals," 252
Folk Song Society of the North-East, 244; *Bulletin*, 249
Folklore, definitions of, 212-214
Folklore Society of the South-East, 250

Forbes, William, 65
Forbes' *Aberdeen Cantus*, 32
"Friar in the Well, The," 46
Fuguing tunes, 140

"Gaberlunyie Man, The," 117
Gammer Gurton's Needle, 114
Gapped scales. *See* Tunes
Gardner, Emelyn E. and Geraldine J.
    Chickering, 250
Gautier de Coincy, 294
Gay, John, *The Beggar's Opera*, 260,
    295
"Georgie" (Geordie), 108, 109-110, 119
Gerhardt, P., "Nun ruhen alle
    Wälder," 296
"Germany Thomas," 32-33
Gerould, Gordon Hall, *The Ballad of
    Tradition*, 153
Gest of Robyn Hode, 15, 104
"Gil Brenton," 43
"Gil Morrice" ("Gil Morris"), 4, 208
Gilchrist, Anne G., modal scheme, 86n.,
    135
"Gipsy Countess, The," 187
Gladden, Mrs. Texas, 119
Glareanus, 83n.
"Go from my Window," 109-110
"Goddesses," 98, 108-109, 117
Golden Age of British Balladry, 74, 76,
    104
Goldsmith, Oliver, 282
Goldstein, Kenneth, 207
Goodman, Benny, 225
Gordon, Thomas, 65
*Gorgeous Gallery of Gallant Inven-
    tions, The*, 296
Graham, G. F., *Songs of Scotland*, 125
Grainger, Percy, 127
"Green grow the rashes, O," 311
Greenleaf, Elizabeth, and Grace Y.
    Mansfield, *Ballads and Songs of
    Newfoundland*, 191, 250
"Greensleeves," 238, 264
Greig, Gavin, 100, 114, 265, 276; MSS,
    12; and Alexander Keith, *Last Leaves
    of Traditional Ballads*, 43, 126, 153
Grove's *Dictionary of Music*, ed.
    Colles, 293-294
Guido of Arezzo, 289
Guillaume IX, 293
Gummere, Francis, 168
Guthrie, Woodrow Wilson
    ("Woody"), 254
Guthrie MSS., 311

"Gypsy Davie," 185
"Gypsy Davy, 166, 168, 186, 191, 227
"Gypsy Laddie, The," 166, 168

Hailes, Sir David Dalrymple, Lord of
    Session, 2-4, 10-12, 14
Hall, Jack, 22-25
Hall, Sam, 23
Hand, Wayland D., 212
Händel, Georg Friedrich, 286-287
"Hanskin," 262
Hardy, Thomas, *Under the Green-
    wood Tree*, 31
"Hardyknute," 2
Harris, Mrs., 113
Hart, W. M., *Ballad and Epic*, 15; *Eng-
    lish Popular Ballads*, 6n.
Hasse, Johann Adolph, 296
Haydn, Franz Josef, 286
Hayes, William, *Selected Songs Sung
    at Harvard College*, 20-21, 24
Heinrich von Lauffenberg, 295
Henderson, Hamish, and Francis M.
    Collinson, in *Scottish Studies*, 260n.
Henderson, T. F., *The Ballad in Liter-
    ature* (1912), 12
Hendren, J. W., *A Study of Ballad
    Rhythm*, 144n.
"Henry Martin," 88-90, 119, 188, 270
Henry, Mellinger E., 250
Herbert, George, "The Flower," 303-
    304
Herd, David, MSS. Collection, 51, 268
Herrick, Robert, 304-306
Herzog, George, 246
"Hey tutti taiti," 310
"Hind Horn," 50-51, 109, 119
Hogg, James, *Jacobite Relics*, 33
Holmes, Oliver Wendell, "Ballad of an
    Oysterman," 214
Holst, Gustav, 254
"Hootenannies," 253-254
Horace, "Integer vitae," 286, 289
"House Carpenter, The," 167, 190
Housman, A. E., 312
"How should I your true-love know?"
    109-110
Howe's *100 Comic Songs*, 21
Howell, Rednap, "Regulator" Songs,
    213
Hudson's collection of Irish folk-songs,
    100
Hudson, Arthur Palmer, 212, 213, 214;
    work on *North Carolina Folklore*,
    251; *Folk-Songs of Mississippi*, 251
Hughes, Dom Anselm, *New Oxford*

History of Music, cited, 290-292 *passim*

"I cannot eat but little meat," 114
"I hae laid a herring in saut" ("I canna come ilka day to woo"), 125
"I was born almost ten thousand years ago," 30-31
"I would I were in my own country," 98, 117
Idea of a ballad preserved and re-created by traditional singers, 71-72, 105-111, 150, 158, 262; melodic, 61-63, 72, 123, 150, 158, 160-161, 166-167, 169, 228, development in time of, 101-106, stability of, 124-125, in shaped-note hymn tunes, 138, 141-143, stability of melodic ideas, 124-125; textual, 71-72, variations in, 237-241, 258-269
"In dulci jubilo," 294
Incest ballads, 51-53; avoidance of, 72
Incremental repetition. *See* Narrative
"Innsbruck, ich muss dich lassen," 295
Inter-relations of tune and text, 221; refrains, 257-267; textual metrics, 283-287. *See also* Tunes
International Folk Music Council, 95
Isaak, Heinrich, 295
Ives, Burl, 252

"Jack Hall," 22-33 *passim*
"Jack the Chimney Sweep," 21
"Jack the little Scot," 68
Jackson, George Pullen, 250; *Another Sheaf of White Spirituals*, 140-143; *Down-East Spirituals and Others, Spiritual Folk-Songs of Early America*, 133-140; *White Spirituals in the Southern Uplands*, 134-139
"James Harris, or the Daemon Lover," 167
"Jamie Douglas," 271
Jamieson, John, 42, 65, 106, 265
Jamieson, Robert, 66
Lê Jeu de Robin et de Marion, 295
"Jog on, jog on," 262
"John Dory," 114
"John over the Hazel Green," 189
"Johnnie Collins," 190
"Johnny Hall," 22. *See also* "Jack Hall"
Johnson, James, *Scots Musical Museum*, 32, 60, 99, 113, 306-307
Johnson, Samuel, 225, 313
Jones, John Paul, ballad about, 28-33
Joyce, P. W., 100

Jubilus, 288
"Judas," 44, 97

"Kampion," 68
Karpeles, Maud, 147, 249, 250; *Cecil Sharp: His Life and Work*, 273-281
"Katie Morey," 271
Keats, John, "La Belle Dame sans Merci," 42
"Kempy Kay," 50, 267
Kidd, Captain William, ballad about, 24-26
Kidson, Frank, 21, 23, 30, 114, 275; *Traditional Tunes*, 100
"King Herod and the Cock," 110, 119
"King John and the Abbot," 115, 116
Kinloch, George K., 99, 113
Kittredge, George Lyman, 244, 245, 248, 281
Knipp, Mrs., 97, 238

"Lady Cassiles Lilt," 98
"Lady Isabel and the Elf Knight," 49, 53-54, 98, 119, 123, 165-166, 188, 226
"Lady Maisry," 265
"Laetabundus," 292
"Laird o' Elfin," 260
Lais, 294
"Lamkin," 189
"Lang Johnny More," 208
Lanier, Nicholas, 303
Larcombe, Henry, 62-63, 72, 105-106, 148-149
"Lass of Roch Royal," 71
Laudi Spirituali, 295
Laver, Joseph, 62-63
Lawes, William, 303-304
"Lay the bent to the bonny broom," 116, 117
Ledbetter, Hudie ("Leadbelly"), 207
"Leesome Brand," 72
Legacy convention. *See* Narrative
Leich(en), 294
"Lennox Love to Blantyre," 309
"Let all that are to Mirth inclin'd," 110
Leyden MSS., 311
Limburger Chronik, 295
Literacy, effect on ballad singers, 60-61, 66, 147
"Little Musgrave," 73, 129, 206
"Little Sir Hugh," 53, 119, 123-124
"Lizie Wan," 51-53, 73
Lloyd, A. L., 207
Locheimer Liederbuch, 295
Lomax, Alan, 250

Lomax, John, 245, 246, 249, 250; *American Ballads and Folk Songs*, 19
"Lonesome Prairie, The," 109
"Long metre," LM, 38-39, 42
"Lord Bateman," 109, 166, 186
"Lord John and Burd Ellen," 70
"Lord Lovel," 60, 119, 123, 124, 189, 226
"Lord Randal," 7, 8, 10, 16, 164-165, 168, 227, 268
"Lord Thomas and Fair Annet," 204
"Lord Thomas and Fair Eleanor," 49, 60, 90, 98, 119, 123, 163-164, 168, 226
Love theme in ballads, 167
"Love Gregor," 70
Lyric poems not written for songs, 303-306

MacColl, Ewan, 207
McGill, Josephine, *Folk-Songs of the Kentucky Mountains*, 248
MacKenzie, W. R., *Ballads and Sea-Songs from Nova Scotia*, 24, 249
Macniell, Hector, 33
"Mademoiselle from Armentières," 46
Madrigals, 297
"Maid freed from the Gallows, The," 40, 169
"Maid on the Shore, The," 271
"Maid peept out of the window, The," 56n
"Maiden in the mor lay," 292
Mallet, David, 116
Mansfield. *See* Greenleaf, Elizabeth
Marot, Clement, 296
"Marrinys yn Tiger," 32
Marson, Rev. Charles, 275
"Mary Hamilton," 75
Masefield, John, *A Sailor's Garland*, 25
Mason, M. H., 275
Mass communications; effect on folksong, 218, 253, 255-256, 271-272; deleterious effects, 202-206; beneficial effects, 206-210
Measure (in music), historical development of, 290-291
"Mein Gmüt ist mir verwirrt," 296
Melodic idea of ballads. *See* Idea
Melody the source of inspiration for poets, 306-313
Meredith, George, "Love in the Valley," 312
"Mermaid, The," 188
Metre, 38-39, 283-287; 297-303
Miller, "Mitch," 252
"Missing Boat, The," 32n

"Moderator's Dream, The," 23
Modernizing ballads, 269-271
Modes: scales, 79ff.; interconnections between, 81, 85, 87-90, 98, 129-130; associations, emotional, 120-121, 230; ratios, numerical, in British-American tradition, 152-156
"Mois de Mai qu'est arrivé, c'est aujourd'hui qu'il faut chanter," 292
Monody, 292, 293-296, 303
Moore, Marianne, 304
Moore, Thomas, *Irish Melodies*, 312
Morris, Alton C., *Folk-Songs of Florida*, 251
Motets, 290-295
Motherwell, William, 3, 11-12, 49, 99, 113; *Minstrelsy: Ancient and Modern*, 3n
Mozart, Wolfgang Amadeus, "Variations on a Theme from Gluck's 'Pilgrims of Mecca,'" 286
"My Boy Tammy," 268
"My love gave me a cherry," 271

Narrative: conventional formulae, 6-8, 16; surprise element, 6, 165; suspense element, 6, 162, 164-165, 168; climax of relatives, 7, 164; incremental repetition, 7, 67; legacy formula, 7-8, 164, 168; technique, 16, 72; impersonality, 128, 129, 131-132, 209, 254, 272; effect on by repeating tune, 129-132; structure, 131-132; characteristics, 162-168; motivation for action unimportant, 164; phrasal repetition, 168. *See also* Inter-relations of tune and text
Nashe, Thomas, 263
National Archive of Folk Song, Library of Congress, 100
National style in folk-music variations. *See* Regional styles and preferences
Negro spirituals, 134, 137-138
Neidhart von Reuental, 294
Nelson, Admiral Horatio, 28
Newell, W. W., 244, 246
"North-Country Lasse, The," 98, 117
"Northern Lasses Lamentation, The," 117
Normalizing effect of publication of folk-song versions, 203-204. *See also* Commercialism
North Carolina Folklore Society, 211, 217
Notker Balbulus, of St. Gall, 288

"O admirabile Veneris Idolum," 289
"O Roma Nobilis," 289
"O Waly, waly, up the bank," 271
"O Welt, ich muss dich lassen," 296
"Oak and the Ash and the Bonny Ivy Tree, The," 98, 117
"Of a' the airts," 116. *See also* Burns, Robert
"Oh, I had an apple pie," 30
"Oh, the eagles they fly high In Mobile, in Mobile," 30
"Oh, the praties they are small," 30
"Oh, Who Will Shoe That Pretty Little Foot?" 186, 187
L'homme armé, 296
Organum, 289, 290
Oral transmission of ballads, 44, 144, 203, 214, 226-228. *See also* Traditional process
"Outlandish Knight, The," 165-166, 189, 190
Owen, W. A., *Texas Folk Songs*, 251

Pachelbel, Wilhelm, 286
"Packington's Pound," 294
Paradise of Dainty Devices, The, 296
Parker, Archbishop Matthew, *Psalter*, 120-121
Parodies of ballads, 49-58, 95, 266-268
Pastourelles, 293
"Peg o' Ramsey," 220
Percy, Bishop Thomas, 1, 14; Folio, 2, 46-47, 54-55, 270; *Reliques*, 1-4, 74, 239. *See also* "Edward"
Pepys, Samuel, 97; collection of broadsides, 35, 257; *Diary*, 238, 239
"Perspice Christicola," 292
Pervigilium Veneris, 289
Petri, Theodoric, *Piae Cantiones*, 109-110, 118-119
Petric, George, collection of Irish folk tunes, 22, 33, 100
Philips, Ambrose, *Collection of Old Ballads*, 92, 95-96; *Pastorals*, 92
Pinkerton, John, ballad collection, 44
Plainchant, 289-290, 297
Playford, John, 99, *The English Dancing Master*, 46, 56n., 98, 118
Polyphony, 296-297; development of, 289-291
Pope, Alexander, 92; "Summer," 286
"Popular" (defined), 213
"Pretty Polly," 131
"Proses," 288
Psalm tunes, 140. *See also* Sacred songs

Publicity, effect on folk-song, 202. *See also* Commercialism

Quadruplum, 290
"Quan vei l'aloete," 293
"Quodling's Delight," 98, 118

Raleigh, Sir Walter, 35
Ralph Roister Doister, 296
Ramsay, Allan, *Tea Table Miscellany*, 239, 311
Randolph, Vance, 250
Ranges of folk tunes. *See* Tunes
Rankin, James, 74, 77
Ravenscroft, Thomas, *Melismata*, 32, 112, *Deuteromelia*, 112, 114
Reasons why ballads are preserved by folk-singers, 167-169, 241-242, 277
Record companies, 207
Recordings of folk-songs, effect on folk-singers, 202-206. *See also* Commercialism; Mass communications
Rederykers (Dutch troubadours), 296
Refrain: nonsense syllables in, 42, 115, 257-269; influence on tune and text, 42-48, 166, 208, 211; interlaced with text, 43, 45-48; external, scarcity of, 169; moving with tune from text to text, 257-267
Regional styles and preferences in folk-song, 125-127, 147, 153-159, 206, 218, 221, 229, 232-242, 257-269
Religious folk-songs, 133. *See also* Sacred songs; Shaped-note hymnbooks
"Remember O thou man," 31-35
"Remember, sinful youth," 31
"Riddle Wittily Expounded, A," 109
"Riddles Wisely Expounded," 16, 44, 116, 117, 118
Ritchie, Jean, 205-206, 207
Ritchie family, 256
Ritson, Joseph, 2, 42, 66, 69, 76
Robertson, Bell, 59
Robertson, Jeannie, 12, 207
"Robin m'aime," 295
"Robin Hood and Guy of Gisborne," 214
Robin Hood cycle, 15, 47, 74, 104, 115
Robinson, Francis North, 244
Rondeau, 294
"Rose the Red and White Lilly," 68
Ross, G. W., 21
Rota, of Reading, 115
Rowallan MSS., 311

Rowland, Samuel, "The Melancholie Knight," 56
Rufty, Hilton, 135

Sacred songs: intermingled with secular texts, 290-292; set to secular tunes or texts, 292-296
Sanctus, 98, 116
"St. Stephen and Herod," 44
"Saints Bound for Heaven, The," 31
Sam Hall Songster, The, 21
"Samuel Hall," 18-20, 36
Sandburg, Carl, 163; *American Song-Bag*, 31, 249
Sandys, William, *Christmas Carols*, 32
Scarborough, Dorothy, 245, 250; *A Song Catcher in the Southern Mountains*, 189
Schinhan, Jan P., 212, 217-223, 250
Scholarly interest in ballad study, 92-100, 172-182, 211-223; problems for scholars, 172-173; effect of scholarly interest, 276-281; history of scholarly interest, 244-252; scholarly interest in England, 275
Scots Musical Museum. See Johnson, James
"Scots wha hae wi Wallace bled," 310
Scott, Harold, *English Song Book*, 20, 21
Scott, Robert, 43, 66
Scott, Sir Walter, 2, 12, 42, 65, 66, 92, 106, 113, 209; as transmitter of traditional material, 76-77, 209; *Minstrelsy of the Scottish Border*, 44, 65, 209
"Sea Captain, The," 271
"Searching for Lambs," 110
"Seeds of Love, The," 275
Seeger, Charles, 141, 143
Seeger, Peggy, 207
Seeger, Pete, 207, 252
Selection (Sharp's principle), 144, 146-150, 160-161, 278
"Sequences," 288-289, 291, 294, 304; burlesques of, 289
Seven-shaped-note song books, 134; *see also* Shaped-note hymnbooks
Shakespeare, William, 107, 224, 296-297
"Shall I go walk the woods so wild?" 297
Shaped-note hymnbooks, 29, 250; melodic idea in shaped-note hymns, 138, 141-143
Sharp, Cecil, 12, 21-22, 25, 43, 62, 72, 94, 100, 103, 105, 114, 125-127, 133, 144-151, 247-248, 251, 254, 273-281; MSS., at Clare College, Cambridge, 30, modal scheme, 135; *English Folk-Song: Some Conclusions*, 72n, 144, 248, 277; and Maud Karpeles, *English Folk Songs from the Southern Appalachians*, 147, 222, 249, 279; and C. L. Marson, *Folk Songs from Somerset*, 123, 248, 275
Sharpe, Charles Kirkpatrick, 99, 113, 265
Shelton, B. F., 131
Shook, Mrs. Meg, 14
"Sick Tune," 264
Sidney, Sir Philip, 92
Simpson, Claude E., *The English Broadside Ballad and Its Music*, 35n
"Sir Andrew Barton," 119, 270
"Sir Eglamore," 50, 56, 57-58, 267
"Sir Eglamour of Artois (metrical romance), 55
"Sir Hugh," 187
"Sir Lionel," 54, 55-56, 58, 267
"Sir Patrick Spens," 4, 60, 74, 75, 76, 103, 129, 204
"Sir Rylas," 55
Skene MSS., 311
Sloane MS., 271
Smith, C. Alphonso, 245
Smith, Reed, 245
Smyth, Mary W., 246
"Solemn Thought," 31
Southeastern Folklore Society, 244. *See also* Folklore Society of the South-East *Southern Folklore Quarterly*, 250
"Stand up now, Diggers All," 34
Standard version, possibility of, 149. *See also* Idea of a ballad
Stanza pattern: relations between ballads, 29-36; structure of, 38-44, 285-286, influence of refrain on, 208-210, 221
Stewart, George R., 126
Straloch MSS., 311
Sturgis, E. B., and R. Hughes, *Songs from the Hills of Vermont*, 249
Sullivan, Maxine, 238
"Sumer is icumen in," 115, 290, 292, 294
Supernatural elements in ballads, 165-167. *See also* Narrative
Surette, T., 248
Susato, Tylman, *Souterliedekens*, 296
Suspense, surprise, in ballads. *See* Narrative

"Sweet William and Fair Margaret," 119, 123

Taylor, Archer, 212, 213; on "Edward," 16-17, 52
Tempo, effect on tune, 125-126
Texas Folklore Society, 248-249
Texts: causes of alterations in, 67; shortening of, 240-241. See also Narrative; Tune; Variation
Thackeray, William M., 163
Theatricals, ballads adapted for, 262, 268
"There is a Fountain," 110
"They say my love is dead," 33
"Thomas Rymer," 119, 209
Thompson, Nat, 180 Loyal Songs, 56
Thompson, Randall, 95
Thompson, Stith, 212
Thompson, Virgil, 95
Thomson, William, 116, 306-311; Orpheus Caledonius, 112, 311
Thorn-Drury Broadsides, 33
"Three Little Babes, The," 185
"Three maidens a milking did go," 30
"Three Ravens, The," 46, 115, 267
Tiersot, Julien, 293
Tisserand, Jean, "O filii et filiae," 292
Tonic, see Tunes: characteristics
Tottel, Richard, Miscellany, 296
Traditional process, 104, 146, 148; methods, 44-63; "sharp corners" in, 59, 75; optimum behavior of, 75-78, 104-106; interference in, 145-146; study of, 255-256; "modernizing" ballads, 269-271; values in balladry, 271-272. See also Conservatism; Creativity of ballad singers; Idea of a ballad; Oral transmission; Variation
Traherne, Thomas, "Solitude," 304
Transcription, importance of accuracy in, 277
Tropes, 288, 291, 292
Troubadour and trouvère songs, 293-296
"True Lover's Farewell, The," 110
"True Thomas," 108
Tunes: crossing of, 44ff., 59ff., 257ff.; range (authentic, plagal, mixed), importance of, 81, 91, 121, 153-155, 169, 176-177, frequency charts, 192-195; inappropriate with texts, 124ff.; metres of, 156-157, relative proportions in tradition, 169; phrases, number of, 157, 228; cadences, relative stability, 159-160, 177; elements of,

174-177; interaction with texts, 221, with irrelevant refrains, 257 ff.; identity, question of, 228-229. See also Idea of a ballad; Inter-relations of tune and text; Modes
"Tuit cil qui sunt enamourat," 294
Tuotilo of St. Gall, 288
"Twa Brothers, The," 53
"Twa Corbies, The," 50
"Twa Sisters, The," 44-49, 55, 227, 264-267, 269
Tytler, Alexander Fraser, 66, 70
Tytler, William, 66

"Ut queant laxis," 289

"Vale of Clwyd, The," 32
Variation: textual, 9, 11, 237-241, 258-269; tune crossings causing, 44-63; in traditional song, 67-73, 75-76, 101-103, 149; modal changes, 86-90, 98; Sharp's principle, 144-151, 160, 278; national style in, 147, 153-159; boundaries of, 151; melodic, to sustain interest, 204; types of, 227-228
Vaughan Williams, Ralph, 95, 254, 255, 263
"Veni, Sancte Spiritus," 294
"Verbum bonum et suave," 289
Versus popularis, 289, 309
"Victimae paschale laudes," 294
"Vinum bonum cum sapore," 289
Virelais, 295
Volkslied, 295

"Wager, a Wager, A," 185
Wager, William, The Longer Thou Livest, 46, 296
Walker, William, Southern Harmony, 31
Waller, Edmund, "Song," 304
Walpole, Horace, 133-134
Walther von der Vogelweide, "Nu alerst leb'ich mich werde," 294
Wardlaw, Lady, 2, 4
"Wedding of the Frog and the Mouse, The," 46
"Wee Wee Man, The," 268
"Well-a-day, well-a-day," 33, 35
Wells, Evelyn K., The Ballad Tree, 152
"Were I laid on Greeland's Coast," 260
"Westron Wynde," 110
Westrup, Jack Allan, 289, 293, 294
Whall, Captain W. B., 25, 29
White, Josh, 252

White, Newman Ivey, 211-212
Whiting, B. J., 212, 216
"Whummil Bore, The," 49-51, 267
"Wife of Usher's Well, The," 74, 76
Wilkinson, Winston, 250
"William and Margaret," 116
Williams, Alfred, *Folk Songs of the Upper Thames,* 30, 55n
"Willy's fair and Willy's rare," 116
"Willy's Lady," 43, 67
Wilson (John), 303
Wilson, G. P., 212
"Wind hath blown my Plaid away, The," 257, 260
"Winder wie ist nu dein Kraft," 294
Winstanley, William, 34

Wiora, Dr. Walter, 169
"Wondrous Love," 31
"Wraggle-taggle Gipsies, The," 122-123
Wyman, Loraine, and Howard Brockway, *Lonesome Tunes* and *Twenty Kentucky Mountain Songs,* 248

"Yankee Doodle," 98, 227
"Ye Jacobites by name," 32
Yeats, William Butler, 313
"Young Andrew," 131
"Young Barbour," 191
"Young Bekie," 67
"Young Hunting," 53-54, 73, 127
"Young man and a maid, A," 23
"Young Waters," 4, 74